HUMAN COGNITIVE NEUROPSYCHOLOGY

Human Cognitive Neuropsychology

Andrew W. Ellis

and

Andrew W. Young

Department of Psychology, University of Lancaster,
Lancaster LA1 4YF, England

LEA LAWRENCE ERLBAUM ASSOCIATES, PUBLISHERS LEA
Hove and London (UK)   Hillsdale (USA)

Copyright © 1988 by Lawrence Erlbaum Associates Ltd.
All rights reserved. No part of this book may be reproduced in any
form, by photostat, microform, retrieval system, or any other
means without the prior written permission of the publisher.

Reprinted 1989, 1990, 1991

Lawrence Erlbaum Associates Ltd., Publishers
27 Palmeira Mansions
Church Road
Hove
East Sussex, BN3 2FA
U.K.

British Library Cataloguing in Publication Data

Ellis, Andrew W.
Human cognitive neuropsychology.
1. Man. Cognition. Neuropsychological aspects
I. Title II. Young, Andrew W.
153.4

ISBN 0-86377-033-9 (Hbk)
ISBN 0-86377-034-7 (Pbk)

Typeset by Tradespool Ltd., Frome, Somerset
Printed and bound by BPCC Wheatons Ltd., Exeter

Contents

Preface

1st author: "Why don't we write a textbook
of cognitive neuropsychology together?"
2nd author: "Yes, O.K."

That conversation, or something like it, took place one day in October 1982. In November 1982 an outline of this book was sent to the publishers who kindly said "Yes please". In September 1983 they received a letter saying "You should have the book by Christmas". In October 1987, almost five years to the day since that first fateful conversation, they got the book we had promised them.

Our first thanks must therefore go to Michael Forster, Rohays Perry, Patricia Simpson, and the rest of the team at Erlbaum for their patient forebearance, the polite way they enquired after the book's progress each time they bumped into us, and tolerated the increasingly evasive replies they received. If it's any consolation, we firmly believe that the book is now considerably better than anything we could have written in 1983.

There are several reasons for that. One is that the subject has progressed quite dramatically in the intervening years. We now know much more about several of the areas we cover than was known even four years ago, and there is a greater consensus and clarity concerning the kind of enterprise that cognitive neuropsychology should be. A second reason is that we have had more personal experience in cognitive neuropsychology, which has led us in the end to a more detailed treatment of human cognitive neuropsychology than we had originally planned. Many people have helped us gain that experience by discussing issues and introducing us to their patients, and we owe them our thanks. They include Dr. Freda Newcombe of the MRC's Neuropsychology Unit and Dr. E. M. R. Critchley of Preston Royal Infirmary, Maureen Miller, Sian Hallam, and the rest of the Speech Therapy team at the Lancaster Moor Hospital, and Dr. M. B. MacIllmurray of the Lancaster Royal Infirmary. We also thank our collaborators on various case studies—Hadyn Ellis, Edward De Haan, Brenda Flude, Rick Hanley, Dennis Hay, Janice Kay, Diane Miller, Freda Newcombe, and Norma Pearson. Above all, we are indebted to the patients themselves who gave of their time so generously, and who in many cases have become friends of ours. Financial support for these investigations has come from the Economic and Social Research Council, the Medical Research Council, and the Nuffield Foundation.

Many people have helped us by allowing us to reproduce figures or extracts from their work, and often by personally supplying such material. We thank Professor Edoardo Bisiach, Dr. Dan Bub, Dr. John Campion, Professor Ennio De Renzi, Dr. David Howard, Dr. Glyn Humphreys, Professor Marc Jeannerod, Dr. Richard Latto, Dr. Freda Newcombe, Professor Graham Ratcliff, Dr. Jane Riddoch, Dr. P. K. Thomas, Professor Elizabeth Warrington, Professor Larry Weiskrantz, Masson Italia Editori, Oxford University Press, Pergamon Press, and The Press Association. Shiela Whalley, Sylvia Sumner and Tracey Newsham coped admirably with rewrites and modifications of drafts. Our thanks to them.

Max Coltheart, David Howard and Glyn Humphreys provided detailed and perceptive comments on a previous draft, and Hadyn Ellis, Andrew Mayes and Freda Newcombe joined in the difficult task of saving us from error on individual chapters. Any errors that remain are, of course, entirely their fault.

Andy Ellis
Andy Young
Lancaster, December 1987

1 What is Cognitive Neuropsychology?

In any well-made machine one is ignorant of the working of most of the parts—the better they work the less we are conscious of them . . . it is only a fault which draws our attention to the existence of a mechanism at all.
Kenneth Craik, *The Nature of Explanation* (1943)

INTRODUCTION

On 5th August, 1982 a 19-year-old man who we shall refer to by his initials as PH was involved in an accident in which he was knocked off his motorcycle. He lost his right arm, and suffered a severe closed head injury. He was in a coma for over 12 days.

Like many head-injury patients PH has, with the help of rehabilitation services, made quite a good recovery. Some four years after his accident his language abilities seemed normal in conversation, and he could read without difficulty. His I.Q. on verbal tests (91) was probably close to what it was before the accident. His short-term memory abilities were normal and, although he scored poorly on formal tests involving long-term retention, he was able to remember the things that were important to his daily life without apparent difficulty.

However, one of PH's problems was most resistant to rehabilitation; he could not recognise people's faces. As soon as a familiar person spoke he would know who it was but, to PH, all faces seemed unfamiliar. He could tell if a face belonged to a man or a woman, an old or a young person, and he could describe the general appearance and facial features reasonably accurately. But PH had no sense of recognising people who had previously been very familiar to him. In neuropsychological terms, his accident had left PH *prosopagnosic*—able to see, but unable to recognise many once-familiar faces (De Haan, Young, & Newcombe, 1987a).

EST was a well-educated, 65-year old man whose difficulties lay not in perception or recognition, but in speaking. His attempts to converse were hampered by the fact that he could no longer call to mind many words that had once been part of his ordinary, everyday vocabulary. The cause of EST's *anomia* (as his condition is known) was not a head injury, but a large slow-growing tumour in the left hemisphere of his brain which was successfully removed when he was 53 years old. Whereas normal people just occasionally find themselves caught in a "tip of the tongue" state, temporarily unable to remember a word, EST seemed to be trapped in such a state almost every minute because EST's word-finding problems extended to commonplace words like "piano", "spider", and "lamp". He knew perfectly well what such objects were, and what one could do with them, but was often unable to remember what they were called. His understanding of speech was good, and he could comprehend written words, though his attempts to read aloud were hindered by the same word-finding problems as affected his speaking (Kay & Ellis, 1987; Kay & Patterson, 1985).

The difficulties experienced by PH and EST are just two of the vast range of different problems that can be caused by brain injury. In this book we shall encounter many of them, though there are many more that we have not had space to include. Chapter 4, for example, reviews different forms of face recognition disorder, including the sort of pro-sopagnosia suffered by PH, whereas Chapters 5 and 9 examine disorders of speech production, including EST's type of anomia. Other conditions we shall look at include disorders affecting object recognition, spatial knowledge and orientation, speech comprehension, reading, writing, and memory.

Human cognitive neuropsychology is, however, much more than just a catalogue of the different problems that brain injury can give rise to. Cognitive neuropsychologists believe that by studying patients like PH and EST (with their co-operation and consent), fundamental insights can be gained into the way the human mind works. These insights should then feed back to provide a better understanding of the problems of brain-injured patients, and should lead in turn to the development of better therapies (e.g. Howard & Hatfield, 1987).

As an approach to understanding the mind and the brain, cognitive neuropsychology is both old and new—old to the extent that the issues it addresses are ones which have exercised the minds of philosophers, psychologists, neurologists and others for hundreds, even thousands, of years; and new because it is only within the last 15 years or so that cognitive neuropsychology has become established and has articulated its distinctive approach. This chapter is intended to acquaint the reader with what cognitive neuropsychologists are trying to do. We shall discuss the sort of questions they ask, the methods they adopt in trying to answer them, the assumptions they make, and some of the potential pitfalls that await them along the way. In doing so we shall try to be brief for two reasons. First, we believe that the vigour and usefulness of cognitive neuropsychology is best established through illustrating its practical application in different areas: If any converts are to be made, they will be won over by the demonstrations in later chapters of how cognitive neuropsychology can illuminate the processes involved in human perception, language, and memory. Secondly, cognitive neuropsychology is an approach in evolution. Matters to be reviewed in this chapter, such as the appropriate methodology and the underlying assumptions, are matters of lively current debate, and we are only too well aware that opinion on these topics is likely to continue to evolve in the years to come. But the fact that we can make extensive use in the chapters to come of observations and conclusions made by earlier researchers whose theoretical viewpoints were different from our own shows that the main substance of the book has a fair chance of surviving a wide range of changes in theoretical fashion.

QUESTIONS AND POSSIBLE ANSWERS

Assuming we have spent some time investigating a case like the anomic patient EST mentioned earlier, two questions arise naturally:

1. What has happened to this patient to cause him to show the particular symptoms he does?
2. Can his pattern of impaired and intact capabilities teach us anything about the way the normal mind and brain are organised?

If we consider first the question of what has happened to EST to cause his anomia, then it soon becomes clear that the question can be answered in at least two very different ways. Brain scans have shown that the tumour which caused EST's anomia occupied a large area in his left cerebral hemisphere, affecting in particular the temporal and temporoparietal areas (Kay & Patterson, 1985). As we have seen, the consequence of the resulting brain injury was that EST could no longer remember, or "find", many words which had once been well-established parts of his vocabulary. Is it better to say of EST, "He is anomic because of damage to his left cerebral hemisphere" or "He is anomic because of damage to the psychological processes which mediate spoken word finding?" Although there are those who believe that one of these two modes of explanation is intrinsically superior to the other, we would suggest that they are both valid in their own way. Only the second explanation is a cognitive neuropsychological explanation, however. Accordingly, the emphasis in this book will be on *explaining the symptoms of brain-injured patients in terms of impairment to psychological operations which are necessary for normal, efficient perception, language and memory*, though we shall see that there are times when a knowledge of the relevant anatomy and physiology is of positive benefit when it would be churlish to ignore biological evidence.

Our main subject matter, however, is *cognitive* neuropsychology. Cognitive psychology (without the neuro- prefix) is the study of those mental processes which underlie and make possible our everyday ability to recognise familiar objects and familiar people, to find our way around in the world, to speak, read and write, to plan and execute actions, to think, make decisions and remember (Eysenck, 1984; Smyth, Morris, Levy, & Ellis, 1987). Neuropsychology is the study of how particular brain structures and processes mediate behaviour, and encompasses such things as appetites and emotions as well as cognitive aspects of mental life. As its name suggests, cognitive neuropsychology represents a convergence of cognitive psychology and neuropsychology. In Campbell's (1987a) words: "Neuropsychology is *cognitive* to the extent that it purports to clarify the mechanisms of cognitive functions such as thinking, reading, writing, speaking, recognising, or remembering, using evidence from neuropathology."

Cognitive neuropsychology has, then, two basic aims (Coltheart, 1986; Ellis, 1983). The first is *to explain the patterns of impaired and intact cognitive performance seen in brain-injured patients in terms of damage to one or more of the components of a theory or model of normal cognitive functioning*. Thus PH's prosopagnosia and EST's anomia might be explained in terms of damage to one or more of the processes required to effect normal face recognition and speech production, respectively.

The second aim of cognitive neuropsychology is largely responsible for the recent upsurge of interest in the approach. It is *to draw conclusions about normal, intact cognitive processes from the patterns of impaired and intact capabilities seen in brain-injured patients*. In pursuing this second aim, the cognitive neuropsychologist wishes to be in a position to assert that observed patterns of symptoms could not occur if the normal, intact cognitive system were not organised in a certain way. We shall make claims of this sort with respect to patients PH and EST in Chapters 4 and 5.

Dissociations and Associations

Assertions about the way the intact mind must be organised are often based on what are termed *dissociations*. If patient X is impaired on task 1 but performs normally on task 2, then we may claim to have a dissociation between the two tasks. For instance, if task 1 is reading words and task 2 is recognising famous faces, then we would state that patient X shows a dissociation between reading, which is impaired, and face recognition, which is intact. On such evidence alone, many cognitive neuropsychologists would feel justified in saying that the normal cognitive system must be organised with face recognition and written word recognition handled by different sets of cognitive processes, thereby allowing one set to be impaired while the other continues to function normally.

Other cognitive neuropsychologists might be more circumspect, however. They would point out that logically possible alternative accounts of patient X can be put forward. It might be, for example, that written word recognition is in some way easier than face recognition and that X's brain injury has rendered him incapable of difficult recognition tasks, while leaving him still able to perform easy ones. This type of alternative account could be ruled out, however, if a second patient, Y, could be discovered in whom written word recognition was intact whereas face recognition was impaired. That patient when contrasted with patient X would provide us with a *double dissociation* between face recognition and written word recognition. There is no doubt that double dissociations are more reliable indicators that there are cognitive processes involved in the performance of task 1 that are not involved in the performance of task 2, and vice versa (Shallice, 1979a; Teuber, 1955; Weiskrantz, 1968). Double dissociations can also be established without requiring that either patient should perform normally on either task: It would often be sufficient to show that patient Y performed reliably and significantly better on task 1 than on task 2 whereas patient X performed reliably and significantly better on task 2 than on task 1 [for the technically-minded, Jones (1983) discusses cases in which this would *not* be sufficient evidence].

There are times, however, when arguments based on such things as the relative simplicity of two tasks seem so implausible that cognitive neuropsychologists are willing to venture claims about normal cognitive organisation on the basis of single dissociations (where a patient performs well on one set of tasks but badly on another), and we shall encounter several examples of such reasoning later in the book. Also, it would be unwise to regard the search for double dissociations as some sort of royal road to understanding the structure of the mind. Having unearthed a double dissociation, there is a lot of work to be done in determining just what cognitive processes mediate aspects of tasks 1 and 2 independently, and what processes, if any, the two tasks share in common. This requires intensive investigation of the patients in order to discover just why they perform badly when they do, and just where in the total cognitive system their breakdowns have occurred.

Much more problematical than arguments based on either double or single dissociations are arguments based on *associations* between symptoms. It is common in neuropsychology to discover that patients who are impaired on task 1 are also typically impaired on tasks 3, 4 and 5. Now, it might be that this association of deficits occurs because a cognitive process required for the successful execution of task 1 is also required for the successful execution of tasks 3, 4 and 5, so that a patient in whom that process is damaged will experience problems with all these tasks. Unfortunately, deficits can also tend to co-occur for reasons that are of neurological importance, but of less interest specifically to the cognitive neuropsychologist.

It could be, for example, that tasks 1, 3, 4, and 5 have no overlap in terms of the cognitive processes required for their execution, but that four discrete sets of cognitive processes are mediated by four adjacent areas of the brain. If this is so, then a brain injury which damages one of those areas will tend also to damage the others, so that deficits on the four tasks which depend on those four regions will tend to be associated. This point as applied to language disorders was well expressed by Lord Brain (1964, p.7) in the following passage:

> ... let us consider two aspects of language which we will merely call *a* and *b* to indicate that we habitually distinguish them in our own minds and give them different labels. Let us further suppose that they are both depressed [*i.e., impaired*] in a particular aphasic patient. There are several possible explanations of this. The primary disturbance may involve *a*, and the disturbance of *b* may be secondary to this, or conversely, we may implicate some general function *c* and say that both *a* and *b* are particular examples of disorder *c*. These are all functional or dynamic [*cognitive*] interpretations. But there is also the possibility that there is no functional relationship between *a* and *b*. They are involved together merely because their pathways, though separate in terms of neurones, run close enough together to be damaged by the same lesion.

Associations which occur for anatomical reasons rather than cognitive-psychological reasons will be encountered on several occasions in this book. They are revealed in their true colours when the exceptional patient is discovered whose lesion affects some but not all of the anatomically adjacent regions and which, therefore, affects some but not all of the cognitive tasks mediated by those regions. In sum, theoretical arguments based on observed associations between symptoms can be very appealing because there are often good psychological reasons for expecting two or more deficits to co-occur as a result of damage to a single cognitive process, but such arguments should always be advanced with caution and are never as secure as arguments based on dissociations.

COGNITIVE NEUROPSYCHOLOGICAL METHODS

We have just seen that *differences* between patients play a very important role in the development of theories in cognitive neuropsychology. In contrast, similarities between patients, in the form of shared sets of associated symptoms, are viewed with caution if not suspicion. Several important dissociations between symptoms have been discovered in patients whom traditional neuropsychology would have grouped together as members of the same syndrome category.

This difference in emphasis is perhaps what most distinguishes modern cognitive neuropsychology from traditional neuropsychology. The latter approach used common co-occurrences of symptoms to group patients together into syndromes. Thus patients with language disorders following brain injury (aphasias) were grouped into categories labelled Broca's aphasia, Wernicke's aphasia, conduction aphasia, etc. on the basis of shared symptoms. The assumption made would be that patients with Broca's aphasia are effectively interchangeable, and quite strong claims would sometimes be made concerning symptom complexes that *had* to co-occur (if patient Z shows symptom q, she will also show symptoms r, s, and t, etc.).

It is now generally acknowledged in cognitive neuropsychology that traditional syndrome categories are too coarse-grained and often form groupings on the basis of symptoms that co-occur for anatomical rather than functional reasons (Poeck, 1983). This is understandable, because one of the original purposes of such syndromes was to assist in the determination of probable lesion sites in the days before more direct brain scanning techniques became available, but most cognitive neuropsychologists would now accept Caramazza's (1984) advice that "research based on classical syndrome types should not be carried out if the goal of the research is to address issues concerning the structure of cognitive processes".

The problem lies in deciding how best to proceed once one has acknowledged that classical syndromes are unsuitable for cognitive neuropsychological analysis. On this issue cognitive neuropsychologists fall into two broad camps. The first wishes to replace the old, broad groupings with newer, finer, more theoretically motivated categories. These could be developed by subdividing the old syndrome categories to take account of dissociations as they arise, or they could be developed *de novo* (as with the classification of acquired reading disorders into "deep dyslexia", "surface dyslexia", "phonological dyslexia" etc.—see Chapter 8). Shallice (1979a) strongly advocates this approach, though acknowledging that it will inevitably lead to the postulation of ever more syndromes of increasing complexity and specificity.

Other cognitive neuropsychologists react to the manifest inadequacies of the classical syndromes by suggesting that there may simply be no need to group patients into categories in order to practise effective cognitive neuropsychology (e.g. Caramazza, 1984; 1986; Ellis, 1987). If it were possible to group patients into homogeneous categories, then that would represent a valuable saving because cognitive neuropsychologists would only need to produce an explanation for each syndrome, not each individual patient. Unfortunately, advocates of the revised syndrome viewpoint have not yet managed to come up with a single, lasting homogeneous category. Thus, the categories of acquired reading disorder mentioned earlier, which are only 10 or 15 years old at the time of writing, are already fractionating as theoretically important individual differences are found among patients in the same categories. As the rest of this book shows, similar fates are befalling all other attempts to delineate new syndrome categories.

One possible response to this situation is to argue that cognitive neuropsychologists should treat each patient as a unique case requiring separate explanation. Single patients could serve the same role in cognitive neuropsychology as single experiments do in experimental cognitive psychology—each is a separate test of cognitive theory (Ellis, 1987). This does not mean that all comparisons between patients are excluded: There are times in the book, for example, when we wish to highlight similarities between two or more patients. Typically, however, this happens because they share a single particular *symptom* which may be given the same explanation in each case. The point is that the other symptoms these patients show may be very different: The patients are alike in one respect but are different in several others and could not plausibly be combined into a syndrome category. In the remaining chapters of this book, we tend to retain traditional neurological terms (aphasia, dyslexia, agnosia, etc.) simply as a shorthand convenience for referring to particular broad classes of symptoms: We do *not* wish to imply that patients with a common symptom will necessarily show that symptom for the same reason.

We do not wish to labour this point about the usefulness or otherwise of syndrome groupings (which we see as just one of the teething troubles of a new scientific approach trying to establish how best to proceed). Advocates of new syndromes still talk to advocates of the single-patient approach. The two groups share the same theoretical models of reading, object recognition, memory or whatever, and each uses the others' case studies to develop those theories. Although we have our own views on this issue, we have tried not to let them dominate this book, which we hope will find acceptance among cognitive neuropsychologists of all denominations.

Case Studies

What an increasing number of cognitive neuropsychologists now agree upon is that the approach is best served by intensive single-case studies of patients with deficits in different areas of cognitive processing. This stands in contrast to traditional neuropsychology where the dominant approach has often been one in which the performance on one or more tasks of a group of patients of a given type is contrasted either with the performance of another group of patients of a different type or with a group of normal "control" subjects. Such studies commonly report only the average score on each task for each group. Unfortunately, much potentially valuable information can be lost in such an averaging procedure, notably information about individual differences between patients assigned to the same groups (Shallice, 1979a).

Accordingly, even cognitive neuropsychologists who believe in the usefulness of syndrome groupings now tend to present data on each individual patient separately. Many publications in cognitive neuropsychology are devoted to presenting and interpreting data from just one patient with a disorder of particular theoretical interest. Generalisability of theories comes in two ways: First, a theory or model of a particular cognitive function is meant to account for *all* reported cases of disorder of that function, so that the theory is *not* a theory of a single patient; and secondly, these are theories of normal, intact cognitive functioning which are used to explain disorders. As such they must explain all the available data from experimental cognitive psychology as well as all the available neuropsychological data. Few areas of psychology place such exacting demands on their theories.

Shallice (1979a) made several recommendations about how single-case studies should proceed. He suggested, for example, that when comparisons between patients are appropriate they would be facilitated if "baseline" data from a range of standard neuropsychological tests were supplied. Beyond that point the particular tasks given to the patient are likely to be tailor-made and designed to evaluate a particular hypothesis as to the nature of the patient's disorder. Such tests should be given under conditions that are as controlled as possible, and their results should be analysed statistically using tests applied as standard in experimental cognitive psychology. Tasks which are of particular theoretical importance should be given on more than one occasion to establish the replicability of their results, and theoretical conclusions should be supported wherever possible by data from more than one task.

In fact, although we have described traditional neuropsychology as being devoted to group studies, that is an over-simplification. Rare or exceptional disorders have always been reported as single-case studies, and in the decades between about 1870 and 1910 a succession of important case studies were published. As we shall see shortly, there are several respects in which modern cognitive neuropsychology can justly be regarded as a return to this turn-of-the-century approach, though the theories and methods employed have become more sophisticated.

MODULARITY

It has already been argued that if one patient shows an impairment of reading but not face recognition, whereas another shows an impairment of face recognition but not reading, then that double dissociation indicates that there are cognitive processes involved in recognising faces that are not involved in reading words, and vice versa. As the remainder of this book will reveal, such dissociations abound in cognitive neuropsychology. If we follow through the logic of our argument, that means that the cognitive skills of the sort we shall be discussing are mediated by large numbers of semi-independent cognitive processes or systems, each capable of separate impairment.

This view of how the mind and brain are organised has come to be known as the *modularity hypothesis*. According to the modularity hypothesis, our mental life is made possible by the orchestrated activity of multiple cognitive processors or *modules*. There may, for example, be one set of modules responsible for various aspects of face recognition, another set for recognising written words, a third set for maintaining our orientation in the geographical environment, and so on. Every module engages in its own form of processing independently of the activity in modules other than those it is in direct communication with. Modules are also distinct within the brain, so that brain injury can affect the operation of some modules while, at the same time, leaving the operation of other modules intact (hence a patient can, for example, experience difficulties in face recognition following brain injury without necessarily experiencing difficulties with reading).

Current interest in the modularity hypothesis stems in large part from the work of Marr (1976; 1982) and Fodor (1983). Building on his experience in both vision research and the simulation of complex human abilities in computers, Marr suggested that complex systems, like minds and brains, are very likely to evolve towards a modular organisation in the course of their development. This is because it is easier, according to Marr, both to detect and correct errors and to improve complex systems whose organisation is modular. Thus, Marr (1976) writes:

> Any large computation should be split up and implemented as a collection of small subparts that are as nearly independent of one another as the overall task allows. If a process is not designed in this way a small change in one place will have consequences in many other places. This means that the process as a whole becomes extremely difficult to debug or to improve, whether by a human designer or in the course of natural evolution, because a small change to improve one part has to be accompanied by many simultaneous compensatory changes elsewhere.

An Analogy

An analogy may help at this point. Modern hi-fi systems are often highly modular, consisting of separate and separable record decks, cassette decks, radio tuners, amplifiers, speakers, headphones, and so on. In contrast, all-in-one "radiograms" of the sort seen in the 1950s were much less modular. One advantage of the modularity of a modern hi-fi is that it assists in tracing the source of a malfunction because disorders can be confined to particular modules leaving the operation of the others intact. Thus, if the record you are playing sounds dreadful, you can decide whether the fault lies in the deck, amplifier or speakers by trying a cassette, listening through headphones instead of through the speakers, and so on.

Many amplifiers have spare slots which allow you to add on new components as they come on the market (adding a compact disc player to an existing hi-fi for example). All that is required is that the new component should provide an output which is compatible with the requirements of the existing components. Similarly, the modular organisation of our minds and brains may allow us to develop new cognitive components and interface them with old ones to create new skills and capabilities. The development in childhood of modules for reading and writing would be an example; reading and writing have only become widespread in very recent history, yet we will see that they appear to be modularised within the brain. Finally, a new, improved type of record deck may come onto the market. If your system is modular you can simply replace your old deck with one of the new type without needing to touch any of your other components, thereby illustrating Marr's point about modular systems being easier to improve.

Diagrams and Diagram Makers

If you were in the position of wanting to assemble a hi-fi system from scratch then you might find it useful to sketch a simple diagram showing the components you need and how they will interconnect. Diagrams are very useful expository devices wherever modular systems are under consideration (Ellis, 1987; Morton, 1981). They were used extensively by the school of neuropsychologists which flourished between 1870 and 1910 (Morton, 1984).

Figure 1.1 shows the diagram put forward by Lichtheim (1885) as a model of the recognition and production of spoken and written words. It comprises five different "centres" or modules interlinked in certain ways. Centre A is a module whose function is to recognise the spoken forms of words when listening to a speaker and also to provide spoken word-forms when you are speaking yourself. Centre B houses word concepts or meanings, and is similarly employed in both the production and comprehension of language. Centre O, the centre for visual word images, recognises written words and also makes their spellings available in the act of writing. Finally, Centres M and E hold "motor images" ready to guide the groups of muscles which will speak or write words respectively.

Diagrams like this were used to explain different forms of language disorder in terms of damage either to the centres themselves or to the pathways connecting them. A patient who had problems understanding or producing both spoken and written words might, for example, be

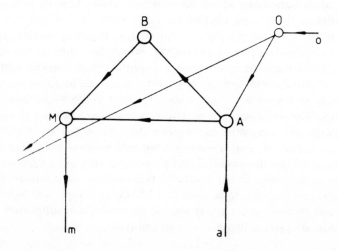

FIG. 1.1   Lichtheim's (1885) model of word recognition and production (reproduced with permission from Howard and Hatfield, 1987).

assumed to have suffered damage to centre B, whereas a patient whose problems lay in articulating words in speech would be said to have an impairment affecting centre M. A patient who could both understand and produce spoken words, but had difficulties in repeating heard words, might be interpreted as having suffered damage to the connection between A and M, and so on.

The popularity of diagrams like Lichtheim's must tell us something about their usefulness for neuropsychologists in practice. They did, however, have their problems (Marshall, 1982; Morton, 1984). First, the diagrams were only of real use in interpreting disorders that affected the comprehension, production or repetition of single words: They had little to say about disorders affecting, for example, grammatical processes involved in sentence construction. Secondly, the theorists had very little idea as to how their centres might actually work. They lacked the vocabulary of computational, information-processing concepts that now enables us to talk about the possible internal operations of the modules we postulate. Thirdly, whereas a modern cognitive theory has to account for data from experimental cognitive psychology as well as data from neuropsychology, the diagrams of the late nineteenth century were only constrained by neuropsychological evidence. The danger was that a diagram could be modified in a fairly *ad hoc* manner in order to fit the particular pattern of impairment seen in any particular patient. Some of these modifications were arbitrary and manifestly unsatisfactory. A theory that can "explain" any patient who comes along simply by redrawing the diagram is unfalsifiable. Unfalsifiable theories may seem attractive to the novice, but because they set no constraints on the claims or predictions that can be made, they are of little real use.

Finally, the majority of the turn-of-the-century diagrams were superimposed upon an outline of the left cerebral hemisphere of the brain. The diagrams therefore incorporated both a cognitive theory as to what the appropriate centres and their interconnections were, and a neuropsychological theory as to where the centres were located in the brain and where the tracts ran between them. If a patient was discovered whose symptoms were not those one would predict, given the site of the patient's brain injury, there was no way of knowing whether the cognitive component of the diagram—the proposed set of centres and connections—was at fault, or whether it was the proposed localisation of the centres and connections that was in error.

Today's cognitive neuropsychologists are much more careful to distinguish between theories as cognitive models and questions as to where a proposed set of modules may be localised within the brain. Some cognitive neuropsychologists refuse almost as a matter of principle to discuss issues of possible localisation; others consider such issues to be of interest but acknowledge that they are separate from the evaluation of the model as a cognitive theory. Our own view is that many of the deficits we will discuss are related to damage to particular areas of the brain. Thus we will mention lesion sites from time to time, but we do *not* give them *explanatory* status.

In his influential book, *The Modularity of Mind*, Fodor (1983) acknowledged several antecedents of the notion of modularity, but curiously failed to mention the nineteenth-century diagram makers. Yet these theorists are arguably closer than anyone to current thinking, as Morton (1984) demonstrates in his point-by-point comparison of nineteenth-century diagrams with information-processing diagrams proposed by cognitive psychologists in recent times. We shall make quite extensive use of modular diagrams in this book to help us understand disorders shown by patients, though some of the weaknesses of nineteenth-century diagrams, such as their problems in giving an account of grammatical and other high-level disorders, remain.

Fodor's Proposed Attributes of Cognitive Modules

In *The Modularity of Mind* Fodor listed what he thought to be the properties of cognitive modules. Important among these was the property of *informational encapsulation*, meaning that a module must carry out its own form of processing in complete ignorance of, and isolation from, the processes going on elsewhere in the total cognitive system. If, for example, there is a module or set of modules which process the emotional expression on a face, and a separate module or set of modules which recognise the face and determine who the person is, then informational encapsulation demands that the modules processing the emotion on the face must operate independently of any activity within those modules processing the identity of the face.

According to Fodor, modules must also be *domain-specific*, meaning that each module can only accept one particular sort of input. For example, the module processing the emotional expression of faces would not also be able to process the emotional tone of voices; such processing would require a separate domain-specific module. As Shallice (1984) pointed out, if the assumptions of informational encapsulation and domain specificity are combined with an assumption of *neurological specificity*, whereby modules are distinctly represented within the brain itself, then cognitive neuropsychology becomes a viable enterprise, because the possibility arises that brain lesions will selectively impair certain modules while leaving the others intact and operating at normal, pre-injury levels of efficiency.

The notions of informational encapsulation and domain specificity are ones which commentators upon Fodor's thesis have found easiest to accept (see, for example, the commentaries which accompany Fodor, 1985). Other properties of modules that Fodor proposed have received less unanimous acclaim. For example, Fodor argued that the operation of modules is *mandatory*. This means that modules are unstoppable— they are beyond voluntary control, and if the appropriate input is present a module will carry out its particular source of processing whether the owner of that module wishes it or not. We shall discover that many modules do indeed show the property of mandatory operation, particularly the modules involved in various aspects of recognition and processing of sensory information, but there may be modules whose operation is not mandatory. For example, the system from which the names of people and things are retrieved appears to have many of the required properties of modules, yet the retrieval of the name of a person or object seems to be more voluntary than mandatory. We cannot stop ourselves recognising a familiar person we see, but we do seem to have some voluntary control over whether or not we activate the module from which the person's name is retrieved. Conceivably, mandatoriness is more a property of input modules than of output modules.

Another property of modules which Fodor suggested but which has come in for some criticism is the notion that cognitive modules are of necessity *innate*, i.e. they are part of our genetic endowment. As Schwartz and Schwartz (1984) among others noted, some of the best cognitive neuropsychological evidence for the existence of modular systems comes from studies of acquired reading and writing disorders (dyslexias and dysgraphias). The skills of reading and writing appear to be made possible by the concerted and orchestrated activity of several cognitive modules each of which is capable of separate impairment, and those modules in the skilled reader and writer apparently behave just like any other cognitive modules. Yet reading and writing are artificial, culturally trans- mitted skills which until recently have only ever been acquired by a very small minority of people, and few psychologists are willing to entertain the notion that the modules required to read and write are part of our biological heritage (though see Marshall, 1987). It in no way threatens Fodor's general thesis to argue that modules can be established through a process of learning as well as being inherited genetically.

One of Fodor's most controversial suggestions was that whereas input processes to do with the perception of the external world (and possibly output processes to do with the control of action upon the world) are modular, there may also be central parts of the mind which are not modular in their organisation. Fodor suggests that higher-level thinking processes such as are involved in reasoning, decision making, the forma- tion of beliefs, etc., are the product of operations which are not informationally encapsulated, not mandatory, not domain-specific, and so on. He even went so far as to suggest that because these central processes are not modular they are not amenable to scientific investigation. Readers interested in pursuing this aspect of Fodor's line of thought are directed to the commentaries in Fodor (1985).

From a cognitive neuropsychological perspective it is true that the dissociation methodology has largely been applied to input and output processes, and dissociations have not been sought among higher-level mental operations. If Fodor is right, then the quest for dissociations among input and output modules will be a quest directed at carving Nature at her joints, but trying to find dissociations among higher mental processes would be like trying to carve a meat loaf at its joints. That said, even if Fodor is right, there is still room for a cognitive neuropsychology of higher mental processes, because dissociations are not the only weapon in the armoury of the cognitive neuropsychologist. One of the techniques that cognitive neuropsychologists use in order to formulate hypotheses about the possible internal workings of cognitive systems is to look at the sorts of errors those systems make when they are partially but not completely disrupted. We shall look, for example, at the sorts of errors made by patients with speech production deficits or spelling impairments in order to try to understand something about the internal workings of modules which mediate the production of spoken and written words. One can equally look at the sorts of errors made by patients with disorders of higher mental functions and the sorts of difficulties they experience on different tasks in order to learn something about how those higher mental functions can be disrupted and impaired. One would hope in the process to learn something about how higher mental processes actually operate. The work of Shallice (1982) and Duncan (1986) represent steps in this direction.

SOME FURTHER ASSUMPTIONS OF COGNITIVE NEUROPSYCHOLOGY

The philosopher of science, Imre Lakatos, has argued that every science has at its core a set of assumptions which are not directly testable (Lakatos, 1974). These assumptions may be right or they may be wrong—the only way that the scientist working in a particular area will know whether its assumptions are right or wrong is by seeing whether the whole approach advances or flounders. As cognitive neuropsychology has become established in recent times, so its practitioners have sought to identify some of the core assumptions upon which it rests. The work of Shallice (1979a; 1981a), Saffran (1982) and Caramazza (1984; 1986) is of particular importance here.

Modularity is arguably one of the core assumptions of cognitive neuropsychology—something which can never be ultimately proved or disproved, but upon whose validity the enterprise as currently articulated rests. Another key assumption, following Shallice (1981a), is what we have already called *neurological specificity*, and what others have called *isomorphism*. This is the assumption that there is some correspondence between the organisation of the mind and the organisation of the brain. In the words of Lashley (1941): "The discovery that the various capacities which independently contribute to intellectual performance do correspond to the spatial distribution of cerebral mechanisms represents a step towards the recognition of similar organisation in neurological and mental events."

This assumption is not one that neuropsychologists in all periods have been willing to make. Brain (1964, p. 6) wrote that:

> The older neurologists, and even some today, thought that the different varieties of aphasia produced by lesions in different situations could be classified in psychological terms... but this presupposes first that in the nervous system speech is organised in such a way that anatomical centres correspond to psychological functions, and then that destruction of such a centre merely impairs a particular psychological element in speech. This view has largely been abandoned.

The view which Brain thought abandoned is one which has been revived by cognitive neuropsychologists and one which underpins much of the cognitive neuropsychological enterprise. This does not mean that it is right, and if it is wrong (as Brain thought) then the early promise of cognitive neuropsychology will not be borne out in its further development. We should note, however, that at minimum all that cognitive neuropsychology needs to claim is that impairments of cognitive processes can be selective. It may well be possible to see selective deficits following injury to systems in which the storage of information is "distributed" rather than being organised into physically discrete centres (modules) corresponding to psychological functions. If so, then cognitive neuropsychology can proceed with its research programme.

Another assumption of cognitive neuropsychology is the assumption of *transparency*, which requires that "The pathological performance observed will provide a basis for discerning which component or module of the system is disrupted" (Caramazza, 1984). That is, careful analysis of the pattern of intact and impaired performance and the pattern of errors shown by a patient after brain injury must be capable of leading us to valid conclusions about the nature and functions of the impaired processing components. To this end, Caramazza (1984) suggests that the performance of a given patient will reflect four factors. These are:

1. The contribution attributable to the "true" effect of the hypothesised disruption of one or more processing components (modules).
2. Normal individual variation in performance.
3. The effects of compensatory operations.
4. Effects that result from disruptions to processing mechanisms other
than the hypothesised component.

Clearly some of these factors present obstacles to the interpretation
of the pattern of symptoms shown by a particular patient. Caramazza's
mention of normal individual variation in performance highlights the fact
that we are not all alike in so-called normality. Even within the normal
population of individuals without brain injuries some people's modules
work better for some things than do other people's, so that some people
are naturally better than others at, say, verbal skills or spatial skills.
Before one attributes a patient's poor performance on certain tasks to
brain injury, it is necessary to satisfy oneself that the patient was not
constitutionally poor on those tasks even before his or her brain injury.
There is a real danger of diagnosing an impairment of geographical
orientation in a patient who always used to get lost when he turned round
twice, or an impairment of spelling in a patient who has never been able
to spell at all well. The usual (but not infallible) way of preventing such
possibilities is to show that the patient's performance is seriously impaired
in comparison to appropriately chosen control subjects.

Caramazza's third factor, that of "compensatory operations", refers
to the widely acknowledged fact that aspects of a brain-injured patient's
performance may reflect cognitive systems working in ways rather different
from those in which they worked before the brain was damaged. For
example, some patients read words in a letter-by-letter manner, naming
each letter before saying what the word is and often before understanding
it (see Chapter 8). Letter-by-letter reading is not something that normal
readers ever do, nor something that these patients would ever have done
before their brain injury; rather it seems to be a way that non-damaged
cognitive systems can operate so as to effect a form of reading in a new
and unusual way when other parts of the system have been damaged.
What matters for cognitive neuropsychology is not that old modules can
be put to new uses, but that new modules should not be coming into
existence following brain injury.

The important assumption that the performance of a brain-injured
patient reflects the total cognitive apparatus minus those systems which
have been impaired, is what Saffran (1982) termed the assumption of
subtractivity. It is assumed—and there is as yet no good evidence to

cast doubt on this assumption—that the mature brain is not capable of sprouting new modules after brain injury. Only if we make this assumption can we use our models and other theoretical accounts of intact cognitive operations to interpret a patient's behaviour in terms of damage to the formerly intact cognitive system. As Caplan (1981) observes: "If the lesioned brain develops systems that are radically different than normal, that is an interesting and medically important fact, but not one relevant to normal functions." The injured brain may develop new *strategies* for coping in a particular task or situation, but it must do so using pre-existing *structures*. We shall encounter several examples of such strategies in the course of the book (e.g. patients who identify people using single salient visual features, or patients who read words by first naming all their letters). Such bizarre strategies need to be explained in terms of old modules and connections being put to new uses, though it is probably fair to say that such abnormal strategies are less helpful than other disorders when it comes to helping us understand the organisation of normal cognitive processes.

Caramazza's (1984) fourth requirement—that effects seen in brain-injured patients should not result from disruptions to processing mechanisms other than those hypothesised to be impaired—alludes to the fact that most brain injuries are substantial and cause damage to multiple processing components. There is a danger of ascribing to one component effects which are in fact due to a second, separate component which also happens to be damaged in that patient. In essence, this is the point made earlier in the chapter that co-occurrences of symptoms are much more hazardous things to base theoretical conclusions upon than are dissociations between symptoms. We will encounter several instances in this book where two or more symptoms, which at one time have plausibly been attributed to the impairment of one cognitive component, have later proved to be dissociable and must now be attributed to impairments to two separate cognitive components.

We should note that the assumption of transparency, whereby a patient's pattern of performance will provide a guide—albeit a complex one—to the nature of the underlying disruption, is one on which opinions have varied quite widely. Heeschen (1985, p. 209) quotes the neuropsychologist Kurt Goldstein as "emphatically pointing out over and over again that the brain-damaged patients' spontaneous behaviour never reflects the deficit itself, but rather the patients' reactions to the deficit". This does not undermine cognitive neuropsychology because "the true behavioural deficit shows up... under more carefully controlled and restricted formal testing conditions", but it suggests that we should be thinking in terms of an assumption of potential if sometimes clouded visibility rather than crystal transparency.

CONVERGING OPERATIONS

We have mentioned a number of similarities between today's cognitive neuropsychology and that practised by the "diagram makers" of the late nineteenth century. There are also, however, some important differences. One of these is that the diagram makers came to a cognitive neuropsychology from a background in medicine and neurology. In contrast, most of today's cognitive neuropsychologists either come from a background in experimental cognitive psychology or work in collaboration with mainstream cognitive psychologists. This means that cognitive neuropsychology is much closer in aims and in theories to experimental cognitive psychology than has ever been the case in the past. This is in part responsible for cognitive neuropsychology's current vigour.

It is noticeable that the subjects on which cognitive neuropsychology cut its teeth in the late 1960s and early 1970s were subjects for which there was a strong tradition in experimental cognitive psychology and for which there were viable theories of normal functioning. For example, Shallice and Warrington (1970) used existing theories of the organisation of short-term memory and long-term memory as a framework within which to interpret the performance of their patient KF in whom short-term verbal recall was impaired although long-term recall was preserved. Shallice and Warrington argued that such a pattern of performance was, in fact, incompatible with prevailing theories of memory structure, such as that put forward by Atkinson and Shiffrin (1968), but was interpretable in terms of a somewhat modified memory model.

Although Shallice and Warrington eventually disagreed with and sought to modify pre-existing memory models, nevertheless those models and techniques which derived from experimental cognitive psychology shaped and guided their investigation of patient KF. Similarly, Marshall and Newcombe (1973) were able to make use of models of normal reading performance which existed at the time in their analysis of different forms of reading disorder (acquired dyslexia). Once again their cognitive neuropsychological work led them to propose modifications to certain existing models, but their work was nevertheless closely guided and shaped by the theories and methods of cognitive psychology. Unlike the diagram makers, who had to devise their own theories of normal performance while simultaneously using those theories to explain different patterns of disorder, the more recent generation of cognitive neuropsychologists have often been able to begin their investigations of disorders in particular areas with reference to theories of normal performance put forward by mainstream experimental cognitive psychologists.

Modern-day cognitive neuropsychologists also bring to the study of patients the techniques of analysis developed in experimental psychology, including techniques for the statistical interpretation of results. Indeed, many cognitive neuropsychologists retain a foot in the experimental camp, because it is not uncommon for work with a patient to generate predictions about how normal subjects will behave in particular tasks or under particular conditions. Cognitive neuropsychologists can find themselves alternating between the hospital ward or patient's home and the cognitive laboratory in their pursuit of the understanding of how a particular area of cognition works.

We noted above that cognitive neuropsychology rests on a number of fundamental assumptions. So, equally, does experimental cognitive psychology. But the assumptions of the two approaches are to some extent different. This means that a conclusion about the nature of cognition which is supported by evidence from both experimental and neuropsychological studies is more reliable than a conclusion which is supported by evidence from only one source, because the conclusion supported by two lines is that much less likely to be artifactual or to rest on a faulty assumption. Seeking support for a theoretical conclusion from two or more different sources is what Garner, Hake, and Eriksen (1956) termed *converging operations*, and the quest for converging operations has provided much of the vigour of cognitive neuropsychology in recent decades.

The quest for converging evidence is seen very clearly in the work of Shallice, McLeod, and Lewis (1985). They sought evidence for the independence of cognitive modules from experiments with normal subjects involving "dual-task" performance. They reasoned that if neuropsychological data suggests that two tasks are dissociable and therefore mediated by separate sets of cognitive modules, then in the normal subject it should be possible for those two sets of modules to sustain their separate tasks independently without detriment to either. Therefore, two tasks which each depend for their execution on different sets of modules should be capable of being executed together simultaneously almost as efficiently as either can be executed on its own. Shallice et al. (1985) tested this prediction in a dual-task experiment where normal subjects were required simultaneously to read aloud written words and to monitor a list of heard names for particular target names. They found that their subjects were capable of reading aloud while monitoring heard names almost as well as they could either read aloud alone or monitor heard names alone. This matches similar work, such as that of Allport, Antonis, and Reynolds (1972) who found that skilled pianists with a little practice could simultaneously repeat passages of prose they were hearing over headphones and sight-read music they had seen beforehand for only 10 seconds with little detriment to either task. This line of convergence promises to provide a good way of assessing whether modules which neuropsychological evidence suggests are capable of functioning independently of one another can in fact do so in the normal, intact person.

A rather different form of convergence between data from patients and data from normal subjects comes when normal subjects display "symptoms" similar to those shown by brain-injured patients. We shall see in Chapter 5 how the word-finding difficulties of some "aphasic" patients closely resemble the occasional difficulties which normal people can experience when caught in a tip-of-the-tongue state. Similarly, in Chapter 7 we shall show how patients with certain forms of writing disorder can make habitual spelling errors which resemble the occasional spelling difficulties of normal subjects. Chapter 8 discusses a form of acquired reading disorder known as "attentional dyslexia" in which patients often report having seen words which are made up of letters taken from words actually present on the written page but rearranged to form a new word (for example, seeing the word *peg* when the words in front of them are *pad* and *leg*). Normal subjects will occasionally make this sort of error when reading (Cowie, 1985) but will make these same errors much more frequently if shown groups of words for very short intervals. That simple experimental manipulation greatly increases the number of errors to a level which can come close to that of "attentional dyslexics" (Allport, 1977). The crucial difference, of course, is that the "attentional dyslexics" make these errors when they have unlimited time to inspect words.

The importance of this sort of converging evidence lies in the support it provides for the subtractivity assumption—the assumption that what we see in a brain-injured patient is just the previous, intact cognitive system minus those components which have been lost or impaired through brain injury. Where the errors made by neurological patients resemble errors made by normal people then we feel confident in saying that the cognitive systems which are impaired in the patient, and give rise to the habitual errors of those patients, are the same systems which very occasionally malfunction in normals, or which can be made to malfunction more often when stressed by various experimental manipulations. We do not need to postulate the growth of new cognitive processes or even of new strategies in the patient in order to explain the occurrence of symptoms which have counterparts in normal behaviour and normal errors.

Converging operations are extremely important in present-day cognitive neuropsychology. The aim is to develop theories of normal, intact cognitive functioning which are also capable of accounting for the different patterns of disorder that can be seen in neurological patients. Sometimes the development of those theories will be better served by laboratory experiments with normal subjects; sometimes by careful study of brain-injured patients. We should be willing to turn to either source of evidence as necessary. The continuing vigour of cognitive neuropsychology will depend to a large extent on whether or not it is able to keep abreast of developments in cognitive psychology. If cognitive neuropsychology were to lose touch with mainstream cognitive science, then it would be in real danger of losing much of its momentum.

We said at the outset of this chapter that we think the strength of cognitive neuropsychology is best appreciated through experience of its achievements in helping to unravel cognitive processes. Accordingly, we shall wind up our introduction at this point in order to turn to a consideration of specific applications of the cognitive neuropsychological approach. Each of the following chapters will end with an Overview, a Summary, and a list of Further Reading. The Overview will make some general theoretical points about the cognitive function under consideration, while the Summary will provide a précis of the main points. Because this entire chapter is, in a sense, an Overview, we shall forego such a section here.

SUMMARY

Cognitive neuropsychology has undergone a revival since around 1970. It is an approach which attempts to understand cognitive functions such as recognising, speaking or remembering through an analysis of the different ways those functions can be impaired following brain injury. More specifically, cognitive neuropsychology seeks to explain the patterns of impaired and intact cognitive performance seen in brain-injured patients in terms of damage to one or more of the components of a theory or model of normal cognitive functioning and, conversely, to draw conclusions about normal, intact cognitive processes from the observed disorders.

Dissociations, in which one aspect of performance is impaired whereas others are preserved, are taken to imply the existence of separate cognitive subsystems or *modules* responsible for different cognitive operations. The hypothesised organisation of these modules may (according to taste) be expressed in terms of an "information processing" diagram. Frequently, observed *associations* between deficits are harder to interpret because of the danger that they may arise for anatomical rather than functional reasons (e.g. cognitively distinct modules depend on adjacent regions of cerebral cortex and thus tend to be impaired together).

In contrast to traditional neuropsychology which tended to study groups of patients, cognitive neuropsychologists typically investigate single cases of theoretical importance. The results of these investigations are interpreted in terms of a set of assumptions which are still being articulated and changed as the approach evolves. The assumption of *isomorphism* states that the cognitive structure of the mind is reflected in, and arises out of, the physiological organisation of the brain. The assumption of *transparency* holds that, given the wit and the time, it will be possible to deduce the nature of the underlying cognitive disorder in a patient from the pattern of preserved and impaired capabilities (including the pattern of errors). This process will be aided by the assumption of *subtractivity* according to which the performance of a brain-injured patient is explained in terms of the capabilities of the normal, intact cognitive system minus those components which have been lost as a result of the injury. In other words, the mature brain is assumed to be incapable of developing new cognitive structures following injury.

Cognitive neuropsychologists believe that we can draw general conclusions about the way the intact mind and brain work from studying neurological patients, but such conclusions can obviously also be drawn from observational and experimental studies of normal subjects. Some theoretical questions may be more easily resolved by the study of patients, others by the study of normals. The most reliable conclusions, however, will be those supported by independent evidence from the two separate lines of enquiry.

FURTHER READING

As yet, general theoretical statements regarding the nature of the cognitive neuropsychological enterprise have been confined to journal articles and book chapters. There are still differences of opinion among practitioners where details are concerned, but a move towards a broad consensus may be detected in the following papers.

We can begin with the two papers which initially excited many people and awakened them to the possibilities of cognitive neuropsychology:

Shallice, T., & Warrington, E. K. (1970). Independent functioning of verbal memory stores: a neuropsychological study. *Quarterly Journal of Experimental Psychology 22*, 261–273. Used date from patient KF to argue against the prevailing view of the organisation of short-term and long-term memory as sequential memory stores in favour of a parallel entry model (see Chapter 10).

Marshall, J. C., & Newcombe, F. (1973). Patterns of paralexia: a psycholinguistic approach. *Journal of Psycholinguistic Research, 2*, 175–199. A review of classical research on reading disorders plus new data supporting a "dual route" model of normal reading processes (see Chapter 8). Introduced, for better or for worse, the terms "visual dyslexia", "surface dyslexia' and "deep dyslexia". Still a joy to read.

Shallice, T. (1979a). Case study approach in neuropsychological research. *Journal of Clinical Neuropsychology, 1*, 183–211. The case for single-case studies, with recommendations on how to conduct and interpret them.

Saffran, E. M. (1982). Neuropsychological approaches to the study of language. *British Journal of Psychology, 73*, 317–337. Applies cognitive neuropsychology to explicating language processes and discusses some of its assumptions.

Caramazza, A. (1984). The logic of neuropsychological research and the problem of patient classification in aphasia. *Brain and Language, 21*, 9–20. A strong case for single-case studies and a detailed consideration of assumptions.

Caramazza, A. (1986). On drawing inferences about the structure of normal cognitive systems from the analysis of patterns of impaired performance: The case for single-patient studies. *Brain and Cognition, 5*, 41–66. The title says most of it. Formal arguments for single-case studies, plus a consideration of some frequently voiced objections.

Ellis, A. W. (1987). Intimations of modularity, or, the modelarity of mind: Doing cognitive neuropsychology without syndromes. In M. Coltheart, G. Sartori & R. Job (Eds), *The cognitive neuropsychology of language*. London: Lawrence Erlbaum Associates. Queries the wisdom of replacing old neuropsychological taxonomies of patients with new cognitive-neuropsychological ones. Argues that the results of case studies should be related directly to theoretical models without the intervention of any sort of syndrome categories.

Wernicke, C. (1874). *Der Aphasische Symptomenkomplex*. Breslau: Cohn & Weigart. (Translated in G. H. Eggert, *Wernicke's works on aphasia*. The Hague: Mouton, 1977.) Carl Wernicke was one of the founders of the school of "diagram makers". Written when he was only 28, this remarkable work is still well worth reading.

2 Object Recognition

INTRODUCTION

The area of neuropsychology that has received the most attention, both from the traditional localisationalist approach and in the more recent studies in which the disorders are considered from a psychological perspective, is language use. There are several reasons for this, including the marked cerebral asymmetries in the control of language which seem well suited to investigation in terms of the localisation of functions in particular areas of the brain. The structural properties of language itself also offer a ready choice of factors to manipulate and investigate in more psychologically oriented studies. In addition, disorders of language are commonly encountered in stroke patients and in other patients with cerebral injuries, and can take remarkably specific forms.

The use of language, however, presupposes something to talk about. So let us begin by considering impairments in an individual's ability to understand the world around her or him; a world of objects and people. In doing this we will first consider the ability to recognise objects (this chapter), then broaden our discussion to examine a wider range of visual and spatial abilities (Chapter 3), and then consider the ability to recognise other people and to interpret their feelings and expressions (Chapter 4). These are vast topics, and in order to keep the range and quantity of material to a manageable level we will concentrate on the understanding of the visually perceived world, and on the face as a source of information used to identify people and interpret their feelings. Although the cognitive analysis of such impairments has not been nearly as widely pursued as has the cognitive analysis of disorders of language, we think that it holds great promise and that there are exciting discoveries to be made. This is not, however, to underestimate the size of the obstacles that will be encountered along the way.

Before considering neuropsychological studies of object recognition, we examine briefly some of the factors involved in recognising objects, and develop a simple theoretical framework to describe the functional components (modules) involved.

UNDERSTANDING OBJECT RECOGNITION

Most people are able to recognise everyday objects with ease across quite wide ranges of distances, orientations and lighting conditions. This is necessary for normal life, because we encounter the objects concerned under many different circumstances. In pointing out that an object can usually be recognised despite such transformations we do not wish to imply that the transformations have no effect. Gross or unusual transformations of distance, lighting or orientation can, for instance, be used to make puzzles in which everyday objects become hard to recognise. Our point is only that the brain's object recognition system has the potential to cope with such transformations and that under everyday conditions their effects are not usually noticed.

We can also readily recognise depictions of objects on a two-dimensional surface in the form of photographs, coloured pictures, or line drawings that may or may not include implied pictorial depth. Realistic depictions of these types make use of some but not all of the cues that can be used to recognise real objects.

Two important points can be deduced from this preliminary consideration of object recognition. The first is that descriptions of the structures of all of the objects we know must in some sense be stored in the brain, so that we are able to recognise one we have met before even if it is seen from a new angle. Object recognition can thus be considered to involve a comparison of the structure of a seen object with the structures of objects that are already known. The second point is that although this comparison will often demand knowledge of the three-dimensional structure of the objects concerned, there are certain cases in which outline shape can be sufficient to effect recognition. Recognition from outline shape probably requires that the object concerned is both well known and has a particularly characteristic shape, and will often also require that it is seen (or depicted) from one of a limited range of viewing positions.

The most powerful theoretical analysis of object recognition to date was presented by Marr (1980, 1982). Marr took as his starting point the assumption that vision involves the computation of efficient symbolic descriptions or representations from images cast by the world upon the retina. The basic questions he addressed were thus those of what types of representations are necessary for vision and what computational problems their construction poses. He suggested an analysis that proceeds through a sequence of three types of representation:

1. An initial representation, which Marr called the primal sketch. He thought that this would represent intensity (brightness) changes across the field of vision, and the two-dimensional geometry of the image. Such features as edges will usually produce abrupt intensity changes.

2. A viewer-centred representation, which Marr called the $2^{1}/_{2}$-D sketch. This would represent the spatial locations of visible surfaces from the viewer's position. Marr's idea was that conventional sources of information concerning depth and location (stereopsis, texture gradients, shading, and so on) are computed as part of the primal sketch and then assembled in the the $2^{1}/_{2}$-D sketch. The disadvantage of the $2^{1}/_{2}$-D sketch is that it lacks generality since it describes the object only from the observer's viewpoint.

3. An object-centred representation, which Marr called the 3-D model representation. This is a representation of the seen objects and surfaces which is independent of the viewer's position, and specifies the real shape of these objects and surfaces and how they are positioned with respect to each other.

Because the object-centred (3-D model) representation specifies the three-dimensional structure of the object in a relatively standard form, recognition by means of looking up this structure in some kind of store of all known object structures would then be possible.

A problem in understanding how objects are recognised that has often received comment concerns the fact that the level in the hierarchy of things in the world at which recognition is required can vary. A motor car might, for instance, be identified under different circumstances as a vehicle, a car, a Ford car, a Ford Escort, or as your friend's car. This point is important because it emphasises the flexibility of the human cognitive system.

We think, however, that the significance of our potential for flexibility of approach in object recognition can be overemphasised. Although it is certainly true that the car can be identified at any of the levels described by someone with the requisite knowledge, it does not follow either that all levels of recognition can be achieved with the same ease or that one level is not typical of everyday use. A particularly convincing case has been made by Rosch and her colleagues that categorisations of concrete objects are not arbitrary, but determined by their natural properties into certain basic categories (Rosch, Mervis, Gray, Johnson, & Boyes-Braem, 1976; Rosch, 1978). The basic category for our example would be "car". These basic categories were found to exist at a level at which objects in different categories could be most readily differentiated from each other in terms of attributes and shapes; they were also the earliest categories to be sorted and named by children. Of particular importance to the present discussion is Rosch et al.'s (1976) finding that objects could be classified as members (or not members) of the basic category more quickly than they could be classified as members (or not members) of superordinate or subordinate categories. Thus you would be quicker to identify your friend's car as a car than as a vehicle (superordinate category) or as a Ford car (subordinate category). This suggests that identification as a member of superordinate or subordinate categories may often be achieved via an initial identification at the basic level.

A MODEL OF OBJECT RECOGNITION AND NAMING

A model of the functional components involved in object recognition and naming consistent with the points we have discussed is presented in Fig. 2.1. This is by no means the only possible theoretical model, but we believe that it is adequate for present purposes. The model makes use of Marr's idea that three levels of representation of the visual input can be distinguished; we have called these initial, viewer-centred and object-centred. It also makes use of the idea that recognition is effected by comparing viewer-centred and object-centred representations to stored structural descriptions of known objects. We have called these stored descriptions object recognition units, and they act as an interface between visual and semantic representations (see Humphreys & Riddoch, 1987b; Seymour, 1979; Warren & Morton, 1982, for related conceptions of object recognition). A visual representation (separated here into initial, viewer-centred and object-centred) describes what the object looks like, whereas a semantic representation specifies its properties and attributes. One recognition unit is held to exist for each known object. This recognition unit can access the object's semantic representation when the visual representation of a seen object corresponds to the description of the object stored in the recognition unit. The object recognition units can be "primed" by recent experience or by context to be more easily activated (i.e. to "expect" certain objects to occur). Like most contemporary theories of object and word recognition (see Seymour, 1979) we tend to think that any particular stimulus has a semantic representation that can be accessed by different types of input (object, picture, written

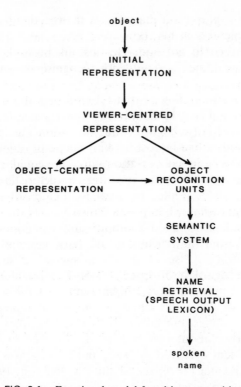

FIG. 2.1.   Functional model for object recognition.

name, spoken name, etc.) rather than a different semantic representation for every type of input.

Object naming, which is a task commonly given to neuropsychological patients, is dealt with in our model by assuming that the semantic system does not contain the object's name, but can retrieve the name from a separate store or "lexicon", which we shall discuss in Chapter 5 under the heading of the "speech output lexicon". There is no direct link between the object recognition units and this name store; all retrieval of object names occurs via a semantic representation.

THE CONCEPT OF AGNOSIA

GL, an 80-year-old salesman, returned exhausted from one of his business trips after a severe storm had blown him against a wooden fence, knocking his head. He retired to bed for a few days, complaining that he was no longer able to see as well as before.

GL's problems were obvious when he got up. Although he could still see, he no longer recognised the things about him. Instead, he looked around in a perplexed manner, as if everything was unfamiliar. He thought that pictures in his room were boxes, and tried to search in them for things he could not find. He mistook his jacket for a pair of trousers, and at mealtimes he could not recognise the pieces of cutlery on the table.

Detailed investigations showed that GL still had almost normal visual acuity for his age, and that he could draw quite accurate copies of seen objects that he could not recognise; thus his vision was in at least some respects intact. Neither had he lost his knowledge of objects; he referred to them appropriately in conversation, and he could recognise them immediately if he handled them, or from characteristic sounds. When shown a whistle, for example, he had no idea what it was, yet he recognised it straight away when it was blown.

GL's problems form a good example of *visual agnosia*. The term agnosia is derived from the Ancient Greek language, and roughly translates as "not-knowing". Use of the term agnosia is usually taken to imply that the recognition disorder is not a consequence of general intellectual deterioration, language impairment, or basic sensory dysfunction at the level we have described as the initial representation. The patient can still see things, but fails to recognise what they are. GL's case is, in fact, of particular interest because it was one of the first to be reported. His accident occurred in 1887, and his case was described in a classic paper by Lissauer (1890; see Shallice & Jackson, 1988).

Agnosias may be in visual (inability to recognise seen objects), tactile (inability to recognise felt objects) or auditory (inability to recognise heard objects) modalities (see Oppenheimer & Newcombe, 1978; Rubens, 1979; Vignolo, 1982). Within a particular modality they can occur for different classes of stimuli such as colours, objects or faces. Often, however, the same patient will be agnosic for more than one modality or for more than one class of stimuli within a particular modality. An excellent review of the clinical features of agnosic disorders is given by Rubens (1979). We will give most attention here to the nature of the underlying cognitive impairments found in cases of agnosia for visually presented objects. These are very disabling, and Humphreys and Riddoch (1987a) provide a sympathetic account of the impact of the condition on everyday life.

There seem to be several different causes of visual object agnosia. Lissauer (1890) himself realised this, and distinguished between what he termed "apperceptive" and "associative" agnosias. He proposed that visual recognition can be separated into apperceptive and associative stages, and that each when impaired has its own characteristic agnosia. The apperceptive stage would correspond to the final stage of purely "perceptual" processing; it was considered to be intact if the patient could accurately copy items s/he could not recognise. The associative stage would give the percept meaning by linking it to previous experience.

Lissauer's apperceptive or associative distinction is still often used as a starting point in identifying the various types of agnosia, but we will not make much use of it here because, as we will see, the issues raised by modern studies of agnosia demand a richer type of theory.

Disconnection Hypotheses

Lissauer's explanation of apperceptive agnosia was in terms of *damage* to the perceptual mechanisms themselves, whereas his explanation of associative agnosia was closer to that of a *disconnection* between intact perception and stored associations. Damage and disconnection continue to be used as explanatory concepts in modern studies of agnosia, and disconnection explanations were given a particular boost by the work of Geschwind (1965a; 1965b), who demonstrated that certain neurological syndromes fit disconnection explanations very neatly.

Although it was not central to his argument, Geschwind (1965b) proposed that visual object agnosia can result from disconnection of areas of the brain responsible for vision and for speech. Such a disconnection could, for instance, happen when serious injury of the posterior part of the left cerebral hemisphere deprived the left hemisphere's speech areas of visual input by destroying simultaneously both the left hemisphere's own visual areas and the connections (via the corpus callosum) to the left hemisphere's speech area from the remaining visual areas of the right cerebral hemisphere. The patient would still have an intact (right hemisphere) visual area and an intact (left hemisphere) speech area, but these intact areas would be disconnected from each other (for most patients there is no right hemisphere speech area). This is actually an over-simplification of Geschwind's suggestion, but it is sufficient to establish the basic point that such disconnections are anatomically possible. More-over, cases of difficulties in object recognition for which disconnection provides a plausible and appealing explanation have certainly been described (e.g. Mack & Boller, 1977; Newcombe & Ratcliff, 1974, case 3; Rubens & Benson, 1971). As we will see, however, disconnection cannot account for the problems of all agnosic patients, and the basic distinction of vision and speech is in any case too simple to cope with the complexity of the issues that emerge. The first cases we will discuss involve shape processing impairments. They are what Lissauer (1890) would have considered to be apperceptive agnosias (but see Warrington, 1987, for a different view), and are not susceptible to disconnection explanations.

SHAPE-PROCESSING IMPAIRMENTS

Benson and Greenberg (1969) reported their observations of a young soldier, Mr S, who had suffered accidental carbon monoxide poisoning. Mr S seems to have possessed an initial representation of visual stimuli that was at least to some extent intact. His visual fields were normal to 10 mm and 3 mm white objects, and he was able to maintain fixation. He could name colours and describe at least some other perceptual qualities; for instance he described a safety pin as being "silver and shiny like a watch or nail clipper". He was said to appear attentive to his surroundings, and he could navigate the hospital corridors successfully in his wheelchair. He was also able to distinguish small differences in stimulus brightness and wavelength on psychophysical testing, and could detect movements of small objects.

On any task requiring shape or form perception, however, Mr S was very severely impaired. His eye movements seemed random when he scanned pictures, and he was virtually unable to recognise objects, pictures of objects, body parts, letters, numbers, faces or geometrical figures from vision alone. He was unable to copy letters or simple figures and could not match a sample figure to an identical figure in a set of four. In marked contrast, he was able to identify and name objects from tactile, olfactory and auditory cues. No defects were noticed in his memory, spontaneous speech, or comprehension.

Mr S showed impaired ability to analyse visual form. We could interpret the case as being one of severe impairment in constructing the viewer-centred representation, because there is some evidence of sparing of the simple perceptual properties given by the initial representation despite almost total deterioration on tasks requiring shape information including copying, matching and identification. Efron (1968) provides further information on Mr S's shape-processing impairment.

A more recent case described by Abadi, Kulikowski, and Meudell (1981), and investigated subsequently by Campion and Latto (1985), however, suggests that impairment of the initial representation might contribute to this type of problem. Like Mr S, Campion and Latto's patient, RC, had suffered accidental carbon monoxide poisoning. He also showed an impairment of object recognition, being able to identify only 17 out of 27 objects with considerable difficulty. He could not copy line drawings, or even trace them with his finger. In contrast, he could negotiate obstacles, reach out for seen objects, name objects from touch or sound, and comment on the colour and texture of seen objects. His visual acuity was normal, yet he maintained that his vision was "not clear".

Initial investigation of RC's visual fields showed only that there was an area of blindness in the lower right-hand portion. Such visual field defects are often found after neurological injury, but this alone could not account for RC's object recognition impairment, because many patients with worse visual field defects do not have the same problem. More careful testing revealed, however, that small areas of blindness were scattered across the whole of RC's field of vision. Campion and Latto (1985) suggest that this "peppering" of the visual field resulted from diffuse damage to the visual cortex of the brain: Because of their cortical origin, RC would not be aware of these numerous small areas of blindness when he looked at things (in the same way as we are not normally aware of the blind spot in our own field of vision where the optic nerve leaves the retina). Figure 2.2 gives an idea of how difficult this hypothesised scattering of blind areas throughout the visual field might make object recognition.

We are touching here on the much debated issue of the contribution of impairments of basic perceptual abilities to agnosias. RC's case makes clear that such impairments may contribute to at least some cases of disordered object recognition ability. The suspicion that all visual object agnosias may be a consequence of subtle (and, by implication, probably overlooked) alterations in perceptual function has been particularly difficult to shake off, but it is now widely accepted that sensory impairments show no necessary relation to object identification difficulties, and that many patients who are in no sense agnosic show greater sensory defects than those who are (Ettlinger, 1956; Young & Ellis, 1988). Moreover, as we will see, even the most careful testing has failed to reveal sensory defects in a few of the agnosic patients who have been described.

RECOGNITION OF DEGRADED STIMULI, AND IMPAIRMENTS OF OBJECT CONSTANCY

Degraded Stimuli

We have already commented on the facility with which normal people can recognise objects across a relatively wide range of perceptual transformations. Several studies of groups of patients with posterior lesions of the left or right cerebral hemispheres have, however, shown that patients with right hemisphere injuries do not show this facility to the same degree as normal people. These patients are not agnosic, in the sense that their everyday recognition abilities are not dramatically affected by the disorder, but they show clear impairments on certain types of task. They experience, for instance, disproportionate difficulty in identifying objects which are drawn overlapping each other (De Renzi & Spinnler, 1966), or in identifying objects from pictures degraded by the removal of some

FIG. 2.2. A: Photograph of a scene, and B: the same photograph covered with a random dot mask to simulate what the world might look like to R.C. It is assumed that the patient would not actually be aware of the dots but would be left with the consequent disruption of contour necessity for form perception. Note the differential masking effect of the same mask on different objects. Thus, the child's face completely disappears, whereas the wheelbarrow remains visible. The bucket contour is disrupted to an intermediate extent. (Reproduced with permission from Campion, 1987.)

edge information (De Renzi & Spinnler, 1966; Warrington & James, 1967a).

A number of other examples of this type could be given. What they all share is the finding that in difficult object recognition tasks the performance of patients with right hemisphere injuries is more affected than the performance of normal control subjects or patients with left hemisphere injuries. Warrington (1982, p. 18) remarks that "the hallmark of this syndrome appears to be a difficulty in perceiving meaningful visual stimuli when the redundancy normally present within the figure is reduced or degraded".

This impairment in difficult recognition tasks does not seem to be a direct consequence of impairment at the level of what we have called the initial representation. Several examples of this point are given by Warrington (1982), who shows that despite their impairment on object identification tasks, patients with right posterior injuries can achieve what she calls an "adequately structured percept". Their impairments in visual sensory efficiency, figure-ground discrimination and contour discrimination are no greater than those of other patients (usually patients with left hemisphere injuries) who do not experience difficulty in object identification tasks.

The difficulties in identification tasks are thus thought to reflect impairments at a post-sensory level of visual information processing, such as the viewer-centred and object-centred representations. The deficits are seen as sufficient to interfere with difficult identification tasks while leaving performance on relatively simple identification tasks within normal limits. Comparable impairments in right hemisphere patients have also been shown for the recognition of degraded letters (Warrington & James, 1967a) and for deciding whether pictures of faces distorted by the exaggeration of lighting effects were those of a man, woman, old man, old woman, boy or girl (Newcombe, 1969; 1974). The parallel between these tasks and those causing impairment of object identification in right hemisphere patients is easy to see, though it should not be too quickly assumed that they all measure the same deficit, because Warrington (1982) has presented evidence for dissociations between comparable impairments with different types of visual stimulus material.

Unusual Views

In a series of papers Warrington (1982; Warrington & Taylor, 1973; 1978) has argued that object recognition requires some means of assigning equivalent stimuli to the same perceptual category, in order to cope with transformations of orientation, lighting, distance, and so on. It is this perceptual categorisation that she thinks defective in patients with posterior injuries of the right cerebral hemisphere. In terms of our own model Warrington's idea of perceptual categorisation involves the combined action of the functional components described as viewer-centred representation, object-centred representation, and object recognition units (i.e. stored descriptions of the structures of familiar objects).

The evidence presented by Warrington and Taylor (1973; 1978) is intriguing. They showed patients photographs of objects taken from conventional and unusual views. Although Warrington and Taylor do not attempt to define what constitutes a conventional or an unusual view, the idea is not difficult to pick up, and an example of what is meant is given in Fig. 2.3. Warrington and Taylor (1973) point out that they chose the unusual views so that they were not necessarily unfamiliar views. Their unusual view of a bucket, for instance, involves looking almost directly into it; yet buckets are not uncommonly seen from this angle.

Two different versions of tests using conventional and unusual views have been devised by Warrington and Taylor. The first version (Warrington & Taylor, 1973) involved photographs of the same 20 common objects taken from both conventional and unusual views. Subjects were first required to identify the object shown in each of the unusual views, and then to identify the same objects from each of the conventional views. Their findings were that few errors were made from the conventional view, but a group of patients with posterior injuries of the right hemisphere were poor at identifying objects from an unconventional view.

We would suggest that at least part of this deficit in identifying objects from unconventional views may be explainable in terms of an impairment in constructing object-centred representations. As already stated, Warrington's idea of perceptual categorisation seems to encompass what we have described as the viewer-centred representation, object-centred representation and object recognition units. However, the unimpaired performance of the patients with right posterior injuries on conventional views suggests that the viewer-centred representation and object recognition units are relatively intact. The key feature of many (though by no means

UNUSUAL VIEW   USUAL VIEW

FIG. 2.3. Examples of usual and unusual views of an object. (Figure kindly supplied by Professor E. K. Warrington.)

all) of the unusual views used by Warrington and Taylor (1973) is most likely to be the foreshortening of the object's principal axis of elongation. This foreshortening would make it particularly difficult to derive an object-centred representation (Marr & Nishihara, 1978) and would thus highlight any impairment at this level.

In the second version of their conventional and unusual views test Warrington and Taylor (1978) presented pairs of photographs of objects, with one conventional view and one unusual view in each pair. The task was to decide whether the photographs in each pair were pictures of the same object; Warrington and Taylor (1978) describe this task as involving matching by physical identity. An impairment in a group of patients with posterior injuries of the right cerebral hemisphere was again found. This result is particularly striking because it implies that these patients cannot form an adequate representation of the object in the unusual view *despite* being able to derive an explicit hypothesis as to what it might be from their unimpaired performance with the conventional view photographs. When the same patients were later asked to identify the objects from photographs of conventional and unusual views presented one at a time, an impairment was again found for the unusual views.

It is clear, then, that patients with posterior (usually parietal lobe) lesions of the right cerebral hemisphere show impairments on some object recognition tasks which do not seem to be a direct consequence of an impairment in the initial representation of visual stimuli. Warrington has interpreted these difficulties as reflecting impaired perceptual categorisation, whereas we have preferred to emphasise the importance of object-centred representations. We see this as a variant of Warrington's explanation rather than a challenge to it. Both accounts locate the impairment at a level of visual information processing that can be described as post-sensory but pre-semantic.

Object Constancy

Humphreys and Riddoch (1984; 1985) have extended Warrington's work by carrying out investigations of individual patients with impairments of object constancy. By object constancy, Humphreys and Riddoch mean the ability to recognise that an object has the same structure across changes in view. They propose that we have two independent means of achieving object constancy; one by making use of an object's distinctive features, and the other by describing its structure relative to its principal axis of elongation. "Unusual" views might then impair object constancy either because they obscure a distinctive feature or because they foreshorten the object, making its principal axis of elongation more difficult to determine.

To disentangle these possibilities Humphreys and Riddoch used a matching task in which two photographs of the same object were presented together with a third photograph showing a visually similar distractor.

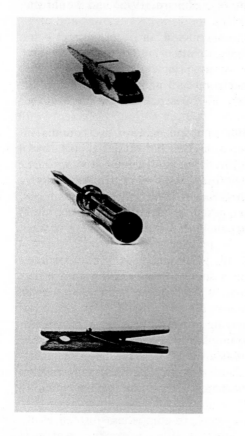
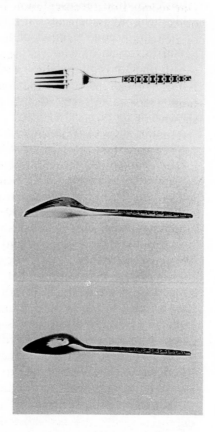

FORESHORTENED MATCH   MINIMAL FEATURE MATCH

FIG. 2.4. Examples of the foreshortened and minimal-feature conditions of Humphreys and Riddoch's (1984) matching task. (Stimuli kindly supplied by Dr. G. Humphreys & Dr. J. Riddoch.)

Patients and control subjects were asked to pick the two photographs which showed the same object. The target objects were carefully chosen to have a primary distinctive feature and a principal axis of elongation. One member of the correct pair of photographs always showed the target object in a "prototypical" view, in which its distinctive feature and axis of elongation were clearly visible. The other member of the correct pair of photographs showed the same object with its axis of elongation foreshortened or with the saliency of its primary distinctive feature reduced; these are called the foreshortened and minimal-feature conditions, respectively. It is easy to get the idea by examining the examples shown in Fig. 2.4.

Humphreys and Riddoch (1984; 1985) present data for five patients— four of these had right posterior cerebral lesions and the fifth, HJA, had a severe visual object agnosia caused by bilateral occipital lobe lesions. Because the performances of the four patients with right hemisphere lesions were so similar we have selected one representative, JL. On tests of basic form perception involving length, orientation and position discrimination with two-dimensional shapes, both JL and HJA were within the normal range of performance.

Data from the matching task for JL, HJA and control subjects are shown in Fig. 2.5, together with data indicating how often JL and HJA could name successfully the objects used from the different views. It was only the foreshortened pictures that created serious problems for JL, and these problems were equally severe whether the task was one of matching or naming. Thus, as we suggested for Warrington's patients with right posterior lesions, JL seems to have difficulty deriving the object-centred representation that would be needed to make a successful match or a successful identification in the foreshortened conditions. Humphreys and Riddoch (1984) in fact note that JL tended to fail to utilise available depth cues with the foreshortened objects, treating them instead as if they were almost two-dimensional, and that JL's performance was improved if extrinsic depth cues (in the form of a textured background) were provided.

HJA's problems are clearly quite different. The most notable feature is that he was much better at matching the objects than at identifying them by name. His performance at matching the foreshortened views was much better than JL's, yet he was as poor as JL at naming them. Thus HJA seems to have access to some form of object-centred representation (because he can match foreshortened views quite well) yet he did not seem to be able to use this very successfully to identify the objects concerned. HJA's case is one of the most fascinating (and thoroughly documented) in the literature of visual agnosia, and we will return to consider the case in detail later in this chapter.

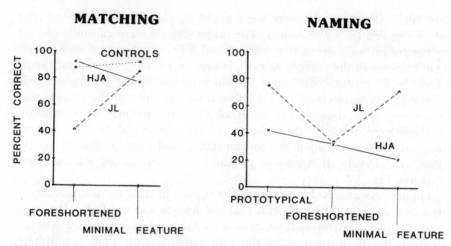

FIG. 2.5. Performance of JL, HJA and control subjects on object matching and naming tasks. Data from Humphreys & Riddoch (1984; 1985); the naming data consider omissions as errors.

SEMANTIC IMPAIRMENTS

Sometimes inability to recognise objects after brain injury can be caused by impairment to the semantic system itself. That is, knowledge of the object's category membership, functions, and so on, is degraded or inaccessible. This can be seen both in the findings of group studies and single-case studies.

Group Studies

Although patients with right hemisphere injuries can show impairments of object recognition to degraded or unusual views, De Renzi, Scotti, and Spinnler (1969) found that it was patients with left (rather than right) hemisphere injuries who were the most impaired when asked to match real objects to pictures of objects with very different appearances but the same names. This task, however, allows the match to be made at the level of object recognition units, semantic representations, or names. This problem of interpretation was eliminated by Warrington and Taylor (1978) who grouped stimuli, so that a photograph of an object was presented together with a photograph of a different object of a somewhat similar appearance and a photograph of another object with a similar function. When they were asked to pick the photograph of the object that matched the original object in function, patients with left and patients with right posterior injuries both showed significant impairments. For the patients with right posterior injuries, however, the impairments were found to be linked to misidentifications of the photographed objects, whereas the patients with the left posterior injuries made few mis-identifications but were still impaired on this matching by function task. Thus there is evidence of dissociable deficits of recognition and classification by function, or in Warrington's (1982) terms, of perceptual and semantic categorisation.

Single-case Studies

Single-case studies of recognition impairments due to damage to the semantic system were initially reported by Taylor and Warrington (1971) and Warrington (1975). The four cases described in these reports all involved progressive cerebral atrophy, and thus present particular prob-lems of description and interpretation because of the changes in the patients' condition. Warrington (1975), however, points out that for these patients at least the pattern of abilities and disabilities remained constant as their condition deteriorated. In effect, what can be done with each patient is to present a "snapshot" of his or her abilities at a certain stage in the disease's progression. From these four cases we have selected that of a former civil servant, AB (Warrington, 1975), for discussion here because of the combination of relatively severe object recognition difficulties and at least some preserved intellectual abilities.

Initially, AB was referred to the National Hospital in London for investigation of his deteriorating memory. He did indeed show impair-ments on conventional memory tests, yet he obtained a verbal I.Q. of 122 (well above average). His understanding of verbal instructions was good and he was able to converse fluently using a somewhat impoverished vocabulary.

Performance on a variety of perceptual tests was within normal limits. AB's visual fields, visual acuity and hearing were normal. He was able to distinguish shapes, and to make figure-ground discriminations at various levels of background noise. He could also match pictures of different views of faces satisfactorily (25/28 correct), and on Warrington and Taylor's (1978) task of matching conventional and unusual views of objects his performance (17/20 correct) was also within normal limits. In our terms this would indicate a preserved ability to derive an adequate object-centred representation.

In contrast to this pattern of remarkably intact perceptual abilities, AB was severely impaired in recognition tasks. Although he could identify colours, numbers, and letters, he was unable to name successfully any of a series of 12 common objects, and could name only 2 of a set of 15 photographs of the faces of contemporary personalities. In addition to these visual object and face recognition problems he was also unable to identify meaningful sounds such as a telephone ringing or a dog barking (2/12 correct). His comprehension of spoken words presented individually (i.e. without any supporting context to aid interpretation) was also impaired. Similarly, although he could read words he often did not understand what he had read, and he was also found to be poor at reading irregular words. He could, for instance, read "classification" but not "nephew". This combination of poor comprehension and difficulty with irregular words suggests that he relied a lot on spelling to sound correspondences in reading single words (see Chapter 8).

As well as being poor at object naming, AB was poor at naming pictures, and this deficit extended to both conventional (11/20 correct) and unusual (12/20 correct) views. When he could not identify an item he would usually state that it was "familiar" or that he had "forgotten" it. The other types of error mentioned by Warrington included being able to identify an object but not name it, being only able to place the item in a superordinate category (identifying a daffodil as "some kind of flower"; a hammer as "some kind of tool"), and substitutions of an incorrect item from the same category (identifying a donkey as a "horse"; a dog as a "cat").

When asked to identify the same items from pictures and spoken words (by naming the objects shown in the pictures or by describing the function of the same objects presented as spoken words) AB was impaired on both tasks, but was a little more successful with spoken words (27/40 correct) than with pictures (19/40 correct). The presence of an impairment on both tasks introduces the possibility favoured by Warrington (1975) that he is suffering from an impairment of semantic memory. This would correspond to an impairment of what we have called the semantic system and would imply some loss of knowledge of the "meanings" of objects (what they do, what they are made of, what category they belong to, where they are found, etc.).

In order to investigate this idea Warrington showed AB 40 photographs of animals and objects. These were given one at a time in random order, and he was asked to decide whether or not each was a photograph of an animal. The animal photographs were then presented one at a time and he was asked whether each one was a bird, whether each one was foreign, and whether each one was bigger than a cat. Similarly, with the object photographs he was asked whether each one was made of metal, used indoors, and heavier than a telephone directory.

The results of these tests are summarised in Table 2.1, together with the performance of five control subjects. AB is clearly impaired on most of the tests, but he is able to judge quite well whether or not photographs are of animals (37/40 correct). This confirms the observation that he could sometimes identify objects only to the level of a superordinate category

TABLE 2.1
Performance of Warrington's (1975) Patient AB on Semantic Judgement Tasks
(Number of Items Correct)

Stimulus Items	Task	Items Presented as Photographs		Items Presented as Spoken Words	
		AB's Performance	*Mean Performance of Control Subjects[a]*	*AB's Performance*	*Mean Performance of Control Subjects[a]*
Animals and objects	Animal?	37/40	39.6	29/40	39.8
Animals	Birds?	13/20	19.6	15/20	19.4
	Foreign?	9/20	18.4	14/20	18.8
	Size?	11/20	16.0	13/20	15.2
Objects	Metal?	16/20	19.8	11/20	19.6
	Indoors?	18/20	19.4	15/20	19.2
	Weight?	8/20	14.8	12/20	15.8

[a]($n=5$)

(e.g. identifying a daffodil as "some kind of flower"). Further evidence of a selective semantic impairment comes from the finding from another task that AB was poor at defining low-frequency concrete words yet able to define low-frequency abstract words. He was, for instance, able to define abstract words like supplication ("making a serious request for help") and pact ("friendly agreement"), while being unable to define needle ("forgotten") or geese ("an animal but I've forgotten precisely").

AB thus presents a pattern of intact initial, viewer-centred and object-centred representations, together with impairments on semantic tasks, suggesting the possibility of a selective impairment of some aspects of semantic memory. Although his memory was also impaired in other ways these additional memory impairments are not in themselves a satisfactory explanation of his recognition difficulties, because even globally amnesic patients are not usually agnosic, as Warrington (1975) and Ratcliff and Newcombe (1982) point out.

Category-specific Semantic Impairments

A remarkable feature of semantic memory impairments is that, for some patients, they can be category-specific. The patient JBR from the series of four patients described by Warrington and Shallice (1984) forms a good example. Like Warrington and Shallice's (1984) other patients, JBR was recovering from herpes simplex encephalitis, which causes extensive damage to the temporal lobes. His scores on intelligence tests were average (Verbal I.Q. 101, Performance I.Q. 103), though probably lower than his premorbid level (he had been an electronics undergraduate). He was amnesic, and disoriented in time and place. Like AB he could match conventional and unusual views well (20/20 correct), but performed poorly on tests of object recognition.

JBR's impairment was, however, particularly noticeable to living things. Table 2.2 shows data obtained when he was asked to identify 48 coloured pictures of animals and plants (living things), and 48 pictures of inanimate objects matched to the animals and plants for frequency of use as a word. He was then asked to define the same items when they

TABLE 2.2

Performance of Warrington and Shallice's (1984) Patient JBR
at Identifying Objects from Coloured Pictures and Defining
Them to Their Spoken Names (Percent Correct)

	Living Things	Inanimate Objects
Recognition from picture	6	90
Successful definition of spoken name	8	79

were presented to him as spoken words instead of pictures, and the data are again shown in Table 2.2. The superiority of inanimate objects over living things is most striking. JBR could define an item such as a compass ("tools for telling direction you are going"), yet produced the response "don't know" when asked what a parrot is. The category-specific impairment was found irrespective of whether JBR was tested on verbal description, naming, mimed responses, or picture–word matching. Often he could get superordinate information to living things (e.g. that a daffodil is a "plant"; a snail is "an insect animal"), but even in terms of access to the superordinate category he was still impaired in comparison with inanimate objects.

Warrington and Shallice (1984) are careful to make clear that the living/non-living distinction may not be the one that captures *every* aspect of these category-specific semantic impairments. JBR, for instance, was poor at identifying (inanimate) musical instruments yet good at (living) body parts. They suggest that semantic systems may be organised differently (and hence vulnerable to selective impairment) for things that have significance in terms of the way we use them (household objects, tools, etc.) and things that we know primarily in terms of their visual form (animals, plants, etc.). For those of us who are not musicians, musical instruments, the inanimate category JBR was poor at identifying, are known primarily from their appearance whereas our own bodies, i.e. the parts of living things JBR could identify well, are used all the time.

PAUSE FOR CONTEMPLATION

So far, we have developed a model (Fig. 2.1) in which an initial representation of a seen object is used to construct viewer-centred and object-centred representations which have parallel access to stored descriptions of the structures of known objects (object recognition units), allowing access to semantic representations. We were then able to use this model to account for cases involving shape-processing impairments (which would traditionally be classified as involving apperceptive agnosia) in terms of impairment to the viewer-centred (and perhaps initial) representations, and to account for other object recognition impairments in terms of impairment to the semantic system itself. We were also able to account for some of the problems experienced by patients with right posterior cerebral lesions by proposing that they experience difficulties in constructing object-centred representations, and were able to explain why these patients are not agnosic (because access to object recognition units from viewer-centred representations remains unimpaired).

If we stopped discussing object recognition impairments now, everything would seem neat. But there are other cases in the literature that do not fit this tidy story so well. Because they force us to reconsider, and perhaps revise, our notions these cases are of exceptional theoretical interest. We will now discuss four such patients, two (MS and HJA) involving "higher-order" perceptual impairment, and two (JF and JB) involving a condition known as optic aphasia.

HIGHER-ORDER PERCEPTUAL IMPAIRMENT

MS had been a police cadet until he suffered a febrile illness. This left him blind in part of his former field of vision and with disturbed colour vision. He also had serious memory difficulties, but he was still able to achieve a verbal I.Q. of 101 (normal level). Object and face recognition were very poor. His case has been described by Newcombe and Ratcliff (1974, case 2) and Ratcliff and Newcombe (1982).

When shown a series of 36 line drawings of objects, MS was only able to name 8 of them correctly. This poor performance cannot be attributed solely to the area of blindness in his left visual field, because most other patients with comparable or even more severe visual field defects would experience little difficulty with a task of this type. For most (20) of these drawings he did not give any suggestions as to what the object might be, but when he did make an error of identification it tended to resemble the stimulus. He thought, for example, that a drawing of an anchor showed an umbrella. The same types of error were evident to photographs and to real objects, though there were signs of improved performance for real objects (in a 10-item test he recognised 4 real objects, 1 photograph and 1 drawing). He was poor at describing the appearance of objects from memory. When asked to recognise objects presented in sense modalities other than vision, MS also showed an impairment in tactual recognition by both left and right hands, but his ability to recognise environmental sounds was within normal limits.

When Newcombe and Ratcliff (1974) asked MS to name each of the 36 objects used in their drawing naming task from a verbal description of its function or use he was able to name 20 correctly. This is certainly an improvement on the eight he could name from drawings, so that it does seem that any semantic or name retrieval problems are not sufficient to account for his agnosia. Further evidence for this conclusion comes from the finding (Ratcliff & Newcombe, 1982) that MS was much better able to make semantic judgements about printed words than pictures, which again suggests an impairment of object recognition over and above any semantic disturbance. However, MS did show uneven performance when asked to define objects himself. He could, for instance, explain successfully what an anchor is ("a brake for ships") but not what a nightingale is (Ratcliff & Newcombe, 1982); the possible parallel with Warrington and Shallice's (1984) patient JBR is obvious. These observations suggest that MS may also be experiencing some disturbance of the semantic system, but that (unlike JBR) it is not in itself sufficient to account for his agnosia.

The impairment of visual object recognition stands in marked contrast to some of MS' other abilities. In particular, we will draw attention to his preserved ability to read, and to his ability to copy drawings and to match identical stimuli. In each of these respects MS was quite unlike patients such as those described by Benson and Greenberg (1969) and Campion and Latto (1985).

On tasks involving naming printed words, MS was very accurate. This preserved ability to read is important because it suggests that the visual analysis needed to recognise words may be different to that required for object recognition, though Humphreys and Riddoch (1987a) have noted that reading *accuracy* is not a particularly sensitive measure, and that at least some agnosic patients may read accurately but letter-by-letter. The question as to the relation between reading impairments and the different types of visual agnosia may thus merit more systematic investigation.

MS also showed good ability to copy drawings and to match identical stimuli. His copy of a picture of an anchor is shown in Fig. 2.6. This was an object he had identified as an umbrella, yet the copy is remarkably accurate. It was achieved, however, only by the use of considerable care and a line-by-line copying strategy; when drawing objects without a model to copy from, his attempts were poor (but not always unrecognisable). When asked to match objects as being the same or different to each other MS performed almost perfectly on visual, tactual and cross-modal (one object presented to vision and one by touch) matches.

His ability to copy and match stimuli successfully suggests that, in contrast to Benson and Greenberg's (1969) patient, MS was able to construct adequate viewer-centred representations of the objects he viewed. Despite the evidence of intact viewer-centred representations, however, MS failed to identify many objects and pictures (such as the anchor) for which shape alone would seem to provide a powerful cue. Thus MS would seem to have an impairment to the stored descriptions of the structures of known objects (object recognition units). This is also suggested by the fact that MS was poor at describing the appearance of objects from memory. In addition, however, object-centred representations seemed to be impaired for MS. This can be seen in his performance on Warrington and Taylor's (1978) task involving the matching of objects photographed from conventional and unusual views. On this task, MS's performance was close to chance level despite his good performance on simpler matching tasks, for which viewer-centred representations would be adequate.

MS's problems in object recognition seem to derive primarily from impairment of "higher" visual functions. We have argued that the principal causes of his visual agnosia might be a combination of impairments of object-centred representations and object recognition units. This view is consistent with those of Newcombe and Ratcliff (1974) and Ratcliff and Newcombe (1982), though our theoretical model differs from theirs in some respects. However, the second case of "higher-order" perceptual impairment we will consider, HJA, cannot be reconciled with our model so easily.

ORIGINAL   COPY

FIG. 2.6.   Copy of a picture of an anchor by MS. He had misidentified the original as an umbrella. (Figure kindly supplied by Dr. F. Newcombe.)

Integrative Agnosia

HJA suffered a stroke when he had an appendicitis operation at the age of 61. Following this stroke he complained of loss of colour vision, impaired reading (initially, he could only read slowly and letter-by-letter), and severe problems in recognising objects and faces. Investigation of his visual fields revealed blindness in the upper-left and -right quadrants (i.e. he had lost the top half of the normal field of vision), but for the lower quadrants acuity was normal. Again, we must note that this visual field defect is not in itself a sufficient explanation of HJA's agnosia; there are other patients with the same visual field loss who can recognise objects without difficulty.

As well as having normal visual acuity, HJA showed normal discrimination of length, orientation and position. He was susceptible to visual illusions such as the Muller-Lyer and Ponzo illusions (which are often thought to depend on implied depth), and he could still see depth from disparity between images presented to each eye (stereopsis). Initial representation of perceptual qualities would thus seem intact.

HJA's object recognition impairments have been carefully investigated by Riddoch and Humphreys (1987a). He was better able to identify real objects (21/32) than photographs of the same objects from a prototypical view (12/32), and worst of all at recognising line drawings. When he could identify a stimulus it was usually only after careful, feature-by-feature examination, leading to response latencies of around 25 seconds for correct responses. All of his errors involved either misidentification as a visually similar item or omission (i.e. failure to come up with an answer). He could not mime the use of objects he could not identify.

Like MS, HJA could copy drawings of objects that he could not recognise. His copy of a drawing of an eagle, which he identified as "a cat sitting up", is shown in Fig. 2.7. To the extent that copying demands use of a viewer-centred representation, HJA's viewer-centred representations seem intact. Moreover, as Fig. 2.5 showed (using data from Humphreys & Riddoch, 1984), HJA's ability to match foreshortened to prototypical views of objects was also unimpaired; thus he seems able to construct some form of object-centred representation.

There was no evidence of any impairment to HJA's semantic system; he was easily able to define objects that he could not recognise. When asked what a duck is, for instance, he said that it:

> is a water bird with the ability to swim, fly and walk. It can be wild or kept domestically for eggs; when wild it can be the target of shooting. In the wild it has a wingspan between 15 and 18 inches and weighs about 2 or 3

HJA

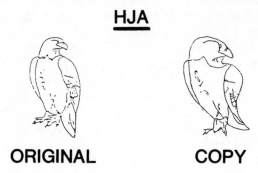

ORIGINAL   COPY

DRAWING FROM MEMORY

FIG. 2.7.   HJA's copy of a picture of an eagle, and his drawing of an eagle from memory. (Reproduced with permission of Oxford University Press from Riddoch and Humphreys, 1987a.)

pounds. Domestic ducks are heavier, up to about 6 pounds perhaps. Wild ducks are multicoloured, mainly brown but with green and yellow breasts. Domestic ducks are white or khaki.

An interesting feature of HJA's object definitions was that, as above, they often included information about the *appearance* of the objects concerned. It seemed as if his stored knowledge of objects (i.e. object recognition units) was intact and accessible from the semantic system, and this was demonstrated convincingly by his ability to draw from memory. Figure 2.7 shows HJA's drawing of an eagle; clearly he remembers what eagles look like. Figure 2.7 is thus very informative about HJA's problems. He can see a drawing of an eagle well enough to copy it accurately, and he can remember what the bird looks like sufficiently well to draw it from memory, yet he cannot recognise an eagle when shown a picture of one. It is as if he can no longer achieve an accurate mapping between his intact perception and his intact stored knowledge of the appearance of objects. We might argue, then, that object recognition units can no longer be accessed properly from viewer-centred or object-centred representations.

This does seem at least in part correct. HJA's ability to decide whether line drawings represented real objects or meaningless objects made by combining different real objects was at chance level (69/120; mean for control subjects 115.7/120). This finding conforms exactly to the view that he is no longer properly able to relate what he sees to his stored knowledge of visual forms.

We could fit HJA to our model by suggesting that intact object recognition units can no longer be accessed effectively from viewer-centred and object-centred representations which are themselves largely intact. To maintain that viewer-centred and object-centred representations are *intact* we would, however, have to overlook an aspect of his attempts at recognition which Riddoch and Humphreys (1987a) see as crucial— the laboured, feature-by-feature descriptions. These were sometimes accompanied by incorrect grouping of the local parts of objects. HJA thought, for instance, that a photograph of a paint-brush with a wooden handle might show "two things close together; a longish wooden stick and a darker, shorter object".

Riddoch and Humphreys (1987a) suggest that HJA finds it difficult to integrate local form information into a coherent overall visual description of the seen object. He picks up the details, but cannot "see" the whole properly. This idea is reminiscent of anecdotes in the literature in which agnosic patients complain that things they look at seem fragmented.

To support this "integration deficit" theory of HJA's difficulties, Riddoch and Humphreys (1987a) point out that his ability to recognise line drawings was reduced both by decreasing exposure duration and by overlapping one drawing on top of another. Moreover, he was better able to decide whether or not a silhouette (i.e. outline shape) represented a real or meaningless object than he was able to make the same decision about line drawings (63/88 silhouettes correct, whereas for line drawings he had been at chance level; mean for controls 77.73/88 silhouettes correct). It is as if the internal detail present in line drawings hindered HJA's performance instead of facilitating it; thus people with normal vision find line drawings easier than silhouettes in this task, but HJA found silhouettes easier than line drawings.

For Riddoch and Humphreys (1987a), then, HJA's perception is impaired, but it is impaired at the highest level of visual analysis. His is an integrative agnosia. He can pick up local features, shape cues, depth cues, and so on, but Riddoch and Humphreys think that he does not readily integrate these into a coherent representation of what he is looking at.

This is an intriguing idea, and we note Young and Deregowski's (1981) suggestion that a similar process is quite generally implicated in picture perception, because under certain conditions children will pick up local depth and feature cues correctly but fail to integrate these into a coherent representation of the depicted object, leading to problems strikingly similar to those experienced permanently by HJA.

One possible way of accommodating the idea of an agnosic integration deficit to our model would be to propose that construction of an adequate object-centred representation involves at least two steps: (1) finding the object's axis of elongation; and (2) integrating local details correctly with respect to this. Patients with posterior lesions of the right hemisphere would then be impaired for the first step, but HJA only for the second step. We would still, though, have to propose that HJA has an additional impairment in accessing object recognition units from viewer-centred representations; perhaps integration is as important to the construction of effective viewer-centred representations as it is to object-centred representations.

More work will be needed before we can know how fruitful such speculations will be (see Humphreys & Riddoch, 1987b, for related suggestions). In the meantime, HJA illustrates well the challenges and insights that a well-documented case study can provide.

OPTIC APHASIA

Optic aphasia was first described by Freund in 1889. The key features of optic aphasia are problems in naming or verbally identifying visually presented objects, which are accompanied by the ability to demonstrate by miming their use that the objects have been recognised, and by unimpaired tactual naming. Thus we are faced in optic aphasia with a naming defect that is specific to the visual modality.

In January, 1970 JF, a retired French electrician, experienced visual disturbances and pins and needles on the right side of his body while driving his car. He had suffered a stroke involving the left posterior cerebral artery. At first he did not seek medical advice and resumed his normal life, though he had become blind in the right side of his former field of vision and unable to read. Some months later, however, he became suspicious and aggressive; he thought that his wife intended to poison him.

In the period following June, 1970 JF was examined at the Salpêtrière Hospital in Paris. He was found to have a complete loss of vision in his right visual field. No disturbances were evident in his spoken language or comprehension, and he obtained a verbal I.Q. of 93 on the Wechsler

Bellevue Test. He was also able to write adequately, both spontaneously and to dictation, and was able to draw well. He was, however, somewhat amnesic and showed a variety of memory difficulties on formal testing, with a Memory Quotient (M.Q.) of 77 on the Wechsler Memory Scale.

JF was found to have problems in naming visually presented stimuli which were carefully investigated by Lhermitte and Beauvois (1973). He was able to name objects presented tactually to his left or right hand (109/120 correct) and he could also name environmental sounds (24/25 correct). He was, however, impaired at naming colours, seen objects (23/30 corrrect), pictures (72/100 correct), and photographs of famous people's faces. He was also severely alexic, being able to name only a few letters and no words at all. When asked to define the spoken name of objects he had misnamed, however, he succeeded on 96 of 100 trials, thus clearly indicating that his object naming difficulty was not due to his impaired memory.

JF's poor performance on visual object naming tasks did not usually derive from failures to produce a name, but from the production of incorrect names. Various types of error were observed by Lhermitte and Beauvois. A number of these were perseverations, in which the name of a previously identified object was repeated; thus he called a fork a comb when it followed a comb in a series of objects, and he called a tomato a strawberry when it occurred a few trials after a strawberry in a series of fruits. He also made a lot of errors in which he produced the name of a semantically related object, including "shoes" for trousers and "grass-hopper" for a slug. Some of his errors were visual in nature, such as "hazel nuts" for coffee beans, and there were others in which it was not entirely clear whether the production of the incorrect names was linked to visual or to semantic factors, or some combination of the two ("glass" for a bottle, "toothbrush" for a comb).

The most notable feature of the case, however, was that JF could indicate that he had understood what a visually presented object was, despite his inability to name it. He did this by miming its use. Thus, for instance, when shown a comb he correctly pretended to use it even though he called it a toothbrush. None of his mimes were found to be incorrect. When asked to draw an object he had just misnamed, he usually drew what he had seen rather than what he had called it. Although he seems to have been aware of his visual field defect and alexia, Lhermitte and Beauvois (1973) state that JF was apparently unaware of his problems in naming visually presented objects.

Optic aphasia poses a challenge to theories that postulate a common set of semantic representations for known objects that can be accessed from any sensory modality. The patient "knows" what seen objects are (in the sense of being able to gesture their use), and knows what felt objects are, but can only name the ones that have been handled.

One way of resolving this paradox is to maintain that different parts of the semantic system can become disconnected from each other. Beauvois (1982) adopts this position. Her claim is that JF has more or less normal vision in the intact part of his visual field, and that visual semantic processes are normal. He also has normal speech and verbal semantic processes, but the visual semantic processes and the verbal semantic processes have become disconnected from each other, whereas tactile input still has access to verbal semantics.

The possibility of separation of visual and verbal semantic processes is supported by Schwartz, Marin, and Saffran's (1979) finding that a patient with a progressive dementing disease, WLP, could mime the use of objects despite a severe impairment of semantic memory. Her mimes were so precise that observers could distinguish easily her "use" of a depicted spoon or fork, pipe or cigarette, and so on. Yet WLP could not identify these objects verbally, or even show understanding of their names in a classification task.

Optic Aphasia as a Semantic Access Impairment

One problem with Beauvois' (1982) account of optic aphasia is how to make more clear the distinction between visual and verbal semantic processes. Work by Riddoch and Humphreys (1987b) has helped by suggesting a somewhat different basis for the distinction and a more precise hypothesis concerning a potential cause of optic aphasia.

Riddoch and Humphreys studied JB, who had sustained a left hemisphere injury in a road traffic accident. This left him unable to read or write, but with intact oral spelling. His speech was not affected, but he was initially amnesic. Although he had a right hemianopia, JB's vision did not seem to be otherwise much affected. He could copy simple drawings, and his ability to match prototypical to minimal-feature or foreshortened views of objects was within the range of control subjects (minimal-feature 26/26; foreshortened 20/26).

JB's ability to name seen objects was poor, and was unaffected by view (42% prototypical view; 40% foreshortened view; 43% minimal-feature view). Like JF, he made several semantic errors. He could, however, provide specific gestures indicating the uses of seen objects that he could not otherwise identify. Object naming from tactile presentation was better than naming from vision.

Thus far, the main difference between JB and the agnosic patient HJA is that whereas JB could mime the functions of the objects he saw, HJA could not. When JB was asked to decide whether line drawings represented real objects or meaningless objects made by combining different real objects, however, he was much better than HJA (HJA 69/120; JB 110/116—JB performed within the range of control subjects). Thus JB was able to access stored knowledge of object structures (object recognition units) from vision, whereas HJA could not do this. JB's performance on this object decision task remained in the normal range even when the task was made very difficult by deriving the meaningless objects from items in the same semantic category (for example, combining features of two different types of animal).

Riddoch and Humphreys (1987b) thus describe JB's impairment as involving semantic access from vision; although he can recognise objects as familiar, he is poorer at accessing semantic knowledge from pictures than from touch or from spoken names. This problem proved to be bidirectional: JB was equally poor at accessing knowledge of an object's appearance from semantics. His ability to draw objects from memory was poor, and he commented that "I know what it (the object he was asked to draw) is, but I just can't picture it."

For JB, then, the ability to mime the use of seen objects occurs in the context of intact access to object recognition units. It would seem that knowledge of how to use objects is linked to their structural rather than their semantic properties. Whether this would also have been true for Lhermitte and Beauvois' (1973) patient JF we do not, of course, know. It may be the case (as we are inclined to think) that intact access to object recognition units is *necessary* for correct gestures to be made, or it may be that there are different forms of optic aphasia. Only further detailed investigations of individual cases can reveal the answer.

Optic aphasia forces us to think more carefully about the different types of information we can access from seen objects. An outline of a possible account of optic aphasia is given in Fig. 2.8. Here we propose that intact miming reflects preserved access to a system of stored motor programs for object use, whereas the naming impairment reflects a disconnection between object recognition units and the (verbal) semantic system.

OVERVIEW

The basic lessons of cognitive neuropsychology, which will be encountered throughout this book, can be learnt from studies of disorders of object recognition.

The first lesson is that quite specific impairments can occur. There are patients who do not recognise the objects they see, yet have well-preserved language, memory, and other intellectual functions. These people are not blind and they can still use their vision effectively for many purposes,

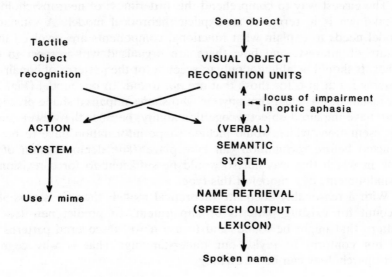

FIG. 2.8.   A possible account of optic aphasia as a disconnection between visual object recognition and the verbal semantic system.

but the things they see have little meaning for them, or meanings that are only attained with difficulty. Such cases are rare, but this rarity is probably due to anatomical reasons (see Chapter 1). The key point is that they can exist at all.

Neuropsychological impairments do not, however, affect object recognition as if it were a single, homogeneous faculty. Instead, what we encounter are different *types* of recognition impairment. One person may be unable to perceive the shapes of seen objects properly, another can perceive shape but fails to form an effective integrated representation that combines local and global features, and another can recognise object forms as familiar and even mime their use, while remaining unable to give any verbal identification. The organisation of complex abilities such as object recognition seems to be into a number of separable functional components or modules, any one of which may be impaired selectively.

Of course, every neuropsychological patient is unique; exactly the same injury is no more likely to recur than people are likely to have the same fingerprints. But the patterns of impairment that are found do not turn out to be unlimited. There are, for instance, no accounts of patients who show impaired processing of shape information and yet recognise seen objects without difficulty. Thus, among the myriad of observed patterns, it is possible to discern a sense of order.

The easiest way to comprehend this orderliness of neuropsychological breakdown is in terms of an explicit theoretical model. A satisfactory model needs to explain what functional components are involved in the ability of interest, and how these are organised with respect to each other. It should be able not only to account for the patterns of impairment observed, but also for those that are *not* found. In our model (Fig. 2.1), for instance, it is clear that anyone who shows impaired shape processing *must* have impaired object recognition ability, because the viewer-centred representations which would include shape information have to be constructed before recognition can take place. The demonstration of one case in which this was not so would be sufficient to force revision (or abandonment) of a model of this type.

With a reasonably adequate theoretical model, then, it is possible to account for existing patterns of impairment, to predict new types of pattern that might be found, and to use newly discovered patterns that do not conform to revise our understanding. That is why cognitive neuropsychology can be so exciting.

SUMMARY

We can think of object recognition as requiring that viewer-centred and object-centred representations of seen objects are matched to stored descriptions of the structures of known objects (object recognition units) which then allow access to semantic representations (see Fig. 2.1). Cases in which there is a severe impairment of form perception and inability to copy seen objects may then be considered to involve impairment of the ability to construct viewer-centred representations. Problems with matching unusual or foreshortened views derive from impaired object-centred representations, but these patients (such as JL) remain able to recognise objects from prototypical views because of their intact viewer-centred representations. Cases of "higher-order" perceptual impairment, in which there may be preserved ability to copy objects that cannot be recognised (such as MS and HJA), may involve a type of integrative agnosia that will need further investigation before they can be related to our theoretical model satisfactorily. Some patients are impaired at object recognition because of damage to the semantic system itself (AB), and these semantic impairments can take category-specific forms (JBR). Optic aphasia (JF and JB) probably represents an impairment that affects access to the semantic system without affecting object recognition units and associated knowledge of object use.

FURTHER READING

Humphreys, G. W., & Riddoch, M. J. (1987). *To see but not to see: A case study of visual agnosia*. London: Lawrence Erlbaum Associates. Readable introduction to HJA's case, with interesting sections explaining the impact of the disorder on his life.

Humphreys, G. W., & Riddoch, M. J. (Eds) (1987). *Visual object processing*. London: Lawrence Erlbaum Associates. Gives more information on studies of object recognition in normal subjects, and how these relate to clinical findings.

Ratcliff, G., & Newcombe, F. (1982). Object recognition: some deductions from the clinical evidence. In A. W. Ellis (Ed.), *Normality and pathology in cognitive functions*. London: Academic Press. One of the first papers to consider object recognition impairments from a cognitive neuropsychological perspective. Contains a detailed case report on MS.

Riddoch, M. J., & Humphreys, G. W. (1987). A case of integrative visual agnosia. *Brain, 110*, 1431–1462. Fascinating investigation of HJA's problems.

Rubens, A. B. (1979). Agnosia. In K. M. Heilman & E. Valenstein (Eds), *Clinical neuropsychology*. New York: Oxford University Press. Excellent introduction from the clinical perspective.

Warrington, E. K. (1982). Neuropsychological studies of object recognition. In D. E. Broadbent & L. Weiskrantz (Eds), *The neuropsychology of cognitive function*. London: Royal Society. Also available in *Philosophical Transactions of the Royal Society, London, B298*, 15–33. Explains Warrington's influential ideas of perceptual and semantic categorisation, and her model of object recognition.

Warrington, E. K., & Shallice, T. (1984). Category specific semantic impairments. *Brain, 107*, 829–854. Includes detailed investigation of JBR, and other patients with semantic impairment.

3

Visual and Spatial Abilities

INTRODUCTION

In Chapter 2 we looked at what cognitive neuropsychological studies have revealed about how we recognise objects. However, for normal life we use vision for a much wider range of purposes. We can recognise other types of stimuli than everyday objects, such as printed words or people's faces, we can see colour and movement, and we can assess accurately the locations of seen objects both with respect to ourselves and in relation to each other.

Our visual experience has such a unified quality that it is initially surprising to discover that, as for object recognition, a range of quite specific impairments of visual information processing can be found after brain injury. The processes responsible for vision are organised into a number of functionally separable modules. This modular organisation makes good sense in terms of keeping the nerve connections involved as tidy as possible and in terms of allowing one process to be modified without affecting others that are unrelated to it (Cowey, 1985; Marr, 1982), and there is good agreement between studies of humans and studies of other species concerning the types of functional module that exist (Cowey, 1982; 1985; Ratcliff & Cowey, 1979; Zeki, 1978). None the less, one cannot help being puzzled as to how our visual experience can have its unified quality when it is produced by a number of separate processing modules. We will not attempt to answer this question here, but will concentrate instead on introducing some of the dissociable disorders that can be observed. Impairments of word and face processing are dealt with elsewhere (Chapters 4, 5, 6, and 7), and in this chapter we examine some of the other deficits that are found. We will not discuss every possible disorder; for those seeking it, a more detailed listing can be found in Benton (1979). Instead, we will illustrate the range of problems that can arise. We begin with colour processing and movement perception, which may be considered to be fairly "basic" visual abilities. These are followed by a discussion of the phenomena associated with "blindsight", which have important implications for our conception of the relation between visual experience and perceptual mechanisms. We then turn to look at impairments affecting abilities that are best considered to be more "spatial" in nature—visual location, spatial attention, and spatial knowledge and thought.

Although modular organisation is a widely agreed feature of visual and spatial abilities, there is as yet no generally accepted theoretical framework that can specify the complete underlying pattern (see Young & Ratcliff, 1983). Obviously, the various processing modules must be interconnected into some kind of coherent system, but we do not yet know how. An important clue, however, is that mechanisms responsible for the recognition of different types of visual pattern seem to be organised into separate systems to those involved in space perception. Thus patients experiencing object recognition difficulties may be relatively unimpaired on spatial tasks, and patients who are spatially disorientated may yet remain able to identify objects without difficulty.

Such observations are borne out by more formal studies. Newcombe and Russell (1969), for instance, studied a group of men with brain lesions due to shrapnel and gunshot wound injuries sustained some 20 years previously. They found that men with right hemisphere injuries could show severe problems in spatial tasks (such as maze learning) or in more directly "visual" tasks likely to relate to pattern recognition, but that these deficits did not relate to each other. Newcombe, Ratcliff, and Damasio (1987) present detailed information on two cases from this series, one with each type of impairment. Such findings, and related studies of the monkey's brain, have been developed by Ungerleider and Mishkin (1982) into the view that there are effectively parallel visual systems in the cerebral cortex responsible for appreciation of an object's identity and its spatial location. Interestingly, Levine, Warach, and Farah (1985) have pointed out that the same dissociation occurs for impairments affecting mental imagery.

COLOUR PROCESSING

Impairments of colour processing due to brain injury can be grouped into three main types affecting what we might roughly describe as colour perception, colour knowledge and colour naming. Of course, many patients experience what would have to be regarded as hybrid impairments under this classification scheme, but this seems justifiable as some relatively pure cases have been described.

Impairments of colour *perception* are called achromatopsias. Patients with cerebral achromatopsia complain that they cannot see colours, and that everything is like a black and white picture, or that colours have lost their brightness (Meadows, 1974b). In some cases the loss of colour perception relates only to part of the field of vision (Damasio, 1985). Even when the whole of the visual field is involved, however, everyday objects can still be recognised provided that colour is not a critical cue; there need not be any impairment of form perception itself. Pallis's (1955) patient, for instance, stated that he could usually identify everyday objects, but gave as examples where his loss of colour perception caused him problems the fact that his shirts all looked dirty and he could not tell them apart, and that he could not tell until he had opened a jar (and smelt or tasted the contents) whether it would contain jam or pickles. Warrington (1987) provides documented cases of dissociations between impairments affecting the processing of colours, locations and shapes.

The cerebral achromatopsias are quite different to the types of colour blindness found in the absence of brain damage, which are due to deficiencies in the retina of the eye (Mollon, 1982). Mollon, Newcombe, Polden, and Ratcliff (1980) showed, for instance, that the patient MS, who experienced achromatopsia as well as his object agnosia (see Chapter 2), none the less retained the usual three functional cone mechanisms with normal spectral sensitivities (cones are the retina's colour-sensitive cells). In threshold tasks MS was found to be able to respond to signals from any of the three classes of cone normally associated with colour blindness; his complete achromatopsia was thus due to a deficit affecting his ability to make proper *use* of the signals that the different types of cone continued to send. He could respond to wavelength without being able to match, sort, or name different hues.

Clinically, achromatopsias are often found in conjunction with problems in recognising familiar faces (prosopagnosia) and familiar places. In some cases, however, colour perception may be impaired without loss of ability to recognise faces or places and, conversely, it remains intact in some reported cases of prosopagnosia (Heywood, Wilson, & Cowey, 1987; Meadows, 1974a; 1974b; see Chapter 4 for further discussion of this point). Thus it seems that these functions are carried out by separate information processing modules, but that these lie in adjacent or even partially overlapping cortical areas that are often damaged simultaneously.

A quite different type of deficit seems to involve impairment of colour *knowledge*. For these patients colour perception is intact, but errors are made in tasks that demand use of stored information about colour.

Patients may be unable to answer from memory questions such as "What colour is a strawberry?", and may choose the wrong coloured crayons if asked to colour in line drawings of the objects concerned (Kinsbourne & Warrington, 1964; Oxbury & Humphrey, 1969, case 2). This deficit often occurs in the context of more general language difficulties (De Renzi, Faglioni, Scotti, & Spinnler, 1972), but, apparently, it can also occur in an isolated form (see Meadows, 1974b). Unlike achromatopsia, the impairment is not found only in "perceptual" tasks, because it is as great in what is apparently a purely verbal task such as stating the colour of a specified object—a task which would not cause an achromatopsic patient particular difficulty.

Impairments of colour knowledge need to be distinguished from problems affecting colour *naming*. Geschwind and Fusillo (1966) described a 58-year-old man who, following a stroke, became unable to name seen colours. This patient could state the usual colours of familiar objects like bananas, or the sky, but he could not put a name to the colour of objects (such as items of clothing) for which there was no learnt association to rely on. Similarly, he could not point to the correct colour when a particular colour name was specified.

These colour naming problems are often found in combination with forms of reading impairment involving letter-by-letter reading, or the complete inability to read. Geschwind and Fusillo's (1966) patient was also unable to read (alexic), and they interpreted his colour naming defects as demanding a similar explanation to his reading problems; in essence, their argument is that there is a disconnection between the brain's visual and language areas. Colour naming problems and alexia do, however, dissociate in rare cases which weaken Geschwind and Fusillo's (1966) argument. For example, Greenblatt (1973) described an alexic patient who could name colours, whereas Mohr, Leicester, Stoddard, and Sidman's (1971) patient could read but was impaired at colour naming. Davidoff and Ostergaard (1984) describe a patient with a colour naming impairment who was none the less able to point to named colours, which again suggests that the explanation of colour anomia is not as simple as disconnection theories often assume. It may prove more enlightening to link impairments of colour naming to other reports of naming disorders specific to certain semantic categories (see Chapter 5).

Colour processing impairments, then, both demonstrate the separability of colour processing from other aspects of vision, and form an interesting and reasonably coherent pattern. Much more work needs to be done, however, before an adequate model of the deficits can be proposed, because there are already signs that the simple classification scheme we have adopted need not always apply (see, especially, Beauvois & Saillant, 1985).

MOVEMENT PERCEPTION

Riddoch (1917) was one of the first people to take a serious interest in disorders of movement perception. He showed that for soldiers with brain injuries due to gunshot and shrapnel wounds there were dissociations between movement perception and form perception abilities in impaired parts of the visual field. In addition, movement perception and form perception could show different courses of recovery. Riddoch (1917) used these findings to argue that movement involves a special type of visual perception.

Isolated disturbances of movement perception are a most uncommon sequel of brain injury, but a very convincing case has been investigated in detail and reported by Zihl, Von Cramon, and Mai (1983). Their patient, LM, complained of a loss of movement perception following a venous thrombosis that produced bilateral lesions of temporo-occipital cortex. She saw the world almost entirely in terms of a series of "snapshots", especially if the movements involved were quite fast. Her perception was affected for movements in all spatial dimensions (horizontal movements, vertical movements, and movements toward or away from her), and the condition was very disabling. Thus LM experienced difficulty in crossing the road because she could no longer judge the movements of cars, yet she could identify the cars themselves without difficulty. She had problems in pouring tea or coffee into a cup because the liquid seemed to be frozen, like a glacier, and she did not know when to stop pouring because she could not see the level in the cup rising. In a room where people were moving about they would seem to LM to be first in one place and then suddenly in another place, and she complained of problems in following conversations because she could not see facial, and especially mouth, movements (people rely on these to a surprising extent, as we will explain in Chapter 4).

On formal tests LM proved to be perfectly able to locate stationary objects by sight; her saccadic eye movements to target lights presented up to 40° from fixation were very accurate. Thus she was able to control her eye movements. Yet her pursuit eye movements to moving targets were markedly abnormal for target velocities greater than 8° per second, with her eyes jumping from one point to another instead of tracking the moving target smoothly. At target velocities below 8° per second LM often did track the target light successfully with her eyes, and when she was successful she always reported seeing movement.

LM also had trouble moving parts of her body under visual control. She could easily trace the path of a raised wire with her finger when she was blindfolded and had to rely on tactile information. But when a sheet of glass was placed over the wire (to eliminate the tactile information) and the blindfold was removed she could only follow the path if she moved her finger slowly.

Other tests carried out by Zihl et al. (1983) confirmed that LM's disorder of movement perception was confined to the visual modality; her perception of movements specified via hearing or touch was unimpaired. Her visual perception of movements in depth was completely abolished but, as we have seen, there was some preservation of movement perception to targets moving slowly along horizontal or vertical axes up to around 15° from fixation. LM did not show visual motion after effects, and she no longer experienced the phi phenomenon, in which *apparent* visual movement is generated between sequentially presented lights.

Despite her impaired ability to see movement, LM remained able to discriminate colours adequately on the Farnsworth-Munsell 100 hue test, and her tachistoscopic recognition thresholds for visually presented objects and words were quite normal. Binocular visual functions, including stereoscopic depth perception were also normal.

BLINDSIGHT

We have described cases in which brain injury can lead to specific impairments of aspects of visual experience, such as colour or movement perception. Now we will consider a quite different type of impairment, in which conscious visual experience is entirely lost for at least part of the field of vision, yet the ability to respond to visual stimuli under certain testing conditions remains. The patient has no sense of seeing these stimuli, yet can make accurate responses if encouraged to guess or given a forced choice. Weiskrantz's term "blindsight" neatly encompasses the paradoxical nature of the condition. Part of the visual field is blind in terms of both standard clinical tests and subjective report, yet behavioural evidence indicates that accurate responses can be made to visual stimuli presented in this blind area. These accurate responses are made without awareness of visual experience on the patient's part.

At this point it is necessary to understand the causes of visual field defects in a little more detail. Loss of vision in part of the normal visual field is a common consequence of injury to posterior regions of the cerebral cortex. Nerve fibres from the retina of each eye project, via the lateral geniculate bodies, to the striate cortex in the occipital lobe of each cerebral hemisphere. The striate cortex is itself organised in a manner described as "retinotopic", meaning that different areas of the visual field are projected onto it in a quite systematic way. Damage to different parts of the geniculo-striate pathway can thus produce loss of sensation in corresponding parts of the visual field. These visual field defects often take the form of hemianopias (loss of vision for stimuli falling to the left or to the right side of fixation), or of impairments to one or more quadrants of the field of vision. Sometimes the central part of the visual field, or macula, is differentially spared or affected (for more details on the causes of visual field defects see Kolb and Whishaw, 1985).

Visual field defects have been investigated carefully for many years, because of their clinical importance. Before the introduction of modern brain imaging techniques, they formed one of the few available methods for determining the loci of cerebral lesions. Many of the neurological conditions described in this book are typically accompanied by characteristic visual field defects. These field defects are, however, coincidental with problems such as achromatopsia and prosopagnosia, and do not themselves directly cause the conditions. The association of particular conditions with particular field defects is often due to the close contiguity of cerebral areas, and in such cases it has no functional significance. Thus, for instance, other patients with the same or with more severe field defects than prosopagnosic patients may remain able to recognise faces without difficulty. For this reason we have not discussed visual field defects in this book except in cases where they have been thought to be, or might reasonably be thought to be, of functional importance in creating the impairment observed.

It has been known for some time that visual field defects can be associated with reduced visual sensitivity rather than an absolute loss. Weiskrantz (1986) reviews many such findings, and we have already noted Riddoch's (1917) observations on movement perception and form perception. One of the most important reports is that by Pöppel, Held, and Frost (1973), who presented a briefly flashed light at different locations in visual field defects caused by gunshot wounds, and asked their ex-servicemen to look toward the flash. Although Pöppel et al.'s (1973) patients thought this an odd request, because they could not consciously "see" anything, their eye movements did in fact approximate to the correct positions.

The key feature of Pöppel et al.'s (1973) technique is that they did not rely on their subjects' reports of what they could see, but instead encouraged them to guess and measured their behaviour to the visual stimulus. This has been the hallmark of the investigations of the patient DB carried out by Weiskrantz and his colleagues (Weiskrantz, Warrington, Sanders, & Marshall, 1974; Weiskrantz, 1980; 1986). DB underwent an operation in 1973 to remove an arteriovenous malformation at the pole of the right occipital lobe that was causing severe and recurrent migraine attacks. This operation involved removal of the striate cortex of the right hemisphere and some of the adjacent calcarine cortex, but left intact other areas of cerebral cortex that would typically be affected in cases of cerebral injury due to stroke, tumour or gunshot wound.

After the operation DB experienced, as would be expected, hemianopia affecting almost the whole of his left field of vision, without sparing of the central macular area. This field defect contracted during the next few years until it occupied the lower left quadrant, but it is the visual information processing abilities found within DB's area of subjective blindness that are of most interest here, rather than its extent or the course of any recovery. Weiskrantz et al. (1974) showed that, like Pöppel et al.'s (1973) patients, DB was able to make eye movements toward a light flashed in his visual field defect that he claimed to be unable to see. These movements were clearly related to the position of the target, though they were not particularly accurate. DB's ability to reach out or point toward the stimulus was, however, much more accurate despite the fact that he was given no feedback as to the correctness or incorrectness of his performance until the entire test was complete. When shown the accuracy of his results at the end of the session, DB was astonished; he thought that he had been guessing. DB was also found to be able to discriminate line orientations, and to make simple form discriminations, such as distinguishing X from O, provided that the stimuli were of sufficient size.

Following the initial report by Weiskrantz et al. (1974), DB has been investigated intensively, and Weiskrantz (1986) reports several further studies which have both confirmed and refined the original findings. As well as being able to locate stimuli presented within the "blind" part of his visual field, DB could detect accurately their presence or absence even when the light stimulus was introduced or extinguished quite slowly. He could also distinguish moving from stationary stimuli. His visual acuity for static stimuli falling within the field defect was found to be poorer than that of his intact field and, unlike normal vision, acuity in the field defect increased as the stimuli were moved to positions further away from fixation. Only limited shape discrimination abilities were found within the visual field defect, and Weiskrantz (1986) suggests that the ability to discriminate simple shapes, such as X or O, found by Weiskrantz et al. (1974) may have been based on DB's ability to discriminate orientation of lines.

Investigations of blindsight pose a number of exacting technical demands, which have been highlighted by Campion, Latto, and Smith (1983). Weiskrantz (1986), however, demonstrates that he has solved these problems satisfactorily, and it should also be noted that studies of blindsight in other patients than DB have revealed broadly comparable patterns of abilities (e.g. Barbur, Ruddock, & Waterfield, 1980; Perenin, 1978; Perenin & Jeannerod, 1978). This comparability of findings from different patients should not, however, be taken to imply that blindsight will be found within *any* visual field defect. The phenomena are only to be expected in field defects caused by lesions of certain types, and it will require extensive work to specify precisely what the necessary and sufficient conditions are.

A key issue concerns whether or not the visual abilities found in blindsight are produced in the geniculo-striate visual system itself, or by alternative visual pathways that may have different functions. Weiskrantz (1986) points out that whereas the geniculo-striate pathway involves about 90% of optic nerve fibres, there are nevertheless at least six other branches of the optic nerve projecting to midbrain and subcortical areas, one of which contains some 100,000 nerve fibres. It is thus possible that the visual abilities found in field defects are supported by one or more of these alternative pathways, and the fact that blindsight seems in some respects to involve a qualitatively different pattern of visual abilities rather than a degradation of those measured in the intact field would support this possibility. Weiskrantz (1986) discusses parallels with studies of other animal species that point in the same direction.

Of particular interest to the cognitive neuropsychologist is the fact that studies of blindsight promise to provide insights into the intriguing question of the relationship between the analysis of visual stimuli and conscious awareness. Several people have used cases of blindsight as a demonstration that awareness is *not* integral to the operation of visual information-processing mechanisms in the way that we commonly suppose (e.g. Marcel, 1983). There are, however, complex issues involved here. Often some degree of practice or "shaping" of responses can be needed before blindsight phenomena can be demonstrated (Weiskrantz, 1980). It is as if patients are able to learn to attend to something, yet that something is seldom described as being like a visual experience. DB, for instance, gradually came to say that he had a sense that "something was there", and roughly where it was, but that he did not in any sense "see" it (Weiskrantz, 1980, p. 374). Another patient, EY, sensed "a definite pinpoint of light" but then claimed that "it does not actually look like a light. It looks like nothing at all" (Weiskrantz, 1980, p. 378).

It is, of course, possible to insist that DB and other patients must in some sense be aware of the visual stimuli to which they respond, and that their descriptions of their experiences are of no scientific value, but this seems to us to take the whole issue into an intractable argument about when we can trust someone else's statement that she or he is—or is not—aware of something. Weiskrantz (1986) himself sidesteps this obstacle by defining blindsight as involving "visual capacity in a field defect in the absence of acknowledged awareness".

Cases of preserved ability to locate stimuli that have not been con-sciously "perceived" are not confined to the visual modality. Paillard, Michel, and Stelmach (1983) studied a patient with a severe impairment of touch perception for the right side of her body. This impairment was so severe that she would sometimes cut or burn herself without noticing, yet she could point to the position where her right arm had been touched even though she was not aware of its having been touched. She commented: "But I don't understand that! You put something here. I don't feel anything and yet I go there with my finger. How does that happen?" (Paillard et al., 1983, p. 550).

Although Paillard et al.'s (1983) patient was considerably better than chance in her ability to locate stimuli she could not feel, her performance was well below that of a control subject. She was also able to make gross discriminations between the sizes of objects palpated (but not subjectively "felt") by her right hand. As Paillard et al. (1983) observe, their case seems to form an interesting analogue of blindsight in the tactile modality.

VISUAL LOCATION

Although disorders affecting visual location had been described previously (e.g. Bálint, 1909), the most detailed of the early reports relate to soldiers who had sustained bullet or shrapnel wounds during the First World War (Holmes, 1918; 1919; Holmes & Horrax, 1919; Riddoch, 1917, case 3; Smith & Holmes, 1916; Yealland, 1916). Even though they did not have the benefit of modern experimental techniques, the descriptions given by Holmes and his colleagues have yet to be bettered.

In the papers he published around this time, Holmes presented his observations of eight people who had disturbances of spatial orientation. Their most obvious problems were in determining the location of seen objects. Holmes (1919, p. 231) described one of them trying to eat a meal:

When he tried to take a piece of bread he brought his hand under the table rather than above it, and on attempting to seize the cup he found his fingers first in the tea, and, in his second attempt on a plate to one side of it.

The disorder was limited to the visual modality, with the patients being able to localise sounds accurately. When blindfolded they were easily able to point in the direction of a noise, or walk toward someone who called them. Similarly, the ability to locate touched objects remained intact. Thus Holmes described one of his patients eating soup, who succeeded in placing the spoon in the bowl only after repeated attempts. Once he had located the bowl, however, he could aways bring the spoon accurately to his mouth. This preserved ability to put a spoon in his mouth shows that the patient remained able to make accurate use of his own bodily sensations for locating things, and it also shows that he had not simply lost proper control over the movements of his muscles. Holmes confirmed these observations by allowing him to touch the soup bowl with his left hand; he then fed himself without difficulty.

Although Holmes's patients had lost the ability to locate seen objects they remained able to identify them:

> When I held up a pocket-knife in front of one man he said at once "that's a pocket-knife"; but though his eyes were directed on it he stretched out his arm in a totally wrong direction when he was told to take hold of it (Holmes, 1919, p. 231).

This provides a striking example of the point that deficits affecting object identification can dissociate from those of a more "spatial" nature.

The picture that we have built up so far is one in which the patients are able to specify object locations from touch or hearing, but not from vision. Despite the inability to derive information about the location of seen objects, they can be identified with ease. This was expressed succinctly by Private M (Holmes, 1918), who explained that though he could see an object he was not sure where it was. Such problems stand in marked contrast to those found in visual object agnosia (see Chapter 2), where patients who are unable to identify objects can usually locate them without difficulty.

We will look more closely at Private M's case, the first to be reported by Holmes (Holmes, 1918, case 1; Smith & Holmes, 1916), and one which is fairly typical. Private M was wounded by a shrapnel bullet. In some respects he recovered rapidly, and did not develop weakness or paralysis of his limbs, or any loss of hearing. His speech was at first a little disturbed, but quickly returned to normal. His intellectual abilities did not seem diminished, but he was unable to remember events that occurred during a period preceding his injury. His emotional reactions, however, were not considered normal as he was inclined to laugh at inappropriate things.

Private M's visual acuity was normal for central vision, and he could detect the presence of a static object to normal limits in his peripheral vision. He could also detect movement in all parts of his visual fields, though he could only do so with difficulty in the lower right quadrant. He could recognise seen objects, and he could also recognise letters and read words and short sentences.

Although Private M's vision would not seem too seriously impaired on the basis of these tests, they were very difficult to carry out because he experienced great problems in controlling the movements of his eyes. He found it difficult to move his eyes in a specified direction; he tended to make incorrect movements or to succeed only after a number of attempts. The inability to control his eye movements properly meant that he had difficulty reading anything other than short sentences. He could not follow a moving object with his eyes, he did not react to objects that were rapidly approaching him, and his eyes did not converge on slowly approaching objects. He had difficulty bringing objects he noticed into the centre of his field of vision, and when they were in central vision he was unable to maintain fixation. He did, however, make accurate eye movements in the direction of unexpected noises.

In addition to these problems of eye movements, Private M was unable to determine the locations of the objects he saw. Although he could detect the presence of moving stimuli he had no sense of their location, and was only aware of "something moving somewhere". There is an interesting contrast here between Private M, who was aware of movement but could not determine its location, and Zihl et al.'s (1983) patient LM, who could determine location but had lost the ability to see many types of movement.

Private M could not reach out accurately to grasp a seen object; sometimes he would project his arm in a totally wrong direction, or he would bring his hand to the appropriate position and then grope about until he came into contact with it. His errors not only took the form of reaching to the left or right of the object, but of stopping short of it or past it. This problem of visual location was worse for objects seen in peripheral than in central vision. For peripheral vision his errors were often gross, but in central vision he could use the groping strategy. Holmes (1918, p. 453) described him getting a box of matches from his locker:

> He sat up in bed, turned his head and eyes towards the locker, stared vacantly at one spot for a moment, then slowly and deliberately moved his eyes into other directions, until, after several seconds, the matchbox, as if by chance, came into his central vision; then he put his hand out to take hold of it, but succeeded in reaching it only after repeated gropings.

What we have described is a problem involving the absolute location of seen objects. However, Private M's problems were just as severe for relative location. He was shown two similar objects (silver and copper coins, or pieces of white and green paper), and then asked if another two objects were in the same relative positions. Whether the objects were positioned to one side of each other, with one above the other, or with one in front of the other, he made many errors. When he was asked to explain why he could not say which of the two objects was the nearer to him he replied: "When I look at one it seems to go further away, when I try to see which is the nearer they seem to change in position every now and then; that one at which I look directly seems to move away" (Holmes, 1918, p. 453).

In contrast to this problem in seeing relative locations, Private M could determine them without difficulty by touch. Thus when his finger was moved between two objects that he could not locate by vision, he could give accurate information immediately about their relative positions.

We are so used to locating objects by vision that it takes an effort to realise how disabled we would be without this ability. Its absence affected Private M across a wide range of activities. He could not count seen objects accurately, because he was unable to keep track of which ones he had already counted. He could only move about slowly and cautiously, and kept bumping into objects, and even walking into walls. When he found an object such as a chair in his way he had great problems in finding his way round it.

As we have already commented, Private M's case is typical of those described by Holmes. In most of these cases the visual location of objects was grossly deficient, yet the patient's experience was not that the world appeared "flat". Individual items were experienced as "normal" solid objects by all except one of the patients Holmes described (Holmes & Horrax, 1919).

Despite their being relatively pure cases, Holmes's patients also often had additional problems. In particular, some had general visual memory difficulties, and all had some degree of loss of topographical memory (for further information on this problem, see the last section of this chapter). We have not discussed these additional problems in detail here because they are all problems that can occur in people who do not experience any difficulty in visual location: Thus we do not think that they contribute to the problems in visual location.

Cases of specific loss of ability to locate seen objects are rare. All of Holmes's patients had bilateral lesions of the parietal lobes, and he commented that he had not seen similar symptoms produced by unilateral lesions. Subsequent studies have, however, shown that disorders of visual location can exist in the visual half field contralateral (i.e. opposite) to a unilateral cerebral lesion (Brain, 1941; Cole, Schutta, & Warrington, 1962; Ratcliff & Davies-Jones, 1972; Riddoch, 1935). Thus patients with left parietal lesions may have a specific difficulty locating objects seen in the right visual field, and patients with right parietal lesions may have a specific difficulty locating objects seen in the left visual field. These location problems can occur in the absence of any other visual defect.

A curious aspect of visual location difficulties is the contrast with blindsight, in which location is performed accurately. In blindsight, however, patients are not aware of seeing anything despite the intact visual location ability, whereas in impairments of visual location the patient cannot locate things accurately that she or he can otherwise see clearly.

It may be the case that it is the same visual location ability which remains intact in blindsight and is impaired in disorders of visual location (see Ratcliff, 1982), but a more intriguing possibility is that there is more than one type of visual location ability and that patients with visual location impairments cannot make use of location abilities equivalent to those available in blindsight. Impairments of visual location are closely related to impairments affecting movement under visual guidance (Damasio & Benton, 1979). Thus, the continued ability of patients with visual location impairments to consciously "see" may interfere with the expression of any residual location abilities.

SPATIAL ATTENTION

Overt and Covert Shifts of Attention

The world about us is extremely complex, and it may at times be useful to use attentional mechanisms to cut down the amount of information we have to deal with. For vision, shifts in attention are often accompanied by eye movements intended to bring the stimulus of interest onto the most sensitive central area of the retina, but shifts of attention to one part of space or another can also be made without eye movements. You can continue to look at a fixed point while directing your attention elsewhere; Posner (1980) calls these shifts in *covert* attention, to distinguish them from shifts involving an *overt* eye movement.

Posner and his colleagues have carried out several investigations of the ability to shift attention in both normal subjects and patients with different types of cerebral injury (e.g. Posner, 1980; Posner, Cohen, & Rafal, 1982; Posner, Walker, Friedrich, & Rafal, 1984; Posner, Rafal, Choate, & Vaughan, 1985). A noteworthy feature of their studies is that they have developed what amounts to a common set of experimental tasks that are given to all groups of subjects.

One of Posner's techniques involves asking people to fixate centrally and, while central fixation is maintained, to press a button as quickly as possible when they detect the presence of a specified stimulus. This stimulus may appear to the left or to the right of the fixated position, and is itself preceded by a cue indicating the left or right position. For normal subjects, detection of the target stimulus is faster if it appears on the cued side. Interestingly, this facilitation is found even when the cue is as likely to be invalid (the target then appears on the opposite side to the cue) as valid (the target then appears on the same side as the cue), so it seems to represent an involuntary attentional reaction outside of conscious strategic control.

Posner et al. (1982) used this general method with patients suffering from a condition known as progressive supranuclear palsy, which interferes with the ability to make voluntary eye movements. They showed that although their responses were rather slow these patients remained able to shift attention covertly, as measured by the facilitatory effect of cueing the target location. Thus the processes responsible for covert orienting of attention are not completely tied to those involved in overt shifts in the form of eye movements; these patients are able to make covert shifts in their visual attention in ways that they would find very difficult to accomplish by means of overt eye movements.

In contrast to the effects of progressive supranuclear palsy, which can leave at least some aspects of covert attentional mechanisms intact, parietal lobe injuries produce marked changes in such abilities. Posner et al. (1984) distinguished three aspects of covert shifts of attention: disengagement of attention from its current focus, moving attention to the target, and engagement of the target. They showed that patients with unilateral parietal lobe injuries find it difficult to disengage their attention from stimuli in the ipsilateral visual field (i.e. in the visual field corresponding to the side of the parietal lesion). Thus patients with right parietal lesions find it difficult to disengage their attention from a right visual field stimulus, but can readily disengage their attention from a left visual field stimulus. In terms of the experiment we described, their reaction times are very slow when the cue is presented to the right and the target appears to the left of fixation, but are unaffected when the cue is presented to the left and the target then appears on the right. Conversely, patients with left parietal lesions find it difficult to disengage their attention from a left but not from a right visual field stimulus.

Visual Extinction

Posner et al.'s (1984) findings form, as they note, an interesting parallel to the phenomenon of visual extinction found after parieto-occipital lesions. Patients with visual extinction can identify a single stimulus presented in any part of the visual field, but when stimuli are presented simultaneously in the left and right visual fields they do not seem to notice the stimulus falling in the visual field opposite (contralateral) to the site of the cerebral lesion. Thus a patient with visual extinction following a right parieto-occipital lesion would be able to identify a pair of scissors when they were presented individually in the left visual field or in the right visual field, but if the scissors fell in the left visual field and a pen was presented simultaneously in the right visual field, he or she would only report seeing the pen.

Visual extinction can happen even though the patient's visual fields may be intact on routine clinical examination (which typically involves testing for perception of a single stimulus). The problem is thus not due to a visual field defect as such, but to a higher-order attentional difficulty. In fact considerable analysis of the "extinguished" stimulus can take place. Volpe, LeDoux, and Gazzaniga (1979) have shown that accurate "same or different" comparisons between the extinguished and unextinguished stimuli are possible even when patients deny the presence of the extinguished stimulus. In our example, the patient would only report seeing a pen after simultaneous presentation of scissors in the left visual field and a pen in the right visual field, but would be able to say that the two stimuli were "different" from each other.

The parallel between visual extinction and Posner et al.'s (1984) demonstration of problems in disengaging attention from stimuli presented in the visual field ipsilateral to the lesion site is clear. Cases of clinically obvious visual extinction are, however, much more common following right rather than left cerebral injury. This observation is not inconsistent with Posner et al.'s (1984) findings, since they noted that although changes in covert orienting of attention were present after left or after right parietal injury, the effects were more marked in the case of right parietal injuries.

Unilateral Neglect and Denial

Visual extinction is closely related to one of the most intriguing of all spatial disorders—unilateral neglect. Like extinction, neglect is usually encountered in patients with right cerebral injuries, for whom it affects the left side of space. Patients with left-sided neglect following right

FIG 3.1.   Performance by a patient with visual neglect on a crossing-out task. She was asked to mark all the circles.

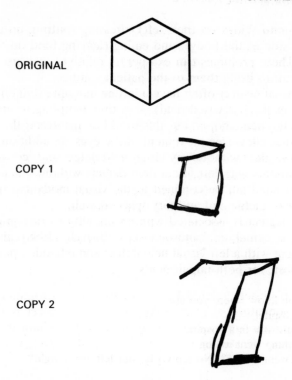

ORIGINAL

COPY 1

COPY 2

FIG. 3.2.   Copies of a figure by a patient with visual neglect. Before copying it she had identified the figure as a cube.

hemisphere injury seem to ignore stimuli that fall to their left. A simple way of demonstrating this is by crossing-out tasks (Albert, 1973). Figure 3.1 shows a page of random circles and crosses: A neglect patient has been asked to put a mark through all the circles. There is a clear (and characteristic) boundary between the area on the right of the page for which the instruction has been followed and that on the left where it is effectively ignored. It is as if the patient has not noticed that the left side of the page is there; yet the right side has been searched diligently.

Neglect can also be detected in drawing and copying tasks. Figure 3.2 shows two attempts by a neglect patient to copy a line drawing of a cube. She easily identified the figure as a cube, yet only the right-hand side has been copied; she was apparently quite satisfied with her efforts, and did not try to change them when given verbal hints as to their inadequacies. Notice that the stimulus figure is symmetrical, so there is no intrinsic reason why the left side should be harder to copy.

Neglect often affects a wide range of everyday activities. Patients may show errors affecting the left side in reading (see Chapter 8), moving around (bumping into things on their left), dressing (putting on clothes only on the right side of the body), and eating (leaving food on the left side of a plate). These problems can exasperate relatives, because it can be curiously difficult to bring them to the patient's notice.

Patients with visual neglect often have a left hemianopia (blindness for stimuli presented in the left visual field). It is thus tempting to attribute their problems to the hemianopia, but this would be incorrect; the defect is found in tasks that allow free movement of the eyes. In addition, some patients show left neglect without any visual field defect and, conversely, there are many patients with left visual field defects without left neglect. Moreover, neglect need not be confined to the visual modality, and can affect the left side of tactile and auditory space as well.

In some cases neglect is associated with an inability to recognise that one is disabled, a denial or "anosognosia". Bisiach (1988) gives an example of a patient with a left visual field defect and left sided paralysis, who was anosognosic for both impairments:

Examiner: Do you know where you are?
Patient: In a hospital.
E: Why are you in a hospital?
P: Something went wrong.
E: What went wrong? [No reply.] Is your left arm alright?
P: Yes.
E: Give me your left hand.
P: Here you are [without performing any movement].
E: Where is it?
P: [Still motionless]... Here, in front of you.
E: [The examiner ostentatiously raises his forefinger in the patient's right visual field and asks]... Grasp my finger with your left hand... Well?... Can't you move your left hand at all?
P: [The patient hesitates]... Just give me time to proceed from thought to action.
E: Why don't you need any time to proceed from thought to action when you use your right hand? Maybe you *can't* move your left hand?
P: I can move it alright. Only,... sometimes there are illogical reactions in behaviour; some positive and some negative...
E: [The examiner places the patient's left hand in the patient's right visual field]... Whose hand is this?
P: Your hand.
E: [The examiner then places the patient's left hand between his own hands]... Whose hands are these?
P: Your hands.

E: How many of them?
P: Three.
E: Ever see a man with *three* hands?
P: A hand is the extremity of an arm. Since you have three arms
            it follows that you must have three hands.

In this example one has the impression of a type of neglect that leaves the patient unaware of the left side of his own body.

A number of different theories have been proposed to try to account for unilateral neglect, and Heilman (1979) provides a useful introduction to these. The term "neglect" implies that the disorder is attentional in nature, so we have chosen to consider it with other disorders of spatial attention. There is some evidence to support an attentional explanation. Riddoch and Humphreys (1983) investigated the effects of cueing in a line bisection task. When asked to bisect horizontal lines patients with unilateral neglect tend to choose a point that is to the right of the true midpoint. Riddoch and Humphreys (1983) showed that this tendency could be reduced if a cue, such as a digit, was presented at the left-hand end of the line, but that cueing was only effective if patients were made to report the cue; the mere presence of a cue did not reduce neglect. Riddoch and Humphreys distinguish between automatic aspects of attentional orienting, which should be elicited by the mere presence of a cue, and the more deliberate attentional demands involved when the cue must be reported. Because cues were only effective when they had to be reported, they suggest that neglect may involve a more serious impairment of automatic than deliberate aspects of attentional orienting.

Riddoch and Humphreys' (1983) work helps to form a link between investigations of neglect and the basic attentional mechanisms studied by Posner and his colleagues. In some symptoms of neglect, however, the disorder must involve very central mechanisms. The studies of Bisiach and Luzzatti (1978) and Bisiach, Capitani, Luzzatti, and Perani (1981) provide dramatic illustrations. Bisiach and his colleagues asked their (Italian) patients to *imagine* that they were in the central square (Piazza del Duomo) of Milan, facing the cathedral, and to describe what they would be able to see. The descriptions given by patients with left neglect were mostly found to involve the buildings on the right side of the square as seen from the patient's imagined viewpoint; buildings on the left of the square were not described. This neglect of the left side of a mental image is a remarkable phenomenon. The patients were then asked to describe the square from a different perspective; they were to imagine themselves standing on the steps of the cathedral, looking away from it. Immediately they described the buildings they had "neglected" to describe before, because these now fell to their right in the imagined view, and neglected to describe the buildings now to their left, which were of course those they had described in response to the initial request! This ingenious control condition neatly demonstrates that the patients' *memory* of the buildings is intact. Thus, they neglect to report buildings that they actually know are there.

Any explanation of Bisiach's findings in terms of an attentional hypothesis would, as we have said, have to involve central attentional mechanisms. Baddeley and Lieberman (1980), for instance, suggest that the process of internally scanning what they call the "visuo-spatial scratch pad" might be defective. Bisiach, however, dislikes the idea of making a distinction between the mental representation of an event and attentional processes that are supposed to "scan" this representation, and suggests instead that it is simpler to think of the deficit as one that involves the *construction of mental representations*. In Bisiach's view neglect is due to damage to an internal spatial framework that then interferes with the patient's ability to form a mental representation of the left side of real or imagined space.

To support this interpretation Bisiach, Luzzatti, and Perani (1979) studied the ability of patients with left neglect to detect differences between successively presented pairs of cloud-like patterns. In one condition of Bisiach et al.'s (1979) study the patterns were presented in their entirety, but in the other condition they were viewed as if passing from left to right or from right to left behind a stationary vertical slit, 1.5 × 12 cm, so that only a strip of one of the patterns was present at any given moment. Unlike control subjects, the neglect patients made more errors when the differences were on the left sides of the patterns, and this was true for both presentation conditions. Thus patients neglected the left side of a pattern even when it was only seen moving past a central area, and this held for both directions of movement, i.e. regardless of whether the left side was the first or the last part of the pattern to be shown. This finding again demonstrates that neglect can affect the left side of internal, mental representations.

The debate between proponents of attentional and representational theories of neglect looks set to continue for some years, and will no doubt reveal many other interesting findings. In our view, however, the central point is that neglect may not be a unitary condition, but a cluster of interrelated deficits that must be teased apart. Thus we doubt whether a unitary explanation of all aspects of neglect should be considered necessary. Not all neglect patients, for instance, neglect the left side of mental images, not all have dressing problems, and only some are anosognosic. It may be that these deficits are only found in the most severe cases, or it may be that they are caused by damage to functionally distinct mechanisms. In favour of this suggestion are the findings of Bisiach and his colleagues indicating dissociations between neglect of personal space (one's own body) and extrapersonal space, and between neglect and anosognosia (Bisiach, Perani, Vallar, & Berti, 1986a; Bisiach, Vallar, Perani, Papagno, & Berti, 1986b).

There are also hints in the literature of dissociations between symptoms of neglect found for the visual and auditory (Bisiach, Cornacchia, Sterzi, & Vallar, 1984) and visual and tactile modalities (Chedru, 1976), and between symptoms found for different materials within the visual modality (Heilman & Watson, 1978), though such dissociations do not, of course, apply to all patients (Caplan, 1985). One problem in investigating them is that neglect is not always a very stable condition. Often it clears up within a few months of the brain injury and, in addition, the performances of neglect patients can be quite variable from day to day, or even within a single testing session. There are some neglect patients with stable symptoms, however, and detailed comparisons between individual cases would seem desirable.

SPATIAL KNOWLEDGE AND SPATIAL THOUGHT

Bisiach and Luzzatti's (1978) study showed that their patients neglected to report buildings on the left of their mental image of Milan's Piazza del Duomo even though they "knew" the position of those buildings, as evidenced by their ability to report previously neglected buildings when they imagined that they were facing in the opposite direction. Thus their spatial knowledge concerning the arrangement of buildings around the square was intact, but their neglect interfered with their ability to express this knowledge in the chosen task.

Other patients, however, may show genuine impairments of spatial knowledge. A more detailed introduction to these impairments can be found in Ratcliff (1982), a comprehensive account is given by De Renzi (1982a), and Benton (1982) provides an interesting survey of the history of ideas about spatial disorders in neurological patients.

We will begin by considering problems in finding one's way about, which clinicians call loss of topographical memory. In fact, there are at least two distinct forms of topographical memory loss. In one form spatial knowledge is preserved, but the patient gets lost easily because he or she cannot recognise the familiar buildings that act as landmarks. Whiteley and Warrington (1977) report a patient, JC, who complained of difficulty in recognising familiar buildings and streets. JC could describe buildings he was looking at, and match simultaneously presented pictures of unfamiliar buildings without difficulty, yet he said that even the street in which he lived seemed unfamiliar, and each day he might be going along it as if for the first time. He had to recognise his own house by the number, or by his car parked outside it. In contrast, he could read maps easily and relied heavily on making maps and plans to get about in his unfamiliar world.

This problem seems like a form of visual recognition difficulty, and indeed it can be found together with problems in familiar face recognition (Landis, Cummings, Benson, & Palmer, 1986; Levine, Warach, & Farah, 1985; see also Chapter 4), so we mention it here only to contrast it with the forms of topographical memory impairment that do involve the loss of spatial knowledge. In these latter forms patients can recognise landmarks, but no longer know how to get from one landmark to another. One of De Renzi, Faglioni, and Villa's (1977b) patients, MA, could not find her way about the hospital ward, and kept stopping to look about her for some familiar landmark to tell her where she was. If she ventured onto a different floor of the hospital she had great trouble finding her way back, and she always got lost in the hospital gardens. Despite her problems remembering routes MA did not show a more general memory impairment, and De Renzi et al. (1977b) contrast her case with that of another patient, RA, who was severely amnesic but quite able to find his way about.

Interestingly, orientation in large-scale spaces may be independently impaired in comparison to other tasks that also seem to have a pronounced "spatial" component. This was demonstrated by Ratcliff and Newcombe (1973) using patients with shrapnel and gunshot wounds. They compared the performance of these patients on finding a path through a maze of 2 × 2 cm blocks (stylus maze) which had been learned by visual guidance, with their performance at following a path between nine points that were 150 cm apart by using a simple map (locomotor maze). Striking dissociations were found. One man with a right parietal lesion, for example, failed to learn the stylus maze task in 25 trials but made only one error on the locomotor maze whereas another man, with a bilateral posterior cerebral lesion, learnt the stylus maze in only 5 trials but made 40 errors (out of a possible 57) on the locomotor maze. Ratcliff and Newcombe (1973) point out that on the locomotor maze task the subject's orientation changes as he walks around, and attribute the poor performance of patients with bilateral posterior lesions to a failure to maintain orientation in a changing environment.

Impairments of spatial knowledge thus fall into different types. We can begin to make a distinction between loss of knowledge of the topography of familiar places, as shown by De Renzi et al.'s (1977b) patient MA, and loss of ability to maintain spatial orientation, as in Ratcliff and Newcombe's (1973) locomotor maze. A patient with impaired knowledge of familiar places might well remain spatially oriented (in the sense of being able to return to his or her starting point) in an unfamiliar place, whereas a patient with impaired spatial orientation would be lost whether the place was familiar or unfamiliar. A further distinction drawn by clinicians is that between personal space (one's own body) and extrapersonal space, where dissociable impairments of spatial knowledge again occur (Ogden, 1985; Semmes, Weinstein, Ghent, & Teuber, 1963).

Dissociations between impairments affecting short-term and long-term memory for spatial locations have also been found. De Renzi, Faglioni, and Previdi (1977a) used a task initially devised by Corsi. The equipment for this task consists of nine wooden cubes fixed at random locations on a small wooden board. The experimenter touches a number of these cubes in sequence, and the subject's task is to reproduce this sequence in the same order; the size of the sequence (in terms of the number of cubes) can be varied in order to determine the subject's immediate memory span. De Renzi et al. (1977a) found that patients with lesions of posterior areas of the left or right cerebral hemispheres could be impaired on this task, but that only patients with right posterior lesions were impaired on a comparable long-term memory task in which they were required to learn a sequence of block positions that was longer than their immediate memory span. Thus the patients with left posterior lesions have impaired short-term but intact long-term memory for spatial locations. Reports of two individual cases of impaired short-term and intact long-term spatial memory can be found in De Renzi and Nichelli (1975).

There are also impairments that affect spatial thought. Morrow, Ratcliff, and Johnston (1985) showed that patients with right cerebral hemisphere lesions who could estimate accurately the distances between arbitrary symbols marked on a piece of paper, and could locate cities correctly on an outline map of the U.S.A., were none the less impaired in comparison to control subjects at estimating the distances between major cities in the U.S.A. (where they lived). Because they could estimate the distances between symbols, and locate the cities involved on a map, their problems could not be due to ignorance of the city locations or inability to estimate distances. Before being asked to estimate the distances between cities, Morrow et al.'s (1985) subjects had been shown an outline map of the U.S.A. and told its overall dimensions in miles. In order to estimate the distances between cities they were asked to make use of a mental image. Morrow et al. emphasise, however, that defective estimation of distances was found for cities on the right (East) side of the U.S.A. as well as for those on the left (West) side; so the phenomenon would seem to be independent of the neglect-related imaging disorder studied by Bisiach and his colleagues.

A neat demonstration of impaired spatial thought was made by Ratcliff (1979), who showed patients with gunshot and shrapnel wounds a drawing of a man with one of the hands marked with a black disc (see Fig. 3.3).

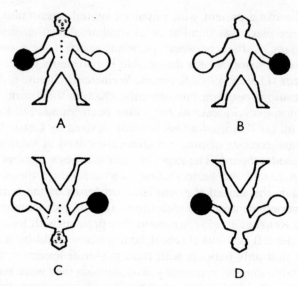

FIG. 3.3. Examples of stimuli used by Ratcliff (1979.) (Reproduced with permission of Pergamon Press from *Neuropsychologia*, 1979, *17*, 51.)

The figure was seen in upright or upside-down orientation, and in front or back view. The patients were asked to indicate whether the black disc marked the man's left or his right hand. Patients with posterior lesions of the right cerebral hemisphere showed a clear impairment on this task, but only when the stimuli were upside-down. Thus they could easily tell left from right when the stimulus was upright, but they seemed unable to "mentally rotate" the upside-down stimuli into their normal orientation.

It would be interesting to know more about the relation between impairments of spatial thought and impairments of spatial short-term memory. If Baddeley's (1983; 1986) conception that spatial short-term memory abilities form part of an organised "working memory" system is correct (see Chapter 10) these types of impairment may well prove to be closely related.

OVERVIEW

Neurophysiologists have been telling us for years that the human visual system has a precise and intricate organisation. Even so, the specificity of some of the disorders of visual and spatial abilities that are beginning to be revealed is very impressive. Highly selective impairments of different aspects of colour processing, movement perception, and visual location have been described. There is evidence, too, that different functional components of the visual system are organised into dissociable systems concerned primarily with the analysis of different types of visual pattern (objects, faces, words, etc.) or with space perception.

Abilities such as visual location might be considered to represent very basic aspects of our analysis of the spatial positioning of the objects around us. However, there is also evidence of modular organisation (as revealed by selective impairments) in the organisation of "higher" spatial abilities. We saw from the evidence reviewed in Chapter 2 that the processes involved in object recognition are highly organised; exactly the same conclusion would seem to be justified with regard to processes involved in space perception, though we have less idea as yet what the outlines of this organisation might be. Identifying the different dissociable impairments of visual and spatial abilities offers the possibility of helping to determine what modular functional components are involved.

Some disorders of visual and spatial abilities, however, turn out to involve different aspects of awareness. In blindsight, for instance, the patient is not aware of seeing anything, yet can make accurate responses based on some form of visual analysis. In visual extinction, patients may deny the presence of one of two simultaneously presented stimuli, yet be able to say whether or not it is the same as or different to one that is overtly reported as present. In visual neglect, awareness of part of external space seems to be compromised, and in anosognosia the patient seems to show an unawareness of one or more of his or her own disabilities. The investigation of such disorders holds great promise for helping us to understand questions about consciousness and awareness that have been puzzled over for centuries, and forms one of the most fascinating areas in contemporary cognitive neuropsychology.

SUMMARY

In this chapter we have examined a number of different types of impairment affecting visual and spatial abilities. Impairments of colour vision were divided into those involving inability to see colour (achromatopsias), impairment of colour knowledge (in which colour perception is intact, but errors occur in tasks that require use of stored information about colour), and difficulties involving colour naming. For movement perception we considered the remarkable case of LM, who had lost the ability to see movement under all except a rather limited range of conditions. To LM most moving things were like a series of arbitrary, static "snapshots". We then discussed contrasting impairments involving spatial location. Blindsight, in which a patient (DB) had no sense of seeing anything presented in the defective areas of his field of vision yet could make accurate judgements of location, was contrasted with a disorder of visual location in which another patient (Private M) was well aware of seeing things and could even recognise them without difficulty, but did not know where they were positioned in external space. "Higher-order" spatial problems were then considered. Some of these involve impairments of spatial attention, and a dissociation between impairments affecting shifts of overt and shifts of covert attention can be observed. Certain aspects of unilateral neglect (such as the influence of cueing) are also consistent with an attentional explanation, but others (such as neglect of mental images) are perhaps more readily explained in terms of a "representational" theory. Neglect is probably a complex phenomenon involving a number of potentially dissociable aspects. For impairments of spatial knowledge a distinction can be drawn between impaired knowledge of the topography of familiar places and impaired ability to maintain spatial orientation. Other types of impairment can affect short-term memory for spatial locations, and spatial thought.

FURTHER READING

Benton, A. (1979). Visuoperceptive, visuospatial, and visuoconstructive disorders. In K. M. Heilman and E. Valenstein (Eds), *Clinical neuropsychology*, pp. 186–232. New York: Oxford University Press. Introduction to the disorders discussed in this chapter from a clinical perspective.

Bisiach, E., & Luzzatti, C. (1978). Unilateral neglect of representational space. *Cortex, 14*, 129–133. A key paper on visual neglect, employing an extremely neat experimental paradigm to elicit a most striking finding.

Cowey, A. (1985). Aspects of cortical organization related to selective attention and selective impairments of visual perception: A tutorial review. In M.I. Posner and O. S. M. Marin (Eds), *Attention and performance*, XI, pp. 41–62. New Jersey: Lawrence Erlbaum Associates. Worth looking at to see just how detailed neurophysiological knowledge of the visual system has become. Its rich organisation suggests that there are many more selective impairments to be discovered.

De Renzi, E. (1982). *Disorders of space exploration and cognition*. Chichester: Wiley. Comprehensive review of spatial impairments, with many interesting clinical insights.

Heilman, K. M. (1979). Neglect and related disorders. In K. M. Heilman and E. Valenstein (Eds), *Clinical neuropsychology*, pp. 268–307. New York: Oxford University Press. Useful introduction to clinical aspects of neglect.

Meadows, J. C. (1974). Disturbed perception of colours associated with localized cerebral lesions. *Brain, 97*, 615–632. Still one of the best papers on impairments of colour vision.

Weiskrantz, L. (1986). *Blindsight: A case study and implications*. Oxford Psychology Series, 12. Oxford: Oxford University Press. Very detailed investigation of DB. Quite technical in places, but will convince you that "hard" science can be very exciting.

4 Face Processing

INTRODUCTION

Other people's faces provide us with a wealth of social information. We are highly skilled at recognising the faces of people we know, and we can assess characteristics such as age or sex fairly accurately even when a face is unfamiliar. We are also adept at interpreting facial expressions, and make much use of these in regulating patterns of social interaction.

Given the range of different types of information we gain from faces, and the variety of uses to which these are put, it is perhaps not too surprising that different types of face processing disorder can be observed in people with cerebral injuries. Investigations of these disorders have been of central importance to the development of functional models of face processing.

A FUNCTIONAL MODEL OF FACE PROCESSING

We will use the functional model presented by Bruce and Young (1986) to organise our discussion of disorders of face processing. Detailed discussion of the studies of normal subjects that support a model of this type can be found in H. D. Ellis (1986a) and Bruce (1988). A slightly simplified version of the Bruce and Young model is shown in schematic form in Fig. 4.1. Bruce and Young (1986) propose that following structural encoding of the face's appearance (which we will equate loosely with formation of a facial percept), different types of information are extracted from the face in parallel. These include the analysis of facial expressions, analysis of the mouth and tongue movements involved in speaking (facial speech analysis), and the types of directed visual processing needed to manipulate facial representations intentionally so that we can, for example, see the similarities and differences between faces of unfamiliar people.

Recognition of familiar faces is also considered by Bruce and Young (1986) to occur in parallel with expression analysis, facial speech analysis, and directed visual processing. They postulate a set of "face recognition units" that form a link between structural encoding of the face's appearance and "person identity nodes" that provide access to stored information concerning known people (their occupations, personal characteristics, etc.). Each face recognition unit is held to contain the structural description of a known person's appearance. The recognition unit "fires" when a seen face resembles the description it holds. Recognition of familiar people from other cues, such as voices, would involve the use of separate access routes to the person identity nodes (not shown in Fig. 4.1). You should be familiar with this type of theoretical model from our discussion of object recognition in Chapter 2.

PROSOPAGNOSIA

The most striking type of face processing disorder is prosopagnosia, or inability to recognise familiar faces. Prosopagnosic patients are often

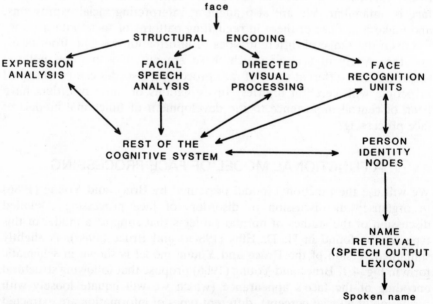

FIG. 4.1.   Functional model for face processing (based on Bruce & Young, 1986.)

unable to identify *any* familiar faces including famous faces, friends, family, and their own faces when seen in a mirror (Hécaen & Angelergues, 1962). Clinical features of this disorder have been summarised by Benton (1980) and Hécaen (1981), and neurological aspects are discussed by Meadows (1974a) and Damasio, Damasio, and Van Hoesen (1982).

Prosopagnosic patients know when they are looking at a face, but cannot say who the face belongs to. Instead they must rely on other cues such as voice, gait, clothing, or context in order to recognise people. Such methods are not very reliable, and it is possible that they are rendered even less effective than they might be by their inconsistency with the defective face recognition mechanisms. Tiberghien and Clerc (1986), for instance, mention that their patient, AH, could identify the voice of a politician on the television without seeing him, but that if AH saw and heard that person at the same time he could no longer recognise him.

Prosopagnosia is, of course, no more a unitary disorder than object agnosia, dyslexia or amnesia. We use the term "prosopagnosia" here simply as a convenient shorthand for "inability to recognise familiar faces" and, as we will show, this may have various causes. Thus, strictly, we should speak of "the prosopagnosias". Identification of the different types of prosopagnosia has, however, been made difficult by the fact that it is especially rare as an isolated deficit. In the historic cases described by Charcot (1883) and Wilbrand (1892), for instance, inability to recognise faces was found in the context of quite widespread perceptual and memory difficulties, and the distinct nature of impairments of familiar face recognition was not generally recognised until Bodamer (1947) published his own observations and coined the term "prosopagnosia". We will examine more closely the relation between impairments affecting the recognition of faces and other types of visual object later in this chapter (pp. 101–105).

Although the different types of prosopagnosic difficulty have yet to be delineated convincingly, it is widely believed that the cases reported to date fall into at least two distinct groups (Hécaen, 1981; De Renzi, 1986). For one group of patients the ability to *perceive* faces is manifestly impaired; in Bruce and Young's terms the defect affects structural encoding. The other group of patients seem to have relatively intact perceptual abilities, but cannot *recognise* or in some other way process the faces they seem to perceive satisfactorily.

DEFECTIVE PERCEPTION OF FACES

The first two patients described by Bodamer (1947) form good examples of prosopagnosia in the context of impaired perception of faces. We will consider his case 2, Unteroffizier (Uffz.) S. This 24-year-old noncommissioned officer was wounded in the head in March 1944. Following this injury he was unable to identify once-familiar faces. He maintained that he could still image the faces of people he knew before his injury, but that the faces of people he was actually looking at all looked the same. They were like strangely flat, white oval plates, with emphatically dark eyes.

Uffz. S could differentiate between faces and most other types of object, but made some errors with animal faces. He identified a rabbit's face from its ears correctly, but thought that a dog's face was that of an unusually hairy human. When looking at people's faces he could pick out individual features correctly, such as the nose, mouth or eyes, but had no sense of the face's individuality. Even very well known faces produced no feeling of familiarity, and he failed to recognise his own mother in a chance meeting.

As well as being unable to recognise individuals, Uffz. S also could not determine the age or sex of seen faces except by inferring these from the hairstyle. His ability to interpret facial expressions was also defective. He said that he could see the movements involved when people made angry or smiling facial expressions, but that these had no meaning for him. When looking in a mirror together with a number of other people Uffz. S could see the movements on his face when he spoke, without recognising the face as his own.

In interpreting the nature of the perceptual disorder involved, Bodamer (1947) placed emphasis on the fact that Uffz. S could distinguish the individual elements of a face but could not appreciate its unique character. Later observers also often return to this idea. As Pallis's (1955, p. 219) patient put it: "I can see the eyes, nose, and mouth quite clearly but they just don't add up. They all seem chalked in, like on a blackboard. I have to tell by the clothes or voice whether it is a man or a woman."

It is difficult to know what to make of such cases of impaired face perception beyond the fact that this can happen. Uffz. S seemed to experience impaired perception both of individual features *and* the facial configuration, whereas from Pallis's (1955) patient's description it would seem that the deficit in seeing the configuration formed by the individual features was perhaps more severe. Pallis's patient's description of his problems is in some ways reminiscent of Riddoch and Humphreys' (1987a) object agnosic patient, HJA (see Chapter 2), who was also prosopagnosic, but Pallis reports that his patient could identify everyday objects without difficulty provided that colour was not a necessary cue (his colour vision was severely impaired). The contrast between the problems of Uffz. S and patients such as Pallis's (1955) patient or HJA suggests that there are probably different types of perceptual deficit that can affect face recognition, and Hay and Young (1982) and H. D. Ellis (1986b) offer suggestions as to what these might be. But the patients are clearly trying to describe types of perceptual experience for which there is no normal shared vocabulary, and it may be unwise to rely too much on their subjective reports.

A further complication is that not all problems affecting face perception cause prosopagnosia. Bodamer (1947) contrasted a third case with his other two patients: This patient saw faces as distorted. He described a nurse's face as having its nose turned sideways by several degrees, one eyebrow higher than the other, the mouth askew, and hair shifted like an ill-fitting cap. This kind of perceptual distortion is often termed "metamorphopsia". According to Bodamer's (1947) third patient, only faces looked distorted in this way; but he remained able to recognise them.

Hécaen and Angelergues (1962) also point out that metamorphopsic patients often remain able to recognise familiar faces to some extent. Perhaps the distortions they experience are not sufficiently severe to prevent recognition (which we know from everyday experience can cope with a wide range of perceptual variations), or perhaps the perceptual impairments that can lead to prosopagnosia are not of the metamorphopsic type.

PROSOPAGNOSIA AS AN IMPAIRMENT OF FACE MEMORY

We have seen that prosopagnosia can arise in a context of impaired perception of faces. For some prosopagnosic patients, however, face perception is relatively intact, leading to the idea that it may be more useful to consider this type of disorder as if it were a material-specific memory impairment (De Renzi, 1982b; Tiberghien & Clerc, 1986; Warrington & James, 1967b; see also Chapter 10 for a discussion of other types of memory impairment). We will consider the patient Mr W, described by Bruyer, Laterre, Seron, Feyereisen, Strypstein, Pierrard, and Rectem (1983).

Mr W was a 54-year-old Belgian farmer who had been unable to identify familiar people for a year. His difficulties in recognising people had initially begun during a spell of hospital treatment for cardiac problems, and had now become stable. His scores on standard intelligence tests did not seem affected (Verbal I.Q. 90; Performance I.Q. 95), but neurological examination (CT scan) revealed bilateral occipital lobe lesions.

Subjectively, Mr W's complaint was that faces seemed "less beautiful" than before and that, although he could still see them and their constitutive parts well, he could not recognise them. Investigation of this complaint showed that he was able to pick out the human faces in an array of photographs of five human faces (photographed with a white hood covering the hairstyle), five dog faces, five car fronts, and five housefronts. He performed this task without error, and could also pick out the dogs, cars, and houses without difficulty. He was able to make accurate copies of line drawings of faces, and to identify correctly the sex of 16 faces (8 male, 8 female) photographed with a white hood covering the hairstyle.

Facial expressions were accurately perceived and interpreted. Mr W could match correctly photographs of faces as showing same or different expressions, could pick out faces having the same expression as a specified target picture, and could judge the appropriateness of facial expressions to pictures meant to elicit an emotional state (a clown, a funeral, etc.).

Mr W's ability to match unfamiliar faces was also good. He could discriminate between pairs of line drawings in which one or more features were altered (13/16 correct, mean score for normal subjects = 14.5). He achieved a normal level of performance when asked to pick out a photographed target face from an array of nine possible faces, and his performance on this task deteriorated in a "normal" manner if the stimuli were blurred. Had his ability to perceive faces already been impaired, blurring might not have produced any further effect. When shown two photographs of the same face in three-quarter and full-face views Mr W correctly stated that the photographs showed the same person on all six trials. He could also match the identities of unfamiliar faces (wearing white hoods so that hairstyle was not a cue) across different expressions. When shown a 4 × 4 matrix of photographs of four different people with each of four different expressions he made 14/16 correct choices of the photographs showing the same person as a target face with a neutral expression.

Given Mr W's ability to discriminate correctly between faces of different unfamiliar people, and to see that different views of the same unfamiliar face belonged to the same person, it is difficult to believe that his problems in recognising familiar people were due to an inability to construct an adequate facial "percept". Instead, it seems that he could no longer use differences that he could see between faces to effect recognition. We do not, however, mean to claim that his perceptual abilities were *entirely* intact. Bruyer et al. (1983) point out, for instance, that Mr W was unable to see bruises on potatoes, and he did sometimes show performances on their tests of face perception that were slightly below normal. These relatively subtle perceptual deficits may, however, have been coincidental; they do not seem sufficient to account for Mr W's recognition problems (patients can have far worse perceptual impairment without showing Mr W's prosopagnosic symptoms).

The face recognition impairment was severe in Mr W's case. When shown photographs of ten famous faces, five of which had been "cued" by being named in a previous discussion, he could only identify one (mean for normal subjects = 9.7). He was shown videotapes of the faces of himself, his doctor, his neuropsychologist, a patient he was friendly with, and two unfamiliar people, all wearing hoods to hide their hairstyles. Mr W could not recognise anyone, and thought that all of the faces were unfamiliar, though he was a little doubtful about his own face. When the hoods were removed he recognised himself after a long delay, thought that his friend's face seemed familiar, and that he might know the neuropsychologist. Even when asked only to decide whether or not faces were those of familiar people Mr W rejected 12 of 20 familiar faces shown to him. The eight faces he accepted as familiar in this task were all those of people he knew personally (and were thus probably of very high familiarity indeed); he invariably rejected celebrities' faces as unfamiliar.

We might summarise Mr W's face recognition problems by saying that in tasks demanding precise identification (e.g. by naming) he was very severely impaired, but that he did seem to retain some sense of the familiarity of faces that had previously been extremely well known to him. His difficulties seemed to lie in accessing previously stored memories concerning the people whose faces he saw—a problem that Damasio et al. (1982) have called "contextual evocation".

The attempts to explain prosopagnosia as a material-specific memory difficulty need to be approached carefully. The claim is *not* simply that prosopagnosics are amnesic. Mr W, for example, could remember perfectly well the people whose faces he could not recognise if he was presented with their names, voices, and so on. His problem was thus one of *access to* these memories from the face itself. In terms of Bruce and Young's (1986) approach Mr W's problem seems to lie in defective operation of face recognition units. His structural encoding processes were relatively intact, as indicated by his near normal performance on tests of face perception, and person identity nodes were also clearly intact because he could recognise people from names and voices, but the recognition units no longer formed an effective link. This conception is analogous to the idea of a material-specific memory difficulty, because face recognition units can be seen as equivalent to a memory store of the faces Mr W had encountered previously.

Mr W certainly did have problems with face memory. Bruyer et al. (1983) demonstrated this by showing him six faces and then asking him to find three that he had just seen in another array of six faces. Whether the faces used were those of familiar or unfamiliar people, Mr W only managed to get one correct. In contrast, when faces with emotional expressions were used in this type of task he did not make any errors because he could use a strategy of labelling the expressions. This shows neatly that it is Mr W's memory for faces, rather than his memory in any general sense, that was defective. The claim is supported by the finding that in paired associate learning tasks Mr W found it easier to associate people's's names with meaningless drawings or even with pictures of car fronts than with faces.

SEMANTIC IMPAIRMENTS

In discussing the view that some cases of prosopagnosia might be considered to involve a material-specific memory problem, we drew attention to the point that prosopagnosia should none the less be distinguished from other forms of amnesia because prosopagnosic patients remain able to remember familiar people and to recognise them from their names or voices. Thus it is access to person identity nodes from faces that is impaired in prosopagnosia, and the memory representations of familiar people remain intact and readily accessible in other ways.

This is not the case for many amnesic patients. A number of studies have shown that amnesic memory deficits can affect memories of familiar people (Marslen-Wilson & Teuber, 1975; Sanders & Warrington, 1971). Such problems affect the recognition of people from their faces but, of course, they extend equally to recognition from names and voices, and problems are also shown in recall tasks involving famous people (Albert, Butters, & Levin, 1979; Hamsher & Roberts, 1985; Meudell, Northen, Snowden, & Neary, 1980b). In cases of semantic memory impairments, such as Warrington's patients AB and JBR (see Chapter 2), failure to recognise overtly familiar people may also occur.

A remarkable impairment affecting the semantic representations of familiar people is seen in the "Capgras syndrome". Capgras syndrome is one of a number of different types of misidentification syndromes (see Joseph, 1986), and was first described by the French psychiatrists Capgras and Reboul-Lachaux in 1923. The Capgras syndrome has been widely believed to be psychodynamic in origin, but recent reports have emphasised that it has a clear organic basis in several cases (e.g. Joseph, 1986; Lewis, 1987; MacCallum, 1973; Weston & Whitlock, 1971; Wilcox & Waziri, 1983).

The key feature of the Capgras syndrome is that the patient believes that one or more familiar people has been "replaced" by an impostor. Often, but not always, this impostor is thought to have harmful intentions. We will make use of the case described by Alexander, Stuss, and Benson (1979). This 44-year-old man suffered a severe brain injury in a road accident, leading to bilateral frontal and extensive right hemisphere damage. Prior to the accident he had been experiencing auditory hallucinations and delusions following a period of prolonged stress, but never acted on them.

When Alexander et al. (1979) met this patient, some two and a half years after his accident, he informed them that he had two families of identical composition. In each family his wife had the same name and very similar appearance and manner. There were five children in each family, with the same names and sexes, though he thought that the children in the original family were about one year younger than in his second family. The change had, he maintained, taken place in December, 1975 (about a month after the accident), when his "new" wife had turned up to take him home from hospital for the weekend. It is perhaps significant that he had not been informed that he was going home that weekend. He said he had not seen his original wife or family since, but he described positive feelings towards both wives and did not seem upset by his first wife's desertion.

Alexander et al. (1979) noted that their patient realised the implausibility of his story, but continued to assert it. He seemed unable to change his beliefs. They quote the following interview (p. 335):

E. Isn't that [two families] unusual?
S. It was unbelievable!
E. How do you account for it?
S. I don't know. I try to understand it myself, and it was virtually impossible.
E. What if I told you I don't believe it?
S. That's perfectly understandable. In fact, when I tell the story, I feel that I'm concocting a story.... It's not quite right. Something is wrong.

Despite being pressed in this way, and told that he was incorrect on several occasions, Alexander et al.'s patient continued to experience the delusion.

The Capgras syndrome may be seen as an example of a general class of "reduplicative paramnesias" (Alexander et al., 1979; Benson, Gardner, & Meadows, 1976; Patterson & Mack, 1985). The term paramnesia is used to refer to a distortion rather than a loss of memory. Capgras' patients reduplicate people, whereas for other reduplication patients it is often places that are affected, with the patient maintaining that their home or hospital is a duplicate of the one they actually live in. For example, Geschwind (1982) quoted the case of a patient in the Beth Israel Hospital in Boston, U.S.A., who said that he was in Concord, New Hampshire. This patient knew that he was in the Beth Israel Hospital, but maintained that he was in a (non-existent) branch of that hospital located in Concord. Sometimes the same patient will reduplicate both people and places (e.g. Patterson & Mack, 1985).

The fact that reduplication can occur to people or to places forms a curious parallel to the observation that defective recognition of places is often found in association with prosopagnosia (Landis et al., 1986). Perhaps this is no more than a coincidence, and it is really the emotional significance of people and of places that underlies the tendency to reduplicate them. Some reports, however, have demonstrated that Capgras' patients show deficits on tests of unfamiliar face matching (Shraberg & Weitzel, 1979; Tzavaras, Luaute, & Bidault, 1986). Although such face processing impairments cannot be sufficient to produce Capgras syndrome, because other patients with equally or more severe impairments do not reduplicate people, it is conceivable that they may play some contributory role.

NAME RETRIEVAL PROBLEMS

In Bruce and Young's (1986) model of face processing access to person identity nodes occurs before name retrieval. Problems involving name retrieval are common in everyday life (Reason & Lucas, 1984; Young, Hay, & Ellis, 1985a), and experiments with normal subjects have shown that people's names are harder to remember than various other kinds of semantic information (Cohen & Faulkner, 1986; McWeeny, Young, Hay, & Ellis, 1987).

Thus we would expect to find examples of patients who, following brain injury, remain able to access semantic information about people but cannot remember their names. This happens in a form of language disorder known as anomia (see Chapter 5), but anomias usually involve not only people's names but also names of objects, places and so on. McKenna and Warrington (1980), however, present a report of an anomia that affected people's names selectively. Their patient, GBL, could only name 3 of 20 photographs of famous people, yet was able to describe accurately who 18 of the 20 people were. In contrast, she correctly named 16 out of 20 European towns and 12 of 12 English towns from their locations on a map.

COVERT RECOGNITION IN PROSOPAGNOSIA

The impairments of familiar face recognition we have already discussed fit Bruce and Young's (1986) model quite well (see Fig. 4.1). Cases of defective face perception (such as Uffz. S) can be considered to involve impaired structural encoding, the material-specific memory deficit (Mr W) would involve face recognition units, semantic impairments would arise at the level of person identity nodes, and there are also distinct problems of name retrieval.

A remarkable feature of some recent studies of prosopagnosic patients, however, is that they can be shown to demonstrate a considerable degree of recognition of familiar faces if tested on tasks that do not demand explicit awareness that recognition has been achieved. The key feature of such tasks would seem to be that recognition is tested *implicitly* (Schacter, McAndrews, & Moscovitch, 1988). These phenomena are not in principle inconsistent with the type of model used here (Fig. 4.1), but they will need to be investigated carefully in order to see how they can be related to it.

Bruyer et al. (1983) tested Mr W's ability to associate names with several types of stimuli. Although Mr W could not identify the faces of celebrities, he found it much easier to learn correct than incorrect names to photographs of their faces. Thus it seems that some degree of recognition of the familiar faces must have taken place; otherwise correct or incorrect names would be equally easy to learn. Curiously, though, it would seem that Mr W was not aware of having recognised the faces.

This phenomenon of "recognition without awareness" in prosopagnosia has been more fully investigated by Bauer (1984), Tranel and Damasio (1985), De Haan, Young, and Newcombe (1987a; 1987b), and Young and De Haan (1988). Bauer (1984) and Tranel and Damasio (1985) used autonomic measures; they found that the skin conductance responses of their prosopagnosic patients showed discrimination between familiar and unfamiliar faces (Tranel & Damasio, 1985) and between correct and incorrect names when viewing a familiar face (Bauer, 1984) even though their patients had no sense of conscious, overt recognition. We will use De Haan et al.'s (1987a; 1987b) work to look more closely at this phenomenon of "covert" recognition in prosopagnosia.

De Haan et al. (1987a; 1987b) worked with PH, who had sustained a severe closed head injury in a motorcycle accident when he was aged 19. His language abilities were well preserved, and he had normal short-term memory, but he showed poor performance on long-term memory tasks and on some visuospatial tasks. He could read satisfactorily, and could recognise many (but not all) seen objects, but he was completely unable to recognise familiar faces. On formal tests he recognised none of 20 highly familiar faces and performed at chance level (18/36 correct) on a task requiring classification of faces as belonging to familiar or unfamiliar people. Even in a forced choice task in which he was only asked to pick which one of two simultaneously presented faces (one familiar, one unfamiliar) was the familiar person, PH still performed at chance level (65/128 correct), yet he was much more accurate (118/128) on a parallel task involving those people's names (Young & De Haan, 1988).

PH's visual acuity was normal for his right eye, but impaired for his left eye, probably because of a longstanding untreated squint. His field of vision for his right eye was somewhat constricted, and there was some loss of contrast sensitivity for all spatial frequencies greater than 1.5 cycles per degree. These visual impairments do not, however, seem sufficient to account for PH's prosopagnosia, because other patients with more severely impaired vision remain able to recognise people. Moreover, PH was able to match different views of unfamiliar faces as belonging to same or different people, and he could interpret facial expressions; his performances on such tasks tended to be impaired in comparison to those of normal people of his age, but well above chance level. His inability to recognise faces could also not be attributed to his other memory problems, because he *could* recognise people from their names. Thus he had not simply "forgotten" the people concerned; in Bruce and Young's (1986) terms, person identity nodes were relatively intact. The nature of his prosopagnosia would thus seem to bear some resemblance to that of Mr W, but for PH the face recognition deficit (on overt tasks) was more severe and occurred in the context of a wider range of other impairments.

Despite his very severe impairment on overt recognition tasks, De Haan et al. (1987a; 1987b) found that PH showed effects of face familiarity on his performance of various tasks that did not demand explicit recognition. Thus when required to judge as rapidly as possible whether two simultaneously presented photographs were of the same or different people he was faster for familiar than unfamiliar faces. As is found for normal subjects (Young, Hay, McWeeny, Flude, & Ellis, 1985b), PH was only faster at matching photographs of familiar faces when matches had to be based on the faces' internal (eyes, nose, mouth) rather than external (hair, chin) features. This normal pattern of responses to familiar and unfamiliar faces was found despite PH's inability to identify explicitly the people involved.

Because PH could recognise printed names without difficulty, De Haan et al. (1987a; 1987b) were able to investigate whether or not the presence of irrelevant "distractor" faces would interfere with name classification. When normal people classify names into semantic categories (for example, as names of politicians or of television personalities) their reaction times are increased by the presence of a distractor face drawn from a different category to the name being classified. PH was also found to show this interference effect in three separate experiments. Figure 4.2 shows examples of stimuli from De Haan et al.'s (1987b) task. Names and faces of four politicians and four television personalities were used as stimuli. These were combined with each other so that a name was presented with the same person's face (SAME PERSON condition), with the face of another person from the same category (RELATED condition; for example, a politician's name with another politician's face), or with the face of another person from the other category (UNRELATED condition; for example, a politician's name with a television personality's face). PH

FIG. 4.2. Examples of stimuli from De Haan, Young, & Newcombe's (1987b) study. The name of the politician David Steel is combined with his own face (top; SAME PERSON), with the face of the politician Peter Walker (middle; RELATED), and with the face of the non-politician Michael Aspel (bottom; UNRELATED). (Reproduced with permission of The Press Association and Masson Italia Editori from *Cortex*, 1987, *23*, 312.)

was asked to decide as quickly as possible whether each *name* was that of a politician or a television personality. He was instructed to ignore the faces. His reaction times, measured from the onset of each stimulus by means of a manual response, are shown in Table 4.1.

TABLE 4.1
Mean Reaction Times (in Milliseconds) for PH's Classification of Names Accompanied by Different Types of Distractor Faces (Data From De Haan, Young, & Newcombe, 1987b)

Type of Face Distractor		
Same Person	Related	Unrelated
1059	1122	1234

Although the same names and faces were used in each condition, and the task only required him to assign the names to one of the sets of four politicians or four television personalities, PH shows a clear interference effect from the faces. His reaction times for classifying the names in the UNRELATED condition are significantly longer than those for classifying the same names in the RELATED condition; the reaction times for the RELATED and SAME PERSON conditions do not differ significantly. This is the same pattern of interference effects as is found in normal subjects for this type of task (Young, Ellis, Flude, McWeeny, & Hay, 1986). PH's reaction times are rather longer than would be usual for normal people, but a general slowing of reaction time is not uncommon after closed head injury (Van Zomeren & Deelman, 1978). The more important point is that the *patterning* of PH's reaction times across the different conditions looks normal.

The faces used by De Haan et al. (1987b) had been carefully matched so that cues such as age or hairstyle would not allow politicians and television personalities to be discriminated from each other. When PH was asked to classify explicitly these faces as those of politicians or television personalities he performed at chance level (30/48 correct). Thus the faces interfered with his ability to classify names despite the fact that accurate overt classification of these faces was not possible.

De Haan et al. (1987a) also showed that, like Mr W, PH learnt true face–name pairings (face + person's actual name) more easily than untrue (face + another person's name) pairings, and that the same finding held for face–occupation pairings. In addition, he learnt true pairings of faces and names more easily than untrue pairings even when tested with faces of people he had only met *since* his accident (and that he had, in consequence, *never* recognised overtly). Thus his face recognition system has continued to store representations of familiar faces seen since his accident, despite the fact that explicit recognition is no longer achieved.

Work on covert recognition in prosopagnosia is all quite recent, and it may be some time before its precise implications can be evaluated correctly. It seems unlikely, however, that such effects will be established for all prosopagnosic patients. It is difficult to believe, for instance, that someone with a structural encoding deficit as severe as that experienced by Uffz. S would show "recognition without awareness". A more likely possibility is that future studies will show the phenomenon to be confined to those patients with the "material-specific memory defect" form of the disorder, and possibly only to a subset of these. This would make sense, because there are some parallels to be drawn between covert recognition and the types of memory that truly amnesic patients can show if tested on "implicit" tasks (Schacter, 1987; Schacter et al. 1988; see also Chapter 10). One possibility is that covert recognition represents the performance of a recognition system that is itself relatively intact, but can no longer interact with the rest of the cognitive system in ways that would signal what has been recognised (see Young, 1988, and Young & De Haan, 1988, for further discussion of this idea).

SPECIFICITY OF FACE RECOGNITION IMPAIRMENTS

A question that is often discussed concerns the extent to which prosopagnosic disorders are *specific* to face recognition. The issue is not yet fully resolved, largely because the condition is seldom encountered in a "pure" form. A number of prosopagnosic patients can read, so they have not lost the ability to recognise *any* visual stimulus. But there are usually additional types of visual recognition difficulty present, particularly achromatopsia (loss of colour vision) and object agnosia. These disorders do not, however, inevitably occur together. Pallis's (1955) patient, for example, showed impairment of colour vision and prosopagnosia but not object agnosia, whereas a patient described by Levine (1978) had object agnosia and prosopagnosia but not loss of colour vision. Occasionally, too, a patient is reported for whom prosopagnosia is present without severe object agnosia *or* achromatopsia. Mr W would serve as an example of this. He could recognise objects without difficulty, and only showed errors of colour naming in relatively subtle tasks (saying, for instance, that brown was "dark red" and that grey was "pale blue").

Although a number of prosopagnosic patients do not show signs of object agnosia, many object agnosic patients are also unable to recognise familiar faces. Moreover, when prosopagnosia and visual object agnosia occur together, the prosopagnosia is usually the more severe deficit in the sense that the patient can identify a smaller proportion of faces (often none at all) than objects. Thus it might be thought that there is a kind of hierarchy in which increasingly fine discriminations lead to the identification first of different categories of object (faces, cars, houses, etc.) and then of individual objects *within* each category. Object agnosia would then be seen as a breakdown in the initial between-category recognition mechanism, and prosopagnosia would be considered to involve impairment of within-category recognition.

This hierarchical conception, in which between-category recognition is followed by within-category recognition, has a certain logical appeal, and it is consistent with the observation that prosopagnosia is often found together with a less severe object agnosia. The idea that prosopagnosia involves a general breakdown of within-category recognition is also bolstered by the fact that most prosopagnosic patients also experience difficulties in identifying individual objects in other visually homogeneous categories (Blanc-Garin, 1986). Bornstein (1963), for instance, described a prosopagnosic patient who had also lost the ability to identify species of birds which had formerly been well known to her. She commented that "All the birds look the same." Similarly, Bornstein, Sroka, and Munitz (1969) reported the case of a prosopagnosic farmer who could no longer identify his own livestock. Previously he had been able to recognise his cows as individuals, but he could no longer do this. He could identify his horse because he only kept one, but felt that had there been more horses he would not have been able to recognise those either. Of the prosopagnosic patients we have considered in detail here, Uffz. S could not discriminate between animals with similar outlines, and PH was severely impaired in his ability to identify different types of flowers or cars—we will say more about Mr W later.

Notice, however, that the arguments for a recognition hierarchy rest entirely on the *association* of different deficits. As we noted in Chapter 1, such arguments are weak because there are many possible reasons why deficits might be associated, not all of which have any functional significance. The existence of cases in which deficits that are thought to be causally linked are not found together is sufficient to falsify the argument.

Such cases do seem to exist. There have been reports of patients who show object agnosia without prosopagnosia, or for whom the object agnosia seems more severe than the prosopagnosia. If prosopagnosia was caused by a breakdown of the higher levels in a recognition hierarchy, this could not happen. The high-level recognition mechanisms could not remain intact while the ability to make the allegedly lower-level between-category discriminations involved in object recognition was lost. This is an important point, so it is disappointing that the known cases have not been more thoroughly investigated with respect to their face processing abilities. The observations of preserved face recognition have arisen incidentally in descriptions of patients with visual object agnosias.

The only cases of object agnosia in which face recognition seemed to be fully preserved are those of Hécaen, Goldblum, Masure, and Ramier (1974) and Ferro and Santos (1984). Hécaen et al.'s (1974) patient was able to recognise hospital staff and all photographs of celebrities presented to him, despite his object agnosia. Ferro and Santos's (1984) patient was also able to identify all of the faces shown to him, though he could not always name them. Thus he identified the face of a former Portuguese politician called Pintassilgo (goldfinch) by saying "I know her. This is the lady that was in power. She has the name of a bird" (Ferro & Santos, 1984, p. 124). On object-naming tasks Ferro and Santos's patient could only succeed on 7 out of 30 trials. However, when presented with an object he could not name he could almost always mime its use. Thus it is unclear to us whether this is not a case of optic aphasia (see Chapter 2) rather than visual agnosia *per se*, and the appropriateness of the comparison with face recognition is brought into question as his performance at *naming* faces was also defective.

In the only other relevant published cases known to us there was some impairment of face recognition, but the object recognition problems were more severe (Albert, Reches, & Silverberg, 1975; McCarthy & Warrington, 1986). Matters are further complicated, however, by the fact that the performance of Albert et al.'s (1975) patient on object recognition tasks improved rapidly during the period in which he was being tested. There is some evidence, then, that object agnosia can be dissociated from prosopagnosia, but more detailed investigations of convincing cases of object agnosia without prosopagnosia are needed.

A second type of dissociation that weakens the straightforward "recognition hierarchy" argument is that different types of within-category discrimination can dissociate from each other. Mr W, for instance, was not impaired at making *any* within-category discrimination. Like Bornstein et al.'s (1969) patient he was a farmer, yet Mr W *could* identify his cows and dogs. He could also identify particular houses and streets that were known to him. None the less, he did still have problems with coins, and with playing cards he found it difficult to distinguish suits of the same colour and jacks from kings.

The most "pure" case of prosopagnosia reported to date is that of patient 4 in the series described by De Renzi (1986). This former public notary showed well preserved verbal abilities and could identify objects (30/30), line drawings (30/30), and overlapping figures (36/36) without error. In contrast, he had to rely on voices to recognise relatives and close friends, and his secretaries had to assist him by identifying clients for him. His performance on unfamiliar face-matching tasks (Benton Test) was poor but, as De Renzi (1986) points out, no worse than that of many other patients who are not prosopagnosic. He also performed poorly on tests of face memory.

The specificity of the defect shown by De Renzi's (1986) patient was remarkable. He could pick out his own belongings when they were mixed in with several distractor objects chosen to resemble them. He could identify his own handwriting among nine samples of the same sentence written by other people. He could pick out a Siamese cat among photographs of other cats. He could recognise his own car in a car park. He could sort domestic (Italian) coins from foreign coins. Thus, on all the tests De Renzi used, this patient could make within-category discriminations with ease for all visual stimuli except faces.

The case for the existence of face-specific recognition deficits is thus becoming quite strong. There does seem to be a functionally distinct system for at least some aspects of face processing. A sceptic might, however, want to shift the grounds of the argument by maintaining that face-specific recognition problems can arise in occasional cases simply because face recognition demands the finest of all perceptual discriminations. On this view other within-category discriminations might be preserved because they are not as fine as those demanded by face recognition.

This argument now looks to be wrong. Assal, Favre, and Anderes (1984) described the case of the farmer MX. When seen by Assal et al. in January, 1983, MX complained of problems in recognising places (rooms in his flat, his farm buildings, etc.), his livestock (cows, calves, and heifers), and human faces (friends and family). When formally tested in June and July, 1983, however, his prosopagnosia had recovered. He recognised 18 of 20 faces of famous people, and he obtained normal scores on tests of unfamiliar face matching. He could also interpret facial expressions correctly. The only test involving faces on which he performed at all poorly involved face memory, where his performance was somewhat below that of normal control subjects (26/40 vs 34/40). Assal et al. (1984) point out, however, that his performance on this test was better than that of other patients with right hemisphere injuries (mean 16.5/40) and that when the test was given to a prosopagnosic patient a score of only 8 out of 40 was attained.

It seems, then, that by July, 1983, MX was no longer prosopagnosic; he had recovered his ability to recognise faces. He could also recognise without difficulty individual members of certain other categories of visual stimuli including fruits, flowers, vegetables, and trees. He remained, however, unable to recognise familiar places or to recognise his livestock. He said that places had lost their familiarity, and he made errors in recognising 6 of 10 photographs of local houses. He could not recognise his cows from their heads, coats, or silhouettes. He could remember all their names, but was unable to recognise them. When shown photographs of the "faces" of the cows he only recognised 2 out of 15 correctly, whereas his coworkers managed 10 out of 15 and 14 out of 15 respectively. For pictures of the whole cow he got 3 out of 10 whereas his coworkers each scored 8 out of 10. He could distinguish pictures of cows from other species of animals, but could not distinguish his own cows from other cows.

MX provides another example demonstrating that different types of within-category recognition impairment can dissociate from each other. The particularly interesting thing about MX, however, is that his pattern of ability to recognise human but not cow faces is *exactly the opposite* of that shown by Mr W, who could recognise his livestock but not people.

Evidence is thus beginning to favour the view that the inability to recognise familiar faces is not inevitably linked to other problems of visual recognition. It seems that recognition difficulties involving only faces can occur.

DIFFERENT TYPES OF FACE PROCESSING ABILITY

We have seen that some prosopagnosic patients do not complain of impaired face perception, and are able both to match views of unfamiliar faces and to interpret facial expressions correctly. It might thus be thought that the matching of unfamiliar faces and the analysis of facial expressions are carried out at a level of analysis preceding that at which recognition of familiar faces can be achieved. Bruce and Young (1986), however, prefer to think of familiar face recognition as proceeding *in parallel* with the analysis of facial expressions and with the "directed visual processing" needed to match unfamiliar faces. Evidence in favour of this suggestion can be found both in studies of normal subjects and in studies of the effects of cerebral injuries. For the neuropsychological literature the key point is that there are findings that imply double dissociations between impairments involving familiar face recognition and impairments involving expression analysis or unfamiliar face matching.

Unfamiliar Face Matching

We will begin by considering unfamiliar face matching. Warrington and James (1967b) noted that patients with right cerebral hemisphere lesions tended to show impairments of familiar face recognition and of recognition of unknown faces in an immediate memory task, but that there was no correlation between these two types of deficit. Their immediate memory task involved finding the face that had just been shown in a booklet of eight male and eight female faces; this is quite different to the relatively long-term tasks on which prosopagnosic patients often show defective memory for unfamiliar faces. The absence of a correlation in Warrington and James' (1967b) findings implies that one patient might be impaired at familiar face recognition but not at immediate memory for unfamiliar faces, whereas another patient might be impaired at immediate memory but not at recognition of familiar faces.

This point is clearly seen in the descriptions of two patients given by Malone, Morris, Kay, and Levin (1982). Initially, the first patient was unable to recognise familiar faces, but had regained this ability by the time that formal neuropsychological tests were given (10–22 weeks after the onset of his symptoms), when he was able to identify 14 out of 17 photographs of famous statesmen. On tests requiring the matching of views of unfamiliar faces, however, he was still impaired. The second patient showed the opposite pattern. Although, initially, he was also unable to recognise familiar faces or to match unfamiliar faces, the ability to match unfamiliar faces recovered to a normal level whereas the familiar face recognition impairment persisted (only 5/22 famous faces identified correctly).

Malone et al.'s (1982) second case is comparable to others in which prosopagnosic patients perform at normal levels on tests of unfamiliar face matching (e.g. Benton & Van Allen, 1972; Bruyer et al., 1983). Since Malone et al.'s first case showed exactly the opposite pattern, with impaired unfamiliar face matching being accompanied by intact recognition of familiar faces, the evidence that familiar face recognition is independent from the directed visual processing required for unfamiliar face matching tasks is strong. There is a double dissociation between impairments affecting the recognition of familiar faces and impairments affecting unfamiliar face matching. The only reservation that needs to be expressed is that it is probably advisable to provide more direct evidence of normal matching of unfamiliar faces in prosopagnosic patients. What has been shown to date is that some prosopagnosics can achieve an overall level of performance comparable to that of normal subjects on unfamiliar face matching tasks. It is possible, however, that this may reflect an effective use of unusual strategies.

Newcombe (1979), for instance, found that the prosopagnosic patient she studied seldom made errors in unfamiliar face matching tasks. However, he performed these tasks by a careful and very time-consuming strategy of searching for an informative individual feature such as the hairline. When faces were presented in an oval frame that masked the hairline, Newcombe's patient experienced great difficulty in performing matching tasks. It would thus be useful to know to what extent other prosopagnosic patients rely on such strategies when matching unfamiliar faces.

Expression Analysis

Impairments affecting the analysis of facial expression have also been shown to be dissociable from impairments of face recognition. Bornstein (1963) noted that some prosopagnosic patients show a degree of recovery of ability to identify familiar faces while remaining unable to interpret facial expressions. Similarly, Kurucz and Feldmar (1979) and Kurucz, Feldmar, and Werner (1979) found that certain patients with diffuse brain damage could not interpret facial expressions correctly yet were still able to identify photographs of American Presidents. For these patients there was no correlation between their performance on recognising expression and identity from faces.

These studies indicate that disorders affecting the analysis of facial expressions are dissociable from disorders affecting familiar face recognition. Studies of patients with right hemisphere injuries have also shown that disorders affecting the analysis of facial expressions can dissociate from disorders affecting unfamiliar face matching (see Etcoff, 1985, for a review). In addition, Bowers and Heilman (1984) described a patient who could match pairs of photographs of unfamiliar faces for identity (same or different person) or expression (same or different expressions; these were portrayed by the same actor in the test used), yet showed impaired ability to identify what the facial expressions were (i.e. which emotional state they corresponded to). Thus he could not interpret facial expressions even though he could match them on a purely "visual" basis.

Because of the evidence of dissociable deficits affecting familiar face recognition, unfamiliar face matching, and analysis of facial expressions, Bruce and Young (1986) suggested that following structural encoding of a seen face's appearance different types of information are accessed in parallel. In addition to the parallel operation of face recognition units, directed visual processing, and expression analysis, they also proposed that facial speech analysis is independently achieved.

Lipreading

The importance of seen movements of the lips and tongue to the perception of speech has only been properly appreciated in recent years. Obviously, we are able to hear what someone is saying even when we are not looking at her or his face. This fact may, however, have obscured the extent to which we all "lipread". This point was shown dramatically by McGurk and MacDonald (1976), who demonstrated an illusion in which a mismatch between heard and seen (mouthed) phonemes can result in the perceiver blending the two. If, for instance, the sound "ba" is superimposed on a film of the face of a person saying "ga", people watching the resulting film find that they *hear* the sound as "da". This surprising use of facial speech information is found even in infancy (Kuhl & Meltzoff, 1982; MacKain, Studdert-Kennedy, Spieker, & Stern, 1983), and may form an important part of the process of language acquisition (Studdert-Kennedy, 1983).

A neuropsychological dissociation between expression analysis and facial speech analysis is described by Campbell, Landis, and Regard (1986). The dissociation was observed in two female patients. One lady, D, was prosopagnosic. She could not recognise familiar faces, she was poor at judging what sex they were, and she could not categorise facial expressions correctly. She could, in contrast, achieve a normal level of performance on unfamiliar face matching tasks if given sufficient time. Her visual recognition problems included not only familiar faces but also familiar places, and she could not recognise her own handwriting. Her reading and speech comprehension abilities were, however, unimpaired.

Although D could not determine the meaning of facial expressions she could imitate both emotional and non-emotional expressions accurately, which suggests that the problem in analysing expressions did not have a perceptual basis. She could also judge correctly what phonemes were being mouthed in photographs of the faces of speaking people, and was susceptible to the McGurk and MacDonald (1976) illusion. Thus, despite her problems with expressions, facial speech analysis remained intact.

The second lady, T, had a severe reading impairment (she read letter-by-letter), but did not show impairments on most face processing tasks. She could both recognise familiar faces and interpret correctly their expressions without difficulty. Her analysis of facial speech was, however, defective. She was impaired at judging what phonemes were being mouthed in photographs of faces, and she was *not* susceptible to the McGurk and MacDonald (1976) illusion.

This double dissociation between impairments of facial speech analysis (lipreading) and expression analysis is particularly striking because the information required for lipreading and expression comprehension is, to a considerable extent, extracted from the same area of the face. This reinforces the idea that the reason for the dissociable deficits in face processing lies in the different types of cognitive operations involved, and cannot be entirely attributed to differences in the facial features that must be analysed.

OVERVIEW

The social and biological importance of faces is such that quite extensive areas of neural tissue must be involved in one way or another with face processing tasks. It does not, however, necessarily follow that these parts of the brain should deal with faces exclusively. We could imagine, for instance, that areas of the brain involved in recognising everyday objects might also be employed for the task of recognising the faces we encounter in our daily lives.

As we have seen, the available evidence suggests that this is *not* the case. To some extent, at least, different functional components seem to be involved in face and object recognition. This is probably in response to the different *demands* of face and object recognition. Often when we recognise everyday objects we need only assign them to a general category. We look for a pen, for a tin opener, for the scissors, and so on; it is only sometimes that we need to distinguish between the pen with the blue top that will not work and the one with the chewed end and the fine nib. In addition, we frequently encounter new exemplars of these categories—someone else's scissors, a shopful of pens, etc.—but can immediately classify them into the appropriate category.

The demands of face recognition are quite different. It is of little use to us to look at a photograph in the newspaper and only recognise that it shows a person's face. We want to know *whose* face it is, and we accept that differences between different people can sometimes be slight. For faces, then, we discriminate between the members of a class of rather homogeneous visual stimuli (all with eyes, nose, mouth, and more or less oval shape) and assign individual identities to those we know.

One reason why face recognition and object recognition can show dissociable impairments, then, is probably that different types of perceptual mechanism are needed to cope with recognition tasks that demand between-category or within-category discriminations. It is now becoming clear, however, that there are also dissociations between impairments of different within-category recognition mechanisms, such as those involved in recognising familiar faces and those used to recognise familiar places. The types of information needed to effect the discriminations involved would also seem to be an important factor.

We also need to be able to extract different kinds of information from faces. We can recognise the people we know, examine the appearance of unfamiliar faces, identify facial expressions, and read speech information from mouth and tongue movements. Impairments of these different aspects of face processing can dissociate from each other, suggesting that different functional components are involved; these seem to be arranged so that the different types of information are independently derived.

Disorders of face processing, then, offer a promising area for further investigation by cognitive neuropsychologists, and the findings of neuropsychological studies relate well to those obtained in studies of normal subjects (Bruce & Young, 1986; H. D. Ellis, 1986a; 1986b). A particularly interesting recent finding, however, has been that certain "automatic" aspects of recognition may be preserved in prosopagnosic patients. If tested on tasks that do not require explicit identification, patients such as PH seem to be able to recognise faces, yet they are not aware that any degree of recognition has taken place. Such cases form an intriguing parallel to some of the disorders discussed in Chapter 3, which we noted could also be seen as involving loss of different aspects of awareness. Explaining how this can happen offers an interesting challenge.

SUMMARY

A number of different causes of inability to recognise familiar faces (prosopagnosia) exist. For some patients (Uffz. S) face perception is clearly impaired, and there are probably several types of perceptual disorder. For other patients (Mr W), however, any perceptual impairment is minor, and cannot be seen to play a causative role. This has led to the suggestion that some cases of prosopagnosia should be considered to involve a material-specific memory impairment; this idea can be considered analogous to that of defective operation of face recognition units. Conversely, these are also cases in which inability to recognise faces arises in the context of a more general impairment of semantic memory, and these patients do not overtly recognise familiar people from their names or voices either.

For some prosopagnosic patients, however, a high degree of recognition of familiar faces can be shown to take place if it is measured on tasks that do not demand awareness of recognition. PH, for instance, showed covert recognition of familiar faces in matching, learning, and interference tasks. It would seem that certain automatic aspects of the operation of recognition mechanisms may be preserved without the patient being aware of this.

Face recognition impairments can dissociate from impairments affecting the recognition of other classes of visual stimuli and, in very rare cases, remarkably specific deficits have been found. Specific impairments of different aspects of face processing have also been revealed. Thus there are dissociations between problems affecting recognition of familiar faces, matching of unfamiliar faces, expression analysis, and lipreading. The existence of dissociable impairments suggests that these types of information are extracted from seen faces by functionally independent mechanisms.

FURTHER READING

Bauer, R. M. (1984). Autonomic recognition of names and faces in prosopagnosia: A neuropsychological application of the guilty knowledge test. *Neuropsychologia*, *22*, 457–469. One of the first studies to show "recognition without awareness" in a prosopagnosic patient.

Benton, A. L. (1980). The neuropsychology of facial recognition. *American Psychologist,* *35*, 176–186. Good introduction to face recognition impairments from the clinical perspective, and to dissociable disorders of familiar and unfamiliar face recognition.

Bruce, V. (1988). *Recognising faces.* London: Lawrence Erlbaum Associates. Gives a lot more detail on studies of the "normal" face recognition system.

Bruyer, R., Laterre, C., Seron, X., Feyereisen, P., Strypstein, E., Pierrard, E., & Rectem, D. (1983). A case of prosopagnosia with some preserved covert remembrance of familiar faces. *Brain and Cognition, 2,* 257–284. Detailed report on Mr W's case.

Campbell, R., Landis, T., & Regard, M. (1986). Face recognition and lipreading: A neurological dissociation. *Brain, 109,* 509–521. Interesting and very thorough investigation of dissociable impairments affecting lipreading and face recognition.

Damasio, A. R., Damasio, H., & Van Hoesen, G. W. (1982). Prosopagnosia: Anatomic basis and behavioural mechanisms. *Neurology, 32,* 331–341. Provides detailed discussion of the neurological basis of face recognition impairments, and relates them to a functional model with some similarities to that used here.

Hécaen, H. (1981). The neuropsychology of face recognition. In G. Davies, H. Ellis, & J. Shepherd (Eds), *Perceiving and remembering faces.* New York: Academic Press, pp. 39–54. Introduces the idea of different types of prosopagnosia from the clinical vewpoint.

5 Producing Spoken Words

INTRODUCTION

In the book so far we have focussed on processes of perception and their associated disorders. The human brain can, however, do more than just perceive the world; it can also talk about it, and understand others talking about it. Our capacities for speaking and understanding speech are the subject matter of this chapter, and also Chapters 6 and 9. Let us begin by sketching very briefly some of the cognitive processes we are likely to need in order to be able to talk sensibly about the world around us.

Imagine that the picture shown in Fig. 5.1 has been placed in front of you and that you have been asked to describe the goings on in it. There is a lot happening in the picture so you let your eyes roam over it to take it all in. "Taking it in" here includes doing precisely those operations we have discussed in Chapters 2 to 4—identifying the objects depicted, working out their spatial relationships one to another, and so on. You must also comprehend the actions being performed; the fact that the bull is *chasing* the boy scout, that another scout is *looking* through binoculars while another is *sitting* on the bank. As you inspect the picture you build up an understanding of it. That understanding is not initially couched in words, though it can be *translated* into words; instead you have some form of conceptual representation which is presumably similar to that built up by intelligent non-verbal animals like chimpanzees. What language allows us to do is to communicate the conceptual representation in our heads to others.

In attempting to describe the picture you may decide to start with the

FIG. 5.1.   A complex picture used to elicit speech from aphasic patients. (The attempt of patient RD to describe the picture is given on p.124.)

activity at the top centre. Here there is a scout and a bull, and one is chasing the other. Recognising a bull or a scout serves to activate within you all the stored knowledge you possess about those objects—their *meanings* in a sense. Linguists use the term *semantics* when discussing issues relating to the meanings of words, so we shall refer to the internal representations of the meanings (e.g. properties and uses) of words and things as their *semantic representations*. Semantic representations do not include the spoken names of concepts—those must be retrieved separately. For instance, you may readily recognise the three-legged object in the centre of the scout camp picture, and you may know that its function is to suspend cooking implements over a fire, but if more years have elapsed than you care to admit since you last went camping, then it may take you quite some considerable time to retrieve the name of the object in question (a "trivet"). When you eventually do manage to retrieve that name it is presumably from some form of memory store whose purpose and function is to make available to you the spoken forms of words appropriate to the meanings you wish to express. We shall call this memory store for the pronunciations of words the *speech output lexicon*. Other authors have referred to that store as the "speech output logogen system" (Morton, 1980a; Morton & Patterson, 1980), the "phonological lexicon" (Allport & Funnell, 1981), or the "phonemic word production system" (Ellis, 1984b). Whatever name we give it, the memory store in question normally works efficiently and yields up its contents with ease: Only when a word eludes you or becomes caught on the tip of your tongue do you become aware of the speech output lexicon's role in efficient speech production.

When the spoken forms of words are retrieved from the speech output lexicon it is presumably as strings of speech sounds which can then be articulated. The distinctive sounds that a language uses (English has 46 or so) are called its *phonemes*. Phonemes in English should not be confused with letters: Phonemes are units of the spoken language whereas letters are units of the written language, and there is not a one-to-one correspondence between them. Thus, whereas *lip* has three letters and three phonemes, *teeth* has five letters but still only three phonemes (*t*, *ee*, and *th*). *Bull* has four letters for three phonemes (*b*, *u*, and *ll*), whereas *scout* has five letters for four phonemes (*s*, *c*, *ou*, and *t*).

We can envisage the speech output lexicon as translating between conceptual, semantic representations of words and their phonemic labels or names. In some theories (e.g. Morton, 1980a), when the entry or "node" for a particular word in the lexicon is activated by its meaning, the lexicon releases a phonological (sound-based) "code" which is held in a short-term memory store before being articulated. In other theories (e.g. Stemberger, 1985), when a node in the lexicon is activated it does not release any form of code, but rather transmits *activation* down to nodes at a lower, phoneme level, activating the nodes for those phonemes which make up the word to be spoken. We shall indicate later why we prefer the latter account to the former, but for now we would emphasize their common features, in particular their assumption that the semantic system, the speech output lexicon, and the phoneme level constitute

SEMANTIC
SYSTEM

SPEECH
OUTPUT
LEXICON

PHONEME
LEVEL

Speech

FIG. 5.2.   Simple functional model for word retrieval in speech production (naming).

distinct and separable cognitive components or "modules" which should, therefore, be subject to different types of impairment giving rise to different patterns of symptoms. This common assumption can be represented in simple diagrammatic form as in Fig. 5.2.

There is, of course, more to language than attaching names to concepts; words must be arranged properly into grammatical sentences or they remain just word lists. Some aphasic patients have particular difficulties with the structuring of spoken sentences, and we shall examine these difficulties in Chapter 9. The remainder of this chapter will be devoted to aphasic language disorders that afflict the translation between concepts and sounds (i.e. that afflict word meanings, word retrieval, and articulation). We shall begin by looking at some aphasic "word-finding" disorders which have been studied in some detail, namely the *anomias* and *neologistic jargonaphasia*. We shall then go on to examine how closely the problems and errors of these and other aphasics resemble the occasional word-finding problems experienced by normal people. In Chapter 6 we shall examine the perception and comprehension of spoken words, and will consider the extent to which the production and comprehension of spoken words are mediated by common or distinct cognitive processes.

ANOMIAS

The simple model in Fig. 5.2 assumes that the semantic system, the speech output lexicon, and the phoneme level are distinct cognitive components capable of separate, independent impairment. If this is so, then problems in retrieving and articulating words could arise at any of these three levels, though the precise nature of the patient's difficulties and the accompanying symptoms should help in identifying the locus of the impairment. Note, however, that it may be an unusual patient in whom one level is impaired, whereas the others continue to function completely normally. Brain injuries are often extensive and are no respectors of cognitive theories, so most patients with naming problems are likely to exhibit mixed symptoms arising from impairment to two or more components. That said, there are now sufficient detailed case reports in the literature that we can pick out the exceptional patients with fairly pure deficits. We shall begin with patients whose word-finding problems in speaking can plausibly be attributed to impairment in or around the semantic system.

Anomia Arising at the Semantic Level

The clearest evidence for semantic involvement in naming difficulties comes from reports of patients who can name objects in some semantic categories but not others. In fact we have already mentioned some of these cases in our discussion of object recognition (see pp. 42–47). Warrington and Shallice's (1984) patient, JBR, was considerably better at naming pictures of inanimate objects like a torch or a briefcase than pictures of living things like a parrot or a daffodil. This impairment was not, however, limited to naming because he had problems comprehending both pictures of the living things he could not name and comprehending their spoken names. Three other patients tested in less detail by Warrington and Shallice (1984) showed the same pattern. Warrington and Shallice suggest that JBR and the other patients suffered from a degradation of the semantic representations of certain categories of things (notably living objects), hence those representations were unavailable to sustain either full comprehension of those objects or the comprehension and production of their names.

The naming difficulties of patient MD (Hart, Berndt, & Caramazza, 1985) were focussed on the semantic categories of fruit and vegetables. Thus he could name an abacus and the Sphinx but not a peach or an orange. When asked to sort pictures into semantic categories he had no problems with animals or vehicles, made two errors to food products (classifying butter and cheese as vegetables), and made more errors to fruits and vegetables (classifying 3/24 fruits as vegetables and 6/23 vegetables as fruits). However, unlike Warrington and Shallice's (1984) patients, MD could comprehend the names he was not able to produce. When MD was required to point to one of two pictures drawn from the same semantic category in response to a heard word he made no mistakes on either fruit or vegetables. He could also categorise correctly the written names of fruits and vegetables whose pictures he had been unable to classify.

MD's good performance with heard and read words suggests that the actual semantic representations of fruit and vegetables are not themselves degraded; rather he has problems accessing those representations from objects or pictures and problems using them to initiate spoken naming (he was poor at generating exemplars of fruit and vegetables, so the deficit is not restricted to confrontation naming).

A Non-category-specific Semantic Anomia: Patient JCU

The patients just discussed had naming impairments of semantic origin that were more severe in some semantic domains than others. There are other patients, however, whose naming difficulties also appear to arise in or around the semantic representations, but in whom the deficit does not seem to be any more severe for one category than for another.

Howard and Orchard-Lisle's (1984) patient, JCU, could name very few object pictures unaided, but retrieved many more if given the initial phoneme of the word as a cue. She could also, however, be induced to make semantic naming errors if the initial phoneme of a close associate of the picture was supplied instead (e.g. shown a picture of a tiger and given the cue "l", JCU said "lion"). She rejected spontaneously only 24% of these semantic errors though she rejected 86% of unrelated responses (these were often perseverations of a name produced earlier). In addition, if an experimenter asked of a picture, "Is this an X?", she accepted 56% of close semantic associates but only 2% of unrelated names.

The results of two further tests led Howard and Orchard-Lisle to conclude that JCU's object recognition and comprehension were not defective. In the first test she was required to match one picture to a choice of two others on the basis of real-world associations (e.g. matching a picture of a pyramid to one of a palm tree rather than a deciduous tree). Here JCU scored 18 out of 20 correct. The second test required pictures to be matched on the basis of a shared semantic category (e.g. matching an onion to a pea—both vegetables—rather than to an apple), and JCU scored 16 out of 20 on this test. This was significantly worse than a normal control group, but sufficiently good when combined with her performance on the real-world associations task for Howard and Orchard-Lisle to reject impairment of processes of conceptual recognition as the source of JCU's naming deficit. They argued instead for a semantic impairment; more precisely, they proposed that semantic information available to the patient was insufficient to specify the exact target name, with the result that the phonological forms of close semantic associates were also being activated to the same level in a phonological lexicon. Thus, the semantic information that JCU can use is sufficient to enable her to reject entirely unrelated names profferred by the experimenter, but is often insufficient to allow her to distinguish a semantic associate from the correct name. Thus JCU might experience naming problems because of a general, non-specific impairment to the semantic representations.

Anomia without Semantic Impairment: Patient EST

Kay and Ellis (1987) report the case of a patient, EST, who experienced word-finding problems for words whose meanings were available to him in full detail. He knew precisely what he wanted to say but could not remember many of the words he needed in order to express his thoughts and intentions. His attempt to describe Fig. 5.3 from Goodglass and Kaplan (1972) ran as follows:

> Er... two children, one girl one male... the... the girl, they're in a... and their, their mother was behind them in in, they're in the kitchen... the boy is trying to get... a... er, a part of a cooking... jar.... He's standing on... the lad, the boy is standing on a... standing on a... standing on a... I'm calling it a seat, I can't... I forget what it's, what the name of it is.... It is er a higher, it's a seat, standing on that, 'e's standing on that... this boy is standing on this, seat... getting some of this er stuff to... biscuit to eat. As he is doing that, the post, it's not a post, it's the, seat, is falling down, is falling over...

EST's speech output is fluent and reasonably grammatical but short on specific object (and action) names. Words he cannot access are usually replaced in spontaneous speech by other, more general words, or by circumlocutions which avoid the difficult word. He has considerable difficulty naming pictures of objects though both his understanding of the objects themselves and his understanding of their spoken names was very good. In picture-naming tasks he would often be at pains to show that he recognised pictures he could not name (e.g. of a snowman he said: "It's cold, it's a man... cold... frozen"). He was very good at sorting pictures into semantic categories, even when this could not be done on obvious visual cues (e.g. wild animals vs. domesticated animals). He also performed at normal levels on Howard and Orchard-Lisle's (1984) task which required pictures to be matched on the basis of real-world associations rather than category membership (e.g. matching a picture of a pyramid to a palm tree rather than to a deciduous tree, because pyramids and palm trees both belong in Egypt).

EST's auditory-vocal repetition of words he had previously been unable to access in a naming task was good, though not perfect (43/50), and better than his repetition of invented non-words (25/50). On a task requiring him to select the picture that matched a heard word from a set of four semantically related items he performed flawlessly (25/25) and he also performed at normal levels (50/52) on a version of the "palm trees and pyramids" task where he was required to choose which of two pictures had the closest real-world association to a heard word. Unlike patient JCU discussed earlier, EST would not accept close associates of an object name when proffered by an experimenter (e.g. he would not accept "lion" as the name to match a picture of a tiger).

EST's semantic representations of the object names he had difficulty accessing in spontaneous speech thus seem to have been intact and he was capable of sustaining good comprehension of spoken (and written) words. We cannot, therefore, locate the source of his anomia within the semantic system. A close analysis of his successes and failures in object naming provided clues as to where the impairment might lie.

In six 1-hour sessions spread over as many weeks EST was asked to name a set of 260 line drawings of objects taken from Snodgrass and Vanderwart (1980). He named 97 pictures correctly without hesitation and a further 27 after a delay or after "working up" to the word (e.g. "five in it, begins with a 't', table"). There were a further 22 pictures which EST could not name correctly but for which he produced without cueing what Kay and Ellis (1987) call a "phonological approximation" to the word. Examples of such approximations include "sumberry" for strawberry, "balla" and "ballow" for balloon, and "gritch" and "grief" for grapes.

If EST failed to provide either the correct name or an approximation to the name of a picture he was cued with the initial phoneme of the name. This allowed him to name a further 27 pictures correctly and produce phonological approximations to 37 more. The remaining 50 pictures he remained unable either to name or approximate, though his comments usually made it clear that he recognised the object for what it was.

Of course some words, including some object names, are used more frequently than others. Word-frequency counts (e.g. Francis & Kucera, 1982) provide a rough measure of the relative frequencies of usage of words in the language (rough because they are usually based on written rather than spoken English). A clear pattern emerged when the name frequencies were compared for the pictures eliciting different types of response from EST. Specifically, those pictures he could name immediately had the most frequently used names of all. Next most frequent were the names he produced after a delay, followed by the names for which he could generate, uncued, a phonological approximation. The names he needed to be cued on were least frequent of all. Thus, the probability that EST could name an object seems to be related to the number of times he is likely to have used that name in the course of his past life.

In fact, a glance at EST's spontaneous speech shows that virtually all the words he uses in normal conversation are of high frequency. This includes the nouns, verbs and adjectives he still has available and also the function words like "the", "on", "not", and "to" that he uses with ease. Marshall (1987) noted that one can create a fair replica of anomic speech using just the 100 most common words in the English language, thus:

> I have one or more of them. It's a... I like them. It must be over there in the... by the... but it's not. My... also made one for some... that he had been with in the... as a... it was before he had his... most of them are like that. They can also be had from the... a man has them, many of them, but a new one would be even more of a.... Did you have one when you were with them? You said that you had one from the time that you were at.... No, if that were so, you could not have made so much... at it all these years. Even then it's not the first new one that I must have been through.

It may be that for *some* anomic aphasics (like EST) what determines their success or failure in accessing a word is not its meaning, nor its grammatical class, but its sheer frequency of usage. EST's good comprehension of words he could not use in speech, the frequency effect he showed, and the presence of phonological approximations led Kay and Ellis (1987) to propose that the source of his anomia lay in a deficit in activating entries for words within the speech output lexicon.

More particularly, Kay and Ellis (1987) supported models like that of Stemberger (1985) in which the role of the speech output lexicon is to channel activation down from the semantic system to the phoneme level, permitting the set of phonemes that comprise a word's spoken form to be activated when that word's semantic representation is activated. It is a common assumption of such models that entries in the lexicon which are frequently activated develop higher *resting* levels of activation. This means that they achieve full activation more quickly and more easily from a given semantic input than do nodes which are less frequently activated. Such a proposal helps to explain why even normal subjects find high-frequency words easier to access than low-frequency words. Thus pictures with commonly used names are named more rapidly than pictures with infrequently used names (Oldfield & Wingfield, 1965) though the two types of picture differ little in terms of speed of recognising them for what they are (Wingfield, 1968). Similarly, slips of the tongue in which normal speakers inadvertently use a wrong word in place of the intended one usually involve the replacement of a less frequent word by a more frequent one (Beattie & Butterworth, 1979).

The frequency bias in EST's speech could be explained by some form of impairment to the lexicon itself, but Kay and Ellis (1987) argue against this on two grounds. First, EST sometimes retrieved a word after extensive effort, and, secondly, he sometimes retrieved a word on one occasion that he had been unable to find on another, earlier occasion. Neither of these observations is new (cf. the patient of Franz, 1930, who when shown a picture of a box of strawberries said: "I like them; I ought to be able to say it. My wife bought some boxes yesterday, and she was making them up into jam. I know, but it has just escaped me... [then after a long pause]... strawberries"), but both suggest that EST's problem is not that certain words have been lost from the speech output lexicon, but that they have become inaccessible. An explanation in terms of inaccessibility would also account for observations of patients who recover from anomia with a speed which suggests re-accessing rather than re-learning their vocabulary (e.g. case 4 of Benson, 1979).

One way to explain how the speech output lexicon might remain intact though many of its entries have become more or less inaccessible is to propose, as Kay and Ellis (1987) did, that following the brain injury, the *amount* of activation reaching the (intact) speech output lexicon from the (intact) semantic system is much reduced (cf. Rochford & Williams, 1965). This reduced activation is still enough to boost up to full activation entries whose resting levels are already high (i.e. entries for frequently-used words), but entries for infrequently-used words whose resting levels are low can no longer be boosted sufficiently to allow all their phonemes to be activated and articulated.

EST could name correctly most pictures with high-frequency names and could make no reasonable attempt at words with low-frequency names. There was a middle range of names, however, for which he could often generate a close approximation. These approximations were sometimes real words, sometimes not (it is not easy to determine whether some approximations like "sludge" for sledge merely happened by chance to be real words in English). In the case of these medium-frequency words, sufficient activation seems to be reaching the phoneme level to activate some, but not all, of the phonemes in the target word. The missing phonemes apparently have to be guessed when an attempt must be made at the word. (N.B. EST made few approximation errors in spontaneous speech: He seemed to know when a word was proving elusive and would typically opt for either an alternative of higher frequency or a circumlocution. Approximations were only common in confrontation naming tasks where the specific names of objects were demanded.)

The notion that EST's speech output lexicon is intact though much of its contents are inaccessible was supported by Kay and Ellis (1987). They showed that EST's auditory-vocal repetition is better for words he can no longer access in his spontaneous speech or naming than for invented non-words created by changing one or two of the consonants of the real words. Thus there was some form of support available from the lexicon to assist the repetition of normally inaccessible words and to boost their repetition accuracy above that of matched non-words. That support would not have been possible had the entries for inaccessible words in the lexicon actually been destroyed.

Semantic versus Output Lexicon Anomias

In sum, then, word-finding difficulties can apparently arise either at the semantic level or at the level of the speech output lexicon. The two forms of anomia seem, however, to have rather different patterns when observed in their pure forms (note that many patients are likely to display a combination of the two sets of symptoms because their brain injury affects both levels).

Patients with semantic level impairments may show a degree of category specificity, having greater naming problems in some semantic domains than others. They make semantic errors in naming and are subsequently poor at detecting those errors as incorrect in comprehension tasks. In general, they perform poorly on comprehension tasks which require precise semantic knowledge. A number of investigators have noted a correlation between the number of semantic errors a patient makes in production and the degree of impairment in comprehension (Butterworth, Howard, & McLoughlin, 1984; Gainotti, 1976; Gainotti, Miceli, Caltagirone, Silveri, & Masullo, 1981). This association has been interpreted as implying that there is just one semantic system employed in both comprehension and production, so that damage to it will be reflected in comparable degrees of impairment to input and output. Such a proposal would help to explain why patients who make semantic errors in speech also make semantic errors in other tasks which do not require spoken responses (Alajouanine, Lhermitte, Ledoux, Renaud, & Vignolo, 1964; Zurif, Caramazza, Myerson, & Galvin, 1974).

On our account, patients with impairment to the output lexicon itself will not show category specificity and will not make semantic naming errors. Their comprehension of the words they find hard to access for speech will be unimpaired. The probability of their being able to produce a word correctly will be strongly affected by its frequency of use, and they will make approximation errors (or "neologisms") to some words they cannot fully access.

NEOLOGISTIC JARGONAPHASIA

The spontaneous speech of anomic aphasics typically contains few phonological approximations, though they may appear in object-naming tasks. There are other aphasics whose spontaneous speech contains large numbers of these errors. They are sometimes regarded as a type of "Wernicke's aphasia", and sometimes treated as a separate group of aphasics termed "neologistic jargonaphasics" (Buckingham & Kertesz, 1976; Butterworth, 1979; 1985; Butterworth, Swallow, & Grimston, 1981; Caramazza, Berndt, & Basili, 1983; Ellis, Miller, & Sin, 1983; Miller & Ellis, 1987). As before, we shall not be concerned with issues of labelling so much as with explaining and interpreting the symptoms of these patients.

The following transcript is part of the attempt by RD, the patient reported by Ellis et al. (1983), to describe the goings on in the scout camp picture (Fig. 5.1). Neologisms are printed in italics, and the target words which RD is presumed to have been attempting are in capital letters within brackets. (A fuller version with the neologisms transcribed in phonemic notation can be found in Ellis et al., 1983):

> A *bun, bun* (BULL)... a *buk* (BULL) is *cherching* (CHASING) a boy or *skert* (SCOUT). A *sk...* boy *skut* (SCOUT) is by a *bone poe* (POST) of pine. A... post... *pone* (POST) with a, er, *tone toe* (LINE?) with *woshingt* (WASHING) hanging on including his socks *saiz* (?). A... a *nek* (TENT) is by the washing. A b-boy is *swi'ing* (SWINGING) on the bank with his hand (FEET) in the *stringt* (STREAM). A table with *orstrum* (SAUCEPAN?) and... I don't know... and a three-legged *stroe* (STOOL) and a *strane* (PAIL)—table, table... near the water. A er *trowlvot* (TRIVET), three-legged er er means for hanging a *tong, tong* (PAN?) on the *fiyest* (FIRE) which is blowed by a boy-boy. A boy *skrut* (SCOUT) is up a tree and looking at... through... *hone*(?) glasses. A man is knocking a paper...paper with a *notist* (NOTICE) by the er t-tent, tent er *tet* (TENT) er tent.

What impairment to the speech production processes could cause such neologisms to occur? We would appear to be able to rule out a conceptual or semantic disorder from the available evidence. RD, whose speech we have just seen an extract of, had very good understanding of written words and pictures. He could sort written words into categories despite being able to read very few of them aloud correctly, and could match pictures to written names. He could also sort pairs of written words into those having similar meanings (e.g. *corner–angle; exhaustion–fatigue*) or dissimilar meanings (e.g. *hurricane–troops; oven–ghost*), and could sort written sentences into those which made sense (e.g. *He sat reading a paper*) and those which, though grammatical, were nonsensical (e.g. *She played her favourite window*). Similarly, JS, the patient reported by Caramazza et al. (1983), could categorise written words and pictures, and could match pictures to words correctly.

We would also seem able to eliminate an articulatory deficit as a cause of JS's and RD's errors. It does not appear to be the case that these patients can retrieve the spoken forms of words correctly which then become distorted during articulation (Buckingham, 1977). Both RD and JS were less likely to produce a neologism as an attempt at a common word than as an attempt at a less common (but still familiar) word, even though the less common word may have been shorter and simpler to articulate than the more common one. Thus in a picture-naming task RD correctly named a "policeman" and a "cigarette" while making errors on the simpler but less common words "frog" and "swan". Word length had little or no effect on whether or not he could say a word correctly, and there was no detectable tendency for incorrect phonemes to resemble the phonemes they replaced (Miller & Ellis, 1987).

It is interesting to look at the grammatical class of the target words which RD mispronounced (which can usually be deduced from their verbal contexts). In the full description of the scout picture from which we have given an extract, Ellis et al. (1983) reckoned that RD made a total of 28 errors. Of these, 24 occupied positions where a noun appears to have been the target (e.g. *trowlvot* for TRIVET), whereas the remaining 4 occupied verb slots (e.g. *cherching* for CHASING). This pattern has been reported by several previous investigators including Green (1969), Buckingham and Kertesz (1976), and Butterworth (1979), and has led a number of theorists to suggest that in patients of this type we are looking at a deficit which has selectively impaired the use of information-transmitting "content words" (nouns, verbs, and adjectives) and spared the use of grammatical "function words" like *a, with, of, and, by*, and *is* (e.g. Garrett, 1982; 1984; Marin, Saffran, & Schwartz, 1976). However, we have already noted that RD and JS were both less prone to make errors on common compared to less common words, and it is a fact of language that function words occur, on average, far more frequently in speech than do content words. When Ellis et al. asked RD to read aloud written content and function words which were equated on frequency of occurrence he was no more successful on the function words (14/20 and 16/24 correct) than on the content words (16/20 and 17/24 correct), suggesting that the apparent preservation of function words in his speech is due to their higher average frequency of usage.

Buckingham and Kertesz (1976) proposed that a word-finding problem similar to that of anomics with output lexicon deficits lies at the heart of "neologistic jargonaphasia". Butterworth (1979) provided support for this proposal by showing that the errors made by his patient KC followed longer pauses than correctly spoken words. The long pauses were construed as indicating an unsuccessful search of the speech output lexicon. The deficit would seem, then, to be at the level of the speech output lexicon. Like the anomics with output lexicon impairments, patients like KC and RD are still able to retrieve the spoken phonological forms of words they have used many times in their lifetimes, including most of the function words. Sometimes only partial information can be retrieved, in which case a phonological approximation error—what Butterworth (1979) calls a "target-related neologism"—is made (such as "balons" for *balloon*, or "peharst" for *perhaps*). Sometimes little or nothing can be retrieved in which case the error may be wildly deviant (e.g. "senstenz" for *penguin*, or "orstrum" for *saucepan*). Individual patients appear to differ in the proportion of target-related neologisms they produce. Some jargonaphasics produce only masses of utterly unintelligible speech, like some foreign tongue: These may be patients who can retrieve no usable phonological information at all from their speech output lexicons (e.g. Perecman and Brown, 1981).

Anomia and Neologistic Jargonaphasia Compared

The account we have just given of RD and other similar patients is effectively the same as the account we gave in the previous section for EST and other anomics with speech output lexicon impairments. Both types of patient can show preserved semantic knowledge with a frequency-related word-finding problem in speech. The chief difference between the two is that the spontaneous speech of neologistic jargonaphasics like RD is littered with approximations to target words whereas anomics like EST only produce high levels of approximation errors in confrontation naming tasks. Part of the explanation of this difference may lie in the speech comprehension of the two types of patient. Understanding of spoken words was effectively nil in RD (a neologistic jargonaphasic), whose comprehension had to be assessed using written words. Caramazza, Berndt, and Basili (1983) analysed in detail the speech perception problems of their patient JS, who was very similar to RD, and attributed his loss of speech comprehension to an inability to make the fine discriminations between speech sounds that speech comprehension demands (see the section on "pure word deafness" in Chapter 6).

Anomics like EST, in contrast, show intact speech perception and comprehension. This may mean that they can monitor the accuracy of their attempts to say words in a way that neologistic jargonaphasics cannot. Thus, RD seemed not to know whether or not he had spoken a word correctly and would sometimes include the correct pronunciation of a word in the course of a sequence of attempts without appearing to know when he got the pronunciation right. Repeated attempts at words showed no tendency to be any better approximations to the target (Miller & Ellis, 1987; see also Joanette, Keller, & Lecours, 1980).

Impaired speech perception can occur in the context of intact speech production in patients with word deafness (e.g. Goldstein, 1974; Saffran, Marin, & Yeni-Komshian, 1976a), so that impairment in neologistic jargonaphasics cannot be held fully responsible for their speech production disorder. We are, however, willing to contemplate the possibility that neologistic jargonaphasia arises through anomia of the output lexicon variety *combined with* a degree of word deafness. Thus, unlike anomic patients, neologistic jargonaphasics can never learn by monitoring their own speech which words cause difficulties and which do not, hence they can never learn that words which are proving hard to access are likely to be mispronounced. Consequently, neologistic jargonaphasics cannot learn to limit their vocabulary to those words they can reliably say correctly. This interpretation has been queried by Butterworth (1985) and Butterworth and Howard (1987). It would be proved wrong if a patient was reported whose speech was like RD's but whose comprehension of the spoken word was intact, especially if the patient was shown to be able to distinguish reliably between correct pronunciations of words and distortions of the sort he or she commonly produced.

Morphology in Neologistic Jargonaphasia

There is one final point to make about neologistic jargonaphasia. Plural words like *ropes, robes*, and *roses* can be split up into their "root morphemes" (*rope, robe*, and *rose*) and the plural morpheme -*s*. Now, if you listen carefully to the pronunciation of *ropes, robes*, and *roses* you will hear that the plural morpheme -*s* is pronounced differently in the three words—"s" in *ropes*, "z" in *robes*, and "iz" in *roses*. The pronunciation given to the plural depends on the phoneme preceding it. A similar thing happens with the past-tense morpheme -*ed*. Listen to the pronunciations of *talked, declared*, and *spouted* and you will hear the -*ed* pronounced "t" in *talked*, "d" in *declared*, and "id" in *spouted*. As with the plural -*s*, the pronunciation given to the past-tense morpheme depends on the phoneme preceding it. Morphemes like -*s* and -*ed* which never occur on their own but only attached to root morphemes like *rope* or *talk* are called bound morphemes or *inflections*. Other common English inflections are -*er* (as in *taller, fatter*), -*est* (as in *shortest, thinnest*), and -*ing* (as in *growing, expanding*).

The relevance of all this to neologistic jargonaphasia can be seen if we ask what happens when a neologistic jargonaphasic tries to say an inflected word. The answer appears to be that whereas the root morpheme may be distorted, the inflection never is. Thus in the scout passage presented earlier, RD says "cherching" for *chasing* with the root *chase* neologised but the *-ing* morpheme present and correct (cf. also "swi'ing" for *swinging*). Many similar examples can be found in the transcripts provided by Buckingham and Kertesz (1976) and Butterworth (1979). The next question is, when the root morpheme of a plural or past-tense target word is jargonised, what form does the inflection take—is it the form appropriate to the correct root morpheme or to the neologised version? For instance, if *declare* were distorted to "dislap", would the past tense come out "dislapd" with the "d" appropriate to "declared", or would it emerge as "dislapt" with the version of the past-tense morpheme appropriate to the preceding "p"? Several studies agree that the pronunciation of variable inflections like *-s* or *-ed* is adapted (or "accommodated") to fit the *neologised* form of the root (see Buckingham & Kertesz, 1976; Butterworth, 1979; Caplan, Kellar, & Locke, 1972; Garrett, 1982). Thus "declared" with a "d" would be neologised to "dislapt" with a "t", as "robes" with a "z" might be neologised to "rofes" with an "s".

Earlier, we interpreted neologisms as indicating problems in retrieving the phonemic forms of words from the speech output lexicon. The analysis of the fate of inflected forms would appear to permit an additional claim to be made, namely that what are retrieved from the speech output lexicon are uninflected root morphemes. Inflections are then added and accommodated appropriately. *Declares, declared*, and *declaring* do not have separate entries in the speech output lexicon but are assembled in the act of speaking from the root (declare) by the addition of the appropriate inflection. In the neologistic jargonaphasic patient, retrieval from the speech output lexicon is impaired but the processes which supply the inflections remain intact so that what emerges are neologisms with the root incorrect but the inflection correctly affixed and appropriately adapted.

This conclusion about how the *normal* system must be organised is congenial because it agrees with observations on slips of the tongue. One type of speech error normal people occasionally make involves the reversal of two root morphemes, as happened in the case of the speaker who intended to say "She slants her writing" but instead said "She writes her slanting". Here the roots *write* and *slant* have been reversed, but the inflections *-s* and *-ing* have remained true to their intended positions. Now, in speech, both *slant* and *write* end with a "t" so that the appropriate form of the *-s* (which here is a verb marker not a plural) is "s". Morpheme reversals have, however, been reported which both required and got adaptation of the inflection (see Garrett, 1975; 1980). Examples we have heard include normal speakers saying "the forks ('s') of a prong" for "the prongs ('z') of a fork", and "a catful of houses ('iz')" for "a houseful of cats ('s')".

These morpheme exchange errors confirm that root morphemes and inflections are represented separately at some point or points in the speech planning process. The fact that the inflections adapt to the reversed roots implies that the precise forms of inflections are chosen after the stage in planning at which the root morphemes reverse, and therefore that the phonemic forms of roots are retrieved from the speech output lexicon with inflections being added later. The resistance of inflections to distortion may arise because they are effectively very high-frequency items which, like "the", "an", or "is" can always be accessed correctly by neologistic jargonaphasics.

APHASIC AND NORMAL ERRORS IN WORD FINDING AND PRODUCTION

In both anomia and neologistic jargonaphasia there are disorders of word finding and production. In this section we hope to convince the reader that there is nothing exclusively aphasic about the difficulties and errors seen in these patients, or the other word-finding and production problems that have been reported in aphasics. Normal people experience occasional problems in retrieving or articulating words, and we shall focus on two types of problem in particular. The first, to which we have alluded already, is the involuntary and unintentional slip of the tongue. These take a variety of different forms and have been studied in some detail for the insights they can provide into normal speech production processes (see Cutler, 1982; Fromkin, 1973; 1980). We shall argue here that some types of aphasic error represent a heightened tendency to errors which normal people occasionally make as slips of the tongue.

The second type of normal difficulty to which we shall compare aphasic problems occurs when a normal speaker is having a temporary difficulty recalling a word in his or her vocabulary. Everyone is aware of being unable to remember a word from time to time and knows how galling it can be. On some occasions a few seconds' search is enough to retrieve the word, while on others it refuses to come but then "pops up" some minutes or even days later. Sometimes you feel as if you have almost got the word, only for it to fade again into the background. The mental experience in this state is a peculiar one well described by William James (1890) who called it a "gap in consciousness" and wrote that (p. 251):

It is a gap that is intensely active. A sort of wraith is in it, beckoning us in a given direction, making us at moments tingle with the sense of closeness, and then letting us sink back without the longed for term. If wrong names are proposed to us, this singularly definite gap acts immediately so as to negate them. They do not fit its mould.

Psychologists have studied these normal word-finding problems either by collecting naturally occurring instances, or provoking them by having normal speakers try to fit words to definitions or faces (e.g. Brown & McNeill, 1966; Reason & Lucas, 1984; Woodworth, 1938). In such "tip-of-the-tongue" states a speaker will sometimes report a "feeling of knowing" but be unable to generate any attempt at the word. Sometimes other words will be retrieved which resemble the target word in some way but which the speaker will usually know to be wrong. Finally, the sought-for word may be so close to the tip of the speaker's tongue that he or she can say what phoneme it begins with, tap out its number of syllables, or even generate close approximations to it. We shall argue that each of the degrees of closeness and type of error have counterparts among aphasic word-finding problems.

Before going on to argue our case in detail we should acknowledge that there is nothing original in our general claim for similarities between persistent aphasic difficulties and the occasional lapses of normal people. Sigmund Freud, the founder of psychoanalysis, was trained initially as a neurologist and his first published book was in fact a short monograph on aphasia (Freud, 1891). That book contains the germs of a number of ideas that reappeared later in psychoanalytic theory, such as the concept of regression, which first appeared as the now unpopular notion that brain injury might cause language skills to regress to the level of a young child. In *The psychopathology of everyday life* (1901) Freud applied psychoanalytic concepts to the interpretation of slips of the tongue, but in *On aphasia* (1891) it was the similarity between slips of the tongue and aphasic errors which interested him. Freud wrote that:

> the paraphasia [i.e. speech error] in aphasic patients does not differ from the incorrect use and the distortion of words which the healthy person can observe in himself in states of fatigue or divided attention or under the influence of disturbing affects—the kind of thing that frequently happens to our lecturers and causes the listener painful embarrassment.

More recently, Lenneberg (1960) asserted that, "some forms of aphasia are an abnormally augmented and sustained state which in transient conditions is not uncommon in persons without demonstrable pathology". Detailed comparisons between normal and aphasic errors can be found in Soderpalm (1979), Buckingham (1980), Garrett (1984), and Ellis (1985).

We shall begin by considering whether there exists in normal, intact people any transient equivalent of the word-finding problems of anomic aphasics.

Anomic and Normal Word-finding Difficulties

Anomic aphasics, it will be remembered, have great difficulties in word finding. If given an object to name they will recognise it and be able to indicate its use, but will often be unable to name it. They will, however, recognise the name when they hear it spoken. A patient described by Potts (1901):

> understood everything that was said to him and could converse fluently until he was required to name either a person, place or object.... For instance, he was unable to give the name of his married sister, who was with him, but knew when it was pronounced correctly. There was inability to name paper, a penholder, an ink-well and a watch, but he could tell at once what they were used for, and whether or not they were named correctly by another.... He also insisted that he knew the name but could not say it.

Over 100 years ago, Ogle (1867, p. 94) likened this to normal word-finding problems:

> Most of us know what it is to have the pictorial image of some familiar object in our mind, and yet be perfectly unable to call up its name. The idea is there, but the idea does not suggest the proper symbol. The moment, however, some other person uses the word in our presence it is at once perfectly recognised. Now a similar forgetfulness of words, but more extensive—a similar inability, that is, to translate ideas into symbols— constitutes one form of aphasia; a form which I will call Amnemonic [= anomic] aphasia.

We have noted how normal word-finding problems take different forms. The form which seems most closely equivalent to anomia occurs when a normal person reports a strong "feeling of knowing" a word but is unable to generate any sort of attempt at it. The word's meaning is fully known and it has an entry in the speech output lexicon (as demonstrated by the fact that the elusive word often is retrieved some time later). It appears then to be the retrieval process that is at fault. This, of course, is precisely the explanation offered earlier for anomics like EST whose aphasia was attributed to problems in activating entries for words within the speech output lexicon.

Semantic Errors in Normals and Aphasics

When a patient described briefly by Schuell (1950) was asked what he grew on his farm he replied: "way down on the farm—tree—26 acres of hay—oats—barley—*corn*! Twenty-six or seven acres of—hay—oats—about three or four acres of—timothy—*clover*! Oh yes, that's it, about four acres of clover, that's right." Schuell relates how the patient would shake his head and look distressed each time he said a word related in meaning to the word he sought but not the correct target word which, if it were eventually spoken, would be accompanied by "relaxation and a smile of satisfaction".

In the same paper, Schuell (1950) lists and classifies a large number of such *semantic errors* in aphasic speech, most of which occurred in object-naming tasks. Table 5.1 provides a sample of these errors. In a more recent paper, Rinnert and Whitaker (1973) also classify and discuss aphasic semantic errors (in reading as well as speech) and note how they are not restricted to one variety of aphasia but occur in patients with a variety of different speech disorders. Although we know of no reports of patients in whom semantic errors were the *only* aphasic symptom, 42% of the object-naming errors made by the patient reported by Nolan and Caramazza (1982) were related in meaning to the target word. We suggested earlier that semantic errors are characteristic of that form of anomia attributable to deficits at the semantic level.

TABLE 5.1
Semantic Errors in Aphasic Misnaming (from Schuell, 1950)

lion	→ "buffalo"	*sheep*	→ "goat"	*desk*	→ "sink"
comb	→ "hair"	*towel*	→ "wash"	*leaves*	→ "tree"
knife	→ "cut"	*coffee*	→ "sugar"	*dish*	→ "spoon"
strawberries	→ "figs"	*shirt*	→ "dress"	*gloves*	→ "arm"
thimble	→ "thread"	*lamp*	→ "bulb"	*razor*	→ "shave"
gun→"bow and arrow"				*hammer*→"screwdriver"	

Note: Target words are given to the left of the arrow, the patient's error to the right.

Normal people in a tip-of-the-tongue state will sometimes produce strings of words related in meaning to the target word which they nevertheless reject as incorrect. Thus, one person, in a study by Davies (1984), when given the definition of *wharf* said, "dock, jetty, no, oh no, I know it, berth, dock, oh no, no, I do know it but it's not gonna come". When provided with the word "wharf" the speaker immediately recognised it as the target. Another person given the definition of *utopia* said: "Oh, I know this one definitely. I first of all thought about nirvana... paradise, no it's not paradise, something to do with a state. If it comes it'll just come [long pause]. I'm thinking of aquarius so

I don't know if I do know it now. No, it's a place but not a real place, its a perfect place [long pause] . . . utopia!"

Semantic errors also occur as slips of the tongue when a normal speaker involuntarily says a word related in meaning to the intended word. Again, the speaker will often correct these spontaneously, and will certainly acknowledge the slip as an error if questioned. Examples from Fromkin (1973; 1980) include:

I really *like* to—*hate* to get up in the morning . . .

It's at the *bottom*—I mean—*top* of the stack of books . . .

This room is too damn *hot*—*cold* . . .

the *oral*—*written* part of the exam . . .

Three, five and eight are the worst years for *beer*—I mean *wine* . . .

There's a small *Chinese*—I mean *Japanese* restaurant . . .

Butterworth (1980) argued that semantic errors occur as slips of the tongue through inadvertent activation of the wrong entry within a semantically structured lexicon. The same locus has been proposed as the source of semantic errors in some anomic aphasics. Thus, semantic errors may occur as slips of the tongue as a result of a temporary aberration within the semantic system, damage to which in aphasics produces a chronic disposition to make semantic errors (and an inability to detect them *as* errors).

Real Word Errors of Normals and Aphasics that are Similar in Sound to the Target Word

Semantic errors are not the only variety of aphasic misnaming reported by Schuell (1950). Some of her patients made errors in which the error was a real word similar in sound to the target word. Examples include *goat* misnamed as "ghost", *spoon* as "spool", *fountain* as "mountain", *hook* as "book", *chain* as "chair", and *basket* as "gadget". Freud (1891) mentions aphasic errors in which "words of a similar sound are mistakenly used for each other", such as "butter" for *mutter*, or "campher" for *pamphlet*, and Luria (1974) claims that some of his Russian patients showed "a prevalence for phonetic [i.e. sound] similarity over semantic similarity" in their misnamings, citing errors such as "Kolkhoz" (collective farm) for *holost* (bachelor). Green (1969) calls these errors "phonic verbal paraphasias" and gives as an example a patient intending to say "I got the *words* right at the end of my *tongue*" and instead saying "I got the *nerves* right at the end of my *thumb*". Soderpalm (1979, pp. 83–86) provides some Swedish examples.

Buckingham (1980) has noted that it is difficult from the examples given in the literature to exclude positively the possibility that some patients make frequent phoneme substitutions which result fortuitously in real words on some occasions. Butterworth (1979) and Ellis et al. (1983) argue for the occurrence of just such random "jargon homophones" in their neologistic jargonaphasic patients. What is needed—and what we have been unable to find—are case reports of patients whose only similar-sound errors in speech or naming are real words. We would note, however, that normal people make similar-sound errors in word finding and slips of the tongue.

As slips of the tongue, similar-sounding real word slips are called "malapropisms" after a character called Mrs Malaprop in Sheridan's play *The Rivals*. She was an inveterate misuser of words, but in the speech error literature the term has come to be applied to involuntary slips which the speaker, unlike Mrs Malaprop, would acknowledge immediately to be wrong. Examples from Fay and Cutler (1977) include "trampolines" said instead of the intended word "tambourines", "inoculation" instead of "inauguration", "insect" instead of "index", and "ludicrous" instead of "lucrative".

When we are searching for a particular word, similar-sound errors also occur. For example, one subject in Davies' (1984) study given a definition appropriate to *necromancy* said "nepotism... no it's not that but it's like that". Other examples from normal subjects include "vixen" and "viscous" as attempts at *viscera*, "crochet" for *creche*, "rotary" for *rosary*, "sideboard" for *scabbard*, and "colon" for *kernel*. All these were proffered in response to definitions of the italicized words.

How might these similar-sound errors arise in aphasics and normals (as slips of the tongue and in word search)? One possibility is to postulate spreading activation within the speech output lexicon akin to that often held to occur within the semantic system (e.g. Anderson, 1976). The difference would be that whereas spreading activation within the semantic system occurs between the entries for words having similar meanings, within the speech output lexicon activation would spread from the entry for one word to the entries for others having similar *sounds*. Stemberger (1985) suggests that this mutual activation of similar-sounding words in the speech output lexicon is not direct, but occurs via nodes at the phoneme level. In his model, activation flows back up from the phoneme level to the output lexicon as well as flowing down from the lexicon to the phoneme level. Similar-sound errors in normals thus arise as a consequence of rapid two-way interaction between the speech output lexicon and the phoneme level. As Ellis (1985a) notes, similar-sound errors may thus represent a type of mistake which is, paradoxically, characteristic of two *intact* subsystems interacting in a fast and (normally) efficient manner. They may thus tend to disappear when one or other level is impaired, and may never occur as the sole or predominant error form in aphasia.

Neologisms

At first glance it seems unlikely that normal people would ever produce neologisms like those of patients EST or RD discussed above. We have, however, observed a neologistic type of response to be made by normals when searching for a word they temporarily are unable to retrieve. Sometimes a normal person will claim to know a defined word and will generate a series of attempts at it which resemble the target word in the way that so-called "target-related neologisms" resemble their targets. All the instances we have observed of this phenomenon to date have culminated in a full, correctly pronounced word. In one example quoted by Ellis et al. (1983), a normal subject was given the definition *A platform for public speaking* and said "past... pestul... peda... pedestal". Another subject's response to the same definition was "strow... strum... rostrum". To the definition *The part of a steeple where bells are hung* a subject responded "belfrum... belfry", whereas in response to *Wordblindness; difficulty in learning to read or spell* another said, "flexi... plexi... plexia... dyslexia".

Earlier we interpreted target-related neologisms in aphasics as symptomatic of impaired activation reaching the speech output lexicon, with the result that only partial information about the phonemic forms of many words can be retrieved. It would appear that this problem may again be a habitual and disabling exaggeration of a problem which occasionally afflicts the normal person caught in a tip-of-the-tongue state for a little-used word. Even in the case of anomics and neologistic jargonaphasics we have seen how the most frequently used words can usually still be retrieved in their entirety, suggesting that although the band of "infrequently used words" has expanded greatly for them, the most common still remain accessible.

PHONOLOGICAL PROBLEMS IN APHASICS AND NORMALS

Many aphasic patients who may show a variety of other language difficulties have, in addition, problems with sequencing and articulating the phonemes in words. Blumstein (1973) studied the phonemic errors of three groups of aphasics (designated Broca's, conduction, and Wernicke's) and could find no differences between them. All three groups made phoneme substitution errors such as saying "*keams*" for "*teams*" or "ti*n*e" for "ti*m*e", and also phoneme misordering errors which might involve the anticipation of phonemes (e.g. saying "*b*istory *b*ooks" for "*h*istory *b*ooks" or "roa*f* bee*f*" for "roa*s*t bee*f*"), their perseveration (e.g. saying "*f*ront *p*rage" for "*f*ront page"), or reversal (e.g. "*ge*drees" for "*de*grees"). Subsequent studies have reported differences in predispositions to different types of error but with considerable overlap between groups (e.g. Blumstein, Cooper, Goodglass, Statlender, & Gottlieb, 1980; Monoi, Fukusako, Itoh, & Sasanuma, 1983; see Kohn, 1988, for a review). In our view the use of *group* studies rather than selected single-case studies virtually ensures a blurring of real individual differences that may exist between patients.

All the types of phonemic error seen in aphasic patients also occur in normal people as slips of the tongue. Thus in the Appendix to Fromkin's (1973) book *Speech errors as linguistic evidence*, we can find examples of normal phoneme substitutions (e.g. "*b*agnificent" for "*m*agnificent"; "pho*l*etic" for "pho*n*etic"), anticipations (e.g. "*t*addle *t*ennis" for "*p*addle *t*ennis", or "*cuff* of co*ff*ee" for "cu*p* of co*ff*ee"), and reversals (e.g. "u*v*i*n*ersity" for "u*n*i*v*ersity", or "*m*oggy *b*arsh" for "*b*oggy *m*arsh").

In addition to their superficial comparability, fine-grain analyses show more detailed resemblances between normal and aphasic phoneme errors. Details of these similarities are shown in Table 5.2. In normal speakers phoneme misordering errors are often referred to as "Spoonerisms" after William Spooner (1844–1930), who reputedly made large numbers of such errors. Lashley (1951) was impressed by the similarity between normal and aphasic errors and wrote: "In some types of aphasia the tendency to disordered arrangement of words is greatly increased.... Professor Spooner, after whom such slips are named, was probably suffering from a mild form of aphasia." Spooner's life and slips are discussed by Potter (1980), and further comparisons between normal and aphasic phoneme errors can be found in Soderpalm (1979) and Buckingham (1980). We would argue that although some differences between the two sorts of error may exist [for example, in the distance covered by items in movement errors (anticipations, perseverations, and reversals), or in the relative frequencies of the subtypes], there are sufficient similarities for us to regard them as both originating from malfunctions of processes in and around the phoneme level—transient malfunctions in normals, more permanent and more disabling in aphasics.

TABLE 5.2
Fine-grain Similarities between Normal and Aphasic Phoneme Misordering Errors
(see also Soderpalm, 1979; Buckingham, 1980)

1. The target phoneme and the error phoneme that replaces it tend to be articulatorily and
   acoustically similar.
   normals: Nooteboom (1967), MacKay (1970), Garrett (1975).
   aphasics: Green (1969), Lecours & Lhermitte (1969), Blumstein (1973), Martin &
   Rigrodsky (1974), Lecours (1975).

2. The target and error phoneme tend to share similar or identical preceding and/or following
   phonemes.
   normals: Nooteboom (1967).
   aphasics: Lecours & Lhermitte (1969).

3. The target and error phonemes tend to originate from similar positions in their respective
   syllables.
   normals: Nooteboom (1967), MacKay (1970).
   aphasics: Blumstein (1978), Buckingham, Whitaker, & Whitaker (1978).

4. Target and error phonemes tend to originate in content words rather than function words.
   normals: Garrett (1975).
   aphasics: Blumstein (1973).

5. Consonants and vowels do not interchange.
   normals: Fromkin (1971), Garrett (1975).
   aphasics: Fry (1959), Blumstein (1973).

6. Errors rarely result in sequences of phonemes that are not permitted in the speaker's
   language.
   normals: Wells (1951), Boomer & Laver (1968), Garrett (1975).
   aphasics: Blumstein (1978).

7. The probability of two phonemes being involved in a misordering error decreases as the
   separation between them increases.
   normals: Cohen (1966), Nooteboom (1967), MacKay (1970).
   aphasics: Lecours & Lhermitte (1969).

ARTICULATORY DISORDERS

In most of the aphasic phoneme errors just described the phonemes are
articulated reasonably smoothly. There are, however, a final set of speech
production aphasias in which articulation itself—that is, the co-
ordination and control of the articulatory muscle groups—is impaired.
Probably the fullest description of such a disorder was provided in a series
of papers spanning 37 years by Alajouanine, Ombredane, and Durand
(1939), Alajouanine, Pichot, and Durand (1949), and Lecours and Lhermitte (1976). The patient receiving this intensive study was a French–
English bilingual man (E.Fr.) who suffered a stroke at the age of 63. A
few months later his speech comprehension was perfectly normal, as
were his ability to read and write, but his speech production was slow

and laborious with syllables being forced out explosively. In a (translated) letter to his doctor written in January, 1948, E.Fr. observes:

> I can only talk syllabically because my articulation is sluggard [*paresseuse*]. It is no longer automatic but has to be commanded, directed. I have to think of the word I am going to utter, and of the way in which to utter it. If I want to say '*bonjour*', I can no longer do so out of habit; it is no longer automatic.... I must articulate each vowel, each consonant, in short each syllable.

Subsequently, studies of this "phonetic disintegration syndrome" (alternatively known as "pure anarthria" or "aphemia") by Shankweiler and Harris (1966), Lebrun, Buyssens, and Henneaux (1973), and Nebes (1975) leave no doubt that in pure cases all internal language functions can remain intact, and that patients may have internal access to the sounds of words (as illustrated by the ability to make rhyme judgements or tap out the number of syllables in words they cannot say), but they can no longer translate phonemic forms fluently into articulations.

Finally, patients whom traditional classification systems label as "Broca's aphasics" have articulatory problems combined with other, grammatical difficulties that we shall review in Chapter 9. Techniques including computer controlled X-ray microbeams have revealed defective articulatory timing in Broca's aphasics, suggesting that an impairment of articulatory programming accompanies the several other features of this "syndrome" (Kohn, 1988). We shall argue in Chapter 9 that because the several features of "Broca's aphasia" can dissociate one from another, it is not a useful category for cognitive neuropsychological analysis.

OVERVIEW

If you are to name an object you are looking at you must perceive it clearly, recognise and "comprehend" it for what it is, retrieve its name from memory, and articulate it correctly. A normal person may experience a temporary difficulty with any of these stages on a particular occasion. Thus, viewing an object from an unusual angle may create momentary problems in recognition, or a tip-of-the-tongue state may signal a temporary problem of name retrieval. Each of the stages in object recognition and naming may also be more seriously impaired as a consequence of brain injury, so that even an apparently simple process like object naming is subject to several different forms of impairment (Morton, 1985a; Ratcliff & Newcombe, 1982). We reviewed disorders of object perception and recognition in Chapter 2 and have covered name retrieval and production in this chapter. Central semantic processes impinge on both recognition and name production and have consequently intruded into both chapters.

For the cognitive neuropsychologist it is a useful exercise to discover whether or not the impairments seen in brain-injured patients can be explained in terms of exaggerations of tendencies to error seen in normal people. If they can, then one has gained a degree of support for the assumption of *subtractivity*, whereby it is assumed that entirely new cognitive processes do not arise following brain injury (see Chapter 1). We have spent a considerable amount of time in this chapter on similarities between normal and aphasic errors because we feel that disorders of word-finding are a case where exaggeration theory can best be sustained and where the subtractivity assumption can best be corroborated.

Object naming is, of course, only one aspect of the more general process of word retrieval and production which is, in turn, only one aspect of successful speech production. In normal speech, words are arranged into sentences to express particular thoughts, and the words in each sentence are given appropriate intonation and emphasis. Linguists use the term "syntax" to refer to the processes whereby words are ordered into sentences, and the term "prosody" to refer to the intonation, stress, timing, and rhythm of utterances. One of the first achievements of the cognitive neuropsychology of language was to highlight the dissociations that can occur between disorders of word finding and syntax (Caramazza & Berndt, 1978; Marin, Saffran, & Schwartz, 1976; Saffran 1982). As we have seen, "anomic" patients have word-finding problems yet they may show normal syntactic skills. In contrast, patients labelled as "agrammatic" may be able to retrieve words well but can no longer arrange them into grammatical sentences (see Chapter 9). This "double dissociation" shows that separate sets of cognitive modules must exist for word finding and syntax, and accordingly constrains any future model of speech production, whether the model is meant to apply to aphasic or normal speech. As we shall also see in Chapter 9, prosody is subject to its own range of impairments which dissociate from disorders of syntax and word finding, so future models must also allow for a third set of separate processes for the production of prosody. This is, of course, another illustration of cognitive neuropsychological analysis driving the theorist inexorably toward a *modular* view of the total human cognitive apparatus.

SUMMARY

Problems in spoken-word retrieval and production can arise at a number of different levels. In pure cases, one stage may be selectively impaired leaving the others intact, though many patients will have multiple problems affecting several levels.

Impairments at the semantic level may in certain cases affect word retrieval for some semantic categories more than others (e.g. patient MD whose naming problems were specific to fruit and vegetables). Other patients have more general semantic problems. These patients have comprehension as well as production difficulties, suggesting that the same semantic system is involved in both comprehension and production.

Other "anomic" patients (like EST) can show word-finding problems for words whose semantic representations appear to be intact (as demonstrated by intact comprehension of the meanings of those words). The features of these cases, including the greater problems with low-frequency than high-frequency words, may be explained in terms of problems activating entries for words in a speech output lexicon. In this respect the problems of these anomic patients resemble greatly exaggerated and habitual tip-of-the-tongue states where semantic errors and similar-sound errors also occur.

When EST could not fully retrieve a word he could often generate a close approximation to it. These occurred more often in tasks like object naming than in spontaneous speech where EST would avoid difficult words as much as possible. Approximation errors (alias target-related neologisms) occur much more commonly in the speech of patients termed "neologistic jargonaphasics" (like RD). Such patients have profound speech perception difficulties which may prevent them from monitoring their own speech and detecting their own errors. The underlying output impairment appears otherwise to be similar to that of anomic patients like EST, namely a frequency related impairment affecting the activation of words in the speech output lexicon. More specifically, it is root morphemes which are difficult to access: Inflections are retrieved and accommodated correctly to the root, suggesting that root morphemes and inflections may have separate entries in the speech output lexicon (a conclusion supported by analyses of normal slips of the tongue).

Impairments at or below the phoneme level are common in aphasics, but currently we lack the detailed case studies that would allow us to tease apart any different forms of impairment that may exist. Phoneme level errors of substitution and misordering bear a close resemblance to the phonemic slips of the tongue of normal speakers, suggesting an exacerbation in the aphasics of processes which are already somewhat error-prone in normal speakers. Low-level articulatory disorders occur in pure form in patients suffering from "phonetic disintegration" or "pure anarthria", and also occur as a component of the condition referred to as "Broca's aphasia".

FURTHER READING

Saffran, E. M. (1982). Neuropsychological approaches to the study of language. *British Journal of Psychology, 73*, 317–337. Discusses the implications of the double dissociation between disorders of syntax and word-finding, and also the different levels at which word-finding can be disrupted.

Morton, J. (1985). Naming. In S. Newman & R. Epstein (Eds), *Current perspectives in dysphasia*. Edinburgh: Churchill Livingstone. Introduction to the notion of modelling a function like naming and accounting for different disorders in terms of impairments at different levels.

Ellis, A. W. (1985). The production of speech: A cognitive neuropsychological perspective. In A. W. Ellis (Ed.), *Progress in the psychology of language*, Vol. 2. London: Lawrence Erlbaum Associates. Discusses word-finding and its disorders in the context of an "interactive activation" theory of speech production, and details similarities between aphasic and normal errors.

Kohn, S. E. (1988). Phonological production deficits in aphasia. In H. Whitaker (Ed.), *Phonological processes and brain mechanisms*. New York: Springer-Verlag. Useful review of that tradition in neuropsychology which (in our view) would have discovered far more had it not been so firmly wedded to syndrome categories like Broca's, Wernicke's, and conduction aphasia.

6

Recognising and Understanding Spoken Words

INTRODUCTION

Spoken language travels from speaker to hearer as a sound wave. That sound wave is an extremely rich source of information. Without ever seeing a speaker we can often deduce correctly that person's sex, region of origin (from their accent), emotional state (e.g. whether they are happy, sad, or angry), approximate age, and so on. If the speaker is someone known to us we may be able to identify him or her as an individual from their voice and way of talking. There is, of course, linguistic information encoded in the speech wave too. This includes information about individual words, but in addition the syntactic boundaries of sentences or clauses are often signalled by pauses or changes in voice pitch, and even the transition from one general topic to another may be marked in a similar way (Ellis & Beattie, 1986).

We shall, however, principally be concerned here with recognising spoken words and extracting their meaning. Imagine the simple case of recognising a single word, clearly articulated and spoken in isolation. Unless that word is a homophone (like *their* and *there*, *one* and *won*) its sound pattern will be unique to it. To identify the word a listener will need to have stored in memory all the sound patterns of words he or she knows, and be able to compare the pattern just heard with these stored patterns to find the best match. What we are proposing is another word store or lexicon, but this time one involved in the recognition rather than the production of spoken words. We shall call it the *auditory input lexicon*.

There are currently two views prevalent on how the auditory input

143

lexicon might work. One theory proposes that the listener first identifies phonemes (individual speech sounds) in the acoustic wave, and then identifies the word from its constituent phonemes. According to this view individual entries in the auditory input lexicon would be activated by a prior set of phoneme recognisers (e.g. Rumelhart & McClelland, 1981). The second theory, advocated by Klatt (1979) and Marcus (1981) among others, holds that the input to the auditory word recognition system is a low-level, relatively unsegmented description of the speech waveform. While acknowledging that either (or neither) of these theories may turn out to be correct in the long run, we shall tentatively adopt the first as our working hypothesis.

We propose, in Fig. 6.1, that the first stage of auditory word recognition performed by an early *auditory analysis system* attempts to identify phonemes in the speech wave. The results of this analysis are transmitted to the auditory input lexicon where a match is sought against the stored characteristics of known words. If the match is a good one, the appropriate recognition unit in the auditory input lexicon will be activated. It, in turn, will then activate the representation of the meaning of the heard word in the semantic system—the same semantic system that initiates the word production process in speaking via the same speech output lexicon and phoneme level that were discussed in the previous chapter. The arrow between the auditory input lexicon and the semantic system is bidirectional. This allows the semantic system to exert an influence upon the level of activity in the word-units which, in turn, provides a mechanism whereby the semantic context in which a word occurs can affect its ease of identification (see below).

One way to repeat a heard word would be to activate its entry in the speech output lexicon, release the phonemic form, and articulate it. This would be to take a route straight through Fig. 6.1. However, normal people can also repeat aloud unfamiliar words or non-words like "fep" or "flootil", for which there will be no entry in either the auditory input lexicon or the speech output lexicon. In Fig. 6.1, therefore, we need a by-pass route from the acoustic analysis system to the phoneme level. The by-pass route *must* be used to repeat unfamiliar words or non-words. It *could* be used for real words (treating them as if they were non-words), but real words can also be repeated via the input and output lexicons.

Figure 6.1 thus provides three "routes" between hearing a word and saying it. The first route is through word meanings and the two lexicons; the second is provided by the direct link between the auditory analysis system and the phoneme level; and the third route is provided by the arrow linking the auditory input lexicon to the speech output lexicon. This would allow heard words to activate their entries in the speech output lexicons directly, without going via the representations of word

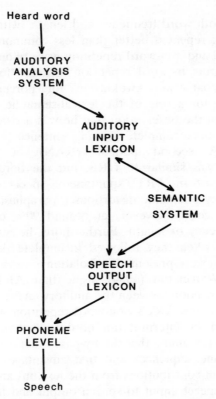

FIG 6.1. Simple functional model for the recognition, comprehension, and repetition of spoken words.

meanings in the semantic system. We will admit here and now that the evidence for such a route is weak. It is included because it allows us to explain in Chapter 7 how certain patients are able to write words to dictation without understanding the meanings of those words.

McCarthy and Warrington (1984) employed a model similar to Fig. 6.1 to explain two different patterns of repetition performance observed in three aphasic patients they studied. Patient ORF was able to repeat words considerably better than non-words of the same length (85% correct for words *vs*. 39% for non-words). Non-words can only be repeated via the link between auditory analysis and the phoneme level, whereas words can be repeated via any of the routes through Fig. 6.1. ORF's superiority for words over non-words suggests some impairment to the connection between the auditory analysis system and the phoneme level, with the routes via the lexicons and semantics assisting word repetition. These latter routes were not completely intact, however: ORF had word-finding problems in speech and naming, and his word repetition was not perfect, being affected by both word frequency and length (with more common, shorter words being repeated better than less common, longer words). Errors in both word and non-word repetition were phonemic distortions. Examples of his errors in word repetition include "fosh" for "wash", "acroldut" for "acrobat", and "kwokutrain" for "porcupine".

Further evidence for a role of the lexical-semantic routes in ORF's repetition came from the observation that he was assisted in repeating a word if it followed an incomplete priming sentence (e.g. The monster was...*hideous*). A second patient (RAN) of McCarthy and Warrington (1984) was similar to ORF, but the third patient (ART) showed a different pattern. ART's spontaneous speech was "halting and effortful", with many phonemic distortions ("paraphasias"). His repetition of words was good, however, at around 90% correct, and was unaffected by frequency or length. Furthermore, he was actually *worse* at repeating words when they followed incomplete priming sentences than when the words were presented in isolation.

McCarthy and Warrington (1984) argue that ART's repetition is mediated by the connection between the auditory analysis system and the phoneme level. Although ART's non-word repetition was not assessed, one would expect on this interpretation no difference between word and non-word repetition (assuming that the by-pass route is insensitive to the wordness of phoneme sequences and that advantages for words over non-words come from contributions from the lexicons and semantics).

Figure 6.1 links speech input to speech output and thus incorporates a model for auditory-vocal repetition. Our central concern in this chapter will, however, be with the recognition and understanding of spoken words, rather than with their simple repetition. We shall consider a number of aphasias in which the recognition and understanding of spoken words is impaired, aphasias known in the literature as pure word deafness, word meaning deafness, auditory phonological agnosia, and deep dysphasia.

PURE WORD DEAFNESS

The Pattern of Symptoms

Hemphill and Stengel (1940) reported the case of a 34-year-old labourer who suffered brain injury after falling from a bus. He could no longer repeat or understand speech addressed to him, and at first was thought to be deaf. This assumption was proved wrong, however, when audiometric testing showed him to be perfectly normal at hearing pure tones. He talked fluently with what are described as "no errors of grammar beyond what is common for his particular dialect and standard of education" [*sic*]. He read well with understanding and could write correctly with good spelling. He complained, however, that much of what he heard conveyed no meaning to him. In his own words: "I can hear you dead plain, but I cannot get what you say. The noises are not quite natural. I can hear but not understand."

Klein and Harper's (1956) patient, RC, showed a similar pattern. Following a stroke this 45-year-old Scottish sheep farmer's spontaneous speech returned almost to normal ("He made occasional slips in conversation, and in the naming of objects, but these mistakes became more and more sporadic"). His reading was "fluent and without mistakes", but he was quite unable to understand speech addressed to him. Audiometric testing showed normal hearing in his right ear with "moderate mixed deafness in the left ear". Though "he could hear everything, even a leaf falling", he said of listening to speech: "It sounds far away. You think you can catch it and it fades away...jumbled together like foreign folk speaking in the distance. You feel it should be louder but when anyone shouts it is still more confusing."

RC could repeat single vowel sounds correctly, but otherwise there was little or no similarity between what was said to him and his repetition. For example, he repeated "collaboration" as "setter", "God save the King" as "as in a mix", and "good morning" as "become". Interestingly, RC is reported as having been able to distinguish the voices of different people familiar to him, and able to say whether someone spoke with the accent of his own region, or from another part of Scotland, or "with a foreigner's accent" (it is not clear whether "foreigner" in this context included the English, though quite likely it did!).

These two patients approximate more or less closely to what is referred to in the neuropsychological literature as "pure word deafness". This involves impaired speech perception in the context of good speech production, reading, and writing (though RC had some spelling difficulties) and, importantly, intact perception of non-verbal environmental sounds. A historical review of cases given this designation is provided by Goldstein (1974); more recent and more detailed case studies can be found in Okada, Hanada, Hattori, and Shoyama (1963), Albert and Bear (1974), Denes and Semenza (1975), Saffran, Marin, and Yeni-Komshian (1976a), Shoumaker, Ajax, and Schenkenberg (1977), and Auerbach, Allard, Naeser, Alexander, and Albert (1982). In fact these cases vary in their purity—some, for example, have problems in the perception of melody, and Denes and Semenza's (1975) patient had difficulty with environmental sounds: What matters is that these associated deficits do not always accompany word deafness. Therefore, we can reasonably ignore them when looking at the possible causes of the *speech* perception problem.

The Psychological Nature of the Deficit

As noted earlier, these patients may have entirely normal perception of the sort of pure tones used in audiometric testing. The localisation of sounds in space was also normal in the patients of Okada et al. (1963), Denes and Semenza (1975), and Auerbach et al. (1982). Recognition of environmental sounds was good in all but the patients of Denes and Semenza (1975) and Auerbach et al. (1982). Clearly, then, we are not dealing with simple deafness in these cases.

Okada et al. (1963) seem to have been the first to make an important observation which others have replicated and discussed, namely that these patients sometimes understood a question or request if it was repeated *very slowly* two or three times. Albert and Bear's (1974) patient himself commented that "words come too quickly". Passage comprehension, though never very good, was reportedly better for this patient at a speech rate of 45 words per minute than 150 words per minute. In one experiment groups of three digits were spoken to him either rapidly with no pause between them or at a slower rate of one per 3 seconds. With the examiner's lips screened from view he identified 95% correctly at the slow rate but only 50% correctly at the faster rate. Auerbach et al.'s (1982) patient also commented that people's voices seemed fast and that it helped when they spoke more slowly.

A second clue as to the underlying cause of the deficit is given in reports of the differential ease with which these patients can identify spoken consonants and vowels. Denes and Semenza's (1975) patient was good at identifying single spoken vowels, but his performance became very poor if a consonant was added to the front of the vowel so that he had to identify a CV syllable. Auerbach et al.'s patient similarly was very good at identifying vowels but poor at consonants. In seeking to explain this discrepancy, Auerbach et al. (1982, p. 283) note that:

> When plotted on a frequency spectrogram, vowels are represented by steady state characteristic frequencies. In natural speech, vowel durations usually average 100 to 150 ms but may last as long as 400 ms. CV combinations with stop consonants such as ba, pa, da, ta, ga or ka all contain early rapid formant transitions. In these CV combinations, the vowels are characterised by steady state formants whereas the consonant is characterised by rapid frequency changes within the first 40 ms of onset of stimulus.

In order to identify and discriminate between spoken consonants you need to be able to make very fine temporal discriminations and track rapidly changing acoustic signals accurately (Miller, 1987). That, arguably, is what at least some word-deaf patients are no longer able to do.

Lateralisation and Modes of Perception

We shall have a little more to say about the nature of pure word deafness and strategies for overcoming it shortly, but it is worth noting at this point that this deficit provides one of the best illustrations of how cognitive neuropsychology can interface with that branch of neuropsychology concerned with the localisation of functions within different regions of the brain. Pure word deafness can follow from a single lesion in the temporal lobe of the left hemisphere, that half of the brain which controls many language functions in the majority of right-handed people. The left and right hemispheres receive their most important auditory inputs from the right and left ears respectively. Words are slightly but measurably better identified if presented to the right ear, and hence to the left hemisphere, than if presented to the left ear and hence to the right hemisphere. This right ear advantage is especially pronounced in the "dichotic listening" paradigm where pairs of words are presented simultaneously, one to each ear, through headphones (Bradshaw & Nettleton, 1983; Bryden, 1982). Where this ties in with pure word deafness is that steady-state vowels do *not* yield a right ear/left hemisphere advantage but are perceived equally well by either ear/hemisphere (Blumstein, Tartter, Michel, Hirsch, & Leiter, 1977; Shankweiler & Studdert-Kennedy, 1967). Most consonants cannot be presented in isolation, but as soon as one employs CV or CVC syllables in a dichotic listening test a right ear advantage emerges. This advantage accrues to the vowel segments of the syllables as well as to the consonants (Darwin, 1971; Godfrey, 1974; Haggard, 1971; Shankweiler & Studdert-Kennedy, 1967; Weiss and House, 1973). This may be because in natural syllables cues as to the identity of the vowel are not restricted to the medial portion, but are instead "smeared throughout the syllable" (Sergent, 1984). That is, the central vowel modifies and colours the consonants before and after it, so a component capable of the fine-grain analysis of consonants will gain additional information regarding the identity of the accompanying vowel.

Shankweiler and Studdert-Kennedy (1967) talk of two different "modes" of perception—a general *auditory* mode, and a speech-related *phonetic* mode. Both hemispheres, they argue, are capable of perceiving in the auditory mode, and the auditory mode is capable of processing steady-state vowels, so such vowels show no ear advantage in dichotic listening. The phonetic mode is, according to Shankweiler and Studdert-Kennedy, a unique possession of the human left hemisphere. This mode is necessary for the accurate perception of the rapidly changing acoustic signals that specify consonants, and so consonants display a right ear advantage. There are other lines of evidence for something like this distinction, for example in the patterns of auditory loss which accompany injury to one or other hemisphere (Oscar-Berman, Zurif, & Blumstein, 1975).

Albert and Bear (1974) presented digits through headphones to the left and right ears of their word-deaf patient. With "monaural presentation" (only one digit at a time to either the left ear or the right ear) performance was equally good with either ear. With "dichotic presentation", where the digits are simultaneously presented in pairs, one to each ear, left ear performance remained good, but right ear performance dropped to almost zero. Saffran et al. (1976a) obtained a similar pattern of "right ear extinction", under dichotic conditions from their patient using monosyllabic names like "Ben", "Chuck", or "Tom" (recall that the right ear is the one that shows the *advantage* in dichotic experiments with normal subjects). These authors argue that their digit and name stimuli can be discriminated reasonably well by the right hemisphere auditory system, and that under monaural presentation conditions stimuli to either ear can gain access to that component (there are, in fact, projections from both ears to both hemispheres, though the projections from each ear to the opposite hemisphere appear dominant). Under dichotic conditions the left ear/right hemisphere connection dominates and suppresses the right ear/right hemisphere connection. Stimuli presented to the right ear can no longer be processed by the injured left hemisphere, so the patient shows right ear extinction.

From the observations made so far it could be argued that the left hemisphere "phonetic" system damaged in word-deaf patients is *only* involved in speech processing. This would be in line with arguments for a special "speech mode" of perception (Mann & Liberman, 1983; Repp, 1982). The case for a *speech-specific* mode of perception has not, however, found universal acceptance (e.g. Schouten, 1980). Two points are possibly relevant to the question of whether the component impaired in word-deaf patients is speech-specific. The first is the point we noted earlier, that these patients benefit greatly from a reduction in speech rate. Slowing speech down may bring the range of temporal discriminations necessary to distinguish consonants within the capabilities of the right hemisphere "auditory" component. That is, a reduction of speech rate by one-half or one-third may permit the right hemisphere auditory component to function as a phonetic one.

Secondly, studies by Albert and Bear (1974) and Auerbach et al. (1982) have shown deficits in word-deaf patients in the processing of rapidly changing *non-speech* stimuli. Normal subjects can distinguish two clicks as separate if there is a silence of just 2 or 3 ms between them. Below such separation the clicks "fuse" into a single percept. (Miller & Taylor, 1948; Patterson, Green, 1970). Albert and Bear's patient fused clicks separated by anything less than 15 ms, whereas Auerbach et al.'s patient required clicks to be separated by at least 30 ms before he could distinguish them. So rather than talking of a left hemisphere phonetic system and a right hemisphere auditory one, it might be better to think of the left hemisphere system as more efficient than the right, capable of finer discriminations to more rapidly changing acoustic patterns. The fact that the right hemisphere system can sustain a degree of speech perception may explain why bilateral lesions have often been thought necessary to cause complete (rather than partial) word deafness (Auerbach et al., 1982; Goldstein, 1974).

If the rapid processing deficit in word deafness extends to non-verbal clicks there may be nothing speech-specific about the impairment; word-deaf patients may no longer be able to analyse *any* rapidly changing acoustic signal. Nevertheless, in everyday life the class of sounds particularly affected by such an impairment are spoken consonants. Without such an ability you can still identify steady-state vowels and environmental noises like cows mooing or telephones ringing. You can also process information extractable from vowel quality in speech: As mentioned earlier, word-deaf patients are often capable of identifying the voices of familiar people, distinguishing male from female voices, and locating individuals geographically from their accent. Denes and Semenza's (1975) patient could distinguish Italian from English or German (which have distinctive vowel repertoires) but not from Latin (which has much the same vowel repertoire).

Finally, word deafness does not *have* to be pure. The spontaneous speech of Caramazza, Berndt, & Basili's (1983) patient, JS, was neologistic jargonaphasic, very like RD of Ellis, Miller, and Sin (1983) whom we discussed in Chapter 5. But JS's speech perception deficit, analysed in detail by Caramazza et al. (1983), corresponds closely to the picture seen in patients with pure word deafness. Thus the features of word deafness may co-exist with other language impairments in many more aphasics than show *pure* word deafness. In line with this suggestion, Lasky, Weidner, and Johnson (1976) and Tallal and Newcombe (1978) both found the speech perception of mixed groups of aphasic patients to be somewhat improved by slower rates of presentation (which we have seen to be a characteristic of pure word deafness).

Use of Lip Information

Returning to the cases of pure(ish) word deafness, several investigators have noted that the patients pay close attention to lip movements in an attempt to supplement their impoverished auditory/phonetic processing ability (Albert & Bear, 1974; Denes & Semenza, 1975; Saffran et al., 1976a). Auerbach et al.'s (1982) patient said: "If I go blind, I won't hear anything!" For Albert and Bear's patient the deterioration in digit identification brought about by fast rates of presentation was considerably lessened if the tester's lips were not concealed from view (rather than falling from 95 to 50% as it did with lips concealed, performance only declined from 98 to 80% with lips visible). This parallels closely the use normal listeners make of lip movement information when speech quality is poor. Cotton (1935) had a speaker sit in a sound-proof booth with glass windows. His speech was transmitted to an audience sat outside, but was distorted by removing high frequencies and adding a loud buzzing noise. With the lighting adjusted so as to make the speaker invisible to the audience, only an occasional word or two could be identified, but when the speaker was made visible his speech was understood without difficulty. Cotton concluded that "there is an important element of visual hearing in all normal individuals". Likewise, Sumby and Pollack (1954) showed that speech distorted by hissing "white" noise is more easily perceived if the speaker's lip and face movements can also be seen.

One might be tempted to suggest that the use made by normal listeners and word-deaf patients of lipread information is akin to having available a poorly written transcript of what is being said—it provides a useful but entirely separate source of information. The studies of McGurk and MacDonald (1976) and Summerfield (1979), however, suggest otherwise. They showed that lip movement information combines with speech wave information very early in the process of perception to determine what is actually *heard*. It is thus possible that lipread information in some genuine sense helps word-deaf patients *hear* better. Auerbach et al.'s (1982) patient may have been closer to the mark than he thought. Maybe if he did go blind he would not *hear* what people were saying.

Use of Context

In addition to making use of lip movement cues, patients with pure word deafness also seem able to use the linguistic context to aid comprehension. Okada et al. (1963) note that their patient fared quite well when asked a series of questions related to a single topic (e.g. "the weather"), but comprehension became suddenly much worse when the topic changed. Saffran et al. (1976a) describe a conversation in which their patient "gets completely lost each time the questioning shifts from his smoking habits to his work experience, to the circumstances of his early life, but is able to respond appropriately once he grasps the general topic of conversation". In an experimental follow-up of this observation Saffran et al. showed that the perception of lists of words was better when the words came from a small number of semantic categories (animals, vehicles, furniture, fruits), with the words in each category being grouped together, than when unrelated words were presented. Also words presented in sentences which provided contextual cues (e.g. "The boy sailed the BOAT") were better identified than the same words presented in isolation ("BOAT").

Like the use made of lipread information, this use of context, as Saffran et al. (1976a) note, is very similar to that made by normal subjects. Miller, Heise, and Lichten (1951) had subjects try to identify words in a background of white noise. Words in isolation were found to be much less identifiable than words in sentence contexts. Even normal "good quality" speech may need supplementing by context. Lieberman (1963) and Pollack and Pickett (1964) sliced single words out of passages of perfectly intelligible conversational speech and found that less than half of them were comprehensible when heard in isolation from their contexts. Marslen-Wilson and Tyler (1975; 1980) had normal subjects listen to passages of undegraded speech and press a button each time particular target words were heard. Reaction times were much shorter in passages of normal, coherent text than in passages with the word order scrambled, where listeners had to rely for word identification entirely on stimulus information and could make no use of context.

In sum, because of a left hemisphere deficit which appears to affect high-speed processing of acoustic signals, word-deaf patients form only a very poor percept of speech—one good enough to distinguish many vowels but few consonants. They supplement the speech wave by use of lip movement information and also by use of context. In both these respects the patients resemble normal people trying to extract information from a noisy signal. In terms of our model, the locus of the deficit is very clearly the auditory analysis system.

"WORD MEANING DEAFNESS"

The second variety of auditory word recognition disorder we shall discuss has been called "word meaning deafness". A young woman aged 26 years and living near Edinburgh, Scotland in the 1890s suffered a stroke 11 days after giving birth to her third child. After a few weeks of recovery she "volunteered statements, spoke spontaneously, asked questions... [and] seemed able to say almost everything she wished to say, [though] she occasionally made use of a wrong word". She "could read aloud anything which was placed before her" such as the sentence, "No issue of a medical journal would be complete at the present time without containing the latest development in this greatest medical experiment of all time." She understood short written sentences, though she seems to have had some problems understanding long sentences or connected text. She experienced great difficulty understanding speech addressed to her, though she was not deaf. As she said on one occasion: "Is it not a strange thing that I can hear the clock ticking and cannot hear you speak? Now let me think what that means."

Thus far the patient sounds like a case of pure word deafness, but what distinguished her from those patients is that she could repeat the spoken words and sentences she could not understand, and she could even write them down to dictation. When asked, "Do you like to come to Edinburgh?", she did not understand the question, but repeated it correctly and wrote down the words she had just repeated. Having written the question down she then understood it by reading it.

This case report comes from Bramwell (1897), writing in the distinguished medical journal *The Lancet*. Despite its age, Bramwell's report remains one of the best descriptions available of a rare condition referred to as "word-meaning deafness". Bramwell's paper has recently been reprinted with commentary (Ellis, 1984a). Other reports of similar patients masquerading under a variety of diagnostic labels can be found in Lichtheim (1885), Goldstein (1915), Symonds (1953), Yamadori and Albert (1973), Luria (1976), and Kohn and Friedman (1986).

Kohn and Friedman (1986) state that a demonstration of word-meaning deafness must meet two conditions. When a word is not understood auditorily:

1. The word must have undergone adequate acoustic analysis as evidenced by correct repetition.
2. The semantic representation of the word must be intact as evidenced by immediate comprehension of the word when presented in written form.

Two patients reported by Kohn and Friedman (1986) displayed word-meaning deafness in mild form. They could understand many spoken words but showed the symptoms of word-meaning deafness for words they did not understand. For example, when asked to point to named objects in a picture, patient HN identified 9 out of 12 without difficulty, but for "cup" said, "cup, cup, C-U-P, cup. What is it?" Eventually he wrote *cup*, read it aloud, said, "Oh, cup", and immediately pointed to the cup in the picture.

Allport and Funnell (1981) consider word-meaning deafness to be "of great theoretical significance" (see also Allport, 1983; 1984). Intact repetition of words and sentences implies an intact early stage of auditory analysis (the stage thought to be impaired in patients with pure word deafness). Intact reading comprehension and spontaneous speech imply an intact semantic system and speech output lexicon. One might be tempted then to argue for an impairment to the auditory input lexicon, but the intact writing to dictation (with subsequent but not immediate comprehension) casts doubt on this interpretation. An alternative account is that word-meaning deafness represents a complete or partial disconnection of the auditory input lexicon from the semantic system. Entries in the auditory input lexicon can still be activated, but they are sometimes unable to cause subsequent activation of the representations of word meanings in the semantic system (Ellis, 1984a). (N.B. We shall discuss the processes that might permit words that are not understood to be written to dictation in Chapter 7.) On this account, at least some patients with severe word meaning deafness should still perform well on an auditory lexical decision task requiring the discrimination of spoken words from non-words. To the best of our knowledge such a test has not yet been carried out.

AUDITORY PHONOLOGICAL AGNOSIA

Beauvois, Dérousné, and Bastard (1980) described a patient with a very unusual and circumscribed language problem. The patient, a 58-year-old man (JL), had entirely normal spontaneous speech except if exhausted or upset, when he had some word finding problems and made occasional paraphasias. His reading aloud was good, if a little slow, and his spontaneous writing was also well preserved. JL complained, however, of some difficulties understanding spoken language, especially with new, technical scientific terms or the new names of people or towns. He reported no difficulty with old, familiar terms and names.

On more formal testing it was discovered that JL's repetition and writing to dictation of real, familiar words was almost perfect, whereas repetition and writing to dictation of invented non-words was very poor. His problem cannot have been a peripheral one because he could perceive real words perfectly well, and performed faultlessly in an "auditory lexical decision task" where he had to judge whether heard items were real words or non-words. JL's problem was not in the pronunciation of non-words either, because he read 40 "long and difficult" non-words without mistake. We are left, therefore, to locate his problem "at the level of acoustic-phonemic conversion, or at the level of the transmission of heard phonemes to spoken phonemes". In terms of our working model (Fig. 6.1) the patient's symptoms are neatly explained if we assume damage to the by-pass route, which in normals can shunt the phonemic descriptions of unfamiliar words directly from the auditory analysis system to the phoneme level, from which they can be outputted. If this by-pass route is impaired in JL his only way of repeating speech will be via the input and output lexicons [as was the case for McCarthy and Warrington's (1984) patients ORF and RAN discussed earlier]. This mode will cope quite happily with familiar words but will baulk at non-words (including new scientific terms and the names of new people or places). In such situations its only strategy will be to respond to a non-word with the most similar-sounding real word—something that JL was, in fact, capable of doing.

CATEGORY-SPECIFIC ACCESS PROBLEMS

The patient described by Yamadori and Albert (1973) showed word-meaning deafness in the sense that he could repeat and spell words he failed to comprehend. He differed from other patients with word-meaning deafness, however, in that his comprehension problems were greater for some semantic categories than others. He had particular difficulty with body parts and the names of objects in the room. Thus, "when asked to point to a chair, the patient stood up, looked around the room, then sat down, spelling to himself 'C-H-A-I-R, C-H-A-I-R'. Crossing his arms on his chest, he finally said, 'I'll have to double check that word later. I don't know'." In contrast, he showed no difficulty in understanding the names of tools, utensils, or items of clothing. (We will discuss how such patients might derive the spellings of words they fail to comprehend in Chapter 7.)

This patient fails one of Kohn and Friedman's (1986) criteria for word-meaning deafness, however, because he showed a similar, though apparently milder, category-specific comprehension problem with written words. He was also anomic, which might lead one to suggest an impairment to the semantic representations themselves. His anomia, however, was *not* category-specific, extending equally across categories of words he could and could not comprehend. Tentatively, one might propose that this patient had a problem in activating semantic representations in certain domains from the auditory input lexicon, but a general, non-specific problem in activating entries in the speech output lexicon from the semantic system.

There are other reports in the literature of patients whose problems in comprehending spoken words are greater for some semantic categories than for others. Goodglass, Klein, Carey, and James (1966) reported several different dissociations between the categories of body parts, objects, actions, colours, letters, and numbers in a study of 135 mixed aphasic patients. Unfortunately, Goodglass et al. used only six items per category in their study, so it is hard to tell genuine dissociations from random noise in the data. More secure is Warrington and McCarthy's (1983) case, VER, who had particular problems comprehending the names of inanimate objects in the context of much better comprehension of food names, flowers, and animals, thus presenting an interesting contrast to Warrington and Shallice's (1984) patient, JBR, whose comprehension of living things was impaired (see Chapter 2). We know that VER's comprehension of written words was also impaired but not, unfortunately, whether it displayed any comparable category-specificity. The repetition of words that VER could not understand was reasonably good.

Warrington and McCarthy (1983) present two arguments to support their contention that VER's deficit was one of accessing intact semantic representations. First, VER's performance in a word-picture matching task was improved by allowing more time between items in the test. This is compatible with the notion of very slow accessing of semantics from the auditory input lexicon. Secondly, although VER's overall level of performance was reasonably stable from one testing session to the next, the particular items she succeeded or failed on varied considerably. That is, there was a high degree of inconsistency in her performance from one session to another. If a patient fails to comprehend a word on one occasion but comprehends it correctly on the next, there are grounds for arguing that the semantic representation of the word was present all along but was temporarily inaccessible on the first occasion (cf. Coughlan & Warrington, 1981; Warrington & Shallice, 1979). It should be noted, though, that all patients reported so far have also experienced anomic word-finding difficulties.

SEMANTIC ERRORS IN REPETITION: "DEEP DYSPHASIA"

In 1973 Marshall and Newcombe reported the existence of an acquired reading disorder which they called "deep dyslexia". We shall look at that disorder in greater detail in Chapter 8, but its most striking feature is the occurrence of semantic errors in reading aloud, for example reading the written word *thermos* as "flask", *postage* as "stamps", or *turtle* as "crocodile".

Auditory analogues of this syndrome have been reported recently, sometimes under the heading of "deep dysphasia" (Goldblum, 1979; 1981; Michel, 1979; Michel & Andreewsky, 1983; Morton, 1980b). These patients make semantic errors when they try to repeat spoken words aloud. Thus Michel and Andreewsky's patient repeated "balloon" as "kite", "red" as "yellow", and "independence" as "meaning" (N.B. these are translations from French). Semantic errors were also made in writing to dictation. It is reported that the patient was sometimes uncertain in his responding but on other occasions was convinced he had just repeated the target word correctly.

Clearly a number of things could be going on here. Spoken words might be activating the correct semantic representations which are then misnamed or, alternatively, the spoken words may only be activating approximate conceptual areas from which the patient chooses a likely word. This latter alternative more easily explains why, when the patient was asked to write "brain", he wrote *"heart, liver, lungs ... "*, making it clear by mime, gesture and three dots after the written words that he was not sure of his answer. When asked to point to the correct body part he could only make a vague movement with his hand over his body. The patient did not make semantic errors when reading aloud or writing the names of pictures. If the above suggestion of faulty access to semantics from the auditory input lexicon is correct, then this last observation suggests separate access routes to semantics for written words and pictures.

The patient's oral repetition showed other features that are also reminiscent of a deep dyslexic's reading. He was better at repeating concrete nouns like "tree" or "pencil" than more abstract nouns like "union" or "hazard". He was poor at repeating grammatical function words like "neither" and "just", and apt too to omit or change inflections like the -er on "gardener" or the -ing on "writing". In addition, he was quite unable to repeat simple non-words, suggesting that, like the auditory phonological agnosic patient discussed earlier, he has lost the use of the non-lexical by-pass route. It may be that loss of a non-lexical route is a necessary condition for the occurrence of semantic errors in repetition, for if the route were present it should be capable of completely taking over the repetition function in a patient in whom the route via semantics is impaired.

The patient reported by Metz-Lutz and Dahl (1984) as a case of "pure word deafness" also made semantic errors in repetition and was poor at non-word repetition. This patient could identify non-verbal sounds correctly, identify melodies, tell whether a sentence was spoken in her native French or in a foreign tongue, and could distinguish statements, questions, commands, and negative sentences on the basis of intonation. Further proof of intact auditory and phonetic processing up to and including the auditory input lexicon is provided by her intact ability to distinguish spoken words from non-words. A likely account of "deep dysphasia", at least for some of these cases, is in terms of impaired access to detailed semantics from the auditory input lexicon combined with an impaired non-lexical, auditory-phonological by-pass route, and also perhaps a syntactic impairment (to account for the difficulty with function words and inflections). If a direct route exists between the auditory input lexicon and the speech output lexicon, then that route must also be impaired in patients who make semantic errors in repeating heard words.

OVERVIEW

If you are engaged in ordinary conversational interaction with someone, then the two most important sources of information are the person's voice and face. The voice conveys several different sorts of information including affective information regarding the speaker's emotional state, identity information regarding *who* is speaking, and verbal or phonetic information regarding the sounds and words being spoken. The same three sorts of information are also encoded in the visual information emanating from the moving face. Thus facial expressions convey affective information, the features of the face convey identity information (who the person is), and lip and other facial movements convey phonetic information about the sounds being spoken.

This chapter is concerned specifically with what might be termed phonetic voice processing (notably the recognition and comprehension of spoken words). Affective voice processing is discussed in Chapter 9, while all three aspects of face processing are reviewed in Chapter 4. This separation of modes of processing, which in normal life operate simultaneously and perhaps interactively, may seem typical of the academic penchant for endless subdivision, yet it is a separation which appears to be honoured in the brain. Each of the three modes of voice and face processing seems capable of being impaired independently of all the rest (Ellis, 1988a).

Patients with "pure word deafness" are impaired on phonetic voice processing yet, as far as one can glean from the case reports, can still identify speakers from voices and can still extract affective information. More convincingly, there is a condition known as "phonagnosia", in which patients are impaired at recognising individual voices while still being able to recognise the words they are saying (Van Lancker & Canter, 1982; Van Lancker, Cummings, Kreiman, & Dobkin, 1988), and another condition (to be discussed in Chapter 9) in which patients can again comprehend the verbal content of speech normally but can no longer deduce the speaker's affective state from the tone of voice. Interestingly, these last two disorders follow right hemisphere injury, whereas pure word deafness requires left hemisphere injury. The dissociations between impairments in the processing of facial identity, facial affect, and facial speech information were discussed in Chapter 4.

Therefore, as you sit conversing with an acquaintance at least six separate sets of cognitive modules are actively engaged in processing the six sorts of information just described. We say six *sets* because we know that phonetic voice processing at least requires a number of modules (Fig. 6.1) and that damage to these different speech modules results in different patterns of symptoms. In this chapter, we have discussed those patterns using a limited set of "syndrome"-type categories like "pure word deafness" and "deep dysphasia", but we suspect this is because disorders of auditory word recognition are as yet underinvestigated. We are confident that as more patients are studied in depth, these categories will first stretch and then disintegrate, leaving us to relate individual patients to theoretical models in the way we must now do for disorders of reading (see Chapter 8).

SUMMARY

Disorders of spoken word recognition dissociate from disorders of visual word recognition (Chapter 8), spoken word production (Chapter 5), lip reading (Chapter 4), voice recognition, and the processing of emotional tone-of-voice (Chapter 9). In fact, the evidence suggests that these disorders are all capable of dissociating one from another, implying the existence of separate cognitive subsystems or modules for each of these types of language processing.

Even disorders of spoken word recognition take different forms. In "pure word deafness" the patient can still read, write and speak well, and can hear and recognise non-speech sounds. Vowel perception is better than the perception of spoken consonants, suggesting an impairment of a (left hemisphere) phonetic system capable of the very fine temporal discriminations that consonant perception demands. Slowing speech down may aid comprehension by bringing the required rate of temporal discriminations within the range of the less specialised right hemisphere auditory analysis system. Patients with "pure word deafness" utilise lip movement cues to assist comprehension, and also make use of the content or topic of the conversation to facilitate word recognition.

Patients with "pure word deafness" cannot repeat spoken words any better than they can understand them. Patients with "word meaning deafness", in contrast, can repeat spoken words they still fail to understand. The patient may even be able to write the word he or she cannot comprehend, then recognise it by reading what has just been written (reading remains intact). The symptoms in these cases suggest a complete or partial disconnection of the auditory input lexicon which recognises heard words from the semantic system which comprehends them.

One case has been reported of a patient with "auditory phonological agnosia" who could understand and repeat spoken words but could not repeat invented non-words. This is interpretable as a disorder affecting a link between auditory analysis and an output phoneme level, a link whose normal purpose is to allow a child or adult to repeat a word he or she has never heard before. Separate impairments of lexical and sublexical routes for repetition are reported by McCarthy and Warrington (1984).

Whereas the comprehension problems of patients with "word meaning deafness" appear to affect all words equally, some patients have been reported with comprehension difficulties that are greater for some semantic categories than others. These may be semantic access disorders rather than impairments of the semantic representations themselves. Impairments in or around the semantic system are also implicated in so-called "deep dysphasia", where patients make semantic errors repeating spoken words.

FURTHER READING

The paucity of research into disorders of auditory word recognition is reflected in the shortage of books or articles that can be recommended as further readings. The following, however, cover aspects of the topic.

Keller, E., & Gopnik, M. (Eds) (1987). *Motor and sensory processes of language.* Hillsdale, NJ: Lawrence Erlbaum Associates. Chapters on aphasic disorders of word recognition and production.

Allport, D. A., MacKay, D. G., Prinz, W., & Scheerer, E. (1987). *Language perception and production: Shared mechanisms in listening, reading and writing.* Cognitive and neuropsychological evidence relating to the independence or otherwise of processes mediating word recognition and production.

Goldstein, M. N. (1974). Auditory agnosia for speech ("Pure word deafness"). *Brain and Language, 1,* 195–204. Useful summary of work in traditional neuropsychology.

Ellis, A. W. (1984). Introduction to Bramwell's (1897) case of word meaning deafness. *Cognitive Neuropsychology, 1,* 245–258. Reproduces Bramwell's fascinating nineteenth-century description of word meaning deafness with an Introduction discussing its significance.

Kohn, S. E., & Friedman, R. B. (1986). Word meaning deafness: A phonological-semantic dissociation. *Cognitive Neuropsychology, 3,* 291–308. Applies the cognitive neuropsychological approach to word meaning deafness.

7 Spelling and Writing

INTRODUCTION

Even the most prolific authors speak more than they write, and for the bulk of the population writing is far and away the least used of their language skills. To be aphasic is to labour under an enormous disadvantage in daily life, and even a specific reading problem can be a considerable handicap, but a specific writing difficulty is generally perceived by the patient as much less of a problem. Perhaps because of the marginal nature of writing as a linguistic skill it has, until recently, received very little attention from neuropsychologists (or, for that matter, from psycholinguists and cognitive psychologists).

In so far as traditional neuropsychologists seem to have thought about writing as a skill, they appear all to have believed it to be closely parasitic upon speech. Neuropsychologists have commonly proposed that in order to write a word you must first say it to yourself, then translate that internal string of sounds into a string of letters, and then write those letters (e.g. Déjerine, 1914; Luria, 1970). Luria (1970, pp. 323–324) expressed this view very clearly when he wrote that:

> Psychologically, the writing process involves several steps. The flow of speech is broken down into individual sounds. The phonemic significance of these sounds is identified and the phonemes represented by letters. Finally, the individual letters are integrated to produce the written word.

This view of writing may be termed a "phonic mediation theory", in that spelling is presumed to be mediated by the phonic (sound) forms of words. Recent advances in cognitive neuropsychology have, however, rendered this theory untenable. First, patients have been reported who can still spell words whose spoken forms they seem quite unable to retrieve from memory (e.g. Bub & Kertesz, 1982a; Caramazza, Berndt, & Basili, 1983; Ellis, Miller, & Sin, 1983; Levine, Calvanio, & Popovics, 1982). Secondly, Shallice (1981) has provided a detailed case study of a "phonological" dysgraphic patient who could no longer generate spellings from sounds but could still spell many familiar words.

SPELLING WITHOUT SOUND

Patient EB (Levine, Calvanio, & Popovics, 1982)

Patient EB reported by Levine, Calvanio, and Popovics (1982) was a 54-year-old engineer who was rendered totally speechless by a stroke. He made strong efforts to talk but "could only produce a few undifferentiated sounds after a great delay". His speech comprehension and reading comprehension by contrast are both described as "excellent but slow". Not only was EB mute, he also appeared to have no "inner speech"; that is, no capacity to generate the spoken forms of words internally.

This lack of inner speech showed itself when EB was given a target picture of an object and then asked to point to the picture in a further set of four whose name rhymed with the target. In an attempt to do this task EB would generate to himself the spellings of all the picture names to see if one had the same final letters as the target word. Thus if the target was a picture of a BEE and one of the set of four pictures to choose among was a TREE, EB could match the two successfully. He failed, however, if the rhyming pair were not spelled alike. Thus he failed to match the pictures BEAR and CHAIR, ROPE and SOAP, or KITE and LIGHT. Rhyme matching was equally impaired for visually dissimilar written word-forms: In such instances EB was "puzzled and insisted he could find no rhyme". He was also unable to match spoken and written non-words.

EB's ability to generate the written names of pictures to himself already implies that his writing was less impaired than his speech. In fact his writing is described as "highly successful", with only a mild and variable agrammatism. He wrote correctly the names of objects, actions, shapes, and colours, though he had an occasional difficulty on one naming test, writing STRING YARD BED for *hammock*, MOOSE RACK for *antlers*, and FIND WAY IN/OUT PUZZLE for a *maze*. Otherwise EB's spelling of real words was excellent and he was able to write extensive passages without assistance. The following is an extract from his attempt to write down his earliest memories after his stroke:

Gradually after what seemed days and days, got back enough strength to pull myself up and sit if I held on. I tilted off to the right and had a hard time maintaining my balance. The nurse and doctor and an orderly helped me up then ... I got to another part of the hospital where there were two doctors asking me questions I couldn't answer. I was scared. Nobody would tell me what happened to me.

It must be remembered that EB could have *said* none of this—his speech was reduced to inarticulate sounds. Further, Levine and his colleagues were unable to uncover evidence that EB had *any* internal access to the sounds of the words he could write. There seems no way that his writing could have been based on inner speech and the assembling of spellings from sounds in the manner long advocated by neuropsychologists.

Patient MH (Bub & Kertesz, 1982a)

We have encountered Bub and Kertesz's (1982a) patient MH in Chapter 5 as a well-described case of anomia. MH's speech was fluent but typically anomic, being circumlocutory and virtually devoid of content words. She could name hardly any pictures of objects and was unable to select out pairs of objects having names that rhymed, appearing to have no inner knowledge of the sounds of these words. Despite this she could *write* the names of objects correctly. Thus in one test, although she could only name one of a set of 20 pictures, she wrote 15 of the names correctly. When she made a spelling error, whether in picture naming or writing to dictation, she did not produce the sort of "phonic" misspelling one would expect from someone who was assembling spellings on the basis of the sounds of words. When her errors were real words they were either morphologically related to the target word (e.g. ACQUIRE for *acquisition*; TESTIMONIAL for *testimony*) or were visually similar (e.g. ABYSS for *abase*; COMPREHENSION for *apprehension*). Other errors were incorrect attempts at words which show substantial knowledge of unpredictable aspects of the target's spelling (e.g. ORCHATRIA for *orchestra*; ARCHETACT for *architect*). Finally, particularly with low-frequency words like *philosophy* or *effusive*, MH was sometimes unable to offer any sort of attempt at the spelling.   Another relevant observation is that although MH could repeat non-words like "brod" or "rosk" reasonably well she was extremely poor at generating appropriate spellings for them. Now, non-words are just possible words one has never met before, and asking someone to spell dictated non-words provides a fairly pure test of that person's ability to spell the way traditional neuropsychologists (and others) thought we spell all words; that is by breaking them down into their component sounds, accessing the appropriate letter or letters for each sound, and assembling the resulting letter string into spelling. MH's inability to do this simple test suggests that the correct spellings of many real words she was able to produce were again not generated by the process of phonic mediation. The non-phonic nature of her spelling errors lends further weight to this claim.

Patients JS (Caramazza, Berndt, & Basili, 1983) and RD (Ellis, Miller, & Sin, 1983)

The previous patient, MH, was anomic, and simply blocked at words she was unable to say. Patients JS and RD were, in contrast, neologistic jargonaphasics, which means that their speech was full of distorted, incorrect attempts at words. In Chapter 5 it was argued that these patients had a deficit affecting their speech output lexicons which left them able to retrieve only partial phonemic information about many words in their vocabularies. They were obliged, then, to generate attempts at the pronunciations of words based on that partial information. Of more direct relevance to present concerns is the fact that both JS and RD were frequently able to spell correctly words they could not say correctly. For instance, when RD was asked to say and then write the names of a set of pictures, he called a penguin a "senstenz" but then immediately wrote its name correctly. Similarly, he called an elephant an "enelust... kenelton" and a screwdriver a "kistro", but wrote both names perfectly (Ellis et al., 1983).

If writing were based on inner pronunciation, then the spellings of patients like RD and JS would surely reproduce their mispronunciations, yet they do not. In fact, when these patients did make misspellings they resembled some of MH's errors in appearing to be based on substantial but incomplete information about the word's spelling. Examples from JS (Caramazza et al., 1983, table 11) include *octopus* misspelled as OPUSPUS, *harp* as HARB... HARF, and *antlers* as ARRTAL: Examples from RD (Ellis et al., 1983, table 9) include *zebra* as ZEBARE, *candle* as CALDLE, and *giraffe* as GARFARA. (N.B. These errors were *not* transcriptions by the patients of their neologistic mispronunciations).

The fact that JS and RD could spell many words they mispronounced provides further evidence against an obligatory phonic mediation theory of spelling. The converging neuropsychological analyses of EB, MH, JS, and RD are important, and we shall be returning to these patients shortly to draw further conclusions about human spelling processes, but each of these case studies was predated by the first neuropsychological case study to cast serious doubt on phonic mediation theories of spelling, namely Shallice's (1981b) description of a case of "phonological" dysgraphia in his patient PR.

"Phonological" Dysgraphia

Patient PR, described by Shallice (1981b), is particularly interesting because his dysgraphia might easily have passed unnoticed and even undetected had not its theoretical significance been appreciated. PR had been a computer salesman before suffering a left hemisphere stroke in his mid-50's. Initially he had the speech disturbance of a "conduction" aphasic (good comprehension, poor repetition, spontaneous speech replete with phonemic errors), but by the time his writing was tested he is described as having quite normal speech comprehension combined with fluent speech production with good word choice and only occasional paraphasic errors.

PR's reading is described as rapid and effortless and he performed at quite high levels on several reading tests. His spontaneous writing is said to have been laboured and slow because of slight motor problems and difficulties of formulation. Nevertheless, he was able to write correctly over 90% of a set of common words dictated to him. He found abstract and less common words more difficult, but even here he was writing 80% or more correctly. PR's errors were predominantly morphological (e.g. "navigation" written as NAVIGATOR; "defect" as DEFECTION) or structurally similar real words which often sounded like the target word (e.g. "custom" misspelled as CUSTARD; "plum" as THUMB; "quart" as CAUGHT).

Although PR made some spelling errors, his writing of most real words (with the exception of function words, which he found difficult) was good. This stood in marked contrast to his extremely poor writing of invented non-words. PR was able to create appropriate spellings for only 2 of 10 four-letter non-words like "spid", and none of 10 six-letter non-words like "felute". Indeed, although he could write individual letters to dictation when given their names (e.g. K for "kay"; H for "aitch") he could not write letters when given their sounds (e.g. K for "kuh"; H for "huh"). Now a failure to write non-words could obviously be due to a failure to perceive them, or perhaps an inability to say them. Neither of these explanations is applicable to PR who could repeat non-words aloud (and therefore could both hear and say them), and was even reasonably good at reading them aloud. When PR *did* manage to write a non-word correctly he often commented that he had used a real word as a mediator; for example he spelled "sim" as SYM via *symbol* and "jund" as JUND via *junta* and *junk*. This strategy sometimes led to errors as when, in his attempt to write "sult" via *assault* he wrote AULT, and when he wrote GN for "na" via *gnat*. That noted, it is PR's good spelling of real words in the context of his virtual inability to spell simple non-words that is crucial to the current argument.

THE GRAPHEMIC OUTPUT LEXICON

None of the patients EB, MH, JS, RD, and PR can have been assembling spellings piecemeal from sound, yet all showed considerably preserved writing ability. Their spellings must, therefore, have been produced by some process other than assembly from sound. It would appear that these patients retrieved (or attempted to retrieve) the spellings of familiar words from some internal long-term memory store whose function in writing is equivalent to that of the speech output lexicon held responsible in Chapter 5 for the retrieval of spoken word-forms in spontaneous speech. We shall refer to this proposed store of word spellings as the *graphemic output lexicon*; alternative names in the literature for the same concept are the graphic or graphemic output logogen system (Ellis, 1982; Morton, 1980a), the orthographic lexicon (Allport & Funnell, 1981; Allport, 1983), and the graphemic word production system (Ellis, 1984b).

The idea being proposed is that each time you learn the spelling of a new word, an entry for that spelling is stored in a discrete portion of your memory that we are calling the graphemic output lexicon. Every time you write that word subsequently, that representation in the graphemic output lexicon will be activated and will make the spelling available to you. The spelling need no longer be assembled from the sound of the word. Having postulated this system we can now begin to ask further questions about it, some of which we will be able to answer by reference to findings in cognitive neuropsychology. Such questions include: How is spelling information represented in the graphemic output lexicon? Is retrieval from that lexicon all-or-nothing, or can one sometimes have partial information available about a word's spelling? Is the graphemic output lexicon a distinct and separate word store from the speech output lexicon? What sort of input or inputs activate entries in the graphemic output lexicon? We shall take these questions one at a time.

The Representation of Information in the Graphemic Output Lexicon

We can imagine a possible system which represents the spellings of words in terms of, say, the sequence of muscular movements necessary to write the word. There are, however, fairly straightforward reasons for rejecting this as a model of the human graphemic output lexicon. The reason is the number of different ways we can "produce" a spelling. Within the handwriting mode, one can print a word in capitals, print it in lower case letters, or write it in cursive (connected) handwriting. Each of these styles has its own letter forms, for example F, f, and f, or B, b, and b, yet to know how to spell a word is to be able to spell it in any of these styles. Further, if you can spell a word you can also spell it aloud and perhaps type it too. Whatever is represented in and retrieved from the graphemic output lexicon is presumably some abstract "graphemic" description of a letter sequence which can then be outputted in each of these different ways (Ellis, 1982).

Neuropsychological support can be found for the proposal that what is retrieved from the graphemic output lexicon is an abstract graphemic code rather than, say, a motor program for letter execution. Rosati and de Bastiani (1979) reported the case of a 62-year-old, Italian farmer and ex-telegraphist with intact speech production, speech comprehension and reading, whose stroke resulted in a fairly pure agraphic disturbance. He could spell words aloud without error (de Bastiani, personal communication), but his attempts to write words were replete with omissions, repetitions and transpositions of letters and letter strokes. This patient's intact spelling aloud attests to his preserved ability to retrieve spellings from his graphemic output lexicon; his deficit must have lain in the selection, sequencing and execution of letter forms for handwriting. Other cases of "pure dysgraphia" with relatively isolated writing problems will be discussed later.

Retrieval from the Graphemic Output Lexicon

Patients JS (Caramazza et al., 1983) and RD (Ellis et al., 1983) were mentioned earlier as cases whose written naming was better than their spoken naming. They could write correctly many words which they mispronounced as neologisms when trying to say them. Nevertheless, spelling was not perfectly preserved in either case: Both produced errors which were interpreted earlier as being based on partial but incomplete knowledge of the correct spellings of words. For example, when RD was shown a picture of a pair of scissors he wrote SICESSE. This error is typical, firstly in that it was not a transcription of his neologistic attempt to say the word, and secondly because it demonstrates substantial knowledge of the idiosyncratic spelling of the word *scissors*. There has been a *c* in the English spelling of *scissors* only since it was put there by spelling "reformers" in the sixteenth century. Those men thought *scissors* was a descendent of the Latin word *scindere* (meaning to cleave) and, therefore, inserted a *c* in the spelling where no *c* had been before. As it happens, they were wrong—scissors is actually descended from the Latin *cædere* (to cut)—but the *c*, which is totally unpredictable from the pronunciation and has to be something you just have to know about the word, has stuck. And RD knew it should be there, just as JS knew that the second sound in *pyramid* is spelled with a *y* though he misspelled the word PYMINIA… PYMINAL… PYAMIAL. Errors demonstrating such "partial lexical knowledge" (Ellis, 1982) are quite common, and seem not to be tied to any particular form of aphasia or dysgraphia.

The Distinctness of the Graphemic Output Lexicon and the Speech Output Lexicon

One can envisage a possible model of word production in which the written and spoken forms of words are two outputs from a single internal word store or lexicon. We would seem, however, to have good neuropsychological grounds for rejecting this notion in favour of a model in which the word store for spoken forms (our speech output lexicon) and the word store for written forms (our graphemic output lexicon) are conceived of as separate and discrete lexicons. In Chapter 5 we followed Saffran (1982), Allport (1983), and others in interpreting certain anomic word-finding problems in speech production as due to a partial disconnection of the speech output lexicon from the semantic system. Now, if retrieving word-forms for speech and writing were but two aspects of the same system in operation, then a patient who experiences word-finding problems in speech should experience similar problems in spelling. We have already seen, however, that this is not always the case. Bub and Kertesz's (1982a) patient MH and Hier and Mohr's (1977) patient AF were severely anomic in speech but had much less severe problems of word finding for writing. This is not possible under a single output lexicon model, but is readily accounted for if the speech and graphemic output lexicons are separate word stores which can be impaired separately and disconnected both from each other and from the other components of the language system.

A further argument for the separability of the two word production systems can be derived from cases JS and RD (Caramazza et al., 1983; Ellis et al., 1983). In the previous section we interpreted their spelling errors as due to their ability on some occasions to retrieve only partial information from their graphemic output lexicons. The phonological errors in the speech of these two patients are susceptible to a similar interpretation—this time as attempts at spoken targets based on partial phonemic information. Now, if there were only one word production system, an impairment affecting it should hamper both speech and writing equally. Speech and writing *were* both affected in JS and RD, but speech more so than writing, and the neologistic errors made in speech were different from those made in writing. One could try to explain this particular pattern on a single output lexicon model were it not for the fact that JS and RD seem to be unusual in having better preserved writing than spelling. The normal pattern among such patients is for spelling to be more severely impaired than speech (Kertesz, 1979). Thus, when contrasted with the more usual pattern, JS and RD provide a "double dissociation" between impairments affecting the speech and graphemic output lexicons, which in turn implies that the two systems are separate components of the total language system. The question of whether we are right to propose distinct lexicons for input and output will be dealt with more fully in Chapter 8.

The Nature of the Input to the Graphemic Word Production System

Each entry in the graphemic output lexicon corresponds to the spelling of a familiar word. The question under consideration here is how are those entries accessed? What inputs from what other systems serve to activate them? One possibility is that they receive their activation from the corresponding units in the speech output lexicon. That is, in writing, we might first activate the semantic representation of a word, then activate its representation in the speech output lexicon, then transmit that activation through one-to-one connections between corresponding representations in the two output lexicons to the graphemic output lexicon. This proposal is an attractive one for at least three reasons. First, when writing we are usually aware of an "inner voice" saying the words as we write them. Thus, we do seem habitually to activate the spoken forms of words as we are activating their graphemic forms. Secondly, a form of involuntary slip of the pen, which most people will be aware of having made from time to time, is unintentionally writing a word which has the same sound, or a similar sound, to the desired target word. Examples from Hotopf (1980) include SCENE written unwittingly when the intended target word was *seen*, THEIR written for *there*, SOUGHT for *sort*, SURGE for *search*, and COULD for *good*. These slips are explicable if the sounds of words play a part in selecting their spellings from the graphemic output lexicon. Note that these slips are *not* due to spellings being incorrectly assembled from sounds, because the errors are always real words, whereas assembling spellings would often yield non-words such as SURCH for *search* (as happens in genuine spelling errors as opposed to slips of the pen), and also because the errors produced are sometimes themselves irregular spellings which would not be generated by phoneme–grapheme (sound-to-letter) conversion procedures (words like COULD and SCENE).

A third reason for believing that the sound of a word plays some part in retrieving spellings from the graphemic output lexicon is that some acquired dysgraphic patients produce among their errors real words which are similar in sound to the targets. Like the normal slips of the pen, these are sometimes themselves irregular spellings (which argues against their having been assembled from the sound of the target words) and, in the case of Shallice's (1981b) phonological dysgraphic patient PR, occurred in the context of an almost complete inability to assemble spellings from sounds. Examples of such errors from PR's writing to dictation include "plum" misspelled as THUMB, "chore" as SHORE, and "quart" as CAUGHT.

Thus there is good evidence for some involvement of the sound patterns of words in retrieving spellings from the graphemic output lexicon (cf. Morton, 1980a), but there are also grounds for doubting that phonology is the *only* source of input to that system. MH (Bub & Kertesz, 1982a) is once again relevant here. She could write correctly words whose sound forms she did know, which argues for a mode of retrieval from the graphemic word production system which does not depend exclusively upon activating phonemic forms in the speech output lexicon.

A similar conclusion is indicated from the pattern of symptoms found in another patient reported by Bub and Kertesz (1982b). The patient in question manifested the symptoms of an acquired dysgraphia sometimes called "deep" dysgraphia, which we shall now consider.

Semantic Errors in Writing: The Case of "Deep Dysgraphia"

In Chapter 5 we looked briefly at a condition sometimes called "deep dysphasia" in which patients make semantic errors when attempting to repeat heard words. "Deep dyslexia", where semantic errors are made in reading aloud, will be discussed in the next chapter. Some "deep dyslexics" have been reported to make semantic errors when trying to write words to dictation. For example, when Newcombe and Marshall's (1980a) patient GR was asked to write "star" he wrote MOON. Eleven out of 31 errors obtained in a writing-to-dictation task were either straightforward semantic errors of this sort or misspelled semantic errors [e.g. "cousin" spelt as NEPHIL (= nephew), or "parrot" as CANISTY (= canary)]. Saffran, Schwartz, and Marin (1976b) report two patients who made errors such as writing TIME for "hours" or ORCHID for "lilac", and Peuser (1978) describes similar errors as being produced by a German patient, but the most complete description of "deep dysgraphia" to date is that provided by Bub and Kertesz (1982b) for their patient JC.

JC was a 21-year-old woman who had suffered a left hemisphere stroke. Her speech was the halting, telegraphic speech of a Broca's aphasic. Her comprehension of single spoken words and yes/no questions was good, though she had problems with longer and more complex sentences (presumably the syntactic deficit characteristic of at least some "Broca's" aphasics—see Chapter 9). What is of greatest current concern, however, is JC's writing. When asked to write to dictation 20 concrete and 20 abstract nouns of roughly equal length and frequency of usage in English, she correctly wrote 17 out of 20 concrete nouns but only 9 out of 20 abstract nouns. Whether a word was regularly or irregularly spelled appeared not to influence JC's performance, but she was fairly poor at writing function words (only 6/20 correct despite the fact noted elsewhere that they are far and away the most common words in the language).

Many of JC's writing errors were semantic errors. For example she wrote "time" as CLOCK, "sky" as SUN, "desk" as CHAIR, but "chair" as TABLE! Her errors with function words were either omissions (i.e. "don't knows") or substitutions of other function words; for example "our" written as MY, and "they" as THEIR. JC was also very poor at writing non-words to dictation, managing only 5 out of 20 four-letter non-words and 0 out of 17 eight-letter non-words.

There are two other noteworthy aspects of JC's "deep" dysgraphia. The first is that unlike, say, Newcombe and Marshall's (1980a) patient GR, it was not accompanied by a deep dyslexia. JC did not make semantic errors when reading aloud; in fact her reading and understanding of single words was very good. Even her non-word reading was far better than her non-word spelling, though she had something of a tendency to read non-words as words, for example reading *dosh* as "gosh", and *cred* as "shred".

The second noteworthy aspect is that JC's deep dysgraphic symptoms had entirely disappeared 6 months after her stroke, when she no longer made semantic writing errors, was as good at spelling abstract nouns as concrete nouns, and even spelled non-words quite well. As Bub and Kertesz (1982b) note, this fact rules out any explanation of her earlier difficulties as due to any developmental difficulties existing in JC before her stroke. It also implies that her symptoms should be explained as having been due to processes becoming temporarily inaccessible or inefficient rather than being totally abolished.

How does JC's pattern of symptoms relate to our question concerning the nature of the inputs to the graphemic output lexicon? We have already argued for one input from the speech output lexicon, and could persist with that if we could provide a satisfactory account of JC's symptoms on such a model. This would necessitate proposing that JC's semantic errors are errors of spoken word retrieval which are then translated into semantic writing errors. There is, however, no evidence that JC was prone to making semantic errors in selecting words for speech. She did not make semantic errors in reading aloud, repeating heard words, or naming objects. Bub and Kertesz (1982b), like Morton (1980a) and Ellis (1982) propose that there is a second direct input from the semantic system to the graphemic output lexicon. It is presumably some impairment to this connection in JC that accounts for her semantic errors in writing and also for the superiority of concrete over abstract words in writing that was not shown in reading or repetition.

JC would appear, therefore, to provide cognitive neuropsychological evidence for a second, semantic input to the graphemic output lexicon. Ellis (1982; 1984b) suggests that occasional errors of this route in normals may be responsible for the small number of semantic slips of the pen (e.g. involuntarily writing SPEAKING for *reading* or LAST WEEK for *next week*) that have been reported by Ellis (1979b) and Hotopf (1987; 1983). Presumably, however, the fact that the desired entry in the graphemic output lexicon is specified from *two* sources, one from the semantic system and one from the speech output lexicon, helps reduce any intrinsic liability to error in the system.

A MODEL FOR SPELLING

What emerges from the foregoing discussion is a theory of writing which can be expressed diagrammatically as in Fig. 7.1. Much of the model (the upper, central, and lower-left portions) is a simple redrawing of the model for auditory word recognition and speech production that we developed in Chapters 5 and 6 (see Fig. 6.1, p. 145). The new elements, added to that model to incorporate a writing facility, are the graphemic output lexicon, the grapheme level, phoneme–grapheme conversion, plus their connections one to another and to the other components of the total system.

To summarise and recapitulate briefly, the auditory analysis system and the auditory input lexicon mediate the recognition of heard words and activate their meanings in the semantic system. To say a word, its entry in the semantic system is used to retrieve its pronunciation (phonemic form) from the speech output lexicon. To write a familiar word whose spelling is known, the entry for that word in the graphemic output lexicon is activated. This activation comes from the semantic system and also from the speech output lexicon. Semantic writing errors are errors in activation from the semantic system; similar-sound errors are errors in activation from the speech output lexicon. What is released from the graphemic output lexicon is a string of graphemes; that is, an abstract description of the letter sequence which can be output as print, handwriting, typing, oral spelling, or whatever.

We must not forget that skilled writers *can* assemble plausible attempts at the spellings of unfamiliar words using procedures for translating spoken (phonemic) forms into letter strings. We have argued that this mode of spelling is not, as some have proposed, the sole strategy for spelling any word, but there is no doubt that it exists as an optional strategy for creating spellings of words not stored in the graphemic output lexicon. We have represented this strategy as being mediated by phoneme–grapheme conversion processes linking the phoneme level to the grapheme

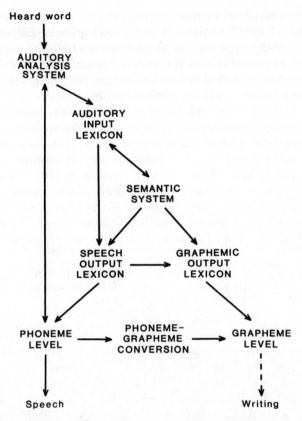

Heard word

FIG. 7.1. Simple functional model for spelling, showing the proposed relations between auditory word recognition, speech production, and spelling.

level. In practice this single box must encompass a number of processes. To assemble a spelling the spoken form of a word must first be broken down into its phonemes (sounds). Each phoneme must then be replaced by the appropriate letter or letters, and the resultant letter string must be stored as it is being created. With a regular word there is a reasonable chance that the assembled attempt will be correct, but the vagaries of English spelling are such that many words are likely to be misspelled this way (Hatfield & Patterson, 1983). The resultant misspellings, diagnostic of the involvement of phoneme–grapheme conversion, will be misspellings which, when pronounced, sound like the target word (e.g. CASSEL for *castle*, or TAYBUL for *table*). Such misspellings are, of course, common in children who have yet to build up a large stock of entries in their graphemic output lexicons and so must resort to assembled spelling more often than a more practiced adult (Ellis, 1984b).

How does our model account for the patients we have already encoun-tered in this chapter? Levine, et al.'s (1982) patient EB, who showed preserved writing in the context of completely abolished overt and inner speech, had presumably lost the use of his speech output lexicon and phoneme level but retained the use of the remaining language components including those used in writing familiar words.

Patient MH of Bub and Kertesz (1982a) was anomic in speech, indicating an impairment in activating entries in the speech output lexicon from the semantic system (cf. Chapter 5, pp. 116–124). She was less anomic in writing, implying less difficulty activating entries in the gra-phemic output lexicon. Some of MH's errors involved "partial lexical knowledge", where only part of the spelling can be retrieved from the graphemic output lexicon (e.g. writing ORCHATRIA for "orchestra"). MH was also unable to assemble spellings for non-words she could repeat correctly, implying impairment to the phoneme–grapheme conversion component.

Shallice's (1981b) "phonological" dysgraphic patient PR who could spell many real words correctly but very few non-words is also assumed to have suffered impairment to the phoneme–grapheme conversion system. Like "phonological" dysgraphics, "deep" dysgraphics have virtually inoperative phoneme–grapheme conversion and must rely en-tirely on whole-word retrieval from the graphemic output lexicon system. Indeed, two of the four "phonological" dysgraphics reported by Ro-eltgen, Sevush, and Heilman (1983) made some semantic errors, so it is not clear where the dividing line between these two putative "syndromes" should be drawn. As elsewhere, we shall interpret and draw conclusions from single patients rather than from "syndrome" categories of uncertain status.

We have argued earlier that an impairment to the route between the semantic system and the graphemic output lexicon must be present for semantic writing errors to occur in any numbers. It is also at least arguable that an impairment to phoneme–grapheme conversion is a necessary condition for the occurrence of semantic errors. For instance, it is hard to imagine that JC would have written CLOCK for "time" or CHAIR for "desk" if intact phoneme–grapheme conversion procedures could have treated "time" and "desk" as non-words and at least generated *t* as the only likely initial letter for "time" and *d* as the only likely initial letter for "desk". We are not arguing that this route prevents semantic errors in normals which might otherwise occur in large numbers, only that a phoneme–grapheme impairment must be present *as well as* a semantic transmission impairment before semantic writing errors will occur.

INTACT SPELLING IN "WORD MEANING DEAFNESS"

In Chapter 6 we encountered the phenomenon of "word meaning deafness", where patients can hear and repeat spoken words but may be unable to understand the words they hear. Of relevance to this chapter is the fact that at least some of these patients may also be able to write correctly the words they fail to understand. If their reading comprehension is intact they can then read what they have just written and so understand what has just been said to them. The example we quoted in Chapter 6 occurred when Bramwell (1897) asked such a patient: "Do you like to come to Edinburgh?" The patient failed to comprehend his question but wrote it down, read it, then replied appropriately (see Ellis, 1984a).

The spelling to dictation without comprehension displayed by these patients is not assembled by phoneme–grapheme conversion, because they do not make "phonic" errors and they spell irregular words correctly (Kohn & Friedman, 1986; Patterson, 1986). The spellings of the words they write without understanding must therefore be retrieved from the graphemic output lexicon. But what is the route from auditory input to writing output that permits such retrieval while by-passing the semantic system? Patterson (1986) proposes a route from the auditory input lexicon to the graphemic output lexicon via the speech output lexicon. The suggestion is that one-to-one connections between entries in the auditory input lexicon and the speech output lexicon allow heard words directly to activate their entries in the speech output lexicon. One-to-one connections of the sort we have already discussed between corresponding entries in the speech output lexicon and the graphemic output lexicon would then allow the spellings of the heard words to be retrieved using a route which is a lexical, whole-word route but which entirely by-passes the representations of word meanings in the semantic system. Although this proposal works, Patterson (1986) admits that the evidence favouring it over alternatives such as direct connections between entries in the auditory input lexicon and the graphemic output lexicon could be stronger.

ASSEMBLING SPELLINGS FROM SOUND: "SURFACE" DYSGRAPHIA

Beauvois and Dérousné (1981) described a French patient, RG, whose writing problems are almost the precise opposite to Shallice's patient PR. Whereas PR wrote words well but non-words very poorly, RG could produce plausible spellings for non-words with ease, but also wrote real words as if they were non-words. That is, he would produce a phonologically plausible spelling for each word, but the vagaries of French spelling meant that those spellings were often incorrect. For example, RG misspelled "habile" as ABILE and HABIL, "fauteuil" as FAUTEUI and FHOTEUIL, "rameau" as RAMO, and "copeau" as COPOT. French, like English, has so few words whose spellings can be predicted with confidence from their pronunciations that the successful speller really must store the spellings of familiar words in memory, not assemble them from sound. If you are a phonological speller of French or English your attempts are much more likely to be correct for regular words than irregular words. This was certainly true of RG who spelled correctly over 90% of regular, predictably-spelled words, but less than 40% of irregular words.

Like RG, Hatfield and Patterson's (1983) patient TP became a phonological speller after a stroke. Her picture is slightly more complex than RG's but perhaps even more informative as a consequence. Because TP's spelling was predominantly phonological she was more successful at spelling regular words than irregular words and many of her spelling errors were straightforwardly "phonic" (e.g. FLUD for "flood", LAF for "laugh", ANSER for "answer", and NEFFUE for "nephew"). The complications in the picture, which show that TP was not always spelling from sound alone, were:

1. She managed to spell correctly on at least one occasion quite a few irregular words, including COUGH, SIGN, AUNT, and ANSWER. This shows that she had not entirely lost the capacity for spelling from memory. (The same probably holds true for RG.)

2. Some of TP's misspellings clearly show partial knowledge of word-specific spellings. One cannot, as TP did, misspell "sword" as SWARD without retrieving from the graphemic output lexicon the fact that *sword* contains an unpronounced *w*, just as one cannot misspell "yacht" as YHAGHT without having retrieved the fact that there is a silent *h* and that the vowel letter is *a* not, as one would expect from the pronunciation, *o*. These errors show that TP could sometimes still retrieve some information about words she could not spell entirely correctly.

3. If a word TP was asked to write was a homophone she would sometimes produce the other member of the homophonic pair as an error, even when the context made it perfectly clear which meaning was meant. Thus she misspelled "sale" as SAIL, "hale" as HAIL, and "pane" as PAIN, though on other occasions she misspelled "hail" as HALE, "pain" as PANE and "plain" as PLANE. Of importance is the fact that sometimes the homophonic misspellings were themselves irregular spellings (e.g. "moan" misspelled as MOWN, "write" as RIGHT, and "sum" as SOME). We have proposed earlier that homophone errors arise from an input to the graphemic output lexicon from the speech output lexicon.

In terms of Fig. 7.1, TP clearly has an impaired graphemic output lexicon. She can no longer access the entries for many words that were undoubtedly once within her spelling vocabulary. There are some words, however, for which she can still retrieve partial information. If a word's spelling is completely inaccessible but has an alternative homophonic spelling, TP can still sometimes access the homophone. Failing that, her last resort is to assemble a plausible attempt at the word's spelling from its sound using her intact processes of phoneme–grapheme conversion.

The pattern shown by TP and RG of many phonic errors with poor spelling of irregular words has been given several different labels by different investigators, including "surface dysgraphia" (by analogy with "surface dyslexia"—see Chapter 8), "lexical" or "orthographic dysgraphia", and "phonological spelling". As we noted in Chapter 1, all this confusing terminology, based as it is in the desire to label syndromes, can be a positive hindrance. Our concern is with explaining patterns of disorders in individual patients in terms of impairment to one or more of the components of a model of normal cognitive processing, and within the framework of that approach all the patients we have just been discussing have impairments that affect the retrieval of the spellings of once-familiar words from the graphemic output lexicon. Because phoneme–grapheme conversion remains intact they can still spell many regular words correctly, can generate misspellings which sound like the target word, and can also generate plausible spellings for invented non-words.

A close inspection of the cases reported so far who show this pattern reveals that in none of them is retrieval from the graphemic output lexicon entirely abolished. All of them remain capable of spelling correctly at least a few highly irregular words. In three cases, the irregular words which remain accessible have been shown to be the more common (high-frequency) irregular words like *talk, noise,* or *head*. The cases in question are MW and JG of Goodman and Caramazza (1986a; 1986b; 1986c; Goodman-Schulman & Caramazza, 1987), and HG of Coltheart and Funnell (1987). We saw in our discussion in Chapter 6, how in some "anomic" and "neologistic jargonaphasic" patients, the retrieval of common (high-frequency) words may be spared when a lexicon (or access to it) is impaired. The retrieval of high-frequency words, both irregular and regular, seems to be similarly spared in these dysgraphic patients when an impairment in or around the graphemic output lexicon prevents the full and correct retrieval of less commonly used (low-frequency) words.

EXTERNALISING THE GRAPHEMIC CODE

Handwriting probably remains the most common way of expressing one's knowledge of spelling, but it is certainly not the only way. Typing, spelling aloud—even Morse code or arranging plastic letters—are alternative ways of tapping spelling skill. We shall assume that the same processes are involved in retrieving the spellings of familiar words or generating plausible spellings for unfamiliar words or non-words, whichever of these alternative modes of output is to be employed. That is, we shall assume that these different modes diverge after the grapheme level.

We shall concentrate here on disorders affecting handwriting at or below the grapheme level in patients whose spelling aloud, for example, remains well preserved. We should note, though, that the alternative output modes seem subject to their own disorders. Thus, Kinsbourne and Warrington (1965) report a patient whose oral spelling was more impaired than his written spelling. Critchley (1942) even reports acquired disorders of Morse and flag signalling in brain-injured naval signalmen.

Ellis (1982) proposed that at least two stages below the grapheme level should be identified in the production of handwriting. These stages are shown in Fig. 7.2. Each letter of the alphabet can take different forms which, following linguistic terminology, we may call "allographs". F, ℨ, f and ℱ are all allographs of the same grapheme which may co-exist in one person's handwriting, as B, b and ℔, or S, s and ﹏ may. In Ellis' model, then, the first step towards externalising a graphemic representation as handwriting involves the selection of the desired allographic form of each letter. This creates a representation at the *allograph level*.

For Ellis (1982) the allographic representation is a quasi-spatial description of the *shape* of each letter-form. The representation at the allographic level does not yet specify the sequence of *strokes* required to create a letter-form on paper. The sequence of strokes comprising a particular allograph is what Van Galen (1980) calls its *graphic motor pattern*. The final stage in Fig. 7.2 is therefore the retrieval or assembly of graphic motor patterns which will guide the movement of the pen in forming the handwriting.

Now a model such as this, however elegant, is only of use if it helps account for aspects of normal or impaired writing performance. Ellis (1982) sought to show how such a model could help account for different types of involuntary "slip of the pen" errors made by normal writers involving misorderings, omissions, additions, or malformations of letters. Here we shall attempt to show how such a model can help explain different types of acquired dysgraphia affecting the production of handwriting. These are what may be termed "peripheral" dysgraphias, because although writing output is impaired, central spelling knowledge appears

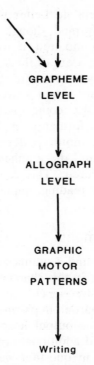

GRAPHEME
LEVEL

ALLOGRAPH
LEVEL

GRAPHIC
MOTOR
PATTERNS

Writing

FIG. 7.2. Processes "downstream" of the grapheme level required to explain the production of handwriting.

to be intact. We shall not attempt an exhaustive survey of the peripheral dysgraphias but will instead discuss selected dysgraphias which seem to affect different stages of planning from the grapheme level to actual writing.

PERIPHERAL DYSGRAPHIAS

Grapheme Level Impairment

Miceli, Silveri, and Caramazza (1985; 1987) describe the case of a 64-year-old lawyer, FV, with no detectable aphasia or dyslexia, whose writing was marred by frequent spelling errors. The errors consisted of additions, deletions, substitutions, and transpositions of letters. Spelling accuracy was unaffected by grammatical class, word frequency or imageability, but long words were less likely to be written correctly by FV than short ones. Although spelling was impaired, copying of written words was intact (even when a delay was introduced between presentation and response). Errors occurred with roughly equal probability across all word positions—initial letters were no better preserved than middle or end ones. Letters were well formed though the words were misspelled. Non-word spelling was also impaired, if anything slightly more than real word spelling, but the errors were of the same sort in both situations.

The deficit in FV must have been after the point at which the familiar word route via the graphemic output lexicon and the non-word route via phoneme–grapheme conversion come together; that is, at or below the grapheme level. Intact letter formation implies normal functioning at and below the level of graphic motor patterns. Miceli et al. (1985; 1987) locate the deficit in or around the grapheme level where abstract letter forms are stored and ordered. The complete preservation of other language skills, in particular reading, implies that the processes impaired in FV are specific to writing.

Allograph Level Impairment

Patient MW of Goodman and Caramazza (1986a; 1986b; 1986c) was mentioned in passing earlier in this chapter as one of those patients who could spell correctly high-frequency but not low-frequency irregular words. On that basis, a partial impairment affecting the retrieval of spellings from the graphemic output lexicon was suggested. However, MW's handwriting contained additional errors that were not seen in his spelling aloud. The errors in question were letter substitutions which caused him, for example, to miswrite "starve" as *starze*, "bump" as *bumd*, and "pierce" as *tierce*.

These letter substitutions also affected MW's attempts to write non-words, though not his attempts to spell them aloud. Thus, for "vand" he wrote *lond*, and for "reesh" he wrote *reech*. The errors, then, are arising at or below the level at which the mechanisms for writing familiar words and non-words converge; that is, at or below the grapheme level. The fact that letter substitutions were absent from MW's spelling aloud excludes the grapheme level as the locus of the impairment. Goodman and Caramazza (1986a; 1986b; 1986c) argue that the fact that MW's letters were correctly shaped, formed and executed also excludes the level of graphic motor patterns and conclude that "the allographic process for assigning the visual shape to a graphemic unit is impaired". So for words and non-words that MW could spell aloud correctly the grapheme level representation was intact and correct. However, that representation could no longer reliably guide the selection of letter shapes (allographs) for writing. Incorrect allographs were sometimes selected, with the result that MW substituted well-formed and well-executed but erroneous letters in the place of intended letters.

Impairment in Selecting Graphic Motor Patterns

A patient whose impairment lies at the level of assembling or retrieving graphic motor patterns should be able to spell aloud correctly, and should know the shapes of the letters required to write a word, but should not always know what sequence of pen movements will serve to create those letters on the page. A patient who seems to approximate this description has been described by Baxter and Warrington (1986). IDT's speech was fluent and his ability to spell words aloud was also normal, yet he was totally unable to write even common, three-letter words correctly. His writing errors, which extended to writing single letters of the alphabet, involved writing incorrect letters, incomplete letters, and forms which looked like fusions of two letters.

IDT's preserved spelling aloud implies an intact grapheme level, and his ability to describe the shapes of letters suggests that he could still activate letter forms at the allograph level. IDT could *copy* words and letters well and did not have more general apraxic disorders of motor planning or execution. Baxter and Warrington (1986, p. 374) conclude from this that IDT's difficulty "occurs at the level which specifies the motor sequences or 'graphic motor pattern'".

Impairment in Executing Graphic Motor Patterns: "Afferent" Dysgraphia

In the final type of "peripheral dysgraphia" we shall discuss, patients seem to get as far as knowing the sequence of movements (the graphic motor pattern) that would create the letters they wish to write, yet they have problems executing those movement sequences correctly. The peripheral dysgraphia in question is often referred to as either "spatial" dysgraphia (Hécaen & Marcie, 1974) or "afferent" dysgraphia (Lebrun, 1976; 1985). These patients usually show a tendency to write down the right-hand side of the page, difficulty maintaining a straight, horizontal writing line, and a tendency to either omit or duplicate letters and strokes in their writing. All of these features can be seen to a degree in the writing samples from patient VB of Ellis, Young, and Flude (1987b) shown in Figs 7.3 and 7.4. Figure 7.3 is a sample of her spontaneous writing done on a horizontally positioned sheet of paper. The tendency to leave a wide left margin and to write down the right-hand side of the page is clear. There is also a slight sloping of the lines, though this was not as pronounced a tendency in VB as in some other "afferent" dysgraphics.

Figure 7.4 shows the characteristic omissions and repetitions in both upper-case (capitals) and cursive handwriting. These errors tend to occur when the patient is attempting to write a sequence of similar or identical

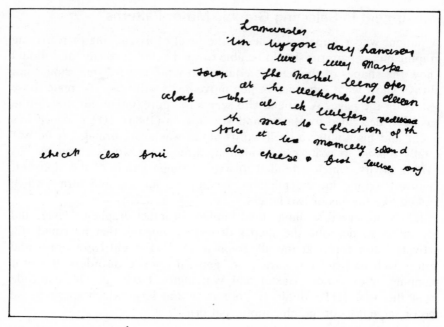

FIG. 7.3. Sample of the spontaneous handwriting of patient VB (from Ellis, Young, & Flude, 1987b).

letters or strokes. Thus doubled letters may be reduced to singles (goggles → gogles) or tripled (gallon → galllon), and strokes will be omitted or added from letters like m or w which contain repeated similar strokes.

As Lebrun (1976) and Ellis et al. (1987b) note, these omissions and repetitions of letters and strokes do not only occur in "afferent" dysgraphics like VB. They occur infrequently in the writing of normal people as involuntary "slips of the pen" (Ellis, 1979b; 1982), and their frequency can be greatly increased in normals by preventing sight of the writing hand and/or by requiring normal writers to perform an additional, secondary task such as counting or tapping with the left hand while writing (Smyth & Silvers, 1987). Ellis et al. (1987b) found that normal subjects writing without being able to see their writing hand, and simultaneously tapping with the fingers of their left hand, made as many errors in writing words to dictation as VB made under normal writing conditions. Furthermore, the normal subjects' errors were of the sort VB herself made— predominantly omissions and repetitions of letters and strokes. Examples of the errors made by the normal subjects are shown in Fig. 7.5.

Therefore, a normal subject writing while without sight of the writing hand and carrying out an additional task such as tapping or counting, effectively becomes an "afferent" dysgraphic. The difference, of course,

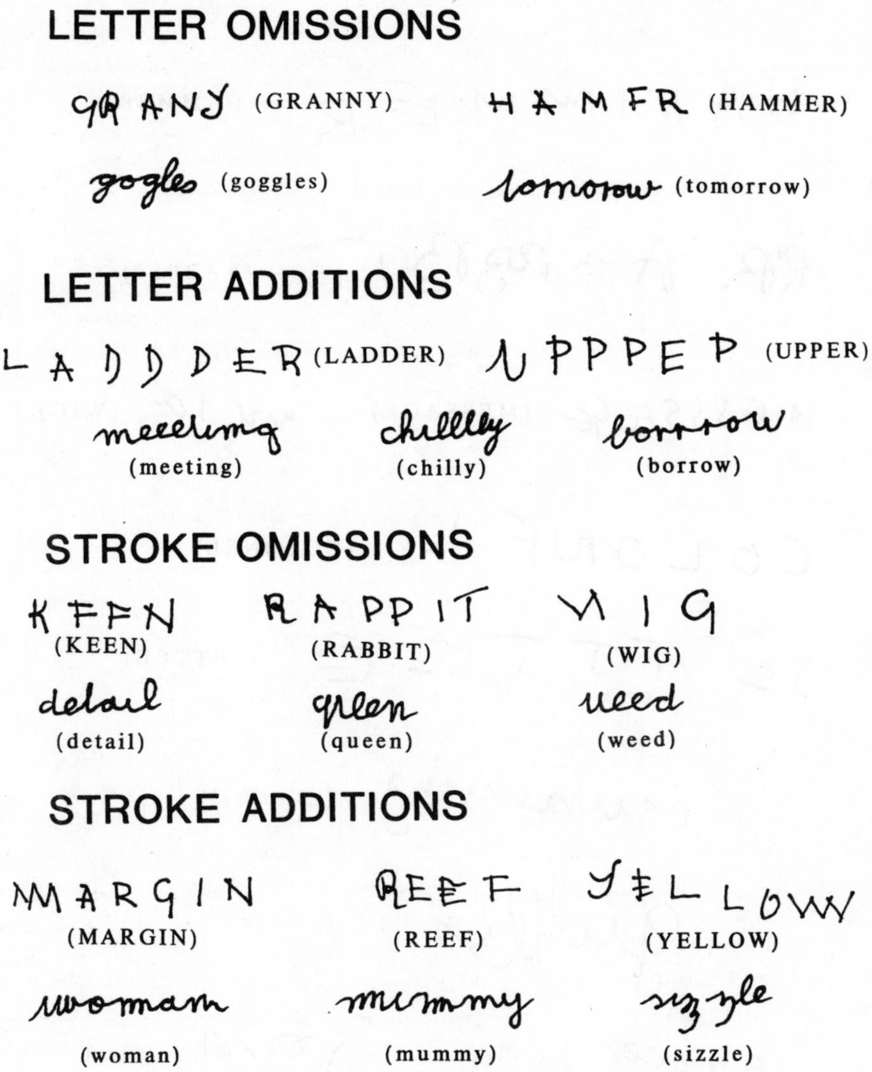

LETTER OMISSIONS

GR ANy (GRANNY)   HAMFR (HAMMER)

gogles (goggles)   tomorow (tomorrow)

LETTER ADDITIONS

L A D D D E R (LADDER)   U PPPE P (UPPER)

meeelimg   chillly   borrrow
(meeting)   (chilly)   (borrow)

STROKE OMISSIONS

KFFN   RAPPIT   VIG
(KEEN)   (RABBIT)   (WIG)

detail   green   weed
(detail)   (queen)   (weed)

STROKE ADDITIONS

MARGIN   REEF   YELLOW
(MARGIN)   (REEF)   (YELLOW)

woman   mummy   sizzle
(woman)   (mummy)   (sizzle)

FIG. 7.4.   Characteristic errors of patient VB (from Ellis, Young, & Flude, 1987b).

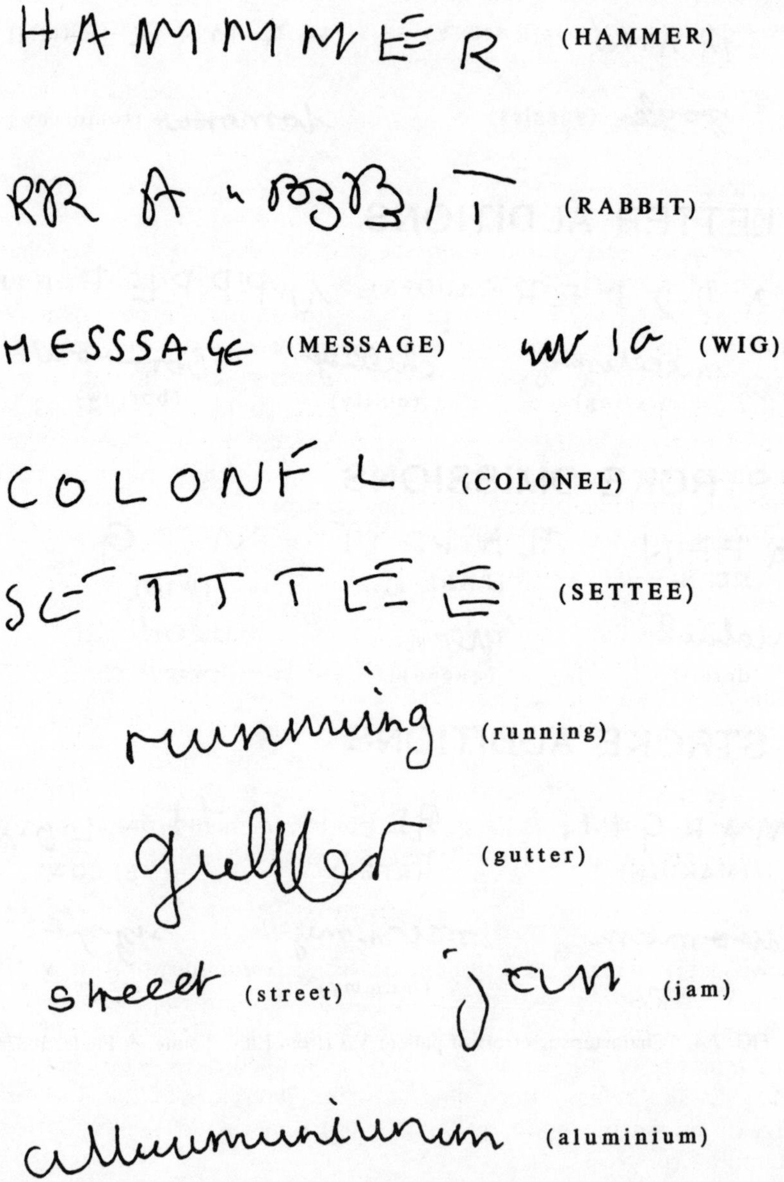

FIG. 7.5. Errors made by normal subjects when asked to write words with eyes closed while simultaneously tapping sequentially the fingers of the left hand (from Ellis, Young, & Flude, 1987b).

is that the truly dysgraphic patient makes these errors under normal writing conditions. How can this striking parallel be explained? Ellis et al. (1987b) suggested that normals become "afferent" dysgraphic when the experimental circumstances prevent them from monitoring and controlling their handwriting through the utilisation of visual feedback (sight of the hand and pen) and kinaesthetic feedback (the feeling of movement of fingers, wrist, and arm). Visual feedback is eliminated by obscuring the sight of the writing hand, and the addition of a secondary task interferes with the writer's ability to attend to kinaesthetic feedback.

Ellis et al. (1987b) showed that, unlike normal subjects, VB's writing was no more error-prone when she had her eyes closed than when she had her eyes open. She thus appears to have been permanently unable to use visual feedback to monitor for errors or help correct them. When, after she had closed her eyes, her forefinger was passively moved so as to form a letter, she was extremely poor at using kinaesthetic information to say what letter had been formed. And she could not distinguish reliably and correctly formed letters between incorrectly formed ones on the basis of kinaesthetic feedback. She thus seems to have also been permanently unable to use kinaesthesis for writing control.

In sum, writing is a complex perceptual-motor skill: Normal subjects use visual and kinaesthetic feedback at least some of the time to control their writing movements. When experimental conditions prevent normals from utilising those sources of feedback, normal writers make errors. Those errors are mostly omissions or repetitions of letters or strokes in sequences of similar items, and the errors may be interpreted as the consequence of a tendency to lose position in the middle of such sequences (Margolin, 1984). The brain injury suffered by "afferent" dysgraphics like VB may have robbed them of the ability to *attend* to visual and kinaesthetic feedback, so that they become permanently prone to errors at those points where close monitoring of writing movements is most needed.

OVERVIEW

If we define writing as a system of visual communication in which the written elements represent elements of the spoken language (words, syllables, or phonemes), then writing is less than 6000 years old. Only a tiny minority of the people who have ever lived have been able to read, and even fewer have been able to write. Accounts of the development of writing can be found in Gelb (1963), Gaur (1984), and Barton and Hamilton (in press).

The skill of writing is culturally transmitted from one generation to the next. The capacity to write is not one for which evolution can have equipped us with any genetically given modules, yet the cognitive neuropsychological evidence reviewed above suggests that writing processes in the skilled adult writer are as highly modularised as the speech-related processes discussed in Chapters 5 and 6. Thus a "surface dysgraphic" patient may lose the capacity to retrieve once-familiar spellings from some form of lexical store without losing the capacity to retrieve spoken word-forms, and without suffering amnesic memory retrieval problems. Similarly, a "phonological dysgraphic" patient may lose the capacity for phoneme–grapheme conversion required to generate plausible spellings for unfamiliar words or non-words without even losing the capacity for grapheme–phoneme conversion in reading (Beauvois and Dérousné, 1981).

The moral to be gleaned from this is that learning can create cognitive processes which are capable of becoming as highly modularised as genetically given modules. This conclusion contradicts Fodor's (1983) notion that modules must be genetically inherited, but the evidence for modularity is probably stronger for writing and reading (see Chapter 8) than for any other aspect of cognition (Ellis, 1987; Schwartz & Schwartz, 1984), so we must now allow that modules can be acquired as well as inherited.

The evidence for writing-specific disorders is stronger for what we have termed "central" dysgraphias than for "peripheral" dysgraphias. Writing is interesting because it begins as a linguistic process and ends as a perceptual-motor one. In the course of that transition the cognitive processes seem to become progressively less specific to writing. Thus "afferent dysgraphia" is probably the way that a general inattention to visual and kinaesthetic feedback affects handwriting, whereas other peripheral dysgraphias not covered here, such as mirror writing or the tiny "micrographic" handwriting of patients with Parkinsonism, similarly illustrate the effects of more general perceptual-motor impairments on handwriting.

SUMMARY

Acquired dysgraphias may be divided for convenience into "central dysgraphias" which affect the capacity to spell familiar or unfamiliar words in any output modality (handwriting, typing, oral spelling, etc.), and "peripheral dysgraphias" which may affect just one output modality, leaving the expression of spelling knowledge through the other modalities intact. But the cognitive neuropsychology of spelling and writing is not built solely upon patients in whom spelling and writing are impaired: patients in whom those skills are intact while other abilities are impaired can be equally important. For example, patients who can spell words correctly despite not having access to their correct spoken forms show that spellings of familiar words are not assembled by phoneme–grapheme conversion (a conclusion strengthened by "phonological dysgraphic" patients like PR—Shallice, 1981b). The spellings of familiar words must be capable of being retrieved as wholes from a graphemic output lexicon, and there must be ways of accessing that lexicon other than through the sound patterns of words.

Figure 7.1 proposes a graphemic output lexicon from which the spellings of familiar words are retrieved that is distinct from the speech output lexicon from which the spoken forms of words are retrieved. Spellings can be retrieved from the graphemic output lexicon using at least two inputs. One input comes direct from the semantic system and allows the meanings of words to activate their spellings without the intervention of sound forms. Disruption of this input is held responsible for semantic writing errors (e.g. time → CLOCK) seen in "deep dysgraphic" patients (and occasionally in normals).

A second input to the graphemic output lexicon comes from the speech output lexicon. Disruption of this input is held responsible for homophone (their → THERE) and similar-sound (plumb → THUMB) errors in which the errors are real, sometimes irregular words which would not be assembled by sublexical phoneme–grapheme conversion. Like semantic errors, these occur occasionally in normal writing as unintended slips of the pen, and at much higher frequencies in the writing of some acquired dysgraphic patients. "Visual" errors (e.g. custom → CUSTARD) may be explained in terms of interactive activation between the graphemic output lexicon and the grapheme level. Morphological errors of a sort that would imply separate representations of morphemes in the graphemic output lexicon have yet to be demonstrated convincingly.

Errors showing partial word-specific lexical knowledge occur in a wide range of qualitatively different acquired dysgraphic patients. They may affect less commonly used (low-frequency) words most, and show that the retrieval of spellings from the graphemic output lexicon is not an all-or-nothing thing. Errors of partial lexical knowledge in spelling may be the logical equivalents of the phonological approximation errors in the speech of some aphasic patients—errors interpretable in terms of partial retrieval of spoken word-forms from the speech output lexicon.

Sublexical phoneme–grapheme conversion of the sort required to assemble a plausible spelling for an unfamiliar word or non-word is represented in Fig. 7.1 in terms of a link between the phoneme level and the grapheme level. This conversion procedure is impaired in "phonological" dysgraphics, and preserved in "surface" dysgraphics for whom retrieval of words from the graphemic output lexicon is impaired. "Surface" dysgraphics are more successful at spelling regular than irregular words, to which they tend to make regularisation errors (e.g. misspelling "biscuit" as BISKET, or "nephew" as NEFFUE). Some theorists would probably prefer to think of lexical and sublexical spelling procedures as more closely intertwined than our model might suggest.

If a writer knows how a word is spelled, then he or she is equally capable of spelling it aloud, typing it (even if slowly), printing it in upper-case (capital) letters, or writing it in cursive handwriting. Because this variety of possible output modalities exists, we suggest that spellings are initially retrieved from the graphemic output lexicon or assembled by phoneme–grapheme conversion as abstract graphemic representations. Processes downstream of the grapheme level convert the graphemic representation progressively into more concrete forms ready for output. In Fig. 7.2 we propose that graphemes first activate particular spatial letter forms at the allograph level and that these then guide the retrieval or assembly of graphic motor patterns which will create the letter forms on paper. Different peripheral dysgraphias are interpretable as impairments affecting one or other of these stages.

FURTHER READING

There are no books devoted to the cognitive neuropsychology of spelling and writing. This reflects in part the paucity of work on spelling and writing in comparison with the mass of work on the psychology of reading. Most appropriate are:

Frith, U. (1980). *Cognitive processes in spelling*. London: Academic Press. Includes John Morton's extension of his influential "logogen model" to writing and Frith's own work on normal people who are good readers but poor spellers.

Ellis, A. W. (1984). *Reading, writing and dyslexia: A cognitive analysis*. London: Lawrence Erlbaum Associates. Chapters on spelling and writing processes in normals and patients.

Three review articles which come to encouragingly similar conclusions are:

Ellis, A. W. (1982). Spelling and writing (and reading and speaking). In A. W. Ellis (Ed.), *Normality and pathology in cognitive functions*. London: Academic Press.

Margolin, D. I. (1984). The neuropsychology of writing and spelling: Semantic, phonological, motor and perceptual processes. *Quarterly Journal of Experimental Psychology, 36A*, 459–489.

Patterson, K. E. (1988). Disorders of spelling. In G. Denes, C. Semenza, P. Bisiacchi, & E. Andreewsky (Eds), *Perspectives in cognitive neuropsychology*. London: Lawrence Erlbaum Associates.

The traditional neuropsychology of writing tended to be guided by rather different concerns from those expressed here. One has therefore to work fairly hard to extract specifically cognitive neuropsychological lessons from those studies. For the curious, access to work in that tradition can be gained through the following two reviews:

Leischner, A. (1969). The agraphias. In P. J. Vinken & G. W. Bruyn (Eds), *Handbook of clinical neurology*, Vol. 4. Amsterdam: North-Holland.

Marcie, P. (1983). Writing disorders associated with focal cortical lesions. In M. Martlew (Ed.), *The psychology of written language*. Chichester: J. Wiley.

8 Reading: And a Composite Model for Word Recognition and Production

INTRODUCTION AND A MODEL

Reading is subject to its own range of acquired disorders in just the same way as are writing, speech perception, and speech production. Disorders of reading consequent upon brain injury are called *acquired dyslexias*. The study of acquired dyslexias was one of the first areas to be investigated intensively from a cognitive neuropsychological perspective, and many qualitatively different forms of acquired dyslexia have been identified, each with different symptoms, different interpretations, and different implications for theories of normal reading. New varieties are still being reported, and our coverage here does not claim to be exhaustive. As in the two previous chapters we shall confine ourselves to disorders identifiable in the processing of single words, and shall defer disorders of the processing of sentences and connected text until Chapter 9. Recent reviews of cognitive neuropsychological investigations of the acquired dyslexias can be found in Coltheart (1981; 1986), Patterson (1981), Newcombe and Marshall (1981), and Ellis (1984b).

In Chapters 5 and 6 we gradually put together a model for the production and comprehension of spoken words, and for the production of written words, culminating in the model shown in Fig. 7.1 (p. 175). This chapter is concerned with reading rather than writing. In Fig. 8.1, the model we shall use in this chapter, processes specific to spelling and writing have been stripped off (for now) and replaced with processes specific to reading. As we shall see, a model for reading needs to preserve those processes which are also involved in speech comprehension and production.

Readers coming straight to this chapter will require a brief explanation of Fig. 8.1. The top left corner of the diagram is concerned with the recognition of spoken words. The auditory input lexicon contains representations of all the words that are familiar in their spoken (heard) forms. In order for a heard word to be identified its representation in the auditory input lexicon must be activated by the sound wave reaching the listeners' ears. The function of the acoustic analysis system is to transform that raw sound wave into a form to which the representations in the auditory input lexicon can respond. Representations of the *meanings* of words are contained within the semantic system. A heard word is only understood when the activation of its entry in the auditory input lexicon triggers the subsequent activation of that word's semantic (meaning) representation in the semantic system.

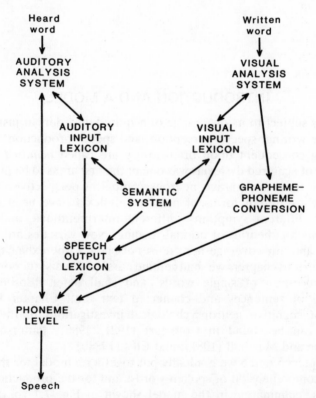

FIG. 8.1. Functional model for the recognition, comprehension and naming of written words in reading.

The lower portion of Fig. 8.1 is concerned with speech production. The speech output lexicon contains those representations of spoken words which are activated when a word is to be spoken (e.g. in spontaneous speech or object naming). Representations in the speech output lexicon are triggered when their meanings in the semantic system become active. This triggering serves, in turn, to activate the sequence of phonemes (distinctive speech sounds) at the phoneme level. Saying a word aloud then simply requires the activated string of phonemes to be articulated.

Words are not, however, always spoken out loud. They can also be "spoken" internally as "inner speech". This is represented in Fig. 8.1 by the arrow on the left-hand side of the diagram which cycles speech back from the phoneme level on the output side to the acoustic analysis system on the input side. Such a link allows a speaker to almost literally hear his or her own voice without anything being said aloud. There are additional advantages in having that connection two-way, thus providing a direct link from the acoustic analysis system to the phoneme level. One such advantage is that it provides a mechanism for repeating aloud words (or invented non-words) which we have never heard or spoken before and which cannot, therefore, have entries in either the auditory input lexicon or the speech output lexicon.

It may seem rather strange to open a chapter on reading with several paragraphs concerned with the comprehension and production of spoken words, but in the course of learning to read cognitive processes dealing with written words are grafted onto those processes we have just outlined which handle spoken words. And, as the chapter progresses, we shall see that although cognitive processes exist which are specific to reading and do not involve spoken word-forms, nevertheless, full, fluent reading also calls upon speech processes in a number of important ways.

Figure 8.1 introduces three new components which are specific to reading—a *visual analysis system*, a *visual input lexicon*, and a component labelled *grapheme–phoneme conversion*. A written word is typically a complex pattern of black lines on a white background. Meaning and sound are imposed by the reader. The function of the first reading component, the visual analysis system, is to identify the component letters of words and note their positions with the word. Identification here is a visual process; it does not involve naming the letters.

We assume that as written words become familiar to a reader, representations of those words are established in a visual input lexicon similar in function to, but separate from, the auditory input lexicon. Thus skilled readers who have learned to recognise many thousands of words "by sight" will have a representation for each word in their visual input lexicons, each representation being activated specifically by its own written word. The visual input lexicon receives its input from the letter recognisers in the visual analysis system and, in turn, activates stored representations of their meanings in the semantic system. For a skilled reader this is the usual route for understanding a familiar written word. Once a word has been comprehended the semantic system can activate the word's spoken form in the speech output lexicon (as in normal speech production), allowing the word to be read aloud. The speech output lexicon is the same component whose role in speech production and spelling has been discussed in Chapters 5 and 7. The route from print to speech via the visual input lexicon, the semantic system, and the speech output lexicon is probably the normal route for reading aloud connected text (see Ellis, 1984b, pp. 55–57).

There must, however, be at least one other route from print to pronunciation. *Pomelo* and *regelate* are both real words in the English language, but they are uncommon ones that most people will not have met before, and for which they are therefore unlikely to have representations in the visual input lexicon. Thanks to the (partially) alphabetic nature of the English spelling system we can, however, attempt a pronunciation for each one. That pronunciation is assembled by first identifying the letters (the job of the visual analysis system again), then converting those letters (or graphemes) into sounds (or phonemes). In our model, a component labelled *grapheme–phoneme conversion* is given the task of translating unfamiliar letter strings into phoneme strings. The input to grapheme–phoneme conversion is letters identified by the visual analysis system, whereas its output serves to activate phonemes at the phoneme level, from whence they can be articulated. We shall see later that there are a number of candidate theories of how unfamiliar letter strings are translated into sounds. For most of this chapter the term "grapheme–phoneme conversion" is meant to be neutral with respect to just how that translation is accomplished.

Grapheme–phoneme conversion is probably used only occasionally by skilled adult readers as the dominant route from print to sound (e.g. in reading an unfamiliar word for the first time), but the young or unskilled reader will encounter many words which are unfamiliar in their printed form and which must therefore be "sounded out" by grapheme–phoneme conversion. The point of doing this is that many words which are visually unfamiliar for the child or unskilled adult reader will be words he or she has *heard* before and whose meaning is known. Converting unfamiliar words into spoken form allows the possibility that they will be recognised auditorily where they were not recognised visually. This auditory recognition most probably involves activating the word's entry in the auditory input lexicon: This could be achieved either by saying the word aloud or by saying it internally using "inner speech".

In Fig. 8.1 an arrow connects the visual input lexicon which recognises familiar written words directly to the speech output lexicon which gives access to their pronunciations. The arrow therefore provides a pathway by which familiar written words may be identified and pronounced as wholes without (or in parallel to) activating their meanings. The justification and purpose of this third pathway from print to sound will be discussed later in this chapter.

Armed with our model we are now ready to survey the range of reading disorders which can occur as a result of injury to the brains of adults who were previously fully literate (the acquired dyslexias). Shallice and Warrington (1980) made a rough, but none the less useful distinction between "peripheral" and "central" acquired dyslexias. Peripheral dyslexias affect early stages in the visual analysis of letters and words, whereas central dyslexias affect deeper processes such as grapheme–phoneme conversion or semantic access. We shall begin our survey with the peripheral dyslexias.

PERIPHERAL DYSLEXIAS

"Neglect" Dyslexia

We have seen in Chapter 4 how brain injury can cause patients to neglect one side of the visual world. That neglect can extend to and affect reading. Kinsbourne and Warrington (1962) reported six patients who showed neglect of the left half of space. In reading they made visual errors which preserved the ends of words but were incorrect at the beginnings (e.g. reading *level* as "novel", *milk* as "chalk", *geography* as "autobiography", and *message* as "passage"). Four of the six patients had visual field defects that left them blind to the left half of the visual world ("left homonymous hemianopia"), but the reading disorder could not be attributed to this factor, first because the same neglect errors also occurred in two patients without blindness in the left visual field and, secondly, because neglect of the leftmost letters of words also occurred when words were presented entirely in the patients' intact right visual fields. Ellis, Flude, and Young (1987a) reported a detailed case study of a single patient, VB, who showed neglect dyslexia. When asked to read passages of text she often read only the right-hand half of each line, neglecting the left half. This tendency could be eliminated by the simple expedient of turning the page through 90° so that the lines of print now ran from bottom to top rather than from left to right.

When reading the right halves of lines of normal, horizontal print VB would misread some words. She made the same sorts of errors when given single printed words to read. With unlimited time to read each word she would misread about 8% of single words; with a time limit of around 2 seconds per word the error rate increased to around 15% of words. Some two-thirds of her errors were of the neglect type (e.g. misreading LOG as "dog", RIVER as "liver", or YELLOW as "pillow"). Other errors were either of a more general visual nature (e.g. misreading WHOM as "thumb", or CHOIR as "anchor"), or were errors in which she misread a word as a non-word (e.g. CABIN as "rabin"; GIRTH as "gorth").

The errors did not seem to be influenced by anything other than visual factors: VB freely produced errors like misreading HARDEN as "warden" where the target word and the error both sound different and belong to different grammatical classes. When VB misread a word she also misunderstood it. Thus when asked to read words and then define them, she misread RICE as "price... how much for a paper or something in a shop", and she misread LIQUID as a "kind of sea creature... squid". The errors seem therefore to happen in early visual processes before word recognition or comprehension occurs.

Although about 12% of VB's neglect errors involved the simple deletion of initial letters (e.g. CAGE misread as "age"; LEVER as "ever"), in the majority of neglect errors she substituted initial letters of the target words with other letters. This occurred even when she was given specially devised lists of words which could be misread by either deleting or substituting the initial letter. Thus she misread ELATE as "plate" not "late", PEACH as "beach" not "each", and JAUNT as "haunt" not "aunt". Furthermore, VB tended to substitute the same number of letters as she had neglected. Thus she would misread TOOL as "fool" with one letter in the error replacing one in the target word, but would very rarely misread, say, TOOL as "school", because that would involve replacing one target letter with three in the error.

Following Shallice (1981a), Ellis, Flude, and Young (1987a) argued that the impairment which led to VB's neglect dyslexic reading errors should be located within the visual analysis system. They proposed that two functions of that system are first to identify the component letters in a word and second to encode the positions of those letters in the word. The need to encode letter positions arises from the fact that the pairs of words may share the same letters and differ only in the positions of those letters (from ON and NO to ORCHESTRA and CARTHORSE). Given the word ELATE, the visual analysis system should therefore both identify each letter and mark it for its within-word position, generating a representation something like $E(1)$, $L(2)$, $A(3)$, $T(4)$, $E(5)$.

When VB neglected the initial letter of a word like ELATE, the *presence* of an initial letter was still reacted to because VB would tend to replace it with another letter rather than simply deleting it. This could happen if, as Ellis et al. (1987a) proposed, VB's neglect affected the encoding of letter identity more than the encoding of letter position. Neglecting the initial letter of ELATE would yield the representation $-(1)$, $L(2)$, $A(3)$, $T(4)$, $E(5)$. Such a representation would be more compatible with the entry in the visual input lexicon for PLATE than with the entry for LATE [which would require $L(1)$, $A(2)$, $T(3)$, $E(4)$]. Finally, Ellis et al. showed that VB's overall accuracy rate to single word targets (over 85%) was better than she could have achieved if she failed to encode the identity of the initial letter of *every* word she tried to read. It would seem that her problem compromised those processes which encoded the identity of the leftmost letters of words, with less or no effect on the processes which encode the position of letters within words.

Though neglect dyslexia, like visual neglect, usually affects elements on the left, a possible (though in some respects unclear) case of *right*-sided "neglect" dyslexia was presented by Warrington and Zangwill (1957). This patient made visual errors which preserved the beginnings of words but not their ends (e.g. reading *beware* as "because", *tongue* as "together", and *obtained* as "oblong"). Patient EA of Friedrich, Walker, and Posner (1985) also made visual errors affecting the ends of words. Some of these errors could be construed as "morphological" (e.g. *provide* misread as "providing"; *electrical* as "electricity"), but Friedrich et al. prefer to interpret these as visual errors which happen to involve the ends of words. The question of whether genuine morphological errors ever occur in acquired dyslexia will be returned to later in this chapter.

An important question concerns the relation of neglect dyslexia to other aspects of visual neglect (see Chapter 2). Ellis et al. (1987a) suggested that the errors found in neglect dyslexia arise when a more general visual neglect happens to compromise the reading process. On this hypothesis there is nothing about neglect dyslexia that is *specific* to reading. This straightforward position is, however, undermined by Costello and Warrington's (1987) report of a patient who misread the beginnings (i.e. the left side) of horizontal words but neglected the *right* side of external space in other tasks. This finding underscores the point discussed in Chapter 2 that there are probably a number of dissociable types of visual neglect.

Attentional Dyslexia

A different form of acquired peripheral dyslexia was reported by Shallice and Warrington (1977). Their two patients were first noticed because although they could read single whole words quite well they were very poor at naming the letters within those words. When these patients were required to identify particular letters in an array their errors tended to be one of the other letters present which the patient was supposed to ignore. So a patient asked to identify the central letter in the sequence BFXQL might say "F" or "L" instead of "X".

The inability of these two patients to ignore irrelevant letters became even clearer when they were asked to read a group of words presented together. Shown a card with WIN and FED on it one patient read them as "fin" and "fed". POT, BIG, and HUT were read as "but", "big", and "hut". In general, the errors involved the migration of letters (not phonemes) from one word into another, so that words the patient reported seeing were made up of letters from the target words combined with letters from other words on the card. Thus, "fin" is a combination of F from FED and -IN from WIN, and "but" is a combination of B from BIG, U from HUT, and T from POT, with all the letters preserving their within-word positions.

Interestingly, this is one of the class of symptoms found in neuro-psychological patients which can also be observed in normal people under certain conditions. Allport (1977) showed groups of words very briefly to normal individuals and obtained a high proportion of letter migration errors (or "visual segmentation errors" as he called them). Shown briefly a card on which were written GLOVE and SPADE a normal person may claim to have *seen* the word GLADE (made up of the GL- from GLOVE and the -ADE of SPADE). These errors of normal readers have since been studied by Shallice and McGill (1978) and Mozer (1983). This work has shown for normals what Shallice and Warrington (1977) also found to be true of their patients, namely that letters tend to migrate from one position in a presented word to the corresponding position in the errone-ously reported word. In addition, Mozer (1983) showed that migrations of letters into a particular word occur less often when the subject focusses attention on that word, a finding which lends support to Shallice and Warrington's (1977) choice of the term "attentional" dyslexia to describe their patients.

We have already talked of the need for the visual analysis system to identify letters *and* code them for their positions within words. To account for these migration errors we must now assign another responsibility to the visual analysis system. Written words are not normally encountered in isolation but in large numbers on a printed page. The visual analysis system must be able to group letters together as belonging to a particular word in a particular position on the page. That perceptual grouping can be sorely tested even under normal conditions, as in the following examples adapted from Wilkins (1910, cited by Woodworth, 1938):

Psychment

Departology

Ronan

Reagald

talder

powcum

Shakesbeth

Macpeare's

Very brief presentations disrupt this perceptual grouping in normal subjects, causing them to report having *seen* Psychology Department when the stimulus was Psychment Departology, or talcum powder when the stimulus was talder powcum. In "attentional" dyslexics the perceptual grouping is permanently disrupted through brain injury and extends to reading under normal conditions. One of Shallice and Warrington's (1977) patients spontaneously observed that "when reading a line of print it helped if he held a piece of paper over other parts of the page". This is precisely the sort of strategy one would recommend both to focus attention on the correct words and to prevent migrations from irrelevant words elsewhere on the page.

Letter-by-letter Reading

Patterson and Kay (1982) give a detailed analysis of the reading behaviour of four patients who showed a phenomenon called "letter-by-letter reading". When presented with a word these patients appeared able to identify it only after naming each letter either aloud or subvocally. Thus, shown *shepherd* a letter-by-letter reader would first name the letters in left-to-right order, and only then be able to name the whole word. Now, there is little in the letter *names* S(ess), H(aitch), E(ee), P(pee), H(aitch), E(ee), R(are), D(dee) to suggest the spoken word "shepherd", and letter-by-letter readers certainly do not proceed by in some way blending together phonemes derived from the letter names.

Some letter-by-letter readers [e.g. Warrington & Shallice's (1980) case, RAV] make few errors when identifying individual letters and will read almost any word successfully given sufficient time. Other patients, however, make rather a lot of errors when trying to identify letters. This, of course, leads to mistakes in identifying the word, for example naming the letters of *spade* as "S,H,A,D,E" then saying "shade" (Patterson & Kay, 1982).

Because such patients' reading proceeds letter-by-letter, the time taken to read a word increases as its length increases. Also, in those patients who are prone to letter misidentifications, the probability of failing to read a word correctly increases as its length increases. Word recognition in general can be a very slow process in letter-by-letter readers— from an average of 7.6 seconds for 3-letter words to 19.5 seconds for

9- or 10-letter words in the *fastest* of Patterson and Kay's (1982) four patients.

Letter-by-letter reading has a long history of study by neuropsychologists and neurologists from Déjerine (1892) onwards, but much of this work has concentrated on locating the anatomical site of the lesion(s) responsible for this dyslexia. Only recently with the work of Warrington and Shallice (1980), Patterson and Kay (1982) and others has a *cognitive* explanation of the disorder been sought.

There are really two questions to be answered if we are to explain letter-by-letter reading. The first is: What deficit(s) to which component(s) has impaired the normal capacity for identifying words as wholes? The second question is: What processes mediate the residual reading abilities of letter-by-letter readers? Regarding the first question, Warrington and Shallice (1980) propose that the deficit in letter-by-letter reading is in what they call the "word-form system" (indeed they dub letter-by-letter reading "word-form" dyslexia). In Warrington and Shallice's schema the word-form system is responsible for segmenting letter strings into recognisable units ranging in size from letters, through syllables and morphemes, to words. Thus it subsumes functions ascribed in our model (Fig. 8.1) to both the visual analysis system and the visual input lexicon. It would not, however, be too gross a violation of Warrington and Shallice's theory to say that, in terms of our model, they propose that letter-by-letter readers are no longer able to gain access to the visual input lexicon from print. They can still identify letters but can no longer activate recognition units in the visual input lexicon from the visual analysis system.

Warrington and Shallice (1980) answer our second question (how are the residual reading abilities sustained?) by proposing that letter-by-letter readers identify written words by some reverse operation of their intact spelling system. Apparently, it is a fact that all letter-by-letter readers who can still identify words correctly after naming their letters also have intact spelling capabilities. Further, two of Patterson and Kay's (1982) letter-by-letter readers were also dysgraphic, and their errors in letter-by-letter recognition mirrored the errors they made in spelling. One case in question was patient TP whom we encountered in Chapter 7 as a case of "surface" dysgraphia—that is, a patient who had lost the capacity to retrieve the spellings of many words from memory (i.e. from her graphemic output lexicon). TP had to resort to assembling plausible spellings from sounds, producing errors like NEFFUE for "nephew" and BISKET for "biscuit". Of relevance here is the fact that TP often made phonological reading errors after naming all the letters of a word correctly. For example, shown *head* she said, "H, E, A, D... heed"; similarly, *city* was read as "C, I, T, Y... kitty", and *ache* was read as "A, C, H, E... aych".

All of these errors are compatible with Warrington and Shallice's notion that letter-by-letter readers read via their spelling system which, in TP's case, is itself disordered (though Patterson and Kay discuss an alternative explanation whereby recognition is still mediated by the visual input lexicon). Much is left unspecified in Warrington and Shallice's account, such as *how* the spelling system is able to work in the reverse of its normal mode, and what role letter *names* play in the reading process, but the interpretation still has much to commend it. Perhaps if we knew more about how *normal* people can identify words they hear being spelled aloud (a curious and little-used skill), we might gain insights into the routes to word identification employed in letter-by-letter reading. A complicating factor is that there seem to be different causes of letter-by-letter reading.

We presented evidence in Chapter 4 to show that at least some prosopagnosic patients with face recognition disorders gain unconscious or "implicit" access to the identities of people whose faces feel utterly unfamiliar to the patient. A phenomenon which seems to be related to this type of observation may occur in some, but probably not all, letter-by-letter readers. Patient ML, studied by Shallice and Saffran (1986), read slowly in a letter-by-letter fashion. If asked to identify five- or six-letter words presented for 2 seconds each he could name very few of them correctly. He could, however, distinguish words from non-words with an accuracy significantly above chance at the same rate of presentation. In fact, his performance on non-words was, at 43%, around chance level, but he classified 87% of words correctly, being more accurate on common (high-frequency) words than on less common (low-frequency) words.

With 2-second presentation times ML could also classify words into semantic categories such as living things *vs*. non-living objects, or names of authors *vs*. names of politicians, at accuracy levels greater than chance, though again he could identify very few of the words explicitly. Shallice and Saffran (1986) propose that ML's route to semantics through the "word-form system" is impaired but not totally abolished. It can sustain levels of performance on lexical decision and semantic categorization tasks which are better than chance, though far from normal, but it cannot sustain explicit word identification. For that ML must resort to a letter-by-letter reading strategy. The letter-by-letter readers studied by Patterson and Kay (1982), however, showed no sign of any capability for "implicit" lexical decision or semantic categorisation and would be assumed on this account to have incurred more complete damage to the normal route to word meanings via the visual input lexicon than was incurred by ML.

"Visual" Dyslexia

One of the most influential papers in the revival of cognitive neuro-psychology was undoubtedly that of Marshall and Newcombe (1973). They reported analyses of six patients who showed three different patterns of acquired reading disorder. The first pattern they called "visual" dyslexia (see also Newcombe & Marshall, 1981). The errors made by these patients take the form of misidentifying one word as another, visually similar one—for example, reading *lend* as "land", *easel* as "aerial", *arrangement* as "argument", or *calm* as "claim". An earlier and very pure case was reported by Casey and Ettlinger (1960).

Marshall and Newcombe (1973) emphasise the "essential normality" of these errors, pointing out that, like the letter segmentation errors mentioned earlier, they can occur in normal readers when words are glimpsed briefly (e.g. Cowie, 1985; Vernon, 1929). "Visual" dyslexics may have difficultes at the level of the visual analysis system. Alternatively, we may be dealing with a problem internal to the visual input lexicon, whereby the correct input in terms of positionally coded letters sometimes triggers the wrong representation. As yet we lack the sort of detailed, experimental case studies that might help tease apart alternative explanations of the characteristic errors of "visual" dyslexics.

Visual dyslexia lies on the borderline between the peripheral and the central acquired dyslexias. The remainder of the acquired dyslexias we shall cover belong clearly in the category of central dyslexias. The first group of central acquired dyslexias we shall look at all involve patients who have an impairment of the normal reading route via the visual input lexicon, semantic system, and speech output lexicon. They still have some capacity for reading aloud though, and by examining their perform-ance we can learn something about the range of alternative routes from print to pronunciation.

READING WITHOUT MEANING?

Patient WLP, described by Schwartz, Saffran, and Marin (1980a), was a 62-year-old woman who suffered from a progressive senile dementia which severely impaired her ability to produce or comprehend either spoken or written language. We have already mentioned her in Chapter 2, where we discussed her preserved ability to mime the use of objects that she could not otherwise identify. In one task WLP was shown the written *name* of an animal, then was required to point to the appropriate picture from a set of four. Her selections were totally random, but she was nevertheless able to read animal names aloud with very few errors. In another task WLP was given a stack of index cards, upon each of which was written the name of a single animal, colour, or body part. She was required to read each word aloud, then place it on one of three piles according to its semantic category. WLP performed this task reasonably well for common names like *horse, red*, or *finger*, but her sorting of less common names like *giraffe, magenta*, or *china* was poor. However, she could still read aloud the words she could not categorise, including irregular words like *leopard, beige*, and *thumb*.

In simple reading tests she read correctly on at least some occasions irregular words such as *blood, climb, come, sugar, wan*, and *gone*. Because they are irregular, the pronunciations of words like these cannot be assembled piecemeal by grapheme–phoneme conversion; they must be recognised as wholes and pronounced as wholes. In terms of our model these words must be identified by the visual input lexicon, and their pronunciations must be retrieved from the speech output lexicon. WLP's performance on semantic memory tasks was very poor (Schwartz, Marin, & Saffran, 1979), and her comments attest her lack of understanding of the words she could still read aloud ("hyena... hyena... what in the heck is that").

Schwartz et al. (1980a) conclude that there is another route from print to sound which takes the form of direct, whole-word connections between corresponding representations in the visual input lexicon and in the speech output lexicon. These connections would thus link together the units in the visual input lexicon which identify *blood, climb, come*, etc. as familiar written words with the units in the speech output lexicon which store (or provide access to) the pronunciations of those words.

This proposal is reminiscent of the argument advanced in Chapter 7 that intact writing to dictation without comprehension in "word meaning deafness" might imply direct connections between corresponding units in the auditory input lexicon and the graphemic output lexicon. We noted alternative explanations in that instance, including the possibility that semantic units mediate the transfer from input to output although the patient cannot act upon the products of semantic processing in the manner required to indicate comprehension in a category-sorting or other task. The same reservations might apply here. Nebes, Martin, and Horn (1984) studied a group of patients with Alzheimer's disease (a form of dementia). As compared with a group of normal elderly patients, the demented patients were poor at generating animal names to request, and their recall of words in a memory test was not aided by cues as to the categories from which the words were drawn. The patients were, however, reasonably good at reading words aloud (as WLP was). Importantly, Nebes et al. (1984) were able to show that they read words aloud faster if they had just read a word related in meaning to the word they were currently being asked to read. The priming effect shown by the demented patients was comparable in magnitude to that shown by the normals. Thus, although

Nebes et al.'s patients showed little conscious understanding of written words, they nevertheless read words like BREAD aloud more quickly if they had just read BUTTER than if they had just read WINDOW. This priming of word naming suggests that what we might be seeing in dementia is a disconnection of the recognition system from awareness, similar to the disconnection that can be seen in some prosopagnosic patients (see pp. 96–101). It thus becomes important to determine whether the priming effect arises in the semantic system itself, or at the input lexicon level. If it is established that demented patients continue to access semantic representations of which the patient has no conscious awareness, then cases like WLP would not provide evidence for direct connections between entries in the visual input lexicon and entries in the speech output lexicon.

That said, the proposal of such direct connections has been widely accepted, and has been incorporated into various influential models of reading (e.g. Morton & Patterson, 1980; Newcombe & Marshall, 1981). In addition, Warren and Morton (1982) have argued that a direct, word-specific route from print to sound may help explain an otherwise puzzling difference between words and pictures in the way they are processed by normal people. In an experiment by Potter and Faulconer (1975) normal subjects were required to classify words or pictures as living or non-living as quickly as possible or, alternatively, to name the words or pictures as quickly as possible. In the classification task pictures were responded to faster than words, but the reverse was true in the naming task, where words were named faster than pictures. Warren and Morton (1982) propose that pictures access the semantic system faster than do words, and so can be classified faster, but that when it comes to naming, the presence of the direct route between the visual input lexicon and the speech output lexicon allows words to be named rapidly, whereas pictures must activate their production units via semantics, which is presumed to be a slower process. Further neuropsychological evidence compatible with the notion of a "direct route" from print to sound will be discussed below.

"SURFACE" DYSLEXIA

Patient WLP, whom we described in the previous section, managed to read many irregular words correctly, but she also showed a tendency, particularly in the later stages of her illness, to break words down and pronounce them in a piecemeal fashion (the way you would if you were trying to pronounce a word you had never seen before). Thus on one occasion WLP pronounced *bury* as "burey" (to rhyme with "fury") though she read it correctly on two other occasions. Similarly, she twice read *deny* as "denny", read *pint* to rhyme with "hint", and pronounced the *w* when reading *sword*.

A patient similar in many respects to WLP was reported by Shallice, Warrington, and McCarthy (1983). This patient (HTR) also suffered from a progressive dementing illness, but she showed an even greater tendency to break words down and assemble a pronunciation as if the words were entirely unfamiliar. Her use of this strategy meant that she was more likely to read regular words aloud correctly than irregular words, and her errors were predominantly "regularisations"; that is, errors caused by treating irregular words as if they were regular (e.g. pronouncing *gauge* as "gorge", *trough* as "truff", *come* as "kome", and *quay* as "kway"). The retention in HTR of a capacity for grapheme–phoneme conversion when whole-word reading began to deteriorate would explain why she continued to be able to read aloud non-words like *wull* or *pild* at a time when she could no longer read correctly many once-familiar real words.

This switch from pronouncing familiar words as wholes to assembling pronunciations piecemeal following brain injury was first discussed in detail by Marshall and Newcombe (1973), who gave it the name of "surface" dyslexia. Marshall and Newcombe's patients JC and ST showed a tendency towards regularisation errors on irregular or ambiguously-spelled words, but they differed from WLP and HTR in certain ways. First of all, they did not have a semantic impairment. Provided they could pronounce a word correctly they could understand it and say what it meant. If their misreading of an irregular word was a word in its own right they would understand and define the word in accordance with their mispronunciation. Thus JC read *listen* as "liston" and commented, "that's the boxer" (this being in the heyday of the American heavyweight Sonny Liston). Similarly, he misread *begin* as "beggin" and then added, "collecting money".

Even though JC and ST were obliged to treat formerly familiar words as unfamiliar and pronounce them as one would an unfamiliar word or non-word, their grasp of grapheme–phoneme conversion also seems to have been impaired to a degree. Thus they often failed to apply the "rule of e" whereby a final *e* in a word like *bite* lengthens the preceding vowel, and so pronounced *bike* as "bik" and *describe* as "describ". Additionally, JC and ST made some visual errors like those of patients we have discussed earlier in this chapter, for example reading *reign* as "region" and *bargain* as "barge".

In terms of our model, JC and ST appear to have suffered impairments to the visual input lexicon and/or its connections to the semantic system. Some words could still be recognised as wholes by the visual input lexicon (hence some irregular words could still be read), but many words were now read by grapheme–phoneme conversion (which was itself mildly impaired). Reliance on grapheme–phoneme conversion produces a patient who is more successful at reading regular words than irregular words, since regular words are by definition words whose pronunciations would be correctly derived by the application of spelling–sound correspondences. Thus when JC was tested on two different sets of regular and irregular words, he read 40 of 80 and 27 of 50 regular words correctly as compared with only 27 of 80 and 14 of 50 irregular words (Newcombe & Marshall, 1984).

The Locus of the Impairment in Cases of "Surface" Dyslexia

In "surface" dyslexia, then, some impairment to the whole-word routes between print and pronunciation causes the patient to rely to a considerable extent on the "sublexical" route, involving what we have called grapheme–phoneme conversion. Effectively, the "surface" dyslexic treats the majority of words he or she is shown as if they were entirely new and unfamiliar, sounding them out, and pronouncing them in piecemeal fashion. The patient has problems with irregular words which, by definition, resist this reading strategy and the errors made tend to be "regularisations" in which words are pronounced as they look rather than being given their conventional pronunciations.

Inspection of Fig. 8.1 will reveal that reliance on grapheme–phoneme conversion will only come about if neither the route from the visual input lexicon to the speech output lexicon via the semantic system nor the direct route between the two lexicons can sustain whole-word recognition and pronunciation. Further inspection of Fig. 8.1 will also reveal that damage at a number of different loci in the model could force a reliance on grapheme–phoneme conversion. In a given patient, the symptoms which accompany the problems with irregular words and the regularisation errors should help us to decide where the impairment(s) lies.

"Surface" dyslexia could arise through damage to the visual input lexicon itself. Words would be unable to contact their representations in that lexicon and so would be unable to activate their meanings as wholes. The auditory input lexicon, semantic system, and speech output lexicon would remain intact, so the patient should have no problems in auditory word recognition and comprehension, should not experience naming problems in speech, and should comprehend those written words that can be pronounced correctly. One patient who seems to fit this description reasonably accurately is JC, the "surface" dyslexic already mentioned who has been described in a series of papers by Marshall and Newcombe (1973; Newcombe & Marshall, 1975; 1981; 1984; see also Holmes, 1973; 1978). JC has good comprehension of spoken words, indicative of an intact auditory input lexicon and semantic system. He also has fluent speech production with only slight word-finding difficulties on low-frequency words. These slight difficulties cannot be held responsible for his "surface" dyslexia because he fails to read many words he can use with ease in his spontaneous speech. A disorder in or around the visual input lexicon seems indicated by JC's symptoms. That diagnosis is reinforced by the fact that as well as making regularisation and other errors of grapheme–phoneme conversion, JC also made frequent visual errors where one word was misread as another (e.g. *apron* misread as "open"; *direction* as "decision"; *precise* as "precious"). In contrast to the laborious grapheme–phoneme errors, these visual errors were typically produced rapidly, though often acknowledged later to be incorrect (Holmes, 1973).

A different locus of impairment is indicated in "surface" dyslexic patients like HTR (Shallice, Warrington, & McCarthy, 1983) described above, or like MP (Bub, Cancelliere, & Kertesz, 1985) and KT (McCarthy & Warrington, 1986). These patients have impaired semantic systems with concomitant difficulties comprehending both spoken and written words, along with "anomic" word-finding problems in spontaneous speech (see pp. 116–119). Each of these patients showed good non-word reading and read highly regular words aloud well, though they often did not understand them.

Bub et al. (1985) carried out an instructive *post-hoc* analysis of their patient MP's ability to read aloud regular and irregular words of different word frequencies. The results are shown in Fig. 8.2. As can be seen, MP's problems with irregular words were only acute when they were of low frequency (i.e. relatively uncommon words). Common, high-frequency irregular words were read with around 80% accuracy.

Bub et al. (1985) also carried out a test in which MP was shown cards on which were printed an irregular word that she had mispronounced consistently on previous occasions (e.g. *leopard*) and a non-word modelled on an irregular word (e.g. *rubtle*). MP's task was to indicate which was the real word. She was able to do this reasonably well (82% correct), suggesting to Bub et al. that the representations of those irregular words she could not read aloud correctly were still present in the visual input lexicon and still able to sustain reasonable performance in this lexical decision task. MP's better reading of high-frequency rather than low-frequency irregular words is attributed by Bub et al. to stronger direct links between corresponding representations in the visual input lexicon and speech output lexicon for frequently encountered words. They suggest that even in normals whole-word reading via the direct, non-semantic route between the visual input and speech output lexicons may become inherently less efficient as word frequency decreases.

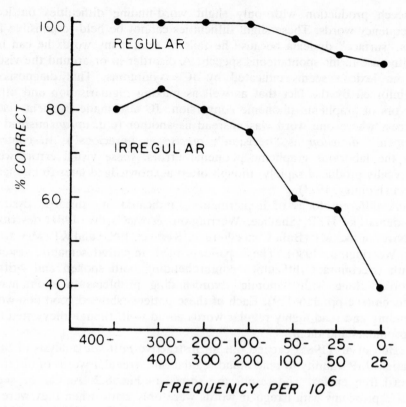

FIG. 8.2.   Effects of word frequency and orthographic regularity on the reading accuracy of patient MP. (Reproduced with permission from Bub, Cancelliere, & Kertesz, 1985.)

So far, then, we have encountered "surface" dyslexia as a consequence of impairment to the visual input lexicon and as a consequence of impairment to the semantic system. Figure 8.1 also permits "surface" dyslexia to arise, however, as a result of an impairment in or around the speech output lexicon. Whole-word reading aloud would be handicapped in such a patient because of difficulties in accessing the pronunciations of words as wholes from the speech output lexicon. The intact visual input lexicon and semantic system would ensure that all familiar written words were recognised and understood, but if the patient was required to read aloud, then those words whose pronunciations could no longer be re-trieved from the speech output lexicon would have to have candidate pronunciations assembled by grapheme–phoneme conversion, with con-comitant difficulties with irregular words and regularisation errors.

Patient MK (Howard & Franklin, 1987) fits this pattern reasonably well. He read regular words aloud better than irregular words, and the majority of his errors were regularisations. However, in a lexical decision task where he was required to distinguish real words from invented non-words he performed at 97.5% accuracy, and made no more errors to irregular words than to regular words. Similarly, when his task was to define words he was shown, rather than to read them aloud, he performed equally well on both regular and irregular words.

MK's ability to identify irregular words as words in the lexical decision task implies intact representations of these words in the visual input lexicon, and his ability to define them as well as he defines regular words implies that their semantic representations are being activated normally. Yet when required to read words aloud he seems to rely heavily on sublexical grapheme–phoneme conversion (hence the regular word advantage and regularisation errors). This suggests that his problems in reading words aloud lies at the stage of retrieving their spoken word-forms as wholes from the speech output lexicon. Other "surface" dyslexics whose problems appear to lie at this stage are described by Kremin (1985), Goldblum (1985), and Kay and Patterson (1985; see also Kay & Ellis, 1987).

We have thus seen that impairment at three different loci (at least) can force a reliance upon sublexical grapheme–phoneme conversion in reading aloud. It is a moot point whether the similarities between these patients (regularity effect in reading aloud and regularisation errors) outweigh their differences sufficiently to make it worth uniting them into a category called "surface dyslexia" (Coltheart & Funnell, 1987). The problem is exacerbated when patients are presented as "surface" dyslexics who show no regularity effect and very few regularisation errors (e.g. Margolin, Marcel, & Carlson, 1985), or when patients shift by imperceptible degrees from being whole-word non-semantic readers to being "surface" dyslexics (e.g. Shallice, Warrington, & McCarthy, 1983). As stated elsewhere in this book, our preferred solution to this dilemma is to avoid syndrome categories except as convenient shorthands and to relate each patient individually to an explicit theoretical model, treating each case as a separate test of that model. The differing reasons why each of the patients described in this section must lean on grapheme–phoneme conversion when reading aloud are explicable in terms of our model, and the question of whether they rightly belong together in a category called "surface dyslexia" is for present purposes of secondary importance.

READING VIA MEANING

From patients who are often unable to read aloud via semantics and must read via alternative routes we now turn to patients in whom it is those alternative routes that are impaired. This second group of central dyslexias involves patients whose brain injury has restricted them to reading via meanings, though in some even that route is affected.

"Phonological" Dyslexia

The first of this group of central dyslexias that we shall consider is of interest because it was only detected after it had been predicted by a cognitive theory. It has very direct and immediate implications for theories of normal reading processes. "Phonological" dyslexia was first reported by Beauvois and Dérousné (1979). Their French patient, RG, was a 64-year-old man whose ability to read real, familiar words was greatly superior to his ability to read invented non-words. Thus in one test he read 40 five- to nine-letter words without making any errors, but managed to read only 4 of 40 four- or five-letter non-words. His errors to non-words were either failed attempts at grapheme–phoneme conversion or visual errors rather like those of the "visual" dyslexics discussed above.

Shallice and Warrington (1980), Patterson (1982), and Funnell (1983) reported subsequent cases of "phonological" dyslexia in English-speaking patients. Patterson's (1982) patient AM was a 62-year-old former supervisor in a printing firm who had only minor problems with speech production and good auditory comprehension. His comprehension and reading aloud of single content words was good, but his reading aloud of non-words was poor. In one session of testing he successfully read aloud 95% of a list of content words, including fairly uncommon words like *decree* and *phrase*, but he managed to read only 8% of a list of non-words correctly. His errors mostly took the form of reading a non-word as a visually similar real word, for example reading *soof* as "soot", and *klack* as "slack, black, flock".

AM made some derivational errors reading real words (e.g. reading *applaud* as "applause", and *sole* as "absolve") and had difficulties with function words, but neither of these occurred in Funnell's (1983) patient WB. This patient had, however, the same difficulty as AM with non-words which he too tended to misread as visually similar real words (e.g. *cobe* read as "comb", *ploon* as "spoon"). Funnell carried out further tests to try to diagnose more closely the nature of WB's problem with unfamiliar non-words. WB was able to segment spoken words into syllables and to isolate the initial phoneme from a spoken word. He could also segment written words into further words on request (e.g. divide *inside* into "in" and "side", or *father* into "fat" and "her"), and could find the hidden word in a written non-word (e.g. *for* in *alforsut*). He did not, however, segment non-words like *tugant* or *pigham* spontaneously into their component real words in order to read them aloud, and had considerable difficulty applying this strategy when encouraged to do so.

Funnell (1983) proposed that WB first inspected a letter string for wordness. If it was a word it could be comprehended and pronounced as a whole via the visual input lexicon. If it was not a word he was at a loss, because he could no longer draw upon grapheme–phoneme conversion procedures. His competence with visual and phonological segmentation suggests that the processes at either side of grapheme–phoneme conversion were reasonably well preserved, but that the *translation* of a letter string into a phoneme string could no longer be effected.

The theoretical implications of WB's dyslexia are clear. He cannot apply grapheme–phoneme conversion procedures to letter strings he has never seen before, yet a letter string which forms a familiar word can be read aloud with comparative ease. Therefore, the processes for pronouncing known words must be separable from those for pronouncing unknown words. Also, access to the meaning of familiar words cannot normally be preceded by a process of piecemeal grapheme–phoneme translation as had been proposed as an account of skilled reading by Meyer and Schvaneveldt (1971), Gough (1972), and others.

Finally, we might note that assembling a pronunciation for an unfamiliar letter string is likely to involve more than one psychological process (Coltheart, 1986). The first process might involve a graphemic segmentation of the letter strings into groups which will map onto single phonemes or syllables (e.g. *THACHIPHORE* into TH – A – CH – I – PH – O(R)E). The second stage might be the actual translation of those segments into a string of phonemes, whereas the third might be the "blending together" of the phonemes into an articulated pronunciation. Funnell's (1983) patient WB may primarily have suffered damage to the second, translation stage, whereas other "phonological" dyslexics may be identified whose primary difficulty lies at one of the other stages. Thus the same set of surface symptoms can, as all clinicians know, arise from different underlying deficits. We must be careful not to assume too readily that patients showing the same symptoms necessarily have the same underlying functional impairment.

"Semantic Access" Dyslexia

Patient AR, reported by Warrington and Shallice (1979), had difficulty naming seen objects though he could name them from descriptions. His reading aloud of single words was reduced to only 30–50% correct, though his spelling to dictation was much better. Of special interest here is what AR could do with words he could not read aloud. Shown the word *beaver* AR said: "could be an animal, I have no idea which one". Shown *cereal* he said: "It is something you eat." He then added: "It seems as if I am almost there, but it seems as if I can't go over the last little bit and finally grasp it."

More detailed testing by Warrington and Shallice (1979) confirmed the impression that AR grasped much, though not all, of the meaning of words he could not read aloud. Thus he could usually categorise correctly a word he could not read aloud as being an animal, or a part of the body, or a foodstuff, etc. Sometimes a semantic prompt helped him name the word. Thus having failed initially to read *pyramid*, he read it correctly after being given the clue "Egypt".

Warrington and Shallice (1979) interpret AR's difficulty as lying between the visual input lexicon and the semantic system (see also Shallice, 1981a). That is, AR could activate the correct representation in the visual input lexicon but often could not negotiate successfully the next step to activating the precise semantic entry. He could usually access the broad area however, providing enough information to succeed in categorisation tasks. Verbal prompts presumably activated the same semantic areas even more from a different access route, helping to form the connection between visual input lexicon and semantic entries. An alternative possibility is that AR's semantic representations were being fully activated, but that his problem lay in gaining *conscious access* to word meanings. We have seen earlier in this chapter how some demented patients may continue to show semantic priming while no longer being consciously aware of the meanings of words they are reading (Nebes, Martin, & Horn, 1984).

As a final point we note that AR had much less difficulty accessing the meanings of heard words. Other patients discussed in Chapter 6 have problems accessing the meanings of heard words but not of seen words. Whatever interpretation is placed upon such access problems, this dissociation supports our policy of regarding the visual and auditory input lexicons as separate components having separate access routes to the semantic system.

"Deep" Dyslexia

Recent interest in the reading disorder known as "deep" dyslexia stems again from the work of Marshall and Newcombe (1966; 1973), but earlier patients in the literature have, with hindsight, been diagnosed retrospectively as cases of "deep" dyslexia (Coltheart, 1980a; Marshall & Newcombe, 1980). The symptom of deep dyslexia which has probably caused most interest is the *semantic error*. A semantic error occurs when a patient reads aloud a printed word as another word similar in meaning. Examples taken from the Appendix to Coltheart, Patterson, and Marshall (1980) are *tandem* read as "cycle", *cost* read as "money", *deed* as "solicitors", *decay* as "rubbish", and *city* as "town".

Patients who make semantic errors in reading also show a number of other characteristics which typically co-occur with the semantic errors and are often considered as defining features of deep dyslexia (Coltheart, 1980a).

These features include:

1. Greater success at reading aloud concrete, imageable words like *butter* or *windmill* than abstract words like *grief* or *wish*, and greater success with content words in general (nouns, verbs, and adjectives) than function words like *was* or *quite*. Errors to function words tend to be other function words (e.g. *was* read as "with", *if* as "yet", *quite* as "perhaps").

2. Frequent visual errors such as misreading *signal* as "single", *decree* as "degree", or *charter* as "garters".

3. "Morphological" (or "derivational") errors such as misreading *edition* as "editor" or *courage* as "courageous".

4. Visual-then-semantic errors, as when a patient misreads *sympathy* as "orchestra", presumably by a visual error to *sympathy* producing the intermediate "symphony" which a semantic error transmuted into "orchestra" (Marshall & Newcombe, 1966). Other likely examples from Patterson (Appendix to Coltheart, Patterson, & Marshall, 1980) include *charter* read as "map" (via *chart*?), *favour* as "taste" (via *flavour*?), and *pivot* as "airplane" (via *pilot*?).

5. Very poor reading of non-words.

What are we to make of this cluster of co-occurring features (including the semantic errors)? At the time of writing there are two main schools of thought regarding deep dyslexia. The first school, exemplified by Morton and Patterson (1980), Newcombe and Marshall (1980a; 1980b), and Shallice and Warrington (1980), takes the same attitude to deep dyslexia that we have taken here to the other acquired dyslexias; that is, it seeks to explain deep dyslexia as the reading performance of a damaged, normal reading system. The alternative school of thought, exemplified by Coltheart (1980b; 1983), Saffran, Bogyo, Schwartz, and Marin (1980a), and Zaidel and Peters (1981), draws attention to the extensive left cerebral hemisphere damage suffered by deep dyslexic patients and suggests that many of the characteristics of deep dyslexia may reflect the involvement of the patient's intact right hemisphere using its limited reading powers. We shall inspect this "right hemisphere hypothesis" of deep dyslexia more closely a little later, but will begin with an examination of the "impaired normal system hypothesis".

First, what is the role in deep dyslexia of the almost total inability to read unfamiliar words or non-words aloud? All investigators agree in construing this inability as an impairment (usually severe) to the processes involved in grapheme–phoneme conversion. Newcombe and Marshall (1980a; 1980b) have, however, gone one step further in suggesting, albeit tentatively, that an impairment to grapheme–phoneme conversion may be *sufficient* to cause semantic errors. They argue that reading via semantics may be a procedure that is inherently prone to semantic errors which are prevented from occurring when normal people read single words aloud by the error-checking function of grapheme–phoneme conversion. Thus a normal reader would never, according to Newcombe and Marshall, read *tandem* as "cycle", because the phoneme level would be receiving a candidate pronunciation via grapheme–phoneme conversion, which would be so different from "cycle" as to inhibit the possible production of "cycle" as a response.

This hypothesis is not without its attractions—semantic errors *have* been observed in normal rapid reading where the speed of reading might be thought to impede grapheme–phoneme conversion (e.g. Morton, 1964)—but it also has its problems. One objection is that "phonological" dyslexics are also poor at reading non-words, yet they make few or no semantic errors (though "phonological" dyslexics are typically not *as* poor at non-word reading as the "deep" dyslexic patients who make semantic errors). A weaker version of the Newcombe and Marshall hypothesis might propose that grapheme–phoneme conversion impairment is a *necessary* condition for the occurrence of semantic errors if not a *sufficient* one. Semantic errors should not occur in a patient with a reasonable capacity for grapheme–phoneme conversion (i.e. a reasonable ability to read non-words aloud). We might note at this point that deep dyslexics must also have an impairment to the whole-word route mediated by the connections between the visual input lexicon and the speech output lexicon. It is only because both this route *and* the route via grapheme–phoneme conversion are inoperative that the patient must read via the semantic route.

Those authors who wish to subscribe to the "impaired normal system" approach, but who do not believe that all of the deep dyslexic symptoms can be blamed on loss of the non-semantic routes, usually propose an additional impairment somewhere around the semantic system. Unfortunately, most of the case studies of deep dyslexics have concentrated solely on reading and have not assessed semantic competence in other areas. If the semantic system is impaired in deep dyslexics, then they should have problems with auditory word comprehension (e.g. of abstract words), and might make semantic errors in other tasks. In one of the few case studies to assess competence more widely, Nolan and Caramazza (1982) found that their patient made semantic errors not only in reading aloud, but also in picture naming (e.g. misnaming a sofa as a "chair"). A central semantic impairment might also ultimately explain the better reading of concrete than abstract words by deep dyslexics, a feature which is presumably due to some difference in the semantic representations of those words.

There is some evidence that the precise nature of the central deficit may vary between patients. Patient GR of Newcombe and Marshall (1980a) made semantic errors when shown a written word and then asked to point to the correct picture in a set which included the correct item plus other, semantically related objects. Thus, if shown the word *fork*, GR might fail to point to the picture of a fork and point instead to the picture of a knife. In contrast, patients PW and DE (Patterson, 1978; 1979; Morton & Patterson, 1980) would make semantic errors in reading aloud but not in word-picture matching (Patterson & Besner, 1984). These and other differences suggest that GR has difficulty accessing precise semantic representations of words from print and sometimes accesses the wrong meanings, whereas PW and DE can access the meanings of the words they are asked to read but make errors when trying to activate the correct representations in the speech output lexicon. This distinction between "input" and "output" forms of "deep" dyslexia was first proposed by Shallice and Warrington (1980).

Morphological Errors

The defining list of symptoms of deep dyslexia includes the presence of so-called morphological errors, such as misreading *angling* as "angler", *worker* as "working", or *salty* as "salt" (Patterson, 1980). These errors are not confined to deep dyslexics, having been observed in several other types of acquired dyslexic patient, but there are problems in how they should be interpreted. For some theorists, the existence of morphological errors in acquired dyslexia supports accounts of normal word recognition which propose that written words are decomposed into their component morphemes before they access the visual input lexicon (e.g. Taft, 1985). By this account, dyslexics who make morphological errors can decompose words into their component morphemes, separating *angling* into *angl-* + *ing*, *worker* into *work-* + *er*, and *salty* into *salt-* + *y*, but have problems with the "bound" morphemes *-ing*, *-er*, and *-y*, and tend to omit or substitute them in reading aloud, resulting in morphological errors (see Caramazza, Miceli, Silveri, & Laudanna, 1985; Job & Sartori, 1984).

Unfortunately, all acquired dyslexic patients so far reported who make morphological errors also make visual errors, semantic errors, or both, and morphological errors are open to alternative construal as either visual or semantic errors. Thus one cannot be confident that a patient who misreads *edition* as "editor" is making a morphological error when that same patient also misreads *gravel* as "grave" and *pupil* as "puppy". Funnell (1987) found that the morphological errors of the two patients she studied were influenced by the variables of word frequency and imageability in precisely the same way as their non-morphological errors, leading Funnell to conclude that the study of morphological errors "has turned out to be a study of a type of visual error in which an embedded word in the stimulus is produced as oral reading response".

Similarly, doubts can be cast over the evidence from experiments on normal subjects that is used to support the notion of obligatory morphological decomposition in visual word recognition (Henderson, 1985). At the time of writing the issue is, however, still being debated strongly, so a firm conclusion one way or the other would be unwise.

Deep Dyslexia and the Right Hemisphere

Returning to the explanation of deep dyslexia, a quite different approach was proposed by Coltheart (1980b; 1983) in his "right hemisphere hypothesis". The hypothesis proposes that word recognition is mediated by a visual input lexicon in the deep dyslexic patient's right hemisphere, though word pronunciations still come from the speech output lexicon in the left hemisphere. Coltheart seeks to support this view by comparing deep dyslexic reading (1) to the capacities claimed for the right hemispheres of "split-brain" patients (whose two cerebral hemispheres have been surgically separated in an operation to relieve epilepsy); (2) to the residual language skills of the few patients whose entire left hemispheres have been surgically removed; and (3) to the capacities of the normal right hemisphere as revealed through experiments on normal subjects in which words are presented briefly to the left or right of a fixation spot (a technique which, for purely anatomical reasons, projects information initially to one or other of the cerebral hemispheres—see Beaumont, 1982; Young, 1982).

Some support can be gained for the right hemisphere hypothesis by making these comparisons. Deep dyslexics cannot read non-words, and neither can the right hemispheres of split-brain patients (Zaidel & Peters, 1981) or normal subjects (Young, Ellis, & Bion, 1984). With normal subjects, abstract words have sometimes been found to lead to a greater right visual half-field (left hemisphere) advantage than concrete words, which is compatible with the suggestion that, whereas all recognition of abstract words is performed by the left hemisphere, the right hemisphere can contribute to the recognition of concrete words (e.g. Bradshaw & Gates, 1978; Day, 1977; Ellis & Shepherd, 1974; Hines, 1976, 1977; Young & Ellis, 1985). Also, two split brain patients studied by Zaidel (1982) made semantic errors when selecting pictures to match printed words, and a patient studied by Gott (1973) made some semantic reading errors after removal of her left hemisphere. The parallels with the semantic errors of deep dyslexic patients are obvious.

Despite these positive lines of comparison, some serious problems for the right hemisphere hypothesis have been raised by Marshall and Patterson (1983) and Patterson and Besner (1984). First, the reading performance of the two deep dyslexics studied by Patterson and Besner (1984) was substantially superior to that of the right hemispheres of any split-brain patients yet reported. Secondly, there has been discussion about whether the few intensively studied split-brain patients are exceptional in the extent of their right hemisphere language capacities (possibly due to early left hemisphere damage). Gazzaniga (1983), for instance, maintains that only 5 of the 44 split-brain patients studied to date have any genuine right hemisphere language. Thirdly, several of the studies which have looked for differences between the two visual half-fields (and hence the two cerebral hemispheres) of normal people in their capacity to identify concrete rather than abstract words have failed to find any difference (see Lambert, 1982; Patterson & Besner, 1984; Young, 1987b for reviews). When differences have been found, they are always such as to imply greater left hemisphere superiority for abstract words, but because this finding is not made consistently it would be unwise to draw firm conclusions from these experiments at present.

The debate as to how deep dyslexia should be interpreted is clearly not over yet. Its resolution is, however, of some importance to cognitive neuropsychology. If what we see in deep dyslexia is the word recognition and comprehension skills of the right hemispheres of normal people (or even a minority of normal people), then we must begin to ask what role, if any, that secondary reading system plays in the normal reading process. It could be that the secondary system is *suppressed* in normal, intact individuals and hence only becomes evident after brain injury (Landis, Regard, Graves, & Goodglass, 1983) but this would leave us to ask with Marshall and Patterson (1983) "How plausible is it that one part of the normal . . . brain should inhibit the performance of another part which is committed (albeit less effectively perhaps) to the same functions? What principle of biological engineering could demand such organisation?" In sum, why develop a right hemisphere reading system only to suppress it?

Additionally, a main aim of cognitive neuropsychology is to be able to draw inferences and conclusions from the performance of brain-injured patients to models and theories of *normal* cognitive processes. If what we see in deep dyslexia is the performance of a secondary, and possibly inessential, right hemisphere reading system, then we are unlikely to be able to draw any conclusions from deep dyslexia about the nature of the normal, dominant (left hemisphere) reading system. Only if deep dyslexia reflects the reading capacities of a damaged normal system (as proposed by the first school of thought we reviewed) will it have much to teach us about the properties of that normal system.

READING AND SPEECH PROCESSES

Access to Semantics Without Access to Sound

We have argued from the reported cases of "phonological" and "deep" dyslexia that grapheme–phoneme conversion processes do not necessarily, or even ordinarily, intervene in extracting the meaning from a printed word (see Coltheart, 1980c). Other patients permit us to go one step further to the conclusion that single written words can be understood without the reader's having any idea of how the word sounds.

One line of evidence comes from neologistic jargonaphasic patients like JS (Caramazza, Berndt, & Basili, 1983) and RD (Ellis, Miller, & Sin, 1983). We first came across these patients in Chapter 5 where we noted how their spontaneous speech is full of distorted approximations to target words ("neologisms"). These distortions also characterised their attempts at reading aloud. Thus JS read *both* as "blukts", *bible* as "mowbl", and *butterfly* as "bowdlfley". Similarly, RD read *biscuit* as "biskyut", *despite* as "rediyvist", and *whether* as "geishta". What matters here, however, is that the inability of JS and RD to pronounce many written words correctly did not prevent them from understanding those words. After RD had read *grief* as "preevd" he added, "one is sad". Shown *depth*, he said, "seft... it's very deep down", and to *chaos* he said, "kwost... people all muddled up... out of order... chost". RD could sort written words into categories (e.g. animals *vs.* musical instruments) despite being able to pronounce very few of them correctly, could judge whether pairs of words had similar or different meanings, and could sort sentences into those like *He sat reading a paper* which made sense, and those like *Passing overhead was a kitchen* which were nonsensical (Ellis et al., 1983). Likewise, JS, despite an ability to read aloud which was if anything worse than RD's, could sort written words from non-words and could reject as nonsensical sentences like *The barber captured the razor* (Caramazza et al., 1983).

Levine, Calvanio, and Popovics' (1982) patient EB was discussed in the previous chapter because he retained the capacity to write despite loss of any access to, or apparent knowledge of, the sounds of words. He could not tell which two of a set of four words sounded the same, or rhymed (a deficit also observed in JS), and tended to choose the pair which looked most alike irrespective of their sounds. His understanding of what he read was, however, apparently intact. He read only slowly, but obtained close to maximum scores on a range of tests of reading comprehension.

Patients like JS, RD, and EB can understand written words despite having little or no access to the sounds of those words. They therefore lend support to the theory that there is a route from print to meaning for familiar words which does not involve the sound of the word in any way. In our model, that route is represented by the direct visual access to semantics that is provided by the visual input lexicon. If a letter string corresponds to a known word it will activate the representation for that word in the visual input lexicon. Activation will then pass directly to the representation of the word's meaning in the semantic system along a route in which sound plays no part.

Inner Speech and Reading

We have said that print can access meanings without any involvement of the sounds of words. And yet in normal reading most people are aware of an "inner voice" saying the words as they are read. Does that inner voice have no role to play? Before trying to answer that question we must first ask how inner speech is generated. The voice in the head pronounces irregular words as happily as it pronounces regular words. That simple observation is sufficient to establish that the inner voice we hear is not relaying the products of the grapheme–phoneme conversion route. Additionally, the inner voice assigns the correct pronunciation to a word like *tear* whose pronunciation depends on which of its two meanings is implied (*Her dress had a tear in it* vs. *Her eye had a tear in it*). This suggests that the inner voice speaks words *after* they have been understood, a proposal which is endorsed by the fact that words in inner speech carry the appropriate emphasis and intonation.

In our model, inner speech is represented by the loop back from the phoneme level below the speech output lexicon to the acoustic analysis system and thence to the auditory input lexicon. Familiar written words are recognised via the visual input lexicon, understood by the semantic system, and pronounced by the speech output lexicon. Those pronunciations can then be recycled from the phoneme level as inner speech, allowing the words to be "heard" as well as seen. Familiar words will then be recognised again, this time by the auditory input lexicon, and their semantic representations will receive a fresh boost. Detailing the procedure in this way makes the whole sequence of operations sound slow and ponderous, but in fact it is probably very rapid and fairly automatic (Jakimik, Cole, & Rudnicky, 1985; Rollins & Hendricks, 1980).

So what happens if a patient has lost the capacity for inner speech? Do any penalties accrue to reading comprehension? There are hints in the neuropsychological literature that there may be some penalties, and these hints converge to some extent with the results of experiments in which normal subjects have been asked to read without benefit of inner speech. It will be recalled that patient JS (Caramazza et al., 1983) produced many distorted neologisms in attempting to read aloud, but could nevertheless perform various semantic judgements on written words and sentences. His performance deteriorated badly, however, when success was made contingent upon the processing of syntactic cues such as word order. He could reliably select a picture to match *The block is under the pyramid*, provided that the other pictures depicted balls under pyramids, say, or blocks beside pyramids. If, however, one of the pictures was of a pyramid under a block he was very likely to select it erroneously. JS understood *pyramid, block*, and *under* as individual words, and provided that comprehension was sufficient to solve the task he was all right. But when he had to use the *order* of the words in the sentence to determine which object was under which other object his performance declined markedly. Similarly, he could reject semantically anomalous sentences like *The barber captured the razor* as ill-formed, but he could not reject a syntactically anomalous sentence like *The girl will dressing the doll* as unacceptable in English. Caramazza et al. (1983) propose on the basis of these observations that phonological information is necessary to provide access to the internal machinery which utilises sentence structure in the service of better text comprehension. A patient with rather similar problems confined to understanding reversible sentences was reported by Caramazza, Basili, Koller, and Berndt (1981). In neither of these cases, however, was the problem shown to be specific to reading and absent from the comprehension of spoken sentences.

Patient MV, reported by Bub, Black, Howell, and Kertesz (1987), could detect both semantic and syntactic (word order) anomalies in spoken sentences. With written sentences, however, she could detect semantic anomalies but not syntactic ones. Thus she would reject a written sentence like *The bird flew up the book* (semantically anomalous) as unacceptable, but not *They gave me ride a home* (syntactically anomalous), though she *could* reject the latter sentence perfectly well if she heard it rather than read it. Analysis of MV's performance on a variety of other tasks suggested that she had an impairment which prevented the silent recycling of phonemic representations as inner speech. Her grammatical deficit specific to reading is precisely what one would predict if Caramazza et al.'s theory is correct.

Finally, the converging evidence from normals that we alluded to earlier comes from experiments like those of Kleiman (1981), Baddeley and Lewis (1981), and Levy (1981). In these experiments normal individuals are required to perform various judgements on written sentences while simultaneously saying something irrelevant such as a string of digits or "the-the-the". The aim of the irrelevant articulation is to inhibit inner speech during reading. The results of these experiments suggest that concurrent articulation impairs the capacity of normal readers to detect syntactic anomalies more than it impairs their ability to detect semantic anomalies.

Thus, single written words can be understood without their sound-patterns having to be evoked first. But the direct link from the visual input lexicon to the semantic system does not appear to engage those syntactic processes necessary for the grammatical analysis of sentences one is reading. Those processes appear to operate upon a speech-based code, so that written sentences which are to undergo syntactic analysis must first be converted into spoken form and then recycled back to auditory comprehension processes. As stated earlier, however, the conversion of print to sound in the normal reading of text is a whole-word, semantically mediated process which does not depend upon sublexical grapheme–phoneme conversion.

OVERVIEW: A COMPOSITE MODEL FOR WORD RECOGNITION AND PRODUCTION

The model for reading used in this chapter (Fig. 8.1) shares components in common with the model for spoken word production in Chapter 5 (Fig. 5.2, p. 116), with the model for spoken word comprehension in Chapter 6 (Fig. 6.1., p. 145), and with the model for spelling and writing in Chapter 7 (Figs 7.1 and 7.2, pp. 175 and 181). Each of those models, however, only drew upon the components necessary for the particular skill under consideration.

Figure 8.3 shows the composite model which emerges if those four separate models are fused together, while Table 8.1 represents an extensive commentary on the composite model, summarising the role of each module and some of the connections, and the symptoms which arise when those components and connections are damaged. We would point out that every one of the modules in Fig. 8.3 can be justified with reference to evidence from both normal subjects and brain-injured patients. Similarly, all the connections are empirically motivated: We have kept the links between modules down to the bare minimum necessary to account for the available evidence.

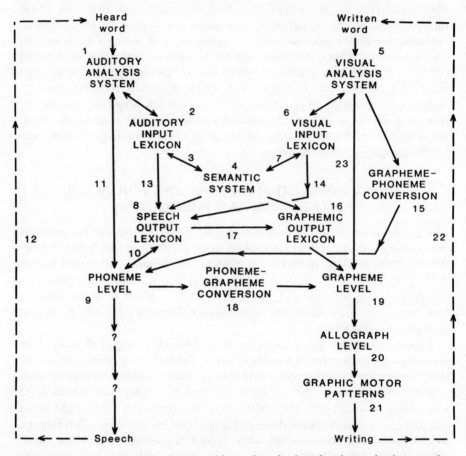

FIG. 8.3. Composite model for the recognition and production of spoken and written words (see Table 8.1 for an explanation of each numbered component and connection).

TABLE 8.1

A Summary of the Functions of all the Components and Some of the Connections in Fig. 8.3, with a Mention of the Disorders which may Arise through Impairment

1. The function of the auditory analysis system is to extract individual speech sounds (possibly phonemes, though there are other candidates) from the speech wave. It does this despite differences in accent, voice, speech rate, etc. and so must have the flexibility to cope with these variations. It must also cope with the fact that speech is often heard against a substantial level of background noise.

The acoustic analysis system may be impaired selectively in some patients with "pure word deafness" (pp. 146–153) who have difficulties understanding and repeating heard words though they can still speak, read, and write normally. They still hear speech, and may be able to identify vowels but not consonants (which require the analysis of rapidly changing acoustic signals). Speech comprehension may be aided by lipreading cues, by context, and by slowing the speech to a rate which may allow the less efficient acoustic analysis system of the right hemisphere to sustain phonetic perception.

2. The function of the auditory input lexicon is to recognise familiar spoken words. It simply signals that a word has been heard before—knowing what the word means requires subsequent activation of its semantic representation in the semantic system.

Selective impairment of the auditory input lexicon would result in a patient who could no longer recognise many or all spoken words but could repeat them correctly using the by-pass route from the acoustic analysis system to the phoneme level. Intact repetition distinguishes this impairment from "pure word deafness" (see 1 above). Speech production should be intact as should most aspects of reading (though not the ability to comprehend misspelled pseudohomophones like "phoks" or "neffue") and most aspects of writing (though the patient should tend to misspell dictated homophones like *peak* and *pique* when these are not understood). Certain patients with "word meaning deafness" (pp. 153–155) may fit this description (though see 3 below).

3. The link between the auditory input lexicon and the semantic system allows heard words which have been recognised as familiar to access their meanings in the semantic system. Selective impairment to this connection will result in a patient who can distinguish heard words from non-words (auditory lexical decision), and can repeat both words and non-words, but fails to understand many words. This failure of auditory word comprehension need not be accompanied by any problems in understanding familiar written words, nor any problems with speech production.

Some patients with "word meaning deafness" who can still write to dictation irregular words they cannot understand may fit this description (pp. 153–155 and p. 177). Impairment of 3 is also seen in patients with "semantic access dysphasia", which may be specific to certain categories of words (pp. 156–158).

4. The semantic system is the (grossly underspecified) component in which word meanings are represented. It corresponds to the "semantic memory" component of many cognitive theories of memory. According to some theorists, the semantic system should be divided into a verbal semantic system where word meanings are represented and a non-verbal semantic system in which such things as one's knowledge of objects and people is stored.

Several different neuropsychological conditions may include semantic system impairments. Among these are dementia, category-specific impairments which compromise equally the production and comprehension of both spoken and written words, "deep dysphasia" where semantic errors are made in auditory-vocal repetition (pp. 157–158), and "deep dyslexia" in which both semantic errors in reading aloud and the characteristic imageability effect

(Continued)

TABLE 8.1
(Continued)

(better reading of concrete than abstract words) have been attributed to semantic system impairments (pp. 212–217).

5. The visual analysis system has three functions: (1) to identify letters in written words (or non-words or letter strings); (2) to encode each letter for its position within its word; and (3) to group perceptually those letters which belong together as part of the same word. One or other of these functions may be disturbed in patients with certain "peripheral" acquired dyslexias. Thus patients with "neglect dyslexia" may fail to identify letters at one end of a word (pp. 195–197), whereas "attentional dyslexics" may have problems with perceptual groupings which result in errors which incorporate letters from two or more words present in the visual field (pp. 197–199).

Normally the visual analysis system can identify several letters simultaneously and in parallel (hence word length has little effect on the recognition of familiar words). On one theory of "letter-by-letter reading" (pp. 199–201) letter identification has been reduced to a serial process with only one letter at a time being transmitted from the visual analysis system to the visual input lexicon (Patterson & Kay, 1982). An alternative theory (Warrington & Shallice, 1980) holds that transmission of information from the visual analysis system to the visual input lexicon is completely severed, so that letter information must be transmitted instead along connection 22 to the spelling system which effects recognition in a slow and laborious manner (possibly back up through the graphemic output lexicon to the semantic system, though this is *highly* speculative).

6. The function of the visual input lexicon in reading is analogous to that of the auditory input lexicon in speech perception. It identifies strings of letters which form familiar written words. It can respond to an unfamiliar word (or non-word) by declaring it unfamiliar, by allowing it to activate the representation of a visual similar real word (hence perhaps allowing a patient to respond "table" to the non-word *toble*), or possibly by initiating an attempt at pronunciation based on analogy with familiar words. The visual input lexicon indicates that a word has been seen before, but if the word is to be understood it must activate its semantic representation in the semantic system (4), and if it is to be pronounced correctly it must activate its spoken form in the speech output lexicon (8).

Impairment to the visual input lexicon may account for visual errors such as misreading *arrangement* as "argument", or *calm* as "clam". These are the predominant error forms in "visual" dyslexia (p. 202), but accompany other symptoms in many other forms of acquired dyslexia.

7. The link between the visual input lexicon and the semantic system allows written words which have been recognised as familiar to access their meanings in the semantic system (4). Selective impairments to this connection will result in a patient who can distinguish written words from non-words (visual lexical decision) but fails to understand many written words, or understands them only slowly and incompletely. Auditory word comprehension, speaking, and writing could remain intact. Patients with "semantic access dyslexia" may approximate to this description (pp. 211–212).

8. The function of the speech output lexicon is to make the spoken form of a word available to a speaker. In speech production this will occur in response to activation from the semantic system; in reading it may occur through a combination of input from the semantic system and more direct connections from the visual intput lexicon (see 14 below).

Evidence from both normal subjects and brain-injured patients suggests that ease of activating entries for words in the speech output lexicon is a function of word frequency, with

(Continued)

TABLE 8.1
(Continued)

commonly used (high-frequency) words being easier to access than less commonly used (low-frequency) words. This pattern may be seen in "anomic" aphasics with word-finding problems for words whose meanings they have full awareness of (pp. 119–124). Such patients may only be able to retrieve reliably high-frequency words, though for less common words they may show partial access, generating approximations to words which can also be seen in normal subjects caught in tip-of-the-tongue states. These neologistic approximations may occur frequently in the speech of patients with "neologistic jargonaphasia", a condition in which word retrieval is also frequency-related (pp. 124–129). Target-related neologisms (phonological approximations) also show that retrieval of word-forms from the speech output lexicon is not an all-or-nothing affair.

9. At the phoneme level are represented individual distinctive speech sounds. These could be positionally coded, as letters are thought to be in the visual analysis system. The phoneme level receives inputs from three different sources. The first is the auditory analysis system. This provides a mechanism for the auditory-vocal repetition of both familiar and unfamiliar words (or non-words)—see 11 below. The second input is from the speech output lexicon: phonemes may be activated in the course of spontaneous speech production or reading aloud or semantically mediated repetition or object naming, and so on. Thirdly, the phoneme level may be activated by grapheme–phoneme conversion when unfamiliar words or non-words are being read aloud (see 15 below).

The phoneme level guides speech production through as yet unspecified processes which end in the articulation of speech sounds. The phoneme level can also guide "sublexical" or "assembled" spelling of words whose spellings are not represented in the graphemic output lexicon (see 16 and 17 below).

Slips of the tongue made by normal speakers involving substitution or misordering of phonemes may be attributed to errors at the phoneme level. One hallmark of such errors seems to be that they involve the replacement of phonemes by other phonetically similar phonemes (e.g. replacement of /b/ by /p/, or /g/ by /k/—see Ellis, 1979a; 1980). Errors arising at this level may also be seen in the speech of some Broca's aphasics and possibly some "conduction" aphasics.

10. The two-way arrow connecting the speech output lexicon to the phoneme level is meant to represent the notion that the lexicon and the phoneme level exist in a state of mutual, interactive activation. This means that as an entry in the speech output lexicon is activating its phonemes at the phoneme level, so activation is fed back up to the speech output lexicon in a form of positive feedback. The normal function of this interactive activation is to hasten the selection of entries in the lexicon and the activation of phonemes at the phoneme level, but it may occasionally err, resulting in the production of errors known as malapropisms, where a word similar to an intended target word is spoken by mistake. These word substitution errors are quite common in normal slips of the tongue and may also occur in aphasic patients. It may also be possible to invoke this interactive activation in order to account for certain spelling errors of normals and acquired dysgraphics in which a real word misspelling is produced which is similar or identical in sound to the intended word. This can be done if we postulate a direct link between corresponding entries in the speech output lexicon and the graphemic output lexicon (16; see also pp. 171–172).

11. Both normal speakers and many aphasic patients are able to repeat aloud unfamiliar words or invented non-words for which there will be no entries in the auditory input lexicon or speech output lexicon. This means that we must postulate a route from input to output

(Continued)

TABLE 8.1
(Continued)

which does not go through the two lexicons: This is provided in the model by the direct link between the auditory analysis system and the phoneme level. Although repetition of unfamiliar words is relatively uncommon in adulthood, it is a necessity which must arise very commonly in childhood where children repeat words they have not heard before in order to question adults about their meaning. In this respect, non-lexical repetition is more important in childhood than in adulthood, as may be non-lexical reading (see 15 below). The provision of a direct link between the auditory analysis system and the phoneme level provides a mechanism whereby unfamiliar words may be repeated without comprehension or recognition. This route is impaired in certain aphasic patients, e.g. "auditory phonological agnosics" and "deep dysphasics", whose repetition of non-words is much worse than their repetition of words.

The link between the auditory analysis system and the phoneme level is represented as a two-way link. This means that activation of phonemes at the phoneme level can be fed back to the auditory analysis system. This could provide a mechanism for what we experience in everyday life as "inner speech", where we appear to hear our own silent speech internally. This inner process of generating what is effectively an acoustic image from a phoneme level representation may also be important in the silent comprehension of written words which have been read aloud using grapheme–phoneme conversion, as when a child reads silently an unfamiliar written word, recognises its sound form as one which has been heard before, and understands the word.

12. As an alternative to the internal feedback from phonemes to the auditory analysis system afforded by 11 above, one may speak a word aloud and monitor one's own speech output by external feedback. The inability to monitor one's own speech and detect one's own errors may be a contributing factor in certain forms of aphasia. Thus it is suggested in Chapter 5 that "neologistic jargonaphasics" may freely produce large numbers of errors in their speech precisely because an accompanying speech perception disorder prevents them from detecting their own errors and therefore from knowing that their own speech is replete with mispronunciations.

13. A direct connection between an auditory input lexicon and a speech output lexicon appears in several models, including the logogen model (e.g. Morton & Patterson, 1980). The evidence for its existence is slim, however, and its presence makes models with separate input and output lexicons harder to distinguish empirically from models with a single input–output lexicon for spoken words (e.g. Allport & Funnell, 1981).

The main argument in favour of this connection is the fact that it helps complete a whole-word route from auditory input to written output that by-passes the semantic system (auditory analysis system to auditory input lexicon to speech output lexicon to graphemic output lexicon to writing or oral spelling). Such a route seems necessary to explain the ability of some patients with "word meaning deafness" to spell to dictation irregular words they appear not to understand (see p. 177). Better evidence for such a connection would be provided by a patient who could repeat words but not non-words without understanding the words he could repeat correctly.

It is a measure of the incomplete development of models such as Fig. 8.3 that we do not feel the need for a comparable connection between the visual input lexicon and the graphemic output lexicon.

14. Patients have been reported who can read aloud irregular words correctly without appearing to understand what those words mean. This has been taken to imply the existence

(Continued)

TABLE 8.1
(Continued)

of a whole-word route from the visual input lexicon to the speech output lexicon, by-passing the semantic system. Unlike route 13, this route is also supported by evidence from normal, intact subjects who are able to read aloud familiar, irregular words faster than they can perform any form of semantic categorisation upon those words. This finding is compatible with the notion that the retrieval of the pronunciation of a word following its recognition by the visual input lexicon can operate simultaneously and in parallel with the retrieval of the word's meaning from the semantic system.

15. Normal readers can read aloud unfamiliar words or non-words which they have never seen before. Hence we must incorporate into our models a route from letter recognition to speech output which does not depend on words being recognised as familiar by the visual input lexicon. One option is to postulate a distinct sublexical route by which unfamiliar words or non-words can be read aloud through a process of dividing a word up into letters or letter groups and translating those visual units into corresponding phoneme strings. This route would be relatively little used by skilled adult readers, but used extensively by children, for whom far fewer words are represented as wholes in the visual input lexicon, or by unskilled adult readers.

Some aspect of grapheme–phoneme conversion is impaired in "phonological dyslexics" who can read aloud real words much better than they can read aloud unfamiliar words or non-words. Grapheme–phoneme conversion is also severely impaired in "deep dyslexics".

On pp. 203–233 we acknowledge the existence of alternative theoretical accounts of how we might read aloud unfamiliar words, including accounts which would effectively merge grapheme–phoneme conversion with the whole-word route (14), which connects the visual input lexicon with the speech output lexicon.

16. The function of the graphemic output lexicon is to store the spellings of familiar words and make them available in the process of writing. It is particularly important for a language like English that spellings should be retrieved as wholes from memory, because of the presence in the language of so many words with irregular, unpredictable spellings. Words can be retrieved from the graphemic output lexicon in response to input from three different sources—the semantic system, the auditory input lexicon, and the speech output lexicon. We have discussed in 10 above the fact that an input from the speech output lexicon may allow us to explain certain types of spelling errors in which words are produced which are similar in sound to the intended word. An input from the semantic system may allow explanation of semantic errors in writing, both as made occasionally by normal subjects and as made in large numbers by "deep dysgraphics". Retrieval of spellings from the graphemic output lexicon is not all-or-nothing: We can see both in normal subjects and in a variety of acquired dysgraphic patients the occurrence of errors which incorporate unpredictable elements of a word's spelling, while nevertheless being incorrect. Arguably, such errors result from incomplete activation of entries in the graphemic output lexicon.

17. The reasons for including a connection between entries in the speech output lexicon and the graphemic output lexicon are discussed in Chapter 7 (pp. 170–172). They include the fact that normal writers will produce involuntary "slips of the pen" occasionally, where an intended word is miswritten as another real word which is identical or similar in sound to it (e.g. writing *scene* for *seen*, or *surge* for *search*). Some dysgraphics produce similar errors at higher frequencies.

The connection also plays a part in explaining how some "word deaf" patients may be able to write to dictation irregular words they do not understand (see 13 above).

(Continued)

TABLE 8.1
(Continued)

18. Skilled writers can devise plausible spellings for unfamiliar words or invented non-words. In English this is a hazardous enterprise given the variability and unreliability of sound-to-spelling correspondences in English. The ability to generate spellings for unfamiliar words is explained in the model in terms of a system of phoneme–grapheme conversion connecting representations at the phoneme level to representations at the grapheme level (i.e. a system for mapping sounds onto spellings).

The hallmark of phoneme–grapheme conversion is the occurrence of "regularisation" errors which sound like the intended target word (e.g. misspelling biscuit as "biskit"). Such errors are seen in large numbers in the spelling of "surface dysgraphic" patients in whom the process of whole-word retrieval from a graphemic output lexicon is impaired. Conversely, phoneme–grapheme conversion is itself impaired in "phonological dysgraphic" patients whose spelling of familiar real words is much better than their spelling of unfamiliar words or non-words.

19. At the grapheme level are somewhat abstract representations of each of the letters used in English. These representations are abstract because it is assumed that the upper- and lower-case versions of a letter will be represented by a single entry at the grapheme level. Selection of particular letter forms and particular modes of spelling output (handwriting, typing, spelling aloud, etc.) is made downstream of the grapheme level.

The grapheme level receives three inputs—one from the visual analysis system permitting words to be copied directly from print, a second from phoneme–grapheme conversion, and a third from the graphemic output lexicon. Certain slips of the pen made by normal writers may be attributed to errors at the grapheme level, as may the more frequent errors of some "peripheral" dysgraphic patients (pp. 181–182).

20 and 21. At the allograph level letters are represented in spatial form. Each grapheme has at least two allographic variants—its upper- and lower-case form. At the level of graphic motor patterns the letters are represented as the movements necessary to create particular allographs. Certain letter-level slips of the pen in normal subjects, and also certain forms of "peripheral" dysgraphia, may be interpreted in terms of problems arising at the allograph level or the level of graphic motor patterns (pp. 182–187).

22. This link from writing back to the visual analysis system represents the external feedback which can be gained by reading one's own writing. Patients with "afferent" dysgraphia appear not to attend sufficiently to external visual feedback, as they also fail to attend sufficiently to internal kinaesthetic feedback. As a result, they make characteristic errors involving repetitions or omissions of strokes or letters in sequences of similar items. The same sorts of errors can be induced in normal subjects by depriving them of visual feedback (e.g. having them write with eyes closed), and these errors may reach levels in normal subjects comparable to those seen in "afferent dysgraphics" if the removal of visual feedback is combined with a secondary task such as tapping or counting while the person is trying to write. The secondary task probably interferes with attention to kinaesthetic feedback in normal subjects (see pp. 183–187).

23. The provision of a direct connection between the visual analysis system and the grapheme level allows words or non-words to be copied without being recognised or understood. The copying in question is not slavishly pictorial, but involves copying of the stimulus material in the subject's own handwriting. Making the connection between the

(Continued)

TABLE 8.1
(Continued)

visual analysis system and the grapheme level two-way provides a mechanism whereby subjects might image visually words retrieved from the graphemic output lexicon or assembled by phoneme–grapheme conversion. This internal feedback would be analogous to the internal feedback from the phoneme level to the auditory analysis system (see 11 above).

Note: Some of the arrows connecting components are two-way, whereas others are shown as unidirectional. The conservative rule we have followed is only to show a connection as two-way if we have *evidence* that two components can exert a *mutual* influence on one another. Thus, two-way arrows connect the auditory and visual analysis systems to the auditory and visual input lexicons as a device for explaining the "top-down" word-superiority effect, whereby phonemes and letters are perceived more rapidly and more accurately in words than in non-words. Similarly, the semantic system has bidirectional connections to the auditory and visual input lexicons to explain semantic priming and other "context effects" (see McClelland, 1987, for a review of such interactive phenomena in language processing). In contrast, there are grounds for believing that grapheme–phoneme conversion is a one-way translation process distinct from phoneme–grapheme conversion. Other connections shown as one-way may, in reality, be two-way connections allowing interactive activation between components.

Part of the apparent complexity of Fig. 8.3 derives from the need to display it in two dimensions—even imagining elements 13, 14, and 15 sitting above or below the plane of the page helps resolve some of the confusion of crossing lines. An alternative riposte to allegations of Byzantine complexity is to note that the composite model is probably a gross over-simplification. Some of the modules proposed will almost certainly need to be subdivided further: The semantic system, for example, covers a multitude of representations and operations, and the visual analysis system carries more weight than a single module should be expected to. Like the models of the late nineteenth-century "diagram makers" mentioned in Chapter 1, Fig. 8.3 is also severely limited in as much as it only addresses the comprehension and production of single spoken or written words. As the next chapter will show, several more modules need to be postulated when we contemplate the comprehension and production of phrases, sentences, and larger linguistic segments. Finally, Fig. 8.3 relates exclusively to verbal processes, yet language processes must interface with perceptual processes such as those involved in object and face recognition discussed in Chapters 2 and 4. The ultimate model of cognition must show how modules mediating those skills tie in with verbal modules, and the reader may care to play around with possible fusions of Fig. 8.3 and Figs 2.1 and 4.1.

Another obvious point is that a model like Fig. 8.3 is only half a theory. The missing half is the specification of how each module works and how it communicates with the other modules to which it is connected. This is the half that was missing from the nineteenth-century diagrams and one of the causes of dissatisfaction with them. The modern diagram maker is rather better off in this regard because the development of computational concepts has provided a vocabulary for talking about the possible internal workings of modules. Thus we now possess theories, some of them implemented in computer simulations, of the possible mechanics of the auditory input lexicon (e.g. McClelland & Elman, 1985; Klatt, 1979; Marslen-Wilson, 1984), the visual input lexicon (e.g. Brown, 1987; McClelland & Rumelhart, 1981; Morton, 1979), the speech output lexicon (e.g. Dell, 1986; Stemberger, 1985), and so on.

Experience teaches us that some people find diagrams like Fig. 8.3 more congenial than others. That is a fact about individual preferences, not about scientific merit. If we are to take the modularity hypothesis seriously, however, and if we are to continue to use diagrams as expository devices, then we had better get used to models like Fig. 8.3.

We shall close this chapter by commenting briefly on two somewhat controversial features of Fig. 8.3—our separation of grapheme–phoneme conversion from the whole-word route from print to sound (represented in Fig. 8.3 by the direct link 14 between the visual input lexicon and the speech output lexicon), and our separation of input from output lexicons.

Grapheme–Phoneme Conversion

In Fig. 8.3 there are two routes from print to sound by which written words can be read aloud without involving the representations of the meanings of those words in the semantic system. The first route is provided by the provision of direct links between corresponding representations in the visual input lexicon and the speech output lexicon (arrow 14 in Fig. 8.3). This route allows familiar written words (i.e. words with entries in the visual input lexicon) to activate directly their pronunciations in the speech output lexicon while their meanings are being activated simultaneously in the semantic system.

The second route is provided by the grapheme–phoneme conversion system (15). It maps letters or letter groups identified by the visual analysis system onto phonemes or phoneme groups at the phoneme level. It provides a mechanism by which pronunciations can be derived in a piecemeal fashion for unfamiliar written words or for invented non-words. According to traditional (i.e. 5 or 6 years old at the time of writing) formulations of grapheme–phoneme conversion, it will yield the correct pronunciation if the word being read aloud is one with regular spelling–sound correspondences, but irregular words will be pronounced as if they were regular (i.e. "regularised").

When these two routes are combined with the route from the visual input lexicon through the semantic system to the speech output lexicon we end up with a total of three routes from print to sound. Some theorists are happy with this (e.g. Howard & Franklin, 1987; Patterson & Morton, 1985), but others wish to reduce the three to two by combining the whole-word non-semantic route with sub-word grapheme–phoneme conversion. This issue is discussed further by Henderson (1985), Humphreys and Evett (1985), Kay (1985), and Patterson and Coltheart (1987).

There is some empirical support for such a move. If grapheme–phoneme conversion were a separate module then it should, by Fodor's (1983) logic, be autonomous and insulated from activities within the whole-word route. It is not, however. Kay and Marcel (1981) showed that the pronunciation given to a non-word by normal readers can be influenced by the real words they have seen recently. Specifically, the pronunciation given to a non-word like NOUCH embedded in a mixed list of words and non-words is influenced by whether the subject has recently read COUCH or TOUCH. Now COUCH and TOUCH are familiar real words which should be recognised by the visual input lexicon and whose pronunciations should be accessed via the direct links to the speech output lexicon. All this should have no effect whatsoever on the grapheme–phoneme conversion system, and in particular that system should be unaffected by the pronunciation given to the irregular word TOUCH. Yet it *is* affected, because reading TOUCH biases subjects towards a different pronunciation of NOUCH than they would otherwise have given.

There are various ways that theories can respond to this sort of evidence. Kay and Marcel (1981) followed Glushko (1979) in arguing that unfamiliar words and non-words are not read aloud by a separate grapheme–phoneme conversion system at all, but are pronounced by a process of *analogy* with familiar words. In terms of our model, a mechanism for reading aloud non-words (or unfamiliar words) by analogy might begin by allowing a non-word to activate entries in the visual input lexicon through resemblance between the non-word and familiar, known words.

For the non-word NOUCH, this set might include words of similar length beginning NO- (e.g. NOISY, NONE, NORMAL) and words ending in -OUCH (e.g. COUCH, POUCH, TOUCH). All those entries would transmit activation to their corresponding entries in the speech output lexicon causing activation of the nodes at the phoneme level for all those words. Eventually the phonemes which win out should be the ones activated by the greatest number of resemblances between the non-word being read and familiar, known words. For NOUCH an initial /n/ would obviously be selected. Because more words ending in -OUCH are pronounced as in COUCH than as in TOUCH, NOUCH would normally be pronounced to rhyme with COUCH, particularly if COUCH or a similar word had been read recently (assuming that words read recently retain a certain primacy). If, however, TOUCH has been seen recently, that may be enough to bias the pronunciation of NOUCH towards a rhyme with TOUCH—precisely the result obtained by Kay and Marcel (1981).

Not all theorists are enamoured with that sort of analogy model. Some have sought to maintain a separate grapheme–phoneme conversion system, but have modified that system to incorporate alternative letter–sound correspondences and to permit some biassing of correspondences by recently encountered familiar words (e.g. Patterson & Morton, 1985).

A third, radical alternative has been proposed by Shallice, Warrington, and McCarthy (1983) and Shallice and McCarthy (1985). In terms of our model they would effectively merge the visual analysis system and visual input lexicon into a visual "word-form" system containing units representing everything from single letters through letter groups and morphemes to whole words. These units would link up to corresponding units in a phonological "word-form" system created by merging the speech output lexicon and the phonemic level. Familiar words would be read aloud by connections between word-sized units in the two word-form systems, and unfamiliar words or non-words by connections between units for letters and letter groups in the two systems. Biassing and analogy effects are explained in terms of interaction between different sized units in the two word-form systems.

At this point the reader might well be asking whether cognitive neuropsychology could not arbitrate between these alternatives, particularly through a consideration of "phonological" dyslexics whose reading of familiar words is much better than their reading of non-words, and "surface" dyslexics who read non-words well but irregular words poorly, and indeed read aloud many once-familiar words as if they were non-words (making regularisation errors to irregular words in the process). There is a double dissociation between whole-word and subword (or "sublexical") reading here, but double dissociations are between tasks, not postulated modules. This double dissociation is between whole-word reading and piecemeal, "assembled" reading (Patterson, 1982). As such, it shows that there are cognitive processes involved in whole-word reading that are not involved in piecemeal reading, and vice versa. But as Patterson and Coltheart (1987) observe, when all of the types of theory outlined above are inspected closely, processes can be found within them which are specific to piecemeal reading which could be impaired in "phonological" dyslexics, and processes are found which are specific to whole-word reading which could be impaired in (some) "surface" dyslexics.

None of the theories is overly embarrassed by the simple fact of a dissociation between whole-word and piecemeal reading. It could be that when the theories are spelled out in detail or implemented as computer models, then differences will emerge in the precise manner in which each would expect the different sorts of reading to break down. At the time of writing such detailed, implemented models are just beginning to emerge (e.g. Brown, 1987; Sejnowski & Rosenberg, 1986), but the predictions for neuropsychological breakdown are yet to be made and tested. It is already apparent, however, that as greater specificity is demanded and achieved, so the boundaries between "dual-route" models, "analogy" models, and "multiple levels" models begin to blur and dissolve. It seems quite likely that if we ever create a model capable of explaining all the relevant experimental and neuropsychological data it will incorporate aspects of all three types of model.

It would be foolhardy of us to back one type of theory of print-to-sound translation over another with the present state of knowledge. We shall content ourselves with having alerted the reader to the fact that our inclusion in Figs 8.1 and 8.3 of a distinct module named "grapheme–phoneme conversion" is done in the knowledge that such a step is controversial and quite possibly unwise.

Input and Output Lexicons

Another feature of Fig. 8.3 which posterity might well judge unwise is its separation of input from output lexicons. Virtually all theorists nowadays wish to distinguish between phonological lexical systems dealing with spoken words and orthographic lexical systems dealing with written words, but not everyone wishes to make the further division into input lexicons handling word recognition and output lexicons handling word production.

Allport and Funnell have argued in a series of papers that the available experimental and neuropsychological evidence can be handled by a model which has one phonological lexicon handling both the recognition and production of spoken words, and one orthographic lexicon handling both the recognition and production of written words (Allport, 1983; 1984; Allport and Funnell, 1981). Their model can be represented diagrammatically as in Fig. 8.4. Morton (1984) has observed that a similar rivalry between models having two or four word "centres" existed among the nineteenth-century diagram makers.

In more recent times, cognitive neuropsychological arguments in favour of a single orthographic lexicon have been advanced by Coltheart and Funnell (1987). They studied a patient HG who was mildly "surface dyslexic" and mildly "surface dysgraphic". In fact, he read irregular words aloud quite well if the lists he was given contained only real words,

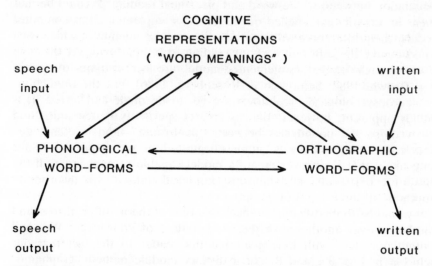

FIG. 8.4. Functional model for the recognition and production of spoken and written words incorporating one phonological and one orthographic lexicon (after Allport & Funnell, 1981).

but if they contained a sprinkling of non-words then he began to make some "regularisation" errors to less common (low-frequency) irregular words; for example, misreading *quay* as "kway", *suede* as "sood", and *colonel* as "kollonel". It seemed as if he failed to recognise these as real words in lists of mixed words and non-words and instead read them aloud using grapheme–phoneme conversion (or analogies, or whatever).

In spelling to dictation he made similar regularisation errors to less common words; for example, misspelling "moan" as *mone* and "blew" as *bloo*. Now, as Coltheart and Funnell (1987) note, HG's particular brand of "surface" dyslexia implies a mild impairment of access of a visual lexicon involved in recognising written words in reading, whereas his "surface" dysgraphia implies a mild impairment of retrieval from an orthographic lexicon involved in producing written words in spelling and writing. If that visual lexicon and orthographic lexicon are one and the same module—a dual-purpose input–output lexicon of the sort proposed by Allport and Funnell (1981)—then the words he has slight problems reading should be the same words as the ones he has problems spelling. Testing this prediction is not quite as easy as it would appear at first glance, because HG's reading and spelling were both affected by word frequency, so one would expect some overlap between sets of words read and spelled successfully or unsuccessfully. When Coltheart and Funnell tested HG's spelling of words he could or could not read reliably they found a remarkably close association between spelling and reading: His spelling performance was better for words he read perfectly than for words he read imperfectly, even when the confounding factor of word frequency was taken into account. On the basis of this finding, Coltheart and Funnell (1987) elected to support the single orthographic lexicon view, while acknowledging the problems involved in using consistency measures to discriminate between one and two lexicon theories.

Set against Coltheart and Funnell (1987) is Campbell's (1987b) argument for separate visual input and graphemic output lexicons. Campbell's starting point is that many normal people misspell some words *consistently*, despite the fact that they see the correct spelling time and again in the course of their reading. One of us drove to Dunfermline nearly every month for 3 years, passing (and using) many road signs, but persisted in writing letters and reports on his visits to Dunfermline. Campbell investigated this phenomenon in two student subjects, JM and RM, both of whom had experienced reading and spelling problems as children and continued to spell rather poorly as adults. Some of their misspellings were consistent from one attempt to the next (e.g. misspelling *talking* as *torking, logical* as *logicle*, and *guarantee* as *garentee*). JM and RM were shown lists of mixed words and non-words where some of the non-words were in fact their own consistent misspellings. On other occasions the correct spellings of those words were presented. The task was one of "lexical decision" with JM and RM being required to decide whether each letter string they read was a word or a non-word.

JM and RM proved to be quite good (around 90%) at judging the correctly spelled words to be words in English. They were poor, however, at rejecting their own consistent misspellings as non-words. In fact they were at chance on this decision (RM 43% correct; JM 48% correct). They were better, though not particularly good (around 75%), at rejecting misspellings generated by the experimenter which they themselves did not make.

Campbell (1987b) maintains that these findings are more easily explained by a model which postulates separate reading (input) and spelling (output) lexicons. She argues that their spelling lexicons (our graphemic output lexicon) only contain their misspellings of words they consistently spell incorrectly, hence those misspellings are all they can generate in writing. Their reading lexicons (our visual input lexicon) will contain the correct spellings, acquired through reading, but are also likely to contain their consistent misspellings, acquired by reading their own written material. The lexical decision task effectively asks whether a letter string is represented in the visual input lexicon: If it is, then it can be assumed to be a real word. But because at least some of JM and RM's consistent misspellings are also represented in their visual input lexicons they are apt to be falsely accepted as real words in English.

As far as reading and spelling are concerned, then, both single and separate lexicon models have their adherents and it is hard to arbitrate between them on current evidence. The situation is similar regarding the issue of one or two lexicons for spoken word recognition and production. If the two alternatives are equally viable, then the scientific principles of parsimony (simplicity) should lead us to prefer single lexicon models. There is, however, at least one observation in the neuropsychological literature which seems more readily explicable in terms of separate auditory input and speech output lexicons, and that is the phenomenon of semantic errors in the repetition attempts of "deep" dysphasics (see pp. 157–158).

Asked simply to repeat the word "crocus", a "deep" dysphasic might say "daffodil". Such repetition is clearly semantically mediated. On a two-lexicon model like Fig. 8.3, this would mean that the more direct route for repetition (11) between the auditory analysis system and the phoneme level is impaired (hence deep dysphasics should be poor at repeating non-words which have no entry in the auditory input lexicon, which they are). Repetition is therefore obliged to proceed via the auditory input lexicon, the semantic system, and the speech output lexicon. Semantic errors would be attributed to an additional impairment in or around the semantic system.

On a one-lexicon model like Fig. 8.4, even where repetition is lexically mediated it can proceed *straight through* the phonological lexicon because the representations in that lexicon which recognise spoken words are also the representations which guide their production. For a semantic error to occur in repetition a representation in the lexicon would have to be activated yet not itself mediate repetition. Rather it would have to transmit activation only up to the (impaired) semantic system which would transmit activation back down to the phonological lexicon, but this time to the entry for a different word of similar meaning which the patient then says.

We are not saying that single-lexicon models could not explain semantic errors in repetition, just that their explanations seem strained in comparison with the accounts which fall readily out of two-lexicon models (Howard & Franklin, 1987). As with the debate over the number of routes from print to sound, the debate over the required number of lexicons is not one we see any sense in taking sides on at present. The interested reader is referred to Monsell (1985) for a review of the scarcely less equivocal evidence to be derived from the experimental cognitive literature.

SUMMARY OF THE COGNITIVE
NEUROPSYCHOLOGY OF READING

The acquired dyslexias may be divided for convenience into peripheral and central dyslexias. Peripheral dyslexias affect early visual processes by which letters are recognised, coded for position and grouped into words. "Neglect dyslexic" patients like VB omit or, more often, substitute letters at the beginnings of words. In VB's case these errors usually involved substituting the correct number of letters, suggesting that her neglect may have affected the encoding of letter identities more than letter positions. Patients with "attentional" dyslexia erroneously combine letters from words simultaneously present on the page. The letters typically retain their within-word positions, suggesting that the impairment may affect the processes which perceptually group letters which belong together as part of the same word. "Letter-by-letter readers" can no longer identify the letters of a word simultaneously and in parallel, and can only identify a word after identifying each letter separately. Warrington and Shallice's (1980) theory proposes that the visual input lexicon which normally recognises familiar words can no longer be accessed and that word recognition is mediated by some form of reversed use of the patients' intact spelling systems.

Central dyslexias affect word recognition, comprehension and naming processes, and/or processes dealing with unfamiliar words or non-words. Patients such as WLP who can read aloud irregular words they fail to understand may provide evidence for word-specific links between corresponding entries in the visual input lexicon and the speech output lexicon.

"Surface" dyslexics rely to a considerable extent on grapheme–phoneme correspondences to read aloud once-familiar words. Accordingly, they read regular words more successfully than irregular words, which they are apt to "regularise". Detailed investigations of single cases show that a number of different impairments can generate these symptoms, including impairment of the visual input lexicon, the semantic system, and the speech output lexicon. The symptoms which accompany the regularity effect and regularisation errors distinguish between these different loci of impairment. It is a moot point whether such different patients belong together in the same "syndrome" category.

The precise nature of the inability to read aloud unfamiliar words or non-words, sometimes termed "phonological" dyslexia, may also vary from patient to patient. These patients show clearly, however, that the recognition of familiar words is not dependent on the availability of low-level grapheme–phoneme conversion procedures.

Problems of a more semantic nature are seen in "semantic access" dyslexics who are unable to gain full, conscious access to word meanings. Semantic problems also occur in "deep" dyslexics in the form of semantic errors and problems reading abstract words. Typically, these patients also make visual errors and are poor at reading non-words, but there are signs that some or all of these symptoms may dissociate. One prevalent view explains "deep" dyslexia in terms of impairment to components of the normal (left hemisphere) reading system; another in terms of the reading capabilities of the right cerebral hemisphere.

Finally, although access to word meanings is possible without the words' sounds, patients who have problems accessing the sound patterns of words may also have problems utilising the grammatical structure of sentences to assist comprehension. It is not yet clear to what extent this is linked to an impairment of auditory-verbal short-term memory.

FURTHER READING

Ellis, A. W. (1984). *Reading, writing and dyslexia: A cognitive analysis*. London: Lawrence Erlbaum Associates. An introduction to modelling skilled reading and writing and their disorders, and to the acquisition of literacy and its impairment in developmental dyslexia.

Coltheart, M., Patterson, K. E., & Marshall, J. C. (1980). *Deep dyslexia*. London: Routledge and Kegan Paul. Already something of a classic in cognitive neuropsychology.

Patterson, K. E., Marshall, J.C., & Coltheart, M. (1985). *Surface dyslexia: Neuropsychological and cognitive analyses of phonological reading*. London: Lawrence Earlbaum Associates. The sequel to *Deep dyslexia*, though the growing awareness of the inadequacies of the syndrome-based approach prevents it from telling such a simple story. Several good case reports plus discussions of phonological reading processes in normals.

9

Further Language and Communication Processes

INTRODUCTION

Language use and its impairments have always occupied a central position within cognitive neuropsychology. We have already discussed work on writing, reading, and the production and comprehension of spoken words, and yet we still have aspects of language to cover. In this chapter we shall begin by discussing briefly the conceptual language disorder known as "semantic jargon". We shall then examine the instructive history of the putative syndrome of "Broca's aphasia" or "agrammatism" which, as we shall see, turns out not to be a syndrome at all (in the sense of being a coherent set of symptoms arising from a single functional impairment) but is instead a cluster of often associated but separable deficits, each requiring a separate explanation. We shall then review a range of language-related disorders, several of which are said to follow injury to the *right* cerebral hemisphere (rather than, as is more normal in the case of language disorders, following left hemisphere injury). Towards the end of the chapter we shall examine briefly disorders of gesture and sign language, ending with a consideration of the nature of language as viewed through the eyes of a cognitive neuropsychologist.

SEMANTIC JARGON

The term "jargon aphasia" is used to refer to speech production which is fluent but very difficult to extract any coherent message from. Butterworth (1985) argues that this term is too vague and all-embracing, covering as it does a range of aphasias for which we would want to provide quite different explanations. Thus, so-called "neologistic jargonaphasia" which we reviewed in Chapter 5 seems to result from a word-finding difficulty in combination with a severe speech comprehension deficit. The patient produces fluent speech, but many words are distorted to the extent that the listener may have great difficulty working out what the patient is trying to say. Such patients may have clear communicative intentions, but those intentions become jargonised in the act of translation into speech (Ellis, Miller, & Sin, 1983).

When looked at closely, the fluent but incoherent speech of patients producing "semantic jargon" is very different from the speech of "neologistic jargonaphasics", in that "semantic jargon" is composed only of real words whereas "neologistic jargon" includes many non-words (often phonological approximations to target words). "Semantic jargon" and "neologistic jargon" are different too from the long strings of meaningless sounds seen in some cases of "phonemic jargon" (Perecman & Brown, 1981). Asked about the job he formerly held (a draughtsman; Kinsbourne & Warrington, 1963, case 2), a "semantic jargonaphasic" said:

> My job was... original... him... concerned with... particulars... of... so that I could tell them exactly what to take, and, where to... take it from... so that I could get away to the... gestures of the conditions of one side... which would give me particular items or discussion according to that...

Similar fluent and reasonably grammatical but semantically opaque speech can be seen in the following extract from case 1 of Brown (1981):

> And I said, this is wrong, I'm going out and doing things and getting ukeleles taken every time and I think I'm doing wrong because I'm supposed to take everything down from the top so that we do four flashes of four volumes before we get down low...

Patients who produce semantic jargon can be fully oriented for time and place, may behave generally in an organised, coherent way, and may perform well on non-verbal tests of intelligence (Kinsbourne & Warrington, 1963). Comprehension impairments seem always to be present, but although these impairments may be orthodox linguistic ones in many patients with semantic jargon, they may take a more subtle form in others. Case 1 of Kinsbourne and Warrington (1963) could obey quite complex commands such as: "When I tap on the table touch the top of your head and put out your tongue." He could also rearrange jumbled words into meaningful sentences like "We started for the country on an early train." When recorded samples of his own jargon spoken by an experimenter were played back to him for comment he rejected them as incomprehensible and in bad English, but when his own speech was played back to him he declared it to be comprehensible and in good English. In general, he appeared entirely unaware of his speech defect and denied that anything was amiss (a form of "anosognosia"—denial of illness).

If we take as a simple example of speech production the situation of describing a real or pictured scene, then we can distinguish three broad stages (Ellis & Beattie, 1986). First the speaker must comprehend the scene in the sense of recognising the components and understanding their relations one to another. Secondly, that understanding must be formulated into a conceptual message in which certain components of the scene and certain relations or actions are selected and arranged coherently. Thirdly, linguistic processes such as syntax and word retrieval must convert the message into a verbal utterance to be spoken or written. At the moment we lack the sort of detailed case reports of patients with semantic jargon that would allow us to locate the deficit with any great confidence, or even assert that the impairment is the same in all cases. That said, the good general orientation and intact non-verbal intelligence of Kinsbourne and Warrington's two cases suggests that the root cause of semantic jargon does not lie in any failure to comprehend the physical world or to have a coherent understanding of it. Similarly, semantic jargon is often grammatically fluent and well articulated in a way that may argue against a straightforwardly linguistic deficit.

What *may* be impaired in patients showing semantic jargon is the capacity to translate a general understanding into the sort of structured, propositional message that can serve as *input* to linguistic processes. The ability of Kinsbourne and Warrington's case 1 to understand the speech of others implies that such a deficit can be unidirectional, affecting production but not comprehension. The presence of *some sort* of comprehension deficit may be important, however (even if it is just a denial that one's *own* speech is impaired), because the willingness of these patients to produce copious quantities of semantic jargon is presumably related to an inability (or unwillingness?) to monitor their own output and detect its incoherence. Because they do not realise that they are talking gibberish they continue to produce it in large quantities.

THE SAGA OF "BROCA'S APHASIA" AND "AGRAMMATISM"

Goodglass and Geschwind (1976) defined Broca's aphasia as a syndrome "marked by effortful, distorted articulation, reduced speech output, and agrammatic syntax but sparing of auditory comprehension. Writing is usually impaired commensurately with speech, but reading is only mildly disturbed." The term "agrammatism" refers to "the dropping out of connective words, auxiliaries, and inflections so that grammar may, in extreme cases, be reduced to rudimentary form—the juxtaposition of one- or two-word sentences" (Goodglass, 1976, pp. 237–239).

"Connective" words and "auxiliaries" in that description are what we have elsewhere called "function words"—words like *and, the, by, through, to*, and *except*, whose presence in a sentence plays an important role in conveying the sentence structure, and hence in communicating the relationships between the "content words" of the sentence, particularly the nouns and verbs. "Inflections", for our purposes, are such as the past tense *-ed* in *walked*, the plural *-s* in *dogs*, and the *-est* in *quickest*; affixes which cannot stand alone but which the grammar demands to be added to words in certain sentence roles.

The effect of omitting function words and inflections is to reduce the resulting speech to strings of words which are often described as "telegraphic" because of their resemblance to the pared-down language of telegrams, where function words and inflections may be omitted to save money. This quality of agrammatic speech is illustrated in the following extract from Goodglass (1976) of the speech of a patient who is trying to explain that he has returned to the hospital to have work done on his gums:

Ah... Monday... ah, Dad and Paul Haney [*referring to himself by his full name*] and Dad... hospital. Two... ah, doctors..., and ah... thirty minutes... and yes... ah... hospital. And, er, Wednesday... nine o'clock. And er Thursday, ten o'clock... doctors. Two doctors... and ah... teeth. Yeah,... fine.

When asked to relate the events in a film, a patient described by Luria (1970) says:

"Ah! Policeman... ah... I know!... cashier!... money... ah! cigarettes... I know... this guy... beer... moustache....

Historically, there was an important spate of work done on aphasic patients of this sort between about 1900 and 1925, mostly in Germany and published in German (e.g. Bonhöffer, 1902; Heibronner, 1906; Isserlin, 1922; Kleist, 1916). Unfortunately, many of the insights gleaned by these aphasiologists were lost and have ended up being rediscovered independently in more recent times (Howard, 1985a; 1985b). These early studies were often intensive investigations of single patients, but research on "Broca's aphasia" or "agrammatism" has tended to be dominated more recently by studies in which the performance of *groups* of agrammatic aphasics on one or more tasks is compared with the performance of normal subjects, or other types of aphasics, or both. Reviews of this work can be found in Caramazza and Berndt (1978), Berndt and Caramazza (1980), Kean (1985), and Howard (1985a). Our treatment of agrammatism will lean heavily on Howard's (1985a) excellent review. We shall begin by summarising some of the findings of the group studies before going on to reflect on some of their problems and shortcomings.

Group Studies of "Agrammatism"

1. Function Words and Inflections. Patients whose speech is "agrammatic" do not omit *all* function words and inflections, only some. Group studies have shown that this omission or retention is not random but is influenced by a number of factors. Some function words and inflections seem intrinsically more prone to omission than others (De Villiers, 1974). Thus Goodglass and Hunt (1958) found twice as many omissions of the inflectional ending -*s* when it occurred as a possessive marker (as in *Dick's*) than when it occurred as a plural marker (as in *bricks*). Gleason, Goodglass, Green, Ackerman, and Hyde (1975) found the plural -*s* and the present participle -*ing* (as in *wishing, kicking*) to be less likely to be omitted than the past tense -*ed* (as in *wished, kicked*). Goodglass and Berko (1960) found the plural -*s* less likely to be omitted when it is expressed as a syllable (as in *horses*) than when it is non-syllabic (as in *goats* or *cows*), and Goodglass, Fodor, and Schulhoff (1967) found more omissions of function words if they were at the beginnings of sentences and/or unstressed than if they occurred within sentences and/or were stressed (sentence position effects have also been found by Gleason et al., 1975, and by Wales & Kinsella, 1981). Friederici (1982) found German prepositions (the equivalents of English function words like *at*, *on*, or *through*) to be more likely to be omitted when their role in a sentence was purely grammatical than when the preposition conveyed referential meaning.

2. Content Words. Although the problems with function words and inflections are usually regarded as prototypical features of agrammatism, the problems experienced by agrammatic patients may not be solely confined to those elements. Myerson and Goodglass (1972) and others have noted that verbs are relatively infrequent in agrammatic speech and often occur in the -*ing* form. Saffran, Schwartz, and Marin (1980b) have suggested that these may be "nounified" verbs which serve to name actions as nouns name things, and cite in evidence sentences like "She is bookening (reading) it" and "The baby bottleing" (is drinking from a bottle). Even nouns may cause problems for agrammatic aphasics: Myerson and Goodglass (1972) found a strong bias towards use of nouns referring to concrete rather than abstract entities, with names of people and places predominating.

3. Sentence Structure. If the use of function words and inflections were the only problem for agrammatic aphasics, then it should be possible to take samples of their speech and recreate straightforwardly their target sentences by adding the missing function words and inflections. It is not. As Howard (1985a) observes: "... on the whole, the content words do not form sentences stripped of their grammatical structures".

Saffran, Schwartz, and Marin (1980c) showed that agrammatic aphasics have problems indicating grammatical relations that are signalled by the order or arrangement of nouns in sentences. Their descriptions of pictures were reasonably good as far as the positioning of nouns was concerned when the pictures showed animate objects as the actors in sentences and inanimate objects as the recipients of the actions (e.g. "The boy pulling a wagon"). But when both the actor and the recipient were animate (e.g. a picture of a horse kicking a cow), the patients chose the wrong noun to initiate the sentence on 35% of occasions. They understood the picture and knew who was doing what to whom, but their ability to use the conventions of English syntax (sentence structure) to express that knowledge seemed impaired.

If agrammatic problems were confined to function words and inflections, then sequences of content words like *large white house* or *give friend dollar* should create no difficulties for them. Yet, as Gleason et al. (1975) showed, agrammatic aphasics find such sequences (Adjective–Adjective–Noun and Verb–Indirect Object–Direct Object) very hard to produce. Like Saffran et al.'s (1980c) observations on word order, this suggests a sentence construction problem over and above the difficulties with function words and inflections.

4. Comprehension. The description of Broca's aphasia given by Goodglass and Geschwind (1976) included agrammatic syntax but also reported "sparing of auditory comprehension". It is not hard to see how the view that language comprehension is spared could come about, for in ordinary clinical or social interactions these patients typically struggle to express themselves in speech yet seem to understand what is said to them without difficulty. Careful testing can show, however, that they often do have language comprehension problems, though these are much less debilitating or obvious in everyday life than are their output difficulties.

Caramazza and Zurif (1976) required their Broca's aphasic subjects to select from a set of alternative pictures the one which matched a sentence they heard. The Broca's aphasics were found to have particular difficulty with sentences whose correct comprehension required the analysis and use of sentence structure. Given the sentence "The man that the woman is hugging is happy", the patients' responses indicated that they knew it to be about a man and a woman, that someone was being hugged, and that someone was happy, but because they could not make use of the sentence structure they could not choose reliably between a picture of a man hugging a woman and a picture of a woman hugging a man. The patients had little difficulty with sentences like "The bicycle that the boy is holding is broken", where the sentence can be interpreted correctly from the content words alone (bicycle... boy... hold... broken), but given an anomalous sentence like "The dog that the man is biting is black", where the grammatical structure of the sentence forces an unusual interpretation, the patients often chose the picture depicting the more likely scenario (i.e. a dog biting a man rather than a man biting a dog). Similarly, Schwartz, Saffran, and Marin (1980b) found agrammatic (alias Broca's) aphasics to have great difficulty interpreting sentences like "The square is above the circle" or "The dancer applauds the clown", where there is nothing in the meanings of the words to help one decide who is above whom or who is applauding whom: Sentence structure must be used to make that decision.

"Agrammatic" aphasics understand the words they hear, then, and very often the meanings of the individual words are enough to guide a correct construal of what the speaker is saying. Consequently, their speech comprehension appears to be relatively intact. Only when correct comprehension is made to depend crucially on cues contained in the sentence structure are their characteristic impairments revealed. We should emphasise, though, that this is a summary of the *average* "agrammatic" aphasic as revealed by the averaged performance of groups of subjects. We shall now see that some patients reveal exceptions to these generalisations.

Dissociations within "Agrammatism"

When agrammatic aphasics are treated as a group, problems with sentence construction and problems with sentence comprehension are seen to accompany the tendency to omit function words and inflections. If we were to treat these all as aspects of one aphasic syndrome then we might be tempted to try to account for them all in terms of a single underlying deficit. Several such attempts have indeed been made (e.g. Berndt and Caramazza, 1980; Kean, 1977, 1979), but their viability has been undermined by the growing evidence that patients may show some of these symptoms without showing the others. If the various features shown to hold for agrammatic aphasics as a group can nevertheless also be shown to be dissociable, with each symptom capable of occurring without the rest, then it would seem more plausible to conclude that what we have is a cluster of deficits which tend to co-occur but which are nevertheless separable and require separate explanations.

1. Dissociation between Agrammatism (Omission of Function Words

*and Inflections) and the Sentence Construction Deficit in Speech Produc-
tion.* One of the many pitfalls lying in wait for the unwary venturer into
this particular literature is a certain inconsistency in the use of the word
"agrammatism". Some authors reserve the term for a particular *symptom*—
the tendency to omit function words and inflections. Others, however,
want it to be the label for a *syndrome*, so that when additional sentence
production or comprehension problems are found to be typically present in patients who omit function words and inflections, the term
"agrammatism" is expanded to encompass those impairments. We shall
adopt the former approach, so that "agrammatism" for us will be a
specific problem (the tendency to omit function words and inflections)
which is capable of being dissociated from other difficulties which may
often accompany it.

Tissot, Mounin, and Lhermitte (1973) argued that different patterns
of speech production impairment could be discerned among "agrammatic" aphasics. One pattern involves classic "telegraphic" speech, with
omissions of function words and inflections but with correct word order
and therefore reasonably comprehensible speech. In a second pattern,
in contrast, language is "reduced to a chaos of words" with disturbed
word order and consequently incomprehensible speech.

Subsequent studies which have contrasted individual aphasic patterns
have shown that the "syntactic" problem with word order and the
"morphological" problem with function words and inflections can indeed
be dissociated. Saffran et al. (1980b) described a patient who made
frequent and appropriate use of function words and inflections but who
could still not arrange words into grammatical sentences. When trying
to describe a picture of a girl giving flowers to her teacher she said:
"Girl... wants to... flowers... flowers and wants to... the
woman... wants to... the girl wants to... the flowers and the
woman." Describing a picture of a woman kissing a man, she said: "The
kiss... the lady kissed... the lady is... the lady and the man
and the lady... kissing." This patient cannot construct grammatical sentences, yet her speech is full of function words and inflections;
that is, she shows the sentence construction deficit without agrammatism. Similar cases have been reported since by Berndt (1987) and Parisi
(1987).

A case showing Tissot et al.'s (1973) converse pattern, with severe
agrammatism but only a mild sentence construction difficulty, was reported by Miceli, Mazzucchi, Menn, and Goodglass (1983). This patient
(their case 2) omitted function words but tended to use incorrect inflections
rather than omitting them. This seems to be characteristic of agrammatism
in languages like Italian and Hebrew which are heavily inflected and in
which, unlike English, words may not have an uninflected form capable

of standing alone (cf. Grodzinsky, 1984). Apart from the severe agrammatism, sentence construction was only mildly impaired in Miceli et al.'s case 2. This contrasted sharply with their case 1, who was much more like Saffran et al.'s (1980b) patient, showing only mild agrammatism in the context of a severe sentence construction deficit.

Miceli et al. (1983) conclude from their two contrasting cases that the sentence construction deficit and the impairment responsible for agrammatism are two separate problems whose degree of severity can vary independently in different patients. Accordingly, they echo Schwartz et al.'s (1980b, p. 235) view that "the constructional and morphological aspects... are dissociable... [and] reflect impairments to separate stages in the production process".

2. Dissociation between Production and Comprehension Impairments. If patients who have constructional or morphological impairments in speech production could be shown invariably to have comparable problems comprehending sentence structure or morphology (e.g. use of function words and inflections) then we would be tempted strongly to posit central syntactic and morphological components, damage to which causes corresponding problems in production and comprehension. Thus, a belief that syntactic problems with sentence structure always co-occurred led Berndt and Caramazza (1980) to argue for a single, central syntactic component whose impairment caused parallel problems in production and comprehension.

We have already seen that comprehension problems commonly co-occur with production problems, so that groups of patients classified as Broca's aphasics or agrammatics on the basis of their speech production show group deficits on comprehension tests, but is that co-occurrence invariable or can patients be found with impairment of production not comprehension, or vice versa?

In Schwartz et al.'s (1980b) study of comprehension in patients whose speech output was agrammatic only one of five patients was able to score above chance consistently, and that was the patient whose speech production was *most severely* impaired. Kolk, Van Grunsven, and Keyser (1985) and Berndt (1987) report two patients whose speech production is severely agrammatic but who performed at or near normal levels on comprehension tests.

It seems likely, then, that some patients may show agrammatic speech production in the presence of intact sentence comprehension, but does the reverse occur? Are there patients whose sentence comprehension is marred by problems with function words and inflections, or problems utilising word order cues, but whose speech production is normal? Two obstacles are encountered in trying to answer this question. The first is that patients with normal speech production would never get classified as "Broca's" or "agrammatic" aphasics, because spontaneous speech is given priority in making such a diagnosis. The second problem is that the comprehension deficits we are looking for may need special tests to detect them and they may not reveal themselves in normal conversational exchanges.

It has often been noted that the comprehension of patients called "conduction" aphasics (whose speech production may include phonemic errors but is certainly not agrammatic) is very similar to the comprehension of many agrammatic aphasics (e.g. Caramazza & Zurif, 1976; Heilman & Scholes, 1976). Howard (1985a) suggests that the conduction aphasic patient MC of Caramazza, Basili, Koller, and Berndt (1981) may fit the description of agrammatic comprehension without agrammatic production. MC's speech was described as "relatively normal", with no tendency to omit function words or inflections and with good control of word order. In sentence comprehension he was, however, very poor at the sort of reversible sentences that often (but not always) cause problems for patients with agrammatic production (sentences like *The cat is being chased by the dog*). However, although MC *may* fit the bill as a patient with agrammatic (or asyntactic) comprehension without comparable problems in production, Caramazza and Berndt (1985) note that MC also had a very restricted repetition span, and suggest that "conduction aphasics" like MC (whose essential symptom is poor repetition in the context of better preserved comprehension and production) may show asyntactic comprehension because they have an impairment to an auditory-verbal short-term memory store which serves as a point of entry to syntactic comprehension processes.

In conclusion, although the status of putative cases of impaired comprehension with intact production may be uncertain, the opposite dissociation of impaired, agrammatic production with intact comprehension seems secure. Parisi (1987) argues that the computational processes required to assemble grammatical sentences are unlikely to be able simply to reverse their direction of operation in order to contribute to sentence comprehension, which will need its own dedicated syntactic processes. Accordingly, Parisi maintains that we should *expect* to discover the sorts of dissociations between production and comprehension impairments that are currently being documented.

"Agrammatism": Some Morals

So where does this all leave "agrammatism", and us? The conclusion drawn by many cognitive neuropsychologists is that the saga of agrammatism is a salutory lesson in how *not* to do cognitive neuropsychology (cf. Badecker & Caramazza, 1985; 1986; Berndt, 1987; Caramazza & Berndt,

1985; Goodglass & Menn, 1985; Howard, 1985a). The initial mistake, these commentators argue, was to take as the object of investigation a "syndrome" which consisted of a cluster of associated but nevertheless dissociable symptoms. That mistake was compounded when the "syndrome" was then studied by presenting tasks to *groups* of subjects. Theories were developed on the basis of group average scores which concealed potentially important individual differences between members of the groups.

Any group of mixed "Broca's aphasics" *will* score below normal on tests of word order in production, tests of syntax in comprehension, and so on, because there is no denying that these impairments are *associated* in such a way that a patient who has one impairment will *tend* to have the others. But the presence of exceptions to that generality shows that the observed frequent co-occurrence is not the result of one underlying functional deficit. More likely the association is attributable to there being several separate functions which happen to be dependent for their successful execution on adjacent regions of cerebral cortex. An injury to the brain which impairs one of those functions will thus tend to impair the others because brain injuries such as strokes are usually crude and undiscriminating, but the occasional patient with impairment to some of these functions but not others will reveal them for the separate and autonomous processes that they are.

In summarising an extensive and insightful review of agrammatism Howard (1985a, pp. 26–27) concludes that:

> Agrammatism has become *reified*: instead of the subject of study being the syntactic problems of aphasic patients, it becomes the "syndrome" of agrammatism. The patients become simply exemplars of the syndrome which is *assumed* to exist.... [This] assumption is faulty. There is sufficient evidence to show that there are a variety of qualitatively different patterns of... impairment. Seen in this light, all the present theories of agrammatism, subtle and sophisticated as they are, are no longer relevant: they are attempts to explain something that may not even exist.

Work so far may thus have revealed several separate language impairments which cognitive neuropsychologists will need to explain:

1. A morphological impairment which creates problems when using function words and inflections in speech production ("agrammatism").
2. A syntactic problem with speech production which shows itself (in English at least) as an inability to order nouns correctly around the verb in a sentence.
3. An impairment affecting the utilisation of sentence structure information in language comprehension.
4. A fourth dissociation is implied by Parisi's (1987) contrast between

patients who have problems with function words and not inflections (e.g. his patients COA and GJ) and patients who have problems with inflections and not function words (e.g. patient AS).

Once the distinctness of these various symptoms has been acknowledged it may be possible to reinterpret some of the earlier group studies as studies of patients who, though they may have been heterogeneous with respect to their other symptoms, mostly showed one or other of these impairments. What is now inadmissible are theories which seek to explain these dissociable symptoms in terms of a single underlying impairment.

Stemberger (1984) makes use of group data to develop his account of the agrammatic tendency to omit function words and inflections in their speech output. Stemberger begins by observing differences in the types of "slip of the tongue" that most commonly affect function words and content words in the speech errors of normal, healthy adults. One interesting difference is that whereas slips of the tongue commonly involve the unintended substitution of one content word for another (e.g. "You'll find the ice-cream in the oven"—intended word, fridge), content words are rarely simply omitted from the intended sentence. Omissions of function words, in contrast, are relatively common ("You wouldn't have to worry that... *about* that"), as are omissions of inflections ("He relax when you go away"—intended word, relaxes). Stemberger notes the similarities between normal speech errors involving function words and inflections, and characteristic agrammatic errors (e.g. the predominance of omissions over substitutions, and the fact that when substitutions of function words do occur they almost always involve the replacement of one function word by another). These similarities are interpreted within an "interactive activation" theory (which we shall not explore here) as suggesting that what we may be seeing in agrammatism is an *exaggeration* of a tendency to error which is already seen in normal people (just as we proposed in Chapter 5 that the word-finding difficulties of some "anomic" aphasics may represent an exaggerated form of the normal "tip-of-the-tongue" state).

Stemberger's (1984) theory may help us explain the omissions of function words and inflections in speech output, but cannot explain the syntactic problem with word order (nor should it be asked to, because the two symptoms are separate and dissociable). It is also not clear how it might explain the dissociation between problems with inflections and function words reported by Parisi (1987). With regard to the syntactic deficit, Schwartz, Linebarger, and Saffran (1985) note that patients with word-order problems *understand* the pictures they are asked to describe, and are thus aware at a conceptual level who is doing what to whom. In other words, comprehension of thematic roles like agent (or performer) of an action and recipient of the action are preserved. What is lost according to Schwartz et al. (1985) is the capacity to *map* those conceptual or thematic roles onto syntactic categories like the subject or object of the verb. As yet, the "mapping hypothesis" lacks detail, but it at least provides a framework to guide future investigation.

"AUTOMATIC" OR "NON-PROPOSITIONAL" SPEECH

Yamadori, Osui, Masuhara, and Okubo (1977) tested 24 right-handed patients with Broca's aphasia for the ability to sing, and discovered that 21 produced good melody and that 12 of these could also produce the lyrics well. Five of the patients whose lyrics were fluent were rated simultaneously as severe Broca's aphasics. Case TO was so aphasic that she could say only her name and a few greetings, yet she sang a song from *The Sound of Music* both excellently and fluently. We have seen a patient ourselves whose spontaneous speech was effectively limited to "Yes" and "No" but who would launch at the drop of a hat into a fluent rendition of the hymn "I am so glad that Jesus loves me".

Song lyrics are not the only bits of language that can be preserved in otherwise very severe aphasics. Zollinger (1935) reports the case of a woman whose entire left cerebral hemisphere had to be removed because of an extensive tumour. During the 17 days that she lived she was severely aphasic, but a few hours after the operation she could say "all right". "Yes" and "no" were added the next day, then "thank you", "sleep", and "please". Smith's (1966) patient also underwent removal of the left cerebral hemisphere and was also severely aphasic. He did, however, utter a range of expletives and short emotional phrases (e.g. "Goddamit!"), and in the fifth month of his operation he showed sudden recall of whole songs (e.g. "Home on the range", and "My counry 'tis of thee"). Other cases are reviewed by Searleman (1983), Code (1987), and Van Lancker (1987).

Jackson (1874) grouped singing, swearing, idioms, cliches, phrases like "thank you" and "good morning", and serial speech such as counting or reciting the days of the week together as *automatic* or *non-propositional* speech. Most normal speech is propositional in the sense that it is made up of sentences assembled *de novo* to express particular thoughts. Non-propositional speech, in contrast, comes "ready-made", so that one can say "Have a nice day" or "Know what I mean" with very little conceptual or semantic contribution.

Hughlings Jackson believed that only the left hemisphere is normally capable of propositional speech, but that both hemispheres can produce non-propositional speech, with the right hemisphere possibly being dominant for such automatic language use. Thus, "the right hemisphere is the one for the most automatic use of words, and the left the one in which automatic use of words merges into voluntary use of words—into speech" (Jackson, 1874, pp. 81–82). Larsen, Skinhoj, and Lassen's (1978) observation of increased blood flow in the right cerebral hemisphere during serial counting is compatible with right hemisphere dominance for automatic speech, though until such time as a case is reported of *loss* of automatic speech following right hemisphere injury it is probably safest to assume that both cerebral hemispheres can produce this sort of speech.

The notion that propositional language can be impaired or lost completely, leaving only automatic or non-propositional speech, is not without its problems. First, there is apparently considerable variation in the amount of "automatic" speech retained by global aphasic patients or patients whose left hemispheres have been removed, suggesting the possibility of individual variation in the normal population in the extent of right hemisphere speech. Secondly, although the distinction between propositional and non-propositional or automatic speech has some intuitive appeal, the distinction has never been defined rigorously within either linguistics or psychology (though, see Van Lancker, 1987). The danger then becomes one of circularity—global aphasics and left hemispherectomy patients have preserved automatic speech, and automatic speech is what is preserved in global aphasics and left hemispherectomy patients. That said, there are examples of speech produced by such cases which could never be classed plausibly as "automatic" or "non-propositional". For example, when Smith's (1966) hemispherectomy patient was asked, "Is it snowing outside?", he replied, "What do you think I am? A mind reader?" That was said, however, 6 months after his operation, and there are hints throughout these reports of genuine acquisition (rather than retention) of propositional language by the right hemisphere following left hemisphere removal.

The situation regarding automatic speech is thus somewhat unclear, but there are clues scattered throughout the literature to suggest that the cognitive processes required to count to ten, say "Have a nice day", or sing the lyrics of "Home on the range", may be separate from the cognitive processes operating when we convert newly-formed ideas into novel utterances.

PROSODY

When a sentence is spoken it acquires aspects and features over and above those it possesses when written down. Those features exist by virtue of the *way* the sentence is spoken. By altering the way we say the same sentence we can change it from a simple statement to a question and then to a command:

You're going out tonight. (statement)
You're going out tonight? (question)
You're going out tonight! (command)

These changes are brought about by changing what linguists refer to as the *prosody* of the sentence, where the term "prosody" covers such things as the emphasis given to certain syllables or words (e.g. contrasting GREENhouse with green HOUSE), the rise and fall of voice pitch (intonation), and the distribution of pauses in the sentence. We can also change our tone of voice in order to say the same sentence in a happy, sad, puzzled, angry, or disbelieving way. This emotive use of tone of voice (and other cues) has been termed *affective prosody*.

Although the bulk of research on language disorders has dealt with such things as word and sentence meanings, syntax, and word retrieval, a growing body of work is showing that prosody is subject to its own range of disorders. And whereas conventional aphasias usually follow injury to the left cerebral hemisphere (Kertesz, 1983), disorders of prosody may often follow injury to the *right* cerebral hemisphere.

The idea that the right hemisphere might play an important role in the expression and interpretation of emotion has a long history (Mills, 1912), though current interest in prosodic impairment stems from the work of Heilman, Scholes, and Watson (1975). This work tended to focus at first on "affective" prosody; that is, the use of tone of voice and other cues to convey emotional states. Heilman et al. found that right hemisphere injured patients could respond well to the content of sentences they heard, but performed at chance levels when required to judge from the speaker's tone of voice whether the speaker was happy, sad, angry, or indifferent. Similarly, Tucker, Watson, and Heilman (1977) reported right hemisphere injured patients who were quite unable to discriminate or repeat an "affective" tone of voice. Both these studies, however, reported averaged data from groups of patients. Potentially important individual differences are often lost in such averaging procedures, and subsequent investigations using more of a case study methodology have indeed revealed a number of qualitatively different patterns of prosodic impairment.

Ross and Mesulam (1979) provided two case reports of patients with impaired affective prosody following right hemisphere injury. Case 1 was a teacher who, on returning to work, experienced difficulty in maintaining classroom discipline. She had formerly relied to a considerable extent on tone of voice to do this, but now she had an "unmodulated, monotonous voice that was devoid of inflections and colouring". Although her comprehension of affective tone of voice was not tested formally, she reported no difficulties in perceiving other people's emotional states from their tone of voice. Case 2 also experienced "marked difficulty in modulating the tone of his voice to match the mood he wanted to impart to the listener", though he reported feeling emotions inwardly.

The possibility raised by Ross and Mesulam's (1979) case 1, that production and comprehension of affective tone of voice can be independently impaired, was assessed by Ross (1981). Ross examined the spontaneous use of affective tone of voice, the repetition of sentences in different tones of voice, and the identification of emotional state (happy, sad, angry, surprised, etc.) from tone of voice. The different patterns of intact and impaired processing of affective prosody obtained by Ross (in admittedly clinical rather than experimental testing) are shown in Table 9.1

Ross's (1981) work conveys the important message that disturbances of prosody take more than one qualitatively different form, even when only the processing of *affective* prosody is considered (see also Ross, Harney, deLacoste-Utamsing, & Purdy, 1981). Weintraub, Mesulam, and Kramer (1981) showed that right hemisphere injured patients can also show deficits (as a *group*) in more linguistic uses of prosody. These included distinguishing compound nouns by stress (GREENhouse *vs.* green HOUSE), discriminating between pairs of sentences differing only in stress or intonation, repeating sentences with varied stress or intonation, and adjusting sentence stress for contrastive emphasis (e.g. the question "Who walked to the store?" requires the answer "The MAN walked

TABLE 9.1

Patterns of Impairment and Preservation in the Spontaneous Use, Repetition, and Identification (Comprehension) of Affective Prosody, and in the Identification of Emotional from Facial Expressions and Gestures (from Ross, 1981)

Patient	Spontaneous Use	Repetition	Identification/ Comprehension	Interpretation of Facial Expressions and Gestures
1	×	×	√	√
2	×	×	√	√
3	×	×	√	√
4	√	×	×	×
5	×	×	×	×
6	×	√	√	√
7	×	√	√	√
8	√	√	×	n.a.
9	×	×/√	×	×
10	×	×	×	√

Note: √ = intact; × = impaired; ×/√ = slightly impaired; n.a. = not assessed.

to the store", with MAN stressed, while the question "Did the man walk to the store or to the station?" requires the answer "The man walked to the STATION", with the stress on STATION.)

Heilman, Bowers, Speedie, and Coslett (1984) pointed out that because Weintraub et al. (1981) had not included a group of *left* hemisphere injured patients they could not prove that the right hemisphere was any more important than the left for the processing of linguistic ("non-affective") prosody. When Heilman et al. (1984) ran a study comparing left hemisphere injured patients, right hemisphere injured patients, and normal controls, they found the right hemisphere group to be more impaired than the left hemisphere group on processing affective prosody, but no difference between the groups on processing linguistic prosody. Both groups were impaired relative to the normal controls on both types of prosody. Emmorey (1987) found the capacity to make the linguistic-prosodic distinction between compound nouns like "GREENhouse" and noun phrases like "green HOUSE" to be impaired by left but not right hemisphere injury.

There are thus questions to be resolved regarding which hemisphere is specialised for which aspects of prosodic processing. Of more relevance to present concerns, though, is evidence from these studies that impairments in the identification of affective and linguistic prosody are indeed dissociable. The task used by Heilman et al. (1984) required patients to listen to speech which had been acoustically filtered in a way which rendered the words unintelligible, while having little effect on tone of voice and prosody. Filtered sentences were spoken as statements, questions, or commands (linguistic prosody) or in a happy, sad, or angry tone of voice (affective prosody). When linguistic prosody was being assessed patients identified the sentence type by pointing to a full stop, question mark, or exclamation mark; for affective prosody they pointed to a happy face, sad face, or angry face. Fortunately, Heilman et al. (1984) provide individual results for each of their patients, and from these we can see that some patients performed better on affective prosody than linguistic prosody (e.g. *Patient L4*: 70% *vs.* 36%; *Patient L5*: 90% *vs.* 53%), while others performed worse (e.g. *Patient R1*: 30% *vs.* 70%; *Patient R4*: 46% *vs.* 83%).

Thus the "comprehension" of linguistic prosody appears to be dissociable from the "comprehension" of affective prosody, which we already know to be dissociable from the repetition and production of affective prosody.

To date research has focussed on establishing the existence of prosodic disorders and on the involvement of the two cerebral hemispheres in prosodic use. From the viewpoint of cognitive neuropsychology, what we now need are explicit information-processing theories of how prosody is produced and comprehended and how it ties in with systems for processing language and other channels of emotional expression. If prosody is anything like other aspects of language, then when we try to develop such models and use them to explain the problems of particular patients, we shall find that prosody is subject to a multitude of impairments and that simple distinctions between affective and linguistic prosody, or between comprehension, production, and repetition, are nowhere near rich enough to capture that diversity. For example, Monrad-Krohn's (1947) case of "dysprosody or altered 'melody of language'" was a Norwegian woman who, following a *left* hemisphere stroke, spoke with a mild agrammatism, and also with an altered intonation which made listeners think she was German. Prosody had not been lost but changed, with unusual emphases and pitch variations suggesting a foreign accent.

"HIGH-LEVEL" LANGUAGE DISORDERS

In this section we turn to a collection of language or language-related disorders which may have little in common with each other except that they are rather "high-level" (often being on the border between language and more general thinking and reasoning) and that, like prosodic disorders, they often follow *right* hemisphere injury rather than the left hemisphere injury we normally associate with language disorders. Indeed, the disorders we shall now review have often been discovered by investigators looking for deficits in right hemisphere injured patients (see Gardner, Brownell, Wapner, & Michelow, 1983, and Searleman, 1983, for reviews).

Two papers published in 1962 by Critchley and by Eisenson pointed to high-level language problems in patients with right hemisphere injuries. Eisenson (1962) reported difficulties on sentence-completion tasks, particularly where abstract concepts were involved, while Critchley (1962) commented upon problems in word finding with frequent resort to circumlocution, difficulties learning novel linguistic material, and severe problems with creative literary work.

Caramazza, Gordon, Zurif, and DeLuca (1976) found that patients with right hemisphere injury can experience difficulties solving verbal problems of the sort: "If John is taller than Bill, who is shorter?" Caramazza et al. (1976) suggest that people may often use imagery to help solve such problems and argue that right hemisphere injury may create problems in the use of visual imagery. Similarly, Hier and Kaplan (1980) found that right hemisphere injured patients performed worse than normal control subjects on spatial reasoning tasks, but qualified this by noting that the deficit occurred in only some of their patients, not others.

Winner and Gardner (1977) found group impairments in patients with right hemisphere injuries on another aspect of "high-level" language comprehension, namely the metaphorical interpretation of sentences. In this study, patients were asked to indicate which of four pictures best matched a metaphorical sentence like *Sometimes you have to give someone a hand*. Winner and Gardner found a tendency among right hemisphere injured patients to select pictures which depicted a literal rather than metaphorical interpretation of the sentence (e.g. a picture of a person offering someone a hand on a tray). Normal control subjects and left hemisphere injured patients rarely selected such literal pictures. Similar tendencies among right hemisphere injured patients towards literal inter-pretations rather than conventional ones have also been found for the interpretation of proverbs like *Don't cry over spilt milk* (Hier & Kaplan, 1980) and idioms like *break the ice* or *kick the bucket* (Myers & Linebaugh, 1981). Swinney and Cutler (1979) and Glass (1983) have suggested on the basis of experimental work with normal subjects that the literal and the figurative meanings of idioms may be computed simultaneously and in parallel. The results just mentioned imply that whereas the left hemisphere may be able to derive a literal interpretation satisfactorily, deriving the figurative meaning may require the additional help of an intact right hemisphere.

Another area where abnormalities have been reported in patients with right hemisphere injuries who are not aphasic by normal criteria is the interpretation and appreciation of verbal humour (Brownell, Michel, Powelson, & Gardner, 1983; see also Gardner, Ling, Flamm, & Silver-man, 1975). In the study by Brownell et al. (1983), subjects heard incomplete jokes and were asked to select the best finishing punchline from a set of alternatives offered. The right hemisphere injured patients could reject sad or neutral "punchlines" as inappropriate, but were as likely to select a "punchline" which was simply bizarre or odd as one which was genuinely humorous. Brownell et al. suggest that these patients are still sensitive to incongruity or incoherence between the "body" of a joke and the punchline, but lack an appreciation of humorous relations. Gardner et al. (1975) found a similar lack of awareness of humour in right hemisphere injured patients' responses to pictorial cartoons, so what we are dealing with here is probably a deficit in the appreciation of humour which affects language comprehension (understanding verbal jokes), but is not specific to it.

Several of the aforementioned features can be seen operating in harness with other features to impair the story recall of right hemisphere injured patients in the study by Gardner et al. (1983). The patients were told a fable-like story which they were asked to retell in their own words. Although, again, none of the patients was aphasic in the conventional sense of that word, their attempts at retelling showed that their story comprehension was not normal. They were more inclined than normal subjects to recall parts of the story verbatim rather than recoding them into their own words. They accepted and rationalised bizarre elements in the story without expressing the amusement these elements elicited in normals, and they had problems comprehending emotions attributed to characters in the tale. They also tended to misorder the elements of the story, producing as a result a less cohesive narrative. Finally, they were deficient in their ability to abstract the moral of the story from the particulars of the plot.

Summarising his own observations on language disorders following right hemisphere injury, Eisenson (1962, p. 53) wrote that, "the right cerebral hemisphere might be involved with super- or extra-ordinary language function, particularly as this function calls upon the need of the individual to deal with relatively abstract established language formulations, to which he must adjust". Many years later it is hard to generate any more precise characterisation of the language deficits shown by groups of right hemisphere injured patients. Once again, a major problem is that the studies have all been *group studies* and have rarely reported data from individual subjects. Thus, although we know that the prototypical patient with language problems following right hemisphere injury will *tend* to have problems completing abstract sentences, problems learning novel material, problems with certain logical tasks, problems interpreting metaphors, proverbs and idioms, problems appreciating verbal humour, problems ordering the elements of a narrative story, and so on, we do not know which of these problems *necessarily* co-occur, and which can be dissociated.

One can believe that a single cognitive deficit could underlie the problems with, say, interpreting metaphors, proverbs, and idioms. At a pinch one might even believe that the same deficit could cause difficulties in extracting the moral of a story (going beyond the literal message). But it is harder to conceive of a cognitive process or component, damage to which would cause these problems *and* problems with verbal humour or ordering the elements of a story. What we badly need before we can do proper cognitive neuropsychology is to know which of these impairments (and here one could throw in the prosodic impairments too) can be dissociated from which of the others, and which apparently co-occur. When we have such data we can begin to speculate about the precise nature of the "high-level" language processing components which reside in the right cerebral hemisphere, and we can begin to relate the impairments of right hemisphere injured patients to information-processing models.

GESTURES AND SIGN LANGUAGE

Language is an important mode of human communication, but it is by no means the only one. In normal life communication is a rich, interwoven blend of speech, facial expressions, body postures, gestures, etc. (Ellis & Beattie, 1986). In deaf people gesture has been developed to the level of a full-blown language (Klima & Bellugi, 1979). In this section we shall explore two of these channels of communication—gesture and sign language—from the cognitive neuropsychological perspective.

Gestures

By "gestures" we mean such things as waving goodbye, nodding the head in agreement, shrugging the shoulders to mean "I don't know", or giving a thumbs-up sign to mean "that's OK" or "Good luck". Gestures like these are symbolic combinations of movements and meanings that are as arbitrary as the connections between words like "dog" and "table" and the objects those words denote. Gestures are acquired like words, as part of the social process of learning to communicate with others (Lock, 1980).

If you were approaching gestures from a naive cognitive neuropsychological direction there are a number of questions it might occur to you to ask. Can the capacity to communicate by gesture occur in isolation, separated from other linguistic or motor disorders? Do aphasics also have problems communicating gesturally, and if they do, are those gestural problems in some way a mirror of their speech difficulties? And so on. Unfortunately, only some of these questions have been addressed by what little research has been done on gestural disorders (see Feyereisen & Seron, 1982a, 1982b; Nespoulos, Perron, & Lecours, 1986; Peterson & Kirshner, 1981).

We do not know, for example, whether brain injury can rob you of the ability to communicate gesturally while leaving speech production, the production of facial expressions, and general movement control intact. Disorders of movements are known as *apraxias*. Within that broad category various subtypes may be identified (Lecours, Nespoulos, Desaulniers, 1986; Roy, 1982). Difficulty with gestures would traditionally be classed under the heading of "ideational apraxia", but that category encompasses *any* difficulty in formulating and executing action plans, and so extends to cover difficulties making cups of coffee as well as difficulties giving a thumbs-up sign appropriately. The fact that clinicians and researchers have not felt the need to subdivide ideational apraxia further *may* mean that gestures do not dissociate from other complex movements, but as we have already seen several times, when viewed under the cognitive neuropsychological microscope, traditional neuropsychological categories often turn out to be heterogeneous clusters of symptoms which commonly co-occur but which can dissociate in key patients. Thus it is quite possible that specific impairments of gestural communication will be discovered once their theoretical significance is appreciated.

The question of whether aphasics also have gestural impairments has received rather more attention. This has often taken the form of assessing the severity of the speech disorder on a linear scale from mild to severe, assessing the severity of the gestural disorder on a similar scale, and then looking to see if the two sets of scores correlate in such a way that more severe aphasia tends to be associated with more severe gestural impairment. Several studies have found a significant association (e.g. De Renzi, Motti, & Nichelli, 1980; Kadish, 1978; Pickett, 1974) though Goodglass and Kaplan (1963) failed to find any such association. Peterson and Kirshner (1981) suggest that an association is found when the sample includes patients with very severe "global" aphasia, but that if the patient sample includes only mild and moderate aphasics then there is no correlation of the aphasia with severity of gestural impairment.

For the cognitive neuropsychologist such evidence is not easy to interpret. First, significant correlations within a group of subjects can conceal the occasional individual who may retain good gestural ability while being severely aphasic (or vice versa). Reports that some severe aphasics can benefit from being taught simple gestural communication systems reinforce this possibility (e.g. Glass, Gazzaniga, & Premack, 1973; Heilman, Rothi, Campanella, & Wolfson, 1979). Secondly, symptoms can co-occur for anatomical rather than cognitive-neuropsychological reasons (a point discussed in Chapter 1 and repeated many times throughout this book). The left cerebral hemisphere is specialised in most people for most aspects of speech production and comprehension, but it is also specialised for the planning and execution of complex motor movements and sequences (Kimura & Archibald, 1974). Impairment to those motor functions is highly likely to affect gestural communication. Therefore, on purely anatomical grounds, even if speech and gesture were entirely separate psychologically, we might expect small lesions of the left hemisphere to cause mild aphasic and mild gestural disorders, whereas large lesions would typically cause severe aphasic and severe gestural disorders, hence the observed correlation when severe aphasics are included in the test group. (N.B. If speech and gesture *are* distinct, then small lesions might affect one function more than the other, depending on the precise site of the injury. This potential for separate impairment might explain the lack of correlation among milder aphasics.)

Ranking patients on a linear scale from mildly to severely aphasic also loses much potentially valuable information because the middle range could be occupied by a truly heterogeneous mixture of anomic aphasics, agrammatic aphasics, jargon aphasics, and so on. It is of more interest to see how gestural communication is affected, if at all, in aphasic patients of different types. Butterworth, Swallow, and Grimston (1981) examined the spontaneous gestures of a "neologistic jargonaphasic" patient, KC, whose speech was littered with distorted approximations to words (neologisms). They found KC's gesturing to be normal, to be associated with content words (nouns, verbs, and adjectives), and to occur during hesitation pauses in his speech. They interpret these observations as compatible with the view that patients like KC have a word-finding difficulty similar to that of some anomic aphasics where they know the meaning they want to convey and can express that meaning gesturally, but can no longer retrieve the correct spoken word-forms to match many of the meanings (see Butterworth, 1979, and pp. 124–129).

Cicone, Wapner, Foldi, Zurif, and Gardner (1979) compared the gestures of two agrammatic "Broca's" aphasics, two "Wernicke's" aphasics with spontaneous speech which was fluent but semantically empty with many neologisms, and four normal control patients. In terms of the total amount of gesturing the two Wernicke's aphasics produced most, the normals produced an intermediate amount, and the two Broca's aphasics produced least. However, although the Wernicke's aphasics produced copious gestures, they were relatively uninformative. There was a lot of attempted pantomiming which failed to convey the patient's intended meaning to observers, but a marked absence of conventional gestures (nods, shrugs, thumbs-ups, etc.). In contrast, although the Broca's aphasics produced relatively few gestures, those they did use were clear and informative, and included a proportion of conventional gestures which was, in fact, higher than the proportion used by the normal subjects.

Cicone et al.'s (1979) observations are compatible with the view that Broca's aphasics have clear communicative intentions and know the meanings they wish to convey, but their attempts to express their intentions in speech are handicapped by the syntactic, morphological, and articulatory impairments which, as we have seen, commonly (though not invariably) co-occur in these patients. Many Wernicke's aphasics, on the other hand, may have high-level problems with message formulation which prevent the assembling of a clear communicative message. The lack of a clear communicative intention reveals itself in both unfocussed, incoherent speech and unfocussed, incoherent gesturing.

The evidence such as it is would seem to suggest, then, that initially we formulate communicative messages in a form which is essentially non- or pre-linguistic. If the message is a fairly simple one, it can be equally well conveyed in words or in gestures: We can nod our heads or say

"Yes", shrug our shoulders or say "I don't know", give a thumbs-up sign or say "That's good". If, however, the message is a more complex propositional one, then it is far easier to convey in speech than in gesture (it would be well-nigh impossible, for example, to convey the meaning of this sentence gesturally). Some Wernicke's aphasics may be impaired in the creation of communicative messages and so are impaired in communicating both gesturally and verbally. For Broca's aphasics, though, the impairments may lie entirely within the language system so that gestural communication, limited though it is, can remain intact.

Sign Language

In the sign language of the deaf, gestural communication has evolved to the status of a full language capable of all the intricacies and nuances of any spoken language. The "words" of sign language are individual gestures which can stand for both concrete and abstract concepts, whereas sentence structure is expressed in the spatial and temporal relations between these words (Klima & Bellugi, 1979). Sign language is different from "finger spelling" (sometimes called "dactylology"), where different hand positions represent different letters of the English alphabet. Finger spelling allows a deaf person to spell out a name or other word for which no standard sign exists, and may be intermixed with sign language proper in everyday communication among the deaf.

That sign language, like spoken language, is predominantly a left hemisphere specialisation is shown by the fact that disorders of sign language use typically follow injury to the left rather than the right cerebral hemisphere (Burr, 1905; Lebrun & Leleux, 1986; Marshall, 1986). Also, signing is much more impaired following temporary anaesthetisation of the left hemisphere by intracarotid injection of sodium amobarbital than following anaesthetisation of the right hemisphere (Homan, Criswell, Wada, & Ross, 1982). We have noted, however, that the planning and execution of complex motor acts is also a left hemisphere specialisation. The question has been asked, therefore, whether disorders of sign language are truly linguistic aphasias or are apraxic disorders of movement (Kimura, 1981). Two lines of evidence suggest that the "sign aphasias" are linguistic rather than apraxic. The first is that although one would expect on anatomical grounds (see above) that many deaf patients suffering from sign aphasia after left hemisphere injury would also be apraxic, nevertheless cases have been reported who have sign aphasia without apraxia (Poizner, Bellugi, & Iragui, 1984). Secondly, sign aphasias come in different varieties which more closely resemble varieties of spoken language aphasia than they resemble varieties of apraxia. That said, the differences between, say, spoken American English and American Sign Language (Ameslan) are such that one should not expect *too* close a correspondence between speech and sign aphasias.

As yet only a small number of cases of sign aphasia have been reported (Lebrun & Leleux, 1986). Following a series of left hemisphere strokes, Leischner's (1943) patient produced many concatenations of signs which did not make sense or were ill-formed, and he had great difficulty understanding the signing of others. The spontaneous signing of Under-wood and Paulson's (1981) sign aphasic was marred by sign-finding errors, substitutions and jargon, but in an interesting parallel with the preser-vation of "automatic speech" in some speaking aphasics, this patient could count from 1 to 10 and recite the Lord's Prayer fluently in sign language.

Three contrasting cases of sign aphasia (PD, KL, and GD) have been described in a series of papers by Kimura, Battison, and Lubert (1976), Chiarello, Knight, and Mandel (1982), Bellugi, Poizner, and Klima (1983), and Poizner et al. (1984). Patient PD was an 81-year-old man who had been deaf since the age of 5 and who developed a sign aphasia following a left hemisphere stroke. His signing remained fluent with good "phras-ing", but he made semantic and grammatical errors in his selection and use of signs. Examples of semantic errors are using the sign for DAUGH-TER instead of WIFE, QUIT instead of DEPART, and BED instead of CHAIR. The grammatical errors are harder to explain without going into the details of sign language, but Bellugi et al. (1983) give as examples PD using an inflected sign meaning "walk for a while" instead of the simple uninflected sign WALK, and using an illegal sign combination which would translate as something like "always brillianting" instead of the simpler BRILLIANT. Other grammatical difficulties and a mild comprehension impairment were also seen in PD.

Patient KL, a 67-year-old woman who had been deaf since the age of 6 months, also continued to sign fluently after a left hemisphere stroke, though paralysis of her right hand meant that she could only sign with her left hand. Like PD, her phrase length and temporal phrasing were normal, but KL's signing errors were different. First, she used pronouns freely (the sign equivalents of "she", "it", "they", etc.) but often failed to specify what they referred to. Secondly, she made errors in the formation of signs involving incorrect handshapes, movements, and loca-tions. For example, the sign ENJOY should be made with a circular movement but was made instead with an up-and-down movement, and the sign SEE was made at the chin instead of at the cheek location. KL's comprehension of signing was severely impaired.

The third patient, GD, was the most severely aphasic patient, being reduced to single sign utterances which were mostly nouns and verbs. GD's single signs were produced effortfully and were always in the simple, uninflected form. Despite the severe output impairment GD's comprehension of signing was only mildly impaired.

As the investigators of these patients note, there are parallels between their sign aphasias and certain aphasias of spoken language. Thus GD's signing resembles that of some "Broca's" or "agrammatic" aphasics, whereas KL's signing has similarities to that of some "Wernicke's" aphasics. More importantly, the differences between GD, KL, and PD are linguistic not motoric.

Users of sign language tend, obviously, to be deaf, and the speech of the profoundly deaf may not be fluent or easy to understand (though they may read the language of their native country well). As a consequence, although it would be interesting to know whether injury to the brain of someone fluent in both signed and spoken languages necessarily affected both forms of language, few opportunities to tackle that issue arise.

Meckler, Mack, and Bennett (1979) report the consequences of brain injury to the hearing son of deaf parents. The patient became globally aphasic with severely impaired comprehension and production of speech, and his comprehension and use of sign language was also severely impaired. Reider's (1941) similar case was more impaired in his use of speech than his use of sign. Cases like these are hard to interpret, however. We have seen that both sign language and spoken language are largely left hemisphere specialisations. Global aphasia only occurs after quite extensive left hemisphere injury (Kertesz, 1979), and such extensive injury is almost bound to affect sign language as well if signed and spoken language occupy the same cerebral hemisphere. The notion of intra-hemispheric sharing is supported by Damasio, Bellugi, Damasio, Poizner, and Van Gilder's (1986) report of how anaesthetising the left hemisphere of a hearing interpreter of sign language produced a temporary aphasia for both spoken English and American Sign Language. Removing part of the patient's right temporal lobe to relieve debilitating seizures had no effect on either signed or spoken language.

Finally, Hamanaka and Ohashi (1974) report the effects of brain injury in a hearing Japanese businessman whose wife was deaf and mute. This woman communicated by means of a sign language used by Japanese Geisha girls "to preserve professional secrecy in the guest room". The sign language employed a gesture for each of the 45 basic syllables of spoken Japanese, and the businessman used this sign language to communicate with his wife. After brain injury the man displayed mild word-finding problems in speaking which were more severe for nouns than for verbs, but no agrammatism, jargon, articulation problems or comprehension deficits. His use of sign language was more impaired, but there are hints of parallels between his signing problems and his word-finding problems in speaking. Briefly, some syllable-signs are derived from gestures which mime an object whose name (a noun) begins with that syllable, whereas others are derived from gestures which mime an action whose name (a verb) begins with that syllable [thus the sign for "ma" involves pointing to the eyebrow (-*mayuge*, a noun), whereas the sign for "ta" involves clapping (-*tataku*, a verb)]. Just as this patient found verbs easier to retrieve in speaking than nouns, so he found signs based on verbs easier to remember than signs based on nouns.

An acquired disorder of Geisha sign language in a Japanese patient may sound about as abstruse as it would be possible to get in cognitive neuropsychology, but it is the only case we know of in which aphasic disorders of speech and signing may be compared within an individual. In this patient the two disorders have interesting similarities, but we should avoid concluding prematurely that such similarities will always exist. The relationship between Geisha sign language and spoken Japanese is much closer than that between, say, American Sign Language and spoken American English, so it is more plausible to argue that they might share cognitive processes. Also, this patient learned his sign language late rather than having been bilingual from early childhood. This too could contribute to greater dependence between the two languages.

OVERVIEW

We have now devoted the best part of five chapters to the cognitive neuropsychology of language. In part this simply reflects the central position that aphasias, dyslexias, and dysgraphias have occupied in the development of cognitive neuropsychology. But such a position would not have arisen were there not such a bewildering variety of qualitatively distinct, yet interpretable and informative, forms of acquired language disorder. We have covered many such disorders in what has by no means been an exhaustive review. The question arises, what general view of human language is implied by the sheer existence of so many different patterns of reading, writing, and speech disorder?

The answer to this question that many cognitive neuropsychologists would subscribe to asserts that language is not a single, unified human faculty; rather speech production, speech comprehension, writing, and reading are capabilities which arise out of the co-ordinated activity of many language-sustaining cognitive processes or "modules".

We have discussed many such modules in this and the preceding chapters: modules for identifying phonemes in the sound wave, for recognising spoken words, for identifying letters in print, for recognising written words, for processing word meanings, sentence structure and prosody, for retrieving spoken and written word-forms in speech and spelling, for co-ordinating the output of phonemes in speaking and the output of letters in writing, and so on. If each of these processes is handled by a separate module (cognitive subsystem), and if each module is capable of being impaired independently of the others, then we can understand how the number of possible distinct patterns of language disorder can become very large. On top of this we must admit the possibility of symptom-patterns arising through complete or partial *disconnection* of intact modules, the possibility that certain modules may be impaired in two or more different ways, and the possibility that certain symptoms may only arise when a particular *combination* of modules is damaged.

Of course we must recognise that patients in whom a single module or connection is damaged will be uncommon: The grossness of most brain injuries will ensure that most patients' symptoms will reflect damage to several different cognitive subsystems. The particular sets damaged in different patients will vary, causing widespread individual differences which are likely to undermine any attempt to group patients into small numbers of homogeneous "syndromes". Patient groupings of one sort or another may be useful for certain purposes (e.g. for determining the probable site of damage, or for designing and evaluating therapies), but the best groupings for one purpose may not be the best for another, and they are unlikely to be easily sanctified by reference to cognitive neuropsychology. As we have said throughout this book, the cognitive neuropsychologist need only be concerned with how the patterns of symptoms displayed by particular patients relate to theories of the normal operation of cognitive processes. Attempts to group patients into syndromes for the purposes of cognitive neuropsychological analysis have thus far only resulted in confusion.

Our everyday use of spoken and written language is made possible by many independent but interacting cognitive components, each handling its own aspect of language use. Normally we are happy for these components to operate entirely automatically, so that all we have to do is formulate ideas and speech follows, or move our eyes along a line of text and understanding follows. In everyday life the existence and operation of these components is only brought to our attention when they malfunction temporarily (as, for example, when we find ourselves caught in a tip-of-the-tongue state). But the implications are never so forcibly driven home as when we contemplate how it is possible for a brain-injured person to have lost the capacity to make use of sentence structure in language understanding while still grasping the meanings of the individual words, or to be unable to write satisfactorily while still being able to talk and read normally.

More generally, a patient may show multiple and severe language problems whereas perception, orientation, thinking, reasoning, memory, and so on may remain intact (though needing, of course, to be tapped non-verbally). Once again, these claims are not best evaluated by comparing groups of aphasic patients with groups of normals (Allport, 1983). For example, group studies have sometimes found average performance on non-verbal tests of reasoning and "intelligence" to be lower in aphasics than normals (e.g. Bay, 1962; Kertesz & McCabe, 1975). Other studies, however, have failed to find any difference, and have failed to find within the aphasic group any correlation between performance on intelligence tests and severity of the language disorder (e.g. Basso, DeRenzi, Faglioni, Scotti, & Spinnler, 1973; Corkin, 1979). Equally important are the few published reports of patients with severe language impairments whose non-verbal intelligence remains high (e.g. Van Harskamp, 1974; Welman & Lanser, 1974; Zangwill, 1964; see also Allport, 1983).

There are clearly many non-linguistic cognitive processes which can continue to function normally even when most of the language modules have been damaged. Impairment to the non-linguistic modules gives rise, of course, to disorders of perception, orientation, thinking, action, memory, and so on, some of which are discussed in Chapters 2 to 4 and Chapter 10 of this book. Those non-linguistic disorders can occur in patients whose language use remains perfectly normal. As a final point we might note that the distinction between linguistic and non-linguistic cognitive modules may not always be easy to draw. Is an impairment in the ability to judge tone-of-voice a linguistic or a non-linguistic impairment? Are impairments in comprehending metaphors or logical sentences exclusively linguistic or do they extend to areas of non-linguistic functioning? And what are we to conclude if patients with certain forms of semantic impairment have problems organising gestural as well as verbal communication, or if patients with impaired phonetic perception are always impaired at the processing of other rapidly-changing, non-verbal acoustic stimuli?

From an evolutionary point of view language is a relatively recent arrival on the scene, and those language-sustaining cognitive modules which are part of our biological endowment are recent acquisitions. Evolution often prefers to adapt old capabilities to serve new purposes rather than to develop completely new ones (Gould, 1980; 1983), so we should not be surprised if, for example, a module for phonetic perception has been adapted from an older and more general capability for processing rapidly-changing acoustic signals, or if processes for handling word meanings also continue to involve themselves in the comprehension or production of arbitrary, symbolic gestures. Nor should we be surprised if we flounder in our attempts to draw hard-and-fast distinctions between language disorders (aphasias) and other forms of cognitive impairment.

SUMMARY

Disorders of speech processing other than those affecting word production and recognition (see Chapters 5 and 6) take many different forms. We have speculated that high-level conceptual impairment may cause the fluent but semantically empty speech of patients with "semantic jargon-aphasia". Patients with so-called "Broca's aphasia" commonly show distorted articulation, impaired use of word order, and "agrammatism" (the omission or substitution of grammatical function words and inflections). Case studies have shown these commonly associated symptoms to be dissociable, and have shown syntactic problems in sentence production to dissociate from problems in comprehension. "Broca's aphasia" is probably best regarded as a collection of symptoms which tend to co-occur for anatomical rather than functional or cognitive reasons.

Nevertheless, some patients with severe aphasias may show preservation of automatic or non-propositional speech (e.g. use of everyday phrases and idioms; reciting the days of the week, or well-learned poems or song lyrics). The right cerebral hemisphere may have some advantage for producing this sort of speech. More conclusive evidence has been reported for a right hemisphere superiority for the comprehension and production of prosody, and a number of different forms of "aprosodia" have been reported following right hemisphere injury. Impairments of affective prosody are dissociable from impairments of linguistic prosody. Other language-related impairments which have been observed to follow right hemisphere injury include solving spatial reasoning problems, interpreting metaphors, proverbs and idioms, and appreciating verbal humour.

Gestural communication is often impaired in aphasic patients, and may mirror the high-level message formulation problems of some "Wernicke's" aphasics. In other aphasic patients, however, gestural communication may be preserved.

Impairments of sign language in the deaf take several different forms which in some ways resemble varieties of spoken-language aphasia. The few reports of aphasias in individuals fluent in both spoken language and sign language do not clarify the nature of the interdependence of the interrelationship between them, but show the linguistic aspects of both forms of language to be left hemisphere specialisations.

FURTHER READING

Lesser, R. (1978). *Linguistic investigations of aphasia.* London: Edward Arnold. Thorough review of the literature on aphasia as far as the mid-1970s.

Newman, S., & Epstein, R. (Eds) (1985). *Current perspectives in dysphasia.* Edinburgh: Churchill Livingstone. Review chapters on several aspects of aphasia including agrammatism, naming, therapy, and recovery.

Code, C. (1987). *Language, aphasia and the right hemisphere*. Chichester: John Wiley. Up-to-date review of the language capabilities of the right cerebral hemisphere.

Kean, M. L. (Ed.) (1985). *Agrammatism*. New York: Academic Press. All extant theories of agrammatism in one volume.

Coltheart, M., Sartori, G., & Job, R. (Eds) (1987). *The cognitive neuropsychology of language*. London: Lawrence Erlbaum Associates. A collection of recent papers on the cognitive neuropsychological analysis of aphasia.

10 Memory

INTRODUCTION

Imagine that you are visiting someone in hospital and that you are attempting to hold a conversation. The patient...

> gives the impression of a person in complete possession of his faculties; he reasons about everything perfectly well, draws correct deductions from given premises, makes witty remarks, plays chess or a game of cards, in a word, comports himself as a mentally sound person. Only after a long conversation with the patient, [you] may note that at times he utterly confuses events and that he remembers absolutely nothing of what goes on around him: he does not remember whether he had his dinner, whether he was out of bed. On occasion the patient forgets what happened to him just an instant ago: you came in, conversed with him, and stepped out for one minute; then you come in again and the patient has absolutely no recollection that you had already been with him. [The patient] may read the same page over and over again sometimes for hours, because [he is] absolutely unable to remember what [he has] read. In conversation [he] may repeat the same thing 20 times, remaining wholly unaware that [he] is repeating the same thing.

This description of *amnesia* (loss of memory) is taken from Korsakoff's classic paper written in 1889 (see Victor & Yakovlev, 1955). Korsakoff was not the first to observe and comment upon memory loss (see Levin, Peters, & Hulkonen, 1983; Schacter & Tulving, 1982), but the present-day tradition of research into amnesia can be traced back to his pioneering work. Reviews of more recent work can be found in Stern (1981), Cermak (1982), Hirst (1982), Meudell and Mayes (1982), Squire (1982, 1987), Squire and Cohen (1984), and Parkin (1987).

The cognitive neuropsychologist looks at amnesia with a view to attempting to explain memory disorders in terms of impairment to aspects of the normal process of learning and remembering, and with a view to asking what the observed patterns of impairment can tell us about the nature of normal, intact memory processes. There are a number of important questions that must be answered in attempting such an analysis of amnesia, notably the question of whether amnesics are all alike, or whether there are significant individual differences of the sort we know to exist among aphasics, agnosics, acquired dyslexics, etc. Such individual differences are arguably easier to discover by carrying out intensive single-case studies than by, for example, comparing groups of amnesics with groups of normals on particular tasks. Unfortunately, from our perspective, there have only been a few detailed case studies in this area, but from those that have been done, and from those studies which compare groups of amnesics of different aetiologies, we can begin to trace the outlines of a plausible cognitive neuropsychology of memory.

FUNDAMENTALS OF MEMORY

The Greek philosopher Plato, in his *Theaetetus*, likened memory to an aviary. Acquiring a new memory is, he said, like adding a new bird to the collection in the aviary, whereas recalling the memory is like catching that same bird for inspection. As Marshall and Fryer (1978) observe in the course of a comparison of old and more recent models of memory, Plato's aviary model enables one to draw an important distinction between storage and recall. A bird (event or item of knowledge) may be in the aviary (memory store), but at a particular instant it may evade capture (recall), though you may succeed in capturing it later (the familiar experience of recalling something which you had earlier been unable to remember).

The metaphor provides several potential reasons why an experienced event may fail to be remembered at some later date. It may be that the bird was never captured and placed in the aviary in the first place (i.e. no representation of the event was ever established in memory). The bird may die in captivity and so be missing when looked for later (i.e. the memory trace of the event may be destroyed in storage). Alternatively, as mentioned above, the bird may be one of thousands in a large aviary and you may be unable to recapture it when you wish to (a recall or retrieval failure).

We may for convenience label these three potential causes of memory failure, a failure of *registration*, a failure of *retention*, and a failure of *retrieval*. Although theories of memory abound, and vary considerably in their particulars, most incorporate these fundamental 3 R's which are logically necessary. It is not difficult to realise that the pattern of an amnesia based on registration failure would be different from, say, a pattern based on retrieval failure. We can sketch out the profile that we would expect each to generate, then survey the literature for reports of patients whose symptoms fit the expected profile.

REGISTRATION AMNESIA?

Suppose a person was suddenly afflicted with a selective inability to establish (register) new memory traces. What would the symptoms be? Memory for events experienced before the onset of the illness should be normal, because retention and retrieval are presumed to be intact, but the patient should have difficulties remembering anything that has happened since the onset of the illness. In terms of a distinction commonly made in the amnesia literature, the patient should show an *anterograde amnesia* (difficulty recalling events that occurred after the onset of the illness) but no *retrograde amnesia* (no difficulty recalling events that occurred before the onset of the illness). The anterograde amnesia could be complete if the registration deficit was a total one, or partial if the deficit was milder.

Has a selective anterograde amnesia indicative of a registration deficit been reported? Liepmann (1910) reported a patient who suffered brain injury in 1870 during the Franco-Prussian war. Apparently, he could remember much of his life before the injury but virtually nothing since. In fact, the last thing he could remember was being a student before he entered the army. Having no memory for anything since, he imagined that he still was a student, and that his parents, who had died many years ago, were still alive. The patient had been an accomplished mathematician and chess player, and retained these skills despite his amnesia.

Syz (1937) reported the case of a man of 45 who fell backwards on his head while shovelling snow from the roof of the factory where he worked. The man suffered a complete, though fortunately only temporary, loss of memory for events since the accident. He could recall details of his life before the accident and retained his knowledge of geography, astronomy, biblical history, etc. He could define words, differentiate between words of similar meaning, and showed no evidence of a perceptual disorder or agnosia. Memory for new events, however, seemed to fade rapidly. Syz (1937, p. 363) comments how, "when performing, for instance, a somewhat involved calculation... he would forget the initial problem before having arrived at the solution. Similarly, in describing pictures that had been shown to him, the impressions would 'fade away' or 'evaporate', as he said, while he was engaged in the process of description."

On 11 March, two months after his accident on 11 January, he remarked: "It should be the 12th of January... but there is something wrong, it is almost spring outside. I saw my wife the last time—if I am to say it as I feel it—yesterday, Friday, on the day of the accident. But when I think it over, I realise that something must have happened in between" (p. 359).

His rapid forgetting was made apparent on his daughter's visits. He "greets her joyfully, kisses her and asks whether she had heard of the accident. The daughter, after a brief conversation, leaves the room and returns after two minutes. The greeting is repeated, he kisses her as before. The patient is very much surprised that the daughter knows everything about the accident.... His daughter leaves the room again, we talk about her for four minutes, when she reenters. [The] patient is emotionally moved again and a similar greeting as before takes place.... [The patient] forgot completely in two minutes that he had seen his daughter and there was no evidence of recall on the second and third repetition" (pp. 361–363).

In time this patient's disorder improved and his memory returned to normal. By 1936, "There are no difficulties with his memory, he only notices that there is a certain difficulty in retaining new names." An attempt was made to find out what the patient recalled of his illness. He remembered the different people who had been in his environment during his stay at the hospital, also that he had suffered from marked headaches, but, he said, "there is a hole. I have tried to fill it out but in vain, so I gave it up" (p. 371).

HM

Perhaps the best known and most intensively studied case of amnesia in recent decades has been patient HM. This man, in his mid-20s, had suffered from major epileptic seizures for many years. In an attempt to relieve these, HM underwent an operation in 1953 involving bilateral resection of the medial portions of the temporal lobes, with partial removal also of the hippocampus and amygdala on each side (midbrain structures now thought to be important in mediating memory processes; Scoville & Milner, 1957). The operation was successful in relieving the seizures, but it left HM with a permanent and profound amnesia.

HM can retain and remember very little of what has happened to him since the operation (an anterograde amnesia). Scoville and Milner (1957, p. 14) state that "he will do the same jigsaw puzzles day after day", and will "read the same magazines over and over again without finding their contents familiar. This patient has even eaten luncheon in front of one of us... without being able to name, a mere half-hour later, a single item of food he had eaten; in fact, he could not remember having eaten luncheon at all." HM describes his situation as "like waking from a dream" and once remarked: "Every day is alone in itself, whatever enjoyment I've had, and whatever sorrow I've had" (Milner, Corkin, & Teuber, 1968, p. 217). Milner et al. (1968, p. 217) comment that, "His experience seems to be that of a person who is just becoming aware of his surroundings without fully comprehending the situation, because he does not remember what went before".

Scoville and Milner (1957) found HM's early memories to be "apparently vivid and intact" and comment upon how, in conversation, he refers constantly to the events of his boyhood. This suggests the lack of a retrograde amnesia, and Marslen-Wilson and Teuber (1975) did indeed find that HM performed at normal levels at recognising photographs of the faces of people who were well known before 1953. There is, however, some loss of memory for events in the years before his operation (Corkin, 1984). He was unable, for example, to remember the death of a favourite uncle 3 years before the operation, and could not remember his time in hospital before his operation.

If HM's recall of events before his operation is not totally intact, then his anterograde amnesia for events since is not absolutely complete either. Marslen-Wilson and Teuber (1975) found him able to recognise 20% of a set of faces of people who had risen to prominence since his operation in 1953, including Elvis Presley, astronaut John Glenn, and Russian president Nikita Khrushchev. In another testing session he identified correctly the face of Kennedy on a coin and recalled such post-operation news events as the death of Pope John XXIII (Milner et al., 1968).

Thus HM shows a degree of retrograde amnesia for events before his operation and some recollection of events since. His retrograde amnesia extends back for several years, but is considerably milder than his profound anterograde amnesia. HM thus corresponds fairly well, though by no means perfectly, to our conception of a "pure" registration amnesic.

NA

NA's injury "resulted from a mock duel with another serviceman, when a miniature fencing foil entered the patient's right nostril and punctured the base of the brain, after taking an obliquely upward course, slightly to the left" (Teuber, Milner, & Vaughan, 1968). NA was born in 1938 and the injury occurred in 1960. When tested by Kaushall, Zetin, and

Squire (1981) he could remember little of what had happened to him since the accident and could also remember little of the 6 months prior to the accident. He was intelligent though (I.Q. = 124), and his recall for events before 1960 was normal (Cohen & Squire, 1981; Squire & Slater, 1978).

Possibly because he only has normal recall for things that happened over 20 years ago, NA gives the impression of living behind the times. He continues to wear his hair in a 1950s crew cut and uses anachronistic phrases. On one occasion he reports having kept himself awake during a 2-hour neurological procedure by thinking of Betty Grable.

NA's memory problems affect his everyday life in many ways. Social relations are difficult because he often cannot remember people from one meeting to the next. He does not enjoy television as he might because he cannot retain the narrative across a commercial break. Cooking is also hard because he cannot keep track of the sequence of steps required by a recipe. The reason why he does not use many external memory aids such as notes is perhaps illustrated by the occasion when, at a testing session, "he repeatedly tried to recall a question that he had wanted to ask. He finally searched his pockets, and found a written note: 'Ask Dr. Squire if my memory is getting better'" (Kaushall et al., 1981, p. 385).

Of some potential theoretical interest is the fact that NA's amnesia is measurably more severe for verbal than for non-verbal material. Teuber et al. (1968) devised a test in which subjects were shown a sequence of items in which some items occurred more than once. The subject's task was to say "Yes" if an item had been seen before, "No" if it had not. In one test the items were meaningless geometrical figures; in a second test they were meaningless syllables or words. Whereas a group of normal control subjects were better at detecting recurring syllables or words than nonsense figures, NA showed the opposite pattern, being better at figures than syllables or words. Thus NA's memory problem affected his verbal recall more than his non-verbal recall. That said, it should be noted that NA performed worse than the normal controls on both tests, so his deficit was not restricted to verbal material.

The four patients we have discussed so far [the Liepmann (1910) case, the Syz (1937) case, HM, and NA] all broadly fit our criteria for "registration" amnesia—impaired acquisition of new memories in the context of good recollection of old ones. Patient BY reported in depth by Winocur, Oxbury, Roberts, Agnetti, and Davis (1984) provides a fifth case. We shall discuss later precisely what form or forms the registration problem seen in these patients might take, and will also discuss the significance of various observations we have made but not commented upon. First, however, we shall review cases of amnesia in which a retrieval impairment seems to play a part.

RETRIEVAL DEFICITS IN AMNESIA?

Despite their differences, the cases described above conform tolerably well to our notion of registration amnesia. We now wish to see if there exist patients interpretable as cases of retrieval amnesia. What would such a case be like? Suppose a patient became suddenly unable to retrieve items from memory, though registration and retention remained intact. Unlike registration amnesia, this deficit would affect old and new memories alike. The patient would be equally unable to remember things learned or experienced before the onset of the illness (retrograde amnesia) and things learned or experienced after the onset (anterograde amnesia).

There is a problem here in that it would not seem possible with such a case to show that registration of memories continued intact, though the memories were no longer accessible. We could only know that registration had continued intact if the patient were eventually to *recover* from the amnesia. If this happened, then all the memory traces of events that happened during the illness should become available, and the patient should be able to remember incidents that happened during the illness as well as before and after. We have been unable to locate such a patient in the literature, so cannot put forward a clear and indisputable case of pure retrieval amnesia. There are, however, cases in which retrieval difficulties undoubtedly form a part of the picture.

The Dana (1894) Case

The very first volume of the prestigious scientific journal *Psychological Review* contains a report by Dana of a case of amnesia following accidental poisoning by domestic gas (carbon monoxide). The patient was a 24-year-old man who

> was quiet and sane in every way.... He dressed himself neatly and with his usual attention to his toilet, understanding apparently the use of various articles of dress. He showed by his conversation at once that he did not know who he was or where he was, and that his conscious memory of everything connected with his past life was gone.... Everything had to be explained to him, such as the qualities and uses of the horse and cow and of the various articles about the house (Dana, 1894, p. 572).

This amnesia was, fortunately, of quite short duration. One morning, about 3 months after the attack,

> he woke up and found his memory restored. He remembered distinctly the events of three months ago: his visit to his *fiancee*, his supper at the club afterwards, his journey home, his shutting his bedroom door and getting into bed. His memory stopped there. He did not recall a thing that had

occurred between times [the gas leak had occurred after he had fallen asleep]. He knew all his family at once and was plainly just the same man as before. But the three months was an entire blank to him. Next day he came to see me [Professor Dana], but he did not know me (I had never seen him before his accident). Not a thing connected with the three months could be recalled. It was so much taken entirely out of his existence (p. 575).

This case is explicable if we argue that during the 3-month period of the amnesia there was a virtual cessation of both registration *and* retrieval. The patient could neither lay down memories for the events occurring around him nor retrieve past memories. When the illness abated both functions returned. He could now retrieve memory traces as normal, and so could remember everything up to the onset of the illness, but because no traces had been registered during the illness there were no memory traces of that period to retrieve. It really was so much taken entirely out of his existence. Other cases of "transient global amnesia" whose symptoms suggest a similar interpretation are reviewed by Whitty (1977), and a case study provided by Gordon and Marin (1979) is also interpreted as a retrieval impairment combined with a registration (or consolidation) impairment.

Traumatic Amnesia

The Dana (1894) case discussed earlier showed a temporary retrograde amnesia resolving to leave just a limited gap in memory. Similar patterns have been reported following blows to the head or other "closed head injuries". For example, a young man reported by Russell (1935) suffered a closed head injury in August, 1933. A week after the accident he was able to converse sensibly but was under the impression that the date was February, 1922 and that he was a schoolboy. Three weeks after the injury he returned to the village where he had lived for the past 2 years but it seemed entirely unfamiliar to him. Gradually, however, his memory for the missing period returned until, eventually, he was able to remember everything to within a few minutes of the accident. Russell and Nathan (1946) present a whole series of similar cases.

The phenomenon of "shrinking retrograde amnesia", where the patient gradually recovers access to old memories, must be reflecting a loss then recovery of retrieval functions. A temporary retrieval impairment gives the only intelligible explanation of a patient's ability to recall an event at time $t1$ before the injury, inability to recall the event at time $t2$ shortly after the injury, and recovered recall ability at time $t3$ when the retrograde amnesia has resolved (Benson & Geschwind, 1967). Williams and Zangwill (1952) studied the form of the recovery from retrograde amnesia and reported how memories originally return as isolated and disconnected "islands". The first memory to return is often for some quite trivial event which occurred some 15–30 minutes before the accident. This recollection can seem hazy, impersonal and "curiously remote" (Whitty & Zangwill, 1977). Other memories re-emerge gradually, often in no particular order, and have to be placed in sequence by the patient until eventually recall of the patient's entire past life is more or less completely re-established. It is common, however, for memory of the accident and the few minutes leading up to it to be lost forever.

In addition to the shrinking retrograde amnesia, head injury often leaves an anterograde or post-traumatic amnesia, so that when the patient is recovered he or she may be unable to remember what happened in the first hours or days after the accident though they were conscious at the time. Fisher's (1966) patient was unconscious for a few seconds at most after falling off her chair and banging her head, and her initial retrograde amnesia cleared almost completely, but she could later remember nothing about the events of the 10 hours following the accident. Similarly, footballers who have been concussed may play on in the game but later remember little or nothing of what happened after the injury (Yarnell & Lynch, 1973).

Once again there would appear to be a combination of registration and retrieval deficits at work in these traumatic amnesias. The retrieval deficit affects the patient's ability to recall events from before the accident but resolves in time. The registration deficit also resolves, but leaves a hole in the patient's memory for the period of its duration. A similar combination of reversible retrograde and anterograde amnesias is seen in cases of "transient global amnesia", a well recognised clinical entity whose organic basis is still unclear (e.g. Evans, 1966; Gordon & Marin, 1979; Shuttleworth & Wise, 1973).

Retrograde Amnesia in Huntington's Disease

Huntington's Disease is a genetically transmitted dementing disorder characterised by involuntary, erratic muscle movements and progressive mental deterioration. Moderately advanced patients show impaired recall of past events. This was demonstrated by Albert, Butters, and Brandt (1981a) using a test which assessed recall and recognition of people and events which had been prominent between 1920 and 1975. The patients with Huntington's Disease were impaired on memory for all decades equally. This contrasts with, for example, patients with alcoholic Korsakoff amnesia whose memory for remote decades is less impaired than their memory for more recent decades.

As Albert (1984) observes, impaired memory for people and events from many years before the onset of the disease is incompatible with an explanation solely in terms of a learning (registration) disorder. It could, however, be accounted for by the proposal that patients with Huntington's Disease are impaired in their ability to *retrieve* old memories. That said, these patients also have a severe anterograde amnesia, so it is impossible to know for certain that the retrieval impairment is not accompanied by a registration impairment in the way we have seen to hold true for transient global amnesia and traumatic amnesia. Nevertheless, these cases and others in which amnesia of sudden onset includes a retrograde component (e.g. Cermak, 1976; Rose & Symonds, 1960; Williams & Smith, 1954) show that retrieval processes are capable of being impaired in amnesia. Given the problems of memory retrieval we all experience from time to time, it would be very surprising if those problems could not be exacerbated and magnified in at least some forms of amnesia.

ALCOHOLIC KORSAKOFF AMNESIA

Cases of amnesia due to sudden injury or illness are comparatively rare. A much more common cause of memory disorders is alcoholism, or rather, a deficiency of the vitamin thiamine which appears to accompany pro-longed alcohol abuse and which causes damage to several thalamic and hypothalamic structures surrounding the third ventricle of the brain, possibly including the dorsomedial nucleus of the thalamus and the mamillary bodies (Butters, 1984). Amnesia resulting from prolonged alcohol abuse is commonly referred to as "Korsakoff's syndrome" and most amnesics studied experimentally have been of this sort. Unfortunately, there are a number of respects in which from a cognitive neuro-psychological perspective they are less ideal than cases where amnesia results from injury or sudden illness. For example, the memory problems of an alcoholic may develop slowly, and the patient may have been experiencing difficulties for many years before he or she is finally admitted to hospital (Goodwin, Crane, & Guze, 1969). This gradual onset makes it difficult to make the conventional distinction between problems in recalling events that occurred before the onset of the amnesia (retrograde amnesia) and problems recalling events that occurred after onset (antero-grade amnesia).

Also, the brain damage in Korsakoff syndrome patients is by no means clearly delimited. Although the damage which follows vitamin deficiency includes those structures like the hippocampus and amygdala, whose intactness appears vital for normal memory functions, it also commonly extends to other parts of the brain, notably the frontal lobes (Squire, 1982). Thus it can be very difficult to determine whether a particular symptom displayed by alcoholic Korsakoff patients is due to their amnesia or to cognitive deficits created by frontal lobe or other brain damage.

Perhaps because of these difficulties agreement has proved much harder to achieve for Korsakoff amnesia than for the amnesia of patients like HM and NA. Whereas a registration account of Korsakoff amnesia has many proponents, so has the notion that the fundamental problem is one of memory retrieval, but it is with registration theories that we shall begin.

Registration Theories of Korsakoff Amnesia

Since the earliest days of enquiry into Korsakoff amnesia there has existed a school of thought which ascribed the disorder to a problem of registration rather than one of recall. Müller and Pilzecker (1900) supported this view, as did Bonhöffer (1901), Burnham (1904), Gregor (1909), Moll (1915), and Bernard (1951), among others. Talland (1965) provides a valuable historical review. We should note that the amnesic patients studied by early advocates of both registration and recall deficits were not all amnesic as a consequence of chronic alcoholism. The expectation among most theorists was that all amnesias would have the same explanation, but it is possible that investigators were led in different directions through studying patients who were themselves different one from another.

While a considerable number of investigators have converged upon some form of registration deficit as a possible cause of amnesia, they have rather diverged again when it came to specifying in a little more detail what precise form that registration defect might take. Many suggestions have been made, but few have received any lasting favour. For example, Craik and Lockhart (1972) proposed a theory of normal learning and remembering which distinguished between "shallow" and "deep" encoding of to-be-remembered material. Roughly speaking, "shallow" encoding focusses upon the physical form of a stimulus (e.g. the appearance of a written word) whereas "deep" encoding focusses on its meaning. Many experiments have shown deep encoding to produce better long-term recall in normals than shallow encoding, but amnesics do not always show such a benefit (e.g. Cermak & Reale, 1978). Cermak and Butters (1973) suggested that a failure to encode experiences to a deep level might lead to the poor recall of past experiences seen in amnesia.

There are several problems, however, with this particular registration account of amnesia. First, as Rozin (1976) pointed out, amnesics can often hold intelligent and intelligible conversations about the here and now. That would not be possible if they do not routinely process words they hear in a "deep" way for their meanings. Secondly, Meudell, Mayes, and Neary (1980a) showed that amnesic recognition memory is better for funny strip cartoons than for unfunny ones. This again would not be possible if the amnesics were not processing the cartoons "deeply" for their "point"—the source of their humour.

Squire (1982) points out that while Korsakoff amnesics may fail to benefit from instructions to encode stimuli deeply, patient NA and patients suffering memory problems as a result of electroconvulsive therapy treatment do show benefits (Wetzel & Squire, 1980). Squire suggests that the failure of Korsakoff amnesics to exhibit rich encoding may be more a reflection of cognitive deficits produced by the frontal lobe damage commonly seen in alcoholic Korsakoff patients than a reflection of their core amnesia.

Retrieval Theories of Korsakoff Amnesia

Over the years numerous theorists have suggested that an impairment of retrieval from long-term memory may lie at the heart of Korsakoff amnesia (e.g. Colella, 1894; Grünthal, 1923, 1924; Schneider, 1912, 1928; Warrington & Weiskrantz, 1970, 1973). We shall start by reviewing briefly some of the lines of evidence which have been held to support a retrieval explanation before evaluating the theory.

First, amnesics sometimes recall incidents they are usually unable to remember, showing that the memory traces for those events were present in their brains even when they were unable to recall them. Coriat (1906, 1907) reports memories being recovered in dreams or "states of abstraction", and Gillespie (1937) is among those who have claimed recovery of amnesic memories under hypnosis. Amnesics not under hypnosis may produce rambling "confabulatory" accounts of their former lives containing much that is fabricated, but also occasional true recollections (Buerger-Prinz & Kaila, 1930/1951; Lewis, 1961; Moll, 1915).

Secondly, if a Korsakoff amnesic is given the same list of items to memorise on two or more occasions, the patient will show "savings" on the second and subsequent learnings, even though he or she will have no conscious recollection of the first learning episode. This was first demonstrated by Brodmann (1902, 1904) and has been confirmed by subsequent investigators (see Lewis, 1961; Talland, 1965; Williams, 1953).

Related to this is the observation that Korsakoff amnesics benefit from prompts or cues presented at the time of recall (Lidz, 1942; Williams, 1953). Warrington and Weiskrantz have reported the beneficial effects of retrieval cues on the performance of amnesic patients in an extensive series of studies. For example, Warrington and Weiskrantz (1970) gave word lists to amnesic and normal subjects to learn. With free and unprompted recall the amnesics managed only 33% correct to the normals' 60% correct. When, however, the first three letters of each word were provided as cues, amnesic performance rose to 60%, and it was statistically indistinguishable from the 66% correct obtained by the normal subjects. Warrington and Weiskrantz (1968) demonstrated that cueing by parts of previously seen line drawings improved performance in Korsakoff amnesics. Mayes, Meudell, and Neary (1978) again found cueing to improve amnesic recall (this time of word lists), but cueing was not enough to bring the amnesics to the level of the normal subjects.

Another argument for a retrieval theory is based on the contrast between the performance of Korsakoff amnesics on tests of recall and their performance on tests of recognition. In a recall paradigm the patient is shown a set of stimuli (e.g. words or pictures) and is later asked to recall the items in the set. In a recognition paradigm the patient is again shown a set of stimuli to memorise, but is later tested by being shown a fresh set of stimuli, some of which were in the original memory set whereas others are new. The patient must judge which items in the test set are old (i.e. were in the memory set) and which are new. Whereas the recall performance of Korsakoff amnesics is very poor, their performance on recognition tests can be very much better, sometimes rivalling that of normal subjects (e.g. Hirst, Johnson, Kim, Phelps, Risse, & Volpe, 1986; Huppert & Piercy, 1976, 1977, 1978; Mayer-Gross, 1943; Starr & Phillips, 1970; Woods & Piercy, 1974; Zubin, 1948).

It is clear that all of the above observations [and others reviewed by Knight & Wooles (1980) and Meudell & Mayes (1982)] are *compatible* with a retrieval deficit account of Korsakoff amnesia. It is reasonable to propose that if Korsakoff amnesics experience difficulty accessing memory traces they might show occasional, rare successes, might benefit from repetition and retrieval practice and so show the "savings" effect, might be aided by cues to assist the recall process, and might perform well in recognition memory tasks which arguably reduce the load upon retrieval operations. However, it can also be argued that poor *registration* of memories could produce exactly the same picture. Memories which are weak or faint as a result of poor registration might still occasionally be recovered in dreams, states of distraction, under hypnosis, or with the aid of cues. Janis (1950) found that amnesics could sometimes recover "lost" memories if they were allowed to "work on" them, but precisely the same is true of normals. For example, Williams and Hollan (1981) asked four subjects who had left high school between 4 and 19 years previously to recall the names of their former classmates over several sessions and found that names continued to be retrieved even after 10 hours of searching and recollecting.

Similarly, the recovery of memories which are weak due to poor registration could show better recognition than recall, and could be aided by cueing in both amnesics and normals. As Squire (1982, p. 249) observes: "The critical issue is not whether performance can be improved at all by such techniques but whether they disproportionately improve the performance of amnesic patients, or are simply effective ways to elicit information from all subjects alike". Schacter and Tulving (1982, p. 9) call this the *rule of differential effects*, arguing that:

> The effect of an experimental manipulation must be greater for amnesics than control subjects before deficits in the memory performance of amnesics can be attributed to corresponding underlying processes. It does not matter how dramatically a particular treatment... affects the operation of a given memory process in a group of amnesics. One can only entertain the hypothesis that amnesia reflects a deficit in a particular process when it can be shown that the memory performance of an appropriate control group is not affected or is affected less markedly, by the same treatment.

In order to ascertain whether the law of differential effects holds, we must look at the results of experiments which have compared the performance of normals and Korsakoff amnesics on memory tasks.

Comparing Normal and Amnesic Memory

Imagine carrying out an experiment to look at the effectiveness of retrieval cues at aiding normal and amnesic recall. Suppose you decide to teach a list of 12 words to each subject, going over them repeatedly until each normal person or amnesic patient can repeat all 12 correctly on two successive attempts. You then wait a few hours and retest each subject. Without prompts or cues the normals manage an average of nine correct but the amnesics only manage three correct. You then supply retrieval prompts (e.g. the first letter of each word, or the category to which it belongs). The normals show a 22% improvement from 9 to 11 correct, but the amnesics leap from 3 to 10 correct (a 230% improvement). Have you satisfied Schacter and Tulving's law of differential effects? After all, the amnesics *have* benefited more than the normals from your retrieval cues.

The problem with an experiment like this (which is similar in design to many of those in the literature) is that an initial, uncued score of 3 out of 12 provides much more room for improvement than a score of 9 out of 12. Potentially, from 3 out of 12 you can achieve a 300% improvement, whereas from 9 out of 12 the most you could achieve is a 33.3% improvement. A fairer comparison would be one in which the *uncued* recall rates of the normals and amnesics are equated (Knight & Wooles, 1980). One way to achieve this is to test the normal subjects after a much longer interval. In the imaginary experiment above we might find that the uncued recall of normal subjects would drop to 3 out of 12 if several days were allowed to elapse between learning and test. The question is, if cues were then provided, would the normal performance still improve by only 22% to an average of 3.66 correct (a differential effect), or would it show an improvement to around 10 out of 12, comparable with the amnesics (no differential effect)?

The strategy of testing normals at longer retention intervals, when their performance level has dropped to around that shown by amnesics at short retention intervals, has been employed by Woods and Piercy (1974), Squire, Wetzel, and Slater (1978), and in an extensive series of studies by Meudell, Mayes and their collaborators (see Mayes & Meudell, 1984; Meudell & Mayes, 1982 for reviews). The general finding of these studies has been that normal, weak memories are in many respects indistinguishable from Korsakoff amnesics' memories. For example, Woods and Piercy (1974) and Squire et al. (1978) found comparable effects of initial letter cueing of word recall in Korsakoff amnesics and normals when the normals were tested at longer retention intervals than the amnesics. Mayes and Meudell (1981) replicated this finding and also noted that for both amnesics and normals, words recalled with the aid of initial letter cues felt unfamiliar, like guesses. In a study of normal and amnesic recognition of famous voices, Meudell et al. (1980b) again found comparable effects of retrieval cues in amnesics and normals when the normals were tested at longer retention intervals.

In sum, there would appear to be no evidence for the law of differential effects as applied to the effects of retrieval cues on amnesia and normal recall. Retrieval cues do not differentially aid amnesic recall, so the fact that amnesics benefit from recall cues cannot be taken as support for the theory that the fundamental deficit in Korsakoff amnesia is a retrieval deficit. In fact, the existence of parallels between amnesic performance and normal weak memories cannot in itself be taken to support any particular theory of the amnesic deficit. Meudell and Mayes (1982, p. 227) comment: "...we believe that an amnesic's memory shortly after learning is probably similar to that of a normal person's after a considerable degree of forgetting. Of course, in the absence of further data, this claim does not discriminate between acquisition [*registration*], storage and retrieval failure explanations of amnesia since normal people could forget for any one of these reasons."

Retrograde Amnesia in Korsakoff Amnesics

If Korsakoff amnesia had a sudden onset, then evidence for a retrograde amnesia for events that happened well before the amnesia began would point clearly to a retrieval deficit in these patients. There is no doubt that Korsakoff patients *do* show retrograde amnesia for several decades before they became clinically amnesic. A striking feature of this retrograde amnesia is that it is *temporally graded*, with memory for more recent time periods being more severely disrupted than memory for earlier time periods. As compared with normal control subjects, Korsakoff amnesics show much less of a decrement in memory for events that occurred 30 or 40 years ago than for events that occurred 10 or 15 years ago. This pattern has been shown to characterise Korsakoff amnesic memory for events from different decades (e.g. Cohen & Squire, 1981; Seltzer & Benson, 1974) and memory for the faces and voices of people who achieved fame or notoriety in different decades (Albert, Butters, & Brandt, 1981b; Albert, Butters, & Levin, 1979; Marslen-Wilson & Teuber, 1975; Meudell, Northen, Snowden, & Neary, 1980).

All this would count as good evidence for a retrieval deficit *if* the memory problems of Korsakoff amnesics had a sudden onset, but they almost certainly do not. Learning difficulties have been demonstrated in alcoholics who are not (yet) clinically amnesic (Parker & Noble, 1977; Ryan, Butters, & Montgomery, 1980), and non-amnesic alcoholics have nevertheless been shown to have the same pattern of better memory for old than for recent decades that Korsakoff amnesics show (Albert, Butters, & Brandt, 1981b; Brandt, Butters, Ryan, & Bayog, 1983; Butters & Albert, 1982; Cohen & Squire, 1981). There is thus the possibility that patients who end up as Korsakoff amnesics have in fact suffered from *registration* difficulties for several decades (ever since they became alcoholic) and that their poor memory for recent decades is due to the fact that as the decades passed they became increasingly impaired at registering new events and people (even assuming that chronic alcoholics pay the same attention to the world about them as do normal people, which is also questionable).

Butters (1984) and Butters and Cermak (1986) have sought to resolve this issue through a rather remarkable case study of an eminent scientist and university professor (PZ) who developed alcoholic Korsakoff amnesia at the age of 65. As a scientist he had published many papers and books in the course of a career spanning 40 years or more, including an extensive autobiography published 2 years before he became clinically amnesic. PZ showed the registration impairments on new learning tasks that one would expect to see in a Korsakoff amnesic, and he also showed a temporally graded retrograde amnesia for famous people from different decades. Using his publications and autobiography, Butters and Cermak were able to assess PZ's memory for scientists who had once been well known to him, and for people, events and works which featured prominently in his autobiography. PZ proved to have precisely the same pattern of temporally graded retrograde amnesia for this personal material as he had for people from the public domain.

Butters and Cermak (1986, p. 270) comment that "there can be little doubt that his [PZ's] severe retrograde amnesia developed acutely with the onset of his amnesic disorder". He did not deteriorate by imperceptible degrees into a full-blown amnesia, but became clinically amnesic fairly suddenly after previously functioning reasonably well. The amnesia extended back to cover material he once had good command of, implying a genuine retrieval problem in at least this case. However, Butters and Cermak (1986) also note that PZ had a history of alcohol abuse going back for 35 years, and admit that during those years he may have suffered a progressive deterioration in his capacity to register new memories. Butters and Cermak do not question the contribution of a registration deficit to PZ's final amnesia (they are *not* advocating a retrieval theory as the complete explanation), but they do believe that their data show clear evidence for a retrieval impairment superimposed upon the registration impairment.

Korsakoff Amnesia: A Summary

We have spent quite some time on alcoholic Korsakoff amnesia, reflecting in part the extent to which research on amnesia has focussed upon this form of memory disorder. As a result of our survey we may draw some tentative conclusions. First, it seems unlikely that the pattern of impairments can be *fully* explained in terms of a retrieval deficit. Much of the evidence that has been adduced to support such an account is at least as compatible with the theory that a registration impairment is a major causal factor in Korsakoff amnesia. That registration deficit probably begins early on in the patient's life and builds up gradually over the years, resulting in a progressive decline in the ability to learn new information.

Butters and Cermark's work on patient PZ seems to establish, however, that a retrieval component constitutes part of the full-blown Korsakoff amnesia. We saw earlier in this chapter that patients with Huntington's Disease may also develop a retrograde amnesia, but in their case it is "flat", being equally severe for distant and recent memories. The retrograde amnesia of the Korsakoff amnesic, in contrast, is temporally graded. Albert (1984) and Butters (1984) propose a two-factor theory according to which the temporally graded retrograde amnesia may be the result of an essentially uniform retrieval deficit *superimposed* upon a longstanding and progressive registration impairment. The older memories of the Korsakoff amnesic were well established and consolidated at the time and are thus more likely to be accessible after the onset of the retrieval impairment than are the more recent memories, weakly established and poorly consolidated after years of alcohol abuse.

This two-factor theory of Korsakoff amnesia would explain why, typically, amnesics perform worse than normals even on remote memories. It also has the potential of reconciling Korsakoff amnesia with other forms of memory disorder in which either the registration impairment or the retrieval impairment predominate. As we shall see in the next section, the registration impairment of Korsakoff amnesics seems comparable with that of amnesics like NA whose retrieval functions are intact.

We should insert a note of caution, though, before moving on. We have been talking about "Korsakoff amnesics" as if they were all alike, rather in contrast to the emphasis on heterogeneity in the rest of the book. Baddeley and Wilson (1986) examined the extent to which personal memories could be evoked in amnesic patients by cue words like *letter* or *find*. Unlike most Korsakoff amnesics, their two patients (AB and MO'C) appeared to have normal access to personal memories when tested in this way, arguing against a retrieval deficit (at least for autobiographical episodes). As Baddeley and Wilson note, Zola-Morgan, Cohen, and Squire (1983) also found relatively normal autobiographical memories in their Korsakoff patients. Thus, whereas all Korsakoff amnesics probably share the registration deficit, the extent and severity of the retrieval impairment may vary considerably from patient to patient, and perhaps also with the type of memory being tested. In the words of Baddeley and Wilson (1986, p. 235), this "serves to emphasise a general point in neuropsychology, namely that common aetiology [*i.e. physical cause of illness*] does not guarantee equivalent cognitive dysfunction". Equally, distinct aetiology does not guarantee distinct cognitive dysfunction.

TWO FORMS OF REGISTRATION DEFICIT?

An inability to establish new, lasting memory traces is thought by many theorists to underlie several, if not all, forms of amnesia. This impairment may be accompanied in some cases by an additional retrieval deficit. It has been suggested, however, that the precise nature of the registration deficit may differ between types of amnesic patient. In particular, some amnesics may show abnormally fast forgetting of learned material whereas others may forget at a normal rate.

Huppert and Piercy (1979) claimed that patient HM showed abnormally fast forgetting. HM studied a sequence of pictures for 16 seconds each. With this exposure duration for each item he could perform at something over 70% correct on a recognition memory test after a retention interval of 10 minutes. Normal control subjects could achieve a similar performance level after 10 minutes given only 1 second exposure to each picture. Huppert and Piercy (1979) then retested the recognition memory of both HM and the control subjects after retention intervals of 1 and 7 days.

HM's performance was seen to decline more rapidly than the performance of the normal controls, suggesting to Huppert and Piercy that HM's rate of forgetting was abnormally fast.

This conclusion has, however, been criticised by Squire and Cohen (1984). They note that HM's level of performance after the 10-minute interval was only just within the normal range and that the evidence for faster forgetting in HM comes largely from the fact that his performance after the 7-day retention interval fell to chance. Between 10 minutes and 1 day the decline in HM's recognition memory performance roughly parallelled that of the controls. In a subsequent study of HM's recognition memory, Freed, Corkin, and Cohen (1984) failed to find any evidence of abnormally rapid forgetting.

Clearer evidence for fast forgetting comes in a study by Squire (1981) of the recognition memory performance of patients who had recently undergone electroconvulsive therapy (ECT) as a treatment for psychiatric disorders. It has been known for some time that memory problems can follow ECT (Miller & Marlin, 1979). Using a picture memory test similar to that of Huppert and Piercy (1979), Squire (1981) showed that patients receiving ECT could achieve comparable (in fact, rather better) performance than control subjects when the patients studied the pictures for 8 seconds per item and the normals for 1 second per item. Over the next 32 hours, however, the recognition memory performance of the ECT patients declined much more rapidly than the controls.

Thus patients who have recently received ECT show abnormally rapid forgetting. In contrast, both alcoholic Korsakoff amnesics and patient NA seem to show normal rates of forgetting once material has been learned to a criterion level. Huppert and Piercy (1978) established comparable levels of recognition memory performance for pictures in Korsakoff amnesics and normal controls after a 10-minute retention interval by allowing the amnesics 4 seconds study time per picture as compared to 1 second per picture for the normals. With comparability of performance after a relatively short delay thus established, recognition memory at 1- and 7-day intervals was found not to differ for the two groups, while remaining above chance at both intervals. Similar results for picture memory were obtained by Squire (1981) and Kopelman (1985) when comparing Korsakoff amnesics and controls, and by Squire (1981) when comparing patient NA and controls.

Although none of these studies addresses the question of what forgetting *is*, or how it arises, it is not hard to accept that abnormally fast forgetting might contribute to the memory problems of ECT patients. The normal forgetting rates of NA and Korsakoff amnesics imply, however, that if one is committed to some form of registration impairment in these cases, then one seems constrained to suggest, as Squire and

Cohen (1984) do, that NA and Korsakoff amnesics are slower to *establish* memory traces—slower, in other words, to learn. Once traces have been established, however, their fate is the same as that of normal memories of comparable strength.

It would be neat and tidy if we could assert that NA and Korsakoff amnesics show slow learning but normal forgetting, whereas ECT patients (and possibly HM) show normal learning but fast forgetting. Unfortunately, for such an elegant theory, the data clearly show that in addition to forgetting faster than normals, ECT patients and HM also *learn* more slowly. In both cases the initial study periods required to achieve criterial performance after 10-minute delays are much longer than are required by normal controls. That said, it may be unreasonable to suggest that normal learning rates could ever accompany abnormally fast forgetting, because forgetting is presumably something which is going on while you are learning the items, not just something which starts to happen after the items have been learned. Forgetting also presumably occurs during the initial 10-minute retention intervals in the above-mentioned studies, so that patients with abnormally fast forgetting would need to learn the items *better* than the controls in the study phase in order to show comparable retention after 10 minutes. (If one could introduce into both the study and retention phases of these experiments a secondary task for the normal subjects which increased their forgetting to a rate comparable with that of the fast-forgetting ECT patients, then one might find that the normals required study times as long as the patients to achieve equal recognition memory performance after the 10-minute retention interval.)

It has been suggested that the registration deficit in at least some amnesics should be interpreted as a difficulty in *consolidating* memory traces—a failure perhaps of a biochemical process which "fixes" newly-formed memory traces. (e.g. Milner, 1966; Squire, Cohen, & Nadel, 1984). McClelland and Rumelhart (1986) offer an account of how such a failure of consolidation could be construed which is both quasi-neurochemical and implemented as a computational model. Following earlier advocates of consolidation theories, McClelland and Rumelhart note how this theory can explain an otherwise puzzling phenomenon, namely the brief retrograde amnesia for events that occurred some months or even a year or two before the onset of the amnesia in patients whose amnesia began *suddenly*. We noted earlier, for example, how HM's memory for events before his operation is generally good but shows some weaknesses for some years before the operation. Similarly, patients with traumatic amnesia often remain permanently unable to recall events leading up to their head injury, even when their memories have otherwise returned to normal.

These observations are explicable if we assume that the consolidation of memory traces is a process which continues for some time, and if we also assume that if consolidation is disrupted, traces for experiences not completely fixed tend to decay and be lost. Depending on how severe the impairment of consolidation is, and how soon (if ever) the process resumes, then we would *expect* a limited retrograde amnesia in patients whose deficit is essentially one of memory registration (consolidation being part of the registration process).

WHAT CAN SURVIVE AMNESIA, AND WHY?

We opened this chapter with Korsakoff's (1889) description of a typical encounter with an amnesic patient. It is worth repeating the first part of that description. Korsakoff observes how the patient "...gives the impression of a person in complete possession of his faculties; he reasons about everything perfectly well, draws correct deductions from given premises, makes witty remarks, plays chess or a game of cards, in a word, comports himself as a mentally sound person" (Victor & Yakovlev, 1955, p. 398). Liepmann's (1910) patient remained an accomplished mathematician and chess player despite his amnesia; Syz's (1937) patient retained his knowledge of geography, astronomy, biblical history, etc.; HM could still do jigsaw puzzles, though he did the same ones day after day. It is obvious that many aspects of cognitive performance can survive despite the presence of a dense amnesia. The question is, is there any logic to the pattern of loss and retention, and if there is, can it shed any light on either the nature of amnesia or the organisation of normal cognitive processes? In the sections that follow we shall evaluate and discuss claims that auditory–verbal short-term memory, semantic memory, skills and perceptual learning may escape impairment in cases of amnesia.

Auditory–Verbal Short-term Memory

If a string of random letters or digits is read out at a pace of about one per second and you are required to repeat the string back in the correct order, then most normal people can repeat between six and eight items before they begin to make mistakes (Miller, 1956). Wechsler (1917) showed that Korsakoff amnesics were as good as normals at immediate recall of digit strings, a result later replicated by Drachman and Arbit (1966) and Butters and Cermak (1980). The amnesic patients HM and NA have also been shown to have normal immediate recall to digits and letters (Teuber, Milner, & Vaughan, 1968; Wickelgren, 1968).

From a cognitive neuropsychological perspective it would be interesting even if only *some* amnesics showed normal immediate recall in the context of deficient long-term recall; the fact that the great majority do is particularly impressive, especially when coupled with reports of patients who show the reverse pattern—impaired immediate recall with normal long-term recall. Warrington and Shallice (1969) provided a detailed case report of a patient, KF, whose digit span was reduced from the normal 6–8 to a maximum of 2. Immediate recall of letters and word strings was comparably impaired. In contrast to this very poor immediate recall, KF's cued recognition memory and his learning of word-pairs were within the normal range, as was his learning of a list of 10 words.

In the late 1960s it was popular to attribute immediate recall to a "short-term memory" (STM) store whose capacity limitations were revealed through limits on digit span, etc. It was thought that perceived stimuli had to pass through STM on their way into long-term memory (LTM) (e.g. Atkinson & Shiffrin, 1968; Waugh & Norman, 1965). But if this were true, then damage to STM should also impair the entry of information into LTM, yet KF's learning rate seemed normal. Shallice and Warrington (1970) proposed that STM and LTM exist as parallel memory stores, so that each can be impaired without affecting the functioning of the other.

Two later studies of KF helped delineate more closely the nature of the impairment of his short-term memory capabilities. Warrington and Shallice (1972) showed that his short-term forgetting of auditory letters and digits was much faster than his forgetting of visual stimuli. Also, with visual presentation, KF did not make the errors involving the substitution of similar-sounding items (e.g. B for P, F for S) that are made by normals and which he himself made with auditory presentation. Warrington and Shallice (1972) argued that KF employed a form of visual storage whenever possible and that his visual (as opposed to auditory) short-term storage capabilities were intact. Later, Shallice and Warrington (1974) showed that KF's deficit was restricted to verbal materials like letters, digits and words, and that his immediate recall of meaningful sounds such as cats mewing or telephones ringing was normal. The short-term store impaired in KF was thus auditory rather than visual, and within the auditory modality verbal rather than non-verbal, hence Shallice and Warrington's final designation of it as the "auditory–verbal short-term store".

There is an obvious parallel between the finding that KF showed impaired short-term yet intact long-term memory for verbal materials and the demonstration of patients with impaired short-term yet intact long-term memory for spatial locations made by De Renzi and his colleagues (De Renzi & Nichelli, 1975; De Renzi et al., 1977a) and discussed in Chapter 3 (pp. 81–84). It is also, however, clear that impairments of auditory–verbal short-term memory and impairments affecting short-term memory for spatial locations are dissociable (De Renzi & Nichelli, 1975), and a number of different types of short-term memory impairment are beginning to be identified. Baddeley and his colleagues have been particularly successful in this enterprise (e.g. Baddeley & Wilson, 1985; Vallar & Baddeley, 1984a, 1984b) and have been able to relate their findings to Baddeley's (1983, 1986) conception that short-term storage involves a working memory system in which a central executive interacts with a number of interrelated subsystems.

Semantic Memory

At the same time that cognitive psychologists were proposing, in the late 1960s and early 1970s, that short-term memory was not a single store, it was also suggested that there might exist more than one type of long-term memory. Influential among these proposals was the theory put forward by Tulving (1972). Tulving drew a distinction between two different sorts of memory. The first are autobiographical memories for episodes in your own past life, as when you think back and recollect some event or occasion in which you participated. Tulving called these *episodic memories*; they are personal memories which are dated in time and located in space— you know when these episodes happened and where. The second type of memories are for items of information you have acquired repeatedly over the years—what the capital of France is; what *reluctant* means; whether pigs have wings. What distinguishes these *semantic memories* from episodic memories is that you are commonly unable to recall where and when you acquired a typical piece of semantic information.

Kinsbourne and Wood (1975) were the first to suggest that we might see in amnesia an impairment to episodic memory with preserved semantic memory. Amnesics, they observed, have difficulty retaining and recollecting incidents and events that have happened to them (episodic memory) yet perform well on tests of factual knowledge or on tests which tap their understanding of word meanings (semantic memory). This observation is undoubtedly a valid one for many amnesics. We have already noted preserved factual knowledge in the cases discussed above. Grünthall (1923, 1924) showed amnesic word associations to be normal, and Baddeley and Warrington (1973) found amnesics to be unimpaired at generating instances from semantic categories such as animals or fruit. A distinction between memories similar to Tulving's (1972) was, in fact, made by Gillespie (1937, p. 749) who argued that

> the kind of remembering involved in saying "I visited Paris in 1925" is different from what is implied in saying "Waterloo was fought in 1815". Both are acts of remembering, but that latter is much simpler than the former. It is an example of the so-called "mechanical" type of memory, as compared with the personal type of remembering. That continuity of

personal identity and memory are separate phenomena is shown by clinical
cases in which mechanical memory, when tested, is found to be intact
but the recollection of everyday events in the patient's life... is
missing.

The distinction between episodic/personal memory and semantic/
mechanical memory is an intuitively appealing one, and if neuropsychological evidence were genuinely to support it then that would be a major
contribution. We have already discussed impairments that do seem to
affect semantic memory in Chapters 2, 5, and 6, and noted that these can
be category-specific. But there are two objections to the theory of impaired
episodic memory with intact semantic memory in amnesia which seriously
call into question its usefulness as an explanation of amnesic loss and
retention. First, many different sorts of "knowledge" can be preserved
in amnesia, from biblical knowledge, through knowledge of how to play
the piano, to knowledge of how to dress oneself. Tulving (1983), like
Parkin (1982), sought to extend the concept of semantic memory to
encompass many or all of these aspects of preserved performance. This
brought the rebuke from Baddeley (1984a, p. 239) that Tulving "simply
labels tasks which amnesics can perform as semantic and then concludes
that their semantic memory performance is intact". If the distinction is
to be productive, then this circularity must be removed, possibly by
restoring the concept of semantic memory back to its original delineation
concerning factual knowledge and knowledge of the meanings of words
and objects.

The more damaging objection arises from the belief discussed earlier
that registration deficits of one form or another comprise a major part
of many or all amnesic disorders. In Korsakoff amnesics the deficit may
have been building up over many years, but as we have seen, memories
for episodes in the patient's early life are usually preserved. The significance
of this point is that most of the information assessed in tests of semantic
memory is information that is normally acquired in the first 20 years or
so of life. One can argue therefore that what we commonly see in amnesia
is the relative preservation of memory traces laid down in early life before
the onset of any registration deficit, traces which include most of the
patients' knowledge of words and the world as well as individual
autobiographical episodes (we note, however, that the existence of
dissociable category-specific deficits demonstrates that age of acquisition
will not be a useful explanatory construct for cases in which semantic
memories are themselves impaired; our point is only that it may explain
the relative preservation of semantic memory in certain forms of amnesia).

For the episodic/semantic distinction to prove useful as an explanation
of amnesia it would be necessary to show that whereas the acquisition

of episodic memories is impaired in amnesic patients, the acquisition of semantic information remains intact. This would not seem to be the case. As Baddeley (1984a, 1984b) notes, amnesics do not seem to update their semantic memories, "frequently being quite unaware of who is the current prime minister or president, where they themselves are, or what is going on in the world about them. They have great difficulty in learning the names of new people, and in finding their way about using anything other than previously learned routes" (Baddeley, 1984a, p. 239).

Gabrieli, Cohen, and Corkin (1983) tried to teach HM the meanings of eight new words. Despite repeating the items 115 times per day for 10 days, HM showed virtually no learning when tested with alternative definitions, synonyms or sentence frames that used the words. Cermak and O'Connor (1983) studied a patient (SS) with a profound anterograde amnesia following an encephalitic illness. He was formerly a pioneer in the field of laser technology and could still discourse knowledgeably on the topic. Cermak and O'Connor (1983) decided, however, to test SS's acquisition of new semantic information about lasers by giving him an article to read about a new laser discovery. He read it and explained its contents as he went along, showing that he could use his existing knowledge to help grasp the new points, but a few moments afterwards he could neither recall the new points nor recognise them when presented by the experimenter. Repeated attempts to teach him new information failed completely.

In the course of their paper Cermak and O'Connor (1983) also make an important point about autobiographical memory. They argue that you can have two sorts of memories about your own past. The first are genuine recollections in which you seem to be able to re-experience a scene or event. The second are facts you know to be true about your past though you cannot remember them personally. Certain things you did or said as a child may, for example, have become part of your family "lore" and may crop up from time to time in family conversations. You may know about these "episodes" though they do not form part of your episodic memory in Tulving's (1972, 1983) sense. Cermak and O'Connor (1983) felt that SS's autobiographical memories were primarily of this last sort rather than true recollections. One might argue on this basis that SS is an exceptional amnesic and that evidence from SS should not be given too great weight when evaluating the relevance to most amnesics of the episodic/semantic distinction. That said, evidence that any form of amnesic patient can register and retain semantic information at normal levels while being unable to register and retain episodic information is lacking (Baddeley, 1984, 1984b; Damasio, Eslinger, Damasio, Van Hoesen, & Cornell, 1985; Squire & Cohen, 1984), yet it is upon such evidence that the relevance of the distinction must depend.

Skills

Another capacity which has been held to remain intact in amnesic patients is "skills"—things like piano playing, carving wood, or playing golf. The same point applies here as to semantic memory: Do amnesics merely retain skills acquired before the onset of their memory problems, or do they retain also the capacity to acquire new skills at normal rates? There is no doubt that old skills can be preserved, as for example the piano-playing skills of Dana's (1894) patient, or the golfing skills of Schacter's (1983) case.

There is also ample documentation of amnesics acquiring new skills. The patient reported by Dunn (1845) learned dressmaking but had to be reminded each morning of her unfinished work as well as her ability to carry it out. Dana's (1894) patient learned billiards and carving, NA has developed model-building skills since his accident (Teuber et al., 1968), and the amnesic patient of Starr and Phillips (1970) learned new piano pieces. What matters crucially, however, is whether they can acquire new skills *at normal rates*. On this the evidence is mixed. HM showed progressive improvement in his performance on tasks like tracing a pattern in a mirror, learning a tactile "finger maze", and tracking a moving target on a "pursuit rotor", but when his performance was compared with that of normals his rate of learning was found to be markedly inferior (Corkin, 1965, 1968). The patients studied by Cermak, Lewis, Butters, and Goodglass (1973) and Cermak and O'Connor (1983) were also slower than normals at learning finger mazes but these authors point out that normals often assist themselves in this task by memorising a series of verbal instructions about the required sequence of turns; something that amnesics would, of course, have great difficulty in doing.

There is no denying that amnesic patients may be capable of learning very sophisticated new skills. Glisky, Schacter, and Tulving (1986) taught four patients with amnesia following traumatic head injuries to manipulate information on a computer screen, to write, edit and execute simple computer programs, and to store and retrieve information on computer disks. They were all capable of learning to some degree, but their rate of learning was slower than that of normals, and the nature of their learning seemed different from that of the normals. In particular, they were thrown by questions about their skill which did not use the same phrases as the materials from which they had learned, and they failed to generalise their learning to tasks similar but slightly different from those they had mastered. In other words, their learning seemed more inflexible and specific than that of normal subjects.

Considering the emphasis placed by some theorists upon claims of amnesics' preserved capacity for learning perceptual-motor skills, the number of studies reporting this finding is surprisingly small. Such studies must incorporate an appropriate "control group" of normals and must find the rate of amnesic acquisition of the skill to be at normal levels. Cermak et al. (1973) compared nine alcoholic Korsakoff amnesics and nine controls on a finger maze task and on the "pursuit rotor" (an apparatus requiring the subject to track a metal target moving on a turntable with a stylus). As mentioned earlier, the amnesics were slower than the normals at learning the finger maze, but they acquired the pursuit rotor skill at the same rate as the normals. Brooks and Baddeley (1976) replicated this observation and also showed normal rates of learning of jigsaw completions in their amnesics. Cohen and Squire (1980) and Martone, Butters, Payne, Becker, and Sax (1984) found normal rates of learning of the skill of reading mirror-reversed print in Korsakoff amnesics, though their retention of the content of what they read was worse than normal controls.

Finally, Cohen (1984) has claimed that a group of amnesics which included HM could learn how to solve a puzzle known as the "Tower of Hanoi" at a rate comparable to that of normal subjects. The Tower of Hanoi game requires the player to transfer a set of rings one at a time from one peg to another in the minimum possible number of moves. The amnesics improved across four training sessions as much as the normals did, and showed comparable generalisation to a slightly different version of the puzzle. HM showed savings on the task even a year later when he would, of course, have been able to recall little or nothing of the earlier training sessions. In contrast to Cohen's (1984) finding, however, the amnesic patient of Beatty, Salmon, Bernstein, Martone, Lyon, and Butters (1987) was slower than normals at learning the Tower of Hanoi puzzle, so although we may be able to claim that some amnesics show normal learning of this problem-solving skill, we cannot claim that they all do, and we do not yet know what distinguishes those who do from those who do not. From our perspective, though, the observation of normal learning in some amnesics is the crucial one.

More studies are needed in order to delineate what sorts of skills can be acquired at normal rates by what sorts of amnesics, because the few existing studies are currently bearing a considerable theoretical burden. It is also by no means obvious that skills as diverse as mirror reading, jigsaw puzzle solving, and computer programming form a sensible grouping for psychological analysis. Neither is it clear where to draw the line between the skills just reviewed and the more perceptual forms of learning we come to next, which, apparently, may also proceed normally in amnesics.

Perceptual Learning (Repetition Priming)

Confusion commonly arises in the memory literature due to the fact that the word "recognition" is used by cognitive psychologists in at least two different ways. An experimenter can present a stimulus such as a familiar word to a subject, initially for a very brief time and then for progressively longer, until the subject identifies the stimulus. The experimenter can then claim to have measured the presentation time necessary for that subject to "recognise" that stimulus. Used in this sense, to recognise the word PENCIL is to know that that string of letters is familiar and to know what meaning to assign to it. Most amnesic patients do not appear to have any problems recognising in this perceptual sense—they continue to recognise objects and words for what they are and use them appropriately.

The second sense in which cognitive psychologists use the word "recognise" has to do with recognition *memory*. In a typical recognition memory experiment a subject is first shown a list of items to memorise. After an interval the subject is shown a second, "test" list of items and is required to indicate which were in the original memory list and which were not. Here "recognising" a word means identifying it as having been encountered on a particular previous occasion. It is not hard to see that this sense of the word "recognition" is different from the first one. Suppose, for example, the word PENCIL occurred in the second, test list but not in the original memory list. A subject encountering PENCIL should recognise it in our first sense (i.e. acknowledge it to be a familiar word with a known meaning) but ought not to recognise it in our second sense (i.e. should not claim that it was in the memory list).

We now know that the processes mediating these two forms of recognition are different in part, and evidence from amnesic patients has been important in establishing this. It has been known for some time that if you read a word now you will identify it more rapidly and more accurately several minutes or hours later than if you had not had the recent encounter. This phenomenon is known as "repetition priming" (e.g. Neisser, 1954; Winnick & Daniel, 1970). The important point is that "recognition" (in the sense of perceptual identification) can be primed in this way without the subject "recognising" (in the memory sense) that the word being identified now is one he or she identified some time ago. This line of research has developed out of the pioneering studies by Warrington and Weiskrantz (1968, 1970).

Cermak, Talbot, Chandler, and Wolbarst (1985), for instance, required amnesic patients first of all to read aloud a list of concrete nouns presented one at a time for 5 seconds each, then to perform two subsequent tests involving the words. One was a perceptual identification test where words from the memory list, mixed in with new "filler" words, were presented initially for very brief exposures and then for progressively longer times until they were identified correctly. In the second test words from the memory list were again mixed with new filler words, but this time the patient had to say for each word whether or not it had been in the memory list (i.e. a standard recognition memory test). The memory task was presented either before or after the perceptual identification task. Their results showed that whereas amnesic recognition memory performance declined dramatically to well below the level shown by a control group of non-amnesic alcoholics if the memory test occurred after the perceptual identification task, the amount of perceptual priming observed was independent of the presence or absence of an intermediate recognition memory task and remained at a level comparable to that shown by non-amnesic control subjects.

Similar results have been obtained in studies investigating priming in the "fragment completion" task. Here subjects are supplied with fragments of words and are required to supply the missing letters so as to complete the word (e.g. completing P-NC-- as PENCIL, or -IN--W as WINDOW). Performance on this task can be primed in normals by recent experience with the full written forms of the words which later appear as fragments (Tulving, Schacter, & Stark, 1982).

Graf, Squire, and Mandler (1984) gave normals and amnesics word lists to study. They were later tested in one of four ways—free recall of the words, cued recall (the cue being the initial three letters of the words), recognition memory, and fragment completion. The amnesic patients were impaired relative to the normals on the free recall, cued recall and recognition memory tests, but their completion of word fragments was primed as much as the normals and the priming declined with time at the same rate as for the normals. A neat twist in this experiment is that the fragments used in the fragment completion test were the same initial three letters of words as were used as cues in the cued recall test. So if the word MARKET occurred in the study list the amnesics were more likely to complete MAR- as MARKET than if they had not been primed with that word, and this tendency was as strong as for normal subjects, but the amnesics were far poorer than the normals at using MAR- as a cue to *remember* that MARKET had actually occurred in the study list.

The crucial difference between fragment completion and cued recall is that there is no requirement in the fragment completion task to *remember overtly* that the completion word occurred in the study list. Subjects are simply instructed to complete the fragment with the first word that comes to mind. Priming in other tasks which do not require the amnesic to recognise that the primed word has recently been encountered has been demonstrated by Jacoby and Witherspoon (1982), Moscovitch (1982), and Graf, Shimamura, and Squire (1985)—see Shimamura (1986) and Schacter (1987) for reviews. A similar form of perceptual learning without explicit remembering may underlie the demonstration by Johnson, Kim, and Risse (1985) that amnesic patients came to prefer Korean melodies which they heard repeatedly over new ones, even though they could not reliably discriminate old from new.

How can the Pattern of Preservation and Loss in Amnesia best be Explained?

Auditory–verbal short-term memory, the acquisition of certain perceptual-motor skills, and some forms of perceptual priming all seem to be preserved in at least some amnesic patients. Considerable effort has gone into trying to explain why these aspects of amnesic performance can be preserved when other memory functions are so severely impaired.

A common approach is to posit more than one memory system and to argue that whereas certain memory systems are impaired in amnesia, others are preserved. We have already encountered one example of this approach in the proposal that immediate recall of strings of letters, digits or words is mediated by a separate auditory–verbal short-term memory system which is preserved in most amnesics though it may be impaired in other neurological patients (e.g. Shallice, 1979b; Warrington, 1979). Although this suggestion may go some of the way towards explaining the amnesic pattern, there is obviously much that it cannot handle, notably findings of intact perceptual-motor skill acquisition and repetition priming. To explain these, theorists have often gone a step further and proposed distinct *long-term* memory systems.

The problems of attempting to capture the amnesic pattern in terms of Tulving's (1972, 1983) episodic-semantic distinction have already been discussed. Cohen and Squire (1980) suggested that the amnesic pattern might yield to a different distinction, between *procedural* knowledge (or "knowing how") and *declarative* knowledge (or "knowing that"). The idea is that some of our knowledge, including that mobilised in the performance of perceptual-motor skills, involves rules and procedures which run fairly automatically when activated by appropriate inputs or commands. This procedural knowledge is held to be preserved in amnesic patients. Other types of knowledge are more item- or data-based. These include both episodic and semantic knowledge which depend on the encoding, storage, and explicit retrieval of distinct events or facts. The storage and/or retrieval of this "declarative" type of knowledge is held to be impaired in amnesics (see Cohen, 1984; Squire, 1982; Squire & Cohen, 1984, for further discussion).

The procedural/declarative (or "knowing how"/"knowing that") distinction has a venerable history in philosophy (e.g. Ryle, 1949), psychology (e.g. Bergson, 1896; Bruner, 1969), and computer science (e.g. Winograd, 1975), but its extension to amnesia is not without its difficulties. Auditory–verbal short-term storage is not obviously procedural, so the distinction may only apply once such short-term memory systems have been fractionated off from systems mediating longer-term storage. Also, it is not at all clear that priming of perceptual recognition depends on rules and procedures. It may instead depend on priming of the stored representations of the appearance of stimuli (e.g. Ellis, Young, Flude, and Hay, 1987c; McClelland & Rumelhart, 1985). These perceptual memories may be separate again from other sorts of long-term storage (Tulving, 1984).

A rather different approach to the amnesic pattern has been adopted by Jacoby (1984) and Schacter (1985, 1987). On this approach, preservation and loss is explained not in terms of distinct stores or distinct types of knowledge, but in terms of the manner in which knowledge is tapped. Jacoby (1984) argues against the notion of separate memory stores and for a distinction between "incidental" and "intentional" retrieval of information from long-term memory. Amnesics fare well, Jacoby argues, on tasks where past experiences can exert effects of an incidental nature on present performance. Perceptual priming is a clear example: The amnesic is simply required to respond to the present stimulus (e.g. complete a word fragment or identify a letter string), but the fact that the stimulus has been encountered recently facilitates performance, even though the patient cannot remember the previous encounter.

A similar distinction, but this time between "explicit" and "implicit" remembering, has been proposed by Schacter (1985) as relevant to explaining the amnesic pattern. Amnesics, he suggests, can demonstrate learning and recall when not required to remember explicitly what they have learned. Conventional memory testing procedures, he argues, demand that we know we have remembered something—they test memory explicitly. Perceptual-motor skills and perceptual priming do not require explicit recall of what was learned or when, but can still show implicit learning in the form of facilitation of test performance without conscious recollection. Strong evidence in favour of this view comes from Graf et al.'s (1984) study (see p. 299), in which amnesic performance matched that of normal subjects on fragment completion (which does not require remembering the previous encounter with the word, and is thus an implicit test) but was below normal when fragments of the words had to be used as an explicit cue to remembering the previously seen words. Furthermore, these types of implicit learning can be shown in normals to be also independent of conscious recollection of the learning episode (see Schacter, 1987, for a review). Put simply, the implicit/explicit distinction may relate to whether or not we are *aware of remembering* something. Schacter, McAndrews, and Moscovitch (1988) thus point to parallels between amnesia and other types of disorder, including blindsight (see Chapter 3) and prosopagnosia (Chapter 4) in which patients retain capacities that can be shown to be remarkably preserved, yet fail to know that this is the case. These disorders, Schacter et al. (1988) argue, can be considered to involve *specific forms of loss of awareness*.

Jacoby's (1984) intentional/incidental and Schacter's (1985) explicit/ implicit accounts represent a considerable step forward in understanding amnesia, but they are not without their difficulties. The preservation of auditory–verbal short-term memory is not easily encompassed within either of these frameworks, because immediate recall of digit or letter strings is surely both intentional and explicit. That preservation seems better accounted for by a separate stores model, in which case some hybrid of separate stores and modes-of-testing accounts would be needed by any final theory. In addition, the notion that priming and skill learning are preserved in amnesics because testing is incidental or implicit in those tasks currently exists largely as an alternative account to the theory that they are preserved because they are mediated by separate memory systems. Neither account has yet emerged as clearly superior to the other. Finally, believers in the incidental/intentional or implicit/explicit account have currently shown that amnesics can show perceptual priming without conscious recollection, and also that they can be primed by word associations, both old and new (Schacter, 1985, 1987). It has *not* yet been established, as it needs to be, that implicit or incidental testing procedures can reveal the presence in amnesic memory of connected episodes or life events of which they have no conscious recollection.

Commenting on research on amnesia, Morton (1985b, p. 285) observes that, "The pattern of amnesic loss seems to make intuitive sense but every attempt to grasp it formally has failed." Both the multiple stores and modes-of-testing approach seem at times to get tantalisingly close to a really good explanation of amnesic preservation and loss, yet problems remain for each. That said, it is clearly the view of many investigators that exploring processes whose operation remains intact in amnesics despite their memory impairment is one of the most promising research fronts at present. We would not dissent from that view.

OVERVIEW

Although the study of amnesia has engaged more people for a longer time than the study of, say, acquired dyslexia, most commentators feel that progress in the cognitive neuropsychology of memory has been less certain than in an area like reading: We seem neither to have such good explanations of the disorders themselves nor such firm conclusions to draw about the normal state from the analysis of its impairments.

A serious problem is that from the very outset of amnesia research, theorists have tended to think in terms of the "amnesic syndrome", believing that all amnesias would yield to a single explanation, and have treated all amnesic patients as alike and interchangeable. Consequently, the typical research project on amnesia has involved comparing a group of amnesics and a group of normals on one or more tests and reporting only the average scores for the groups. This procedure is, of course, quite different from the single-case methodology that has been dominant and productive in other areas of cognitive neuropsychology, and the averaging across normals and amnesics will obscure any important individual differences in both groups.

This tactic seems to us strange even when one simply compares and contrasts the few single-case studies that *have* been published over the decades. For it to continue now would be bizarre in the extreme when one considers that in every other domain of cognition—visual perception, object recognition, spatial representation, reading, writing, speaking, etc.—heterogeneity of impairments has proved to be the norm. In all of these domains brain injury gives rise to a wide variety of patterns of impairment whose differences one from another are of immense theoretical significance. How odd it would be if long-term memory was the single exception to this rule.

A further point worth making is that many of the cognitive disorders we have dealt with elsewhere in this book can be construed as memory disorders of a sort different from the classical amnesic patient. The anomic aphasic patient, for example, appears to have lost conscious access to the representations in memory of the spoken forms of many words (see pp. 116–124). The patient with "surface" dysgraphia has similarly lost conscious access to the representations in memory of the spellings of many words (see pp. 177–179). Recognition problems covering objects (agnosia), faces (prosopagnosia), or words ("surface" dyslexia; letter-by-letter reading; word meaning deafness) can similarly be considered to involve material-specific forms of memory impairment, causing those stimuli to be no longer recognised. Patients with certain acquired dysgraphias appear to have forgotten the shapes of letters or how to form them (pp. 180–187).

These and other disorders, like the "semantic memory" impairments discussed in Chapters 2, 5, and 6, can stand alongside orthodox amnesia as types of memory disorder, and their omission from most treatments of memory disorders may be one reason why memory has seemed to be only subject to a small number of impairments. That said, there are suggestions in the literature that additional forms of amnesia may exist and await detailed cognitive investigation. For example, the 59-year-old patient reported by Andrews, Poser, and Kessler (1982) "came to" after a blackout and found himself unable to remember anything of the last 40 years though he could recall events from before that time. He could remember nothing of his own personal history for the blank period, did not recognise his house, family or friends, and could not remember how to use modern appliances like televisions, microwave ovens, or showers. He identified Charles Chaplin, Fred Astaire, Jean Harlow, and President Roosevelt from pictures but failed to recognise Orson Welles, Marilyn Monroe, President Johnson, or Snoopy.

The sudden onset of amnesia in a patient with no history of alcohol abuse suggests a retrieval disorder, but any simple retrieval disorder would be expected to affect memory for events experienced after the illness, as well as memory for events before the illness. According to Andrews et al. (1982), however, this did not happen: The patient retained and remembered experiences and facts from after his illness well (though unfortunately his retention of new material was not assessed formally). At the clinical level at least this patient appeared to have an isolated retrograde amnesia. Other similar cases have been reported by Roman-Campos, Poser, and Wood (1980) and Goldberg, Antin, Bilder, Gerstman, Hughes, and Mattis (1981; see also Goldberg & Bilder, 1985; Goldberg, Hughes, Mattis, & Antin, 1982).

Isolated retrograde amnesia does not yield to a simple registration/consolidation or retrieval explanation. Andrews et al.'s (1982) patient could retrieve some knowledge of the missing 40 years in dreams, under hypnosis, or following injection with the drug amytal IV, indicating that the memory traces may have been disrupted or weakened rather than lost completely. It may be that these patients suffer a sudden disruption to all stored memory traces—episodic, semantic, and procedural—a disruption which does not affect the processes of registration and retrieval themselves.

In sum, there are many different neuropsychological conditions relevant to cognitive theories of memory. Memories of some type are crucial to everything we do. Trying to base a cognitive neuropsychology of memory solely on amnesia as traditionally construed could be like trying to base a cognitive neuropsychology of reading solely on a "syndrome" like "surface" dyslexia (the difficulty being confounded by the fact that neither amnesia nor surface dyslexia is a unitary, homogeneous disorder). It is legitimate to take a particular form of memory disorder as your object of investigation, but the theorist interested in the wider issue of inferring how normal memory works from the disorders to which it is prone may need to embrace a wider range of disorders than have conventionally been considered.

Progress may also be hastened by a deeper consideration of what memory is *for*. The psychological study of memory has too often been founded upon the results of laboratory tasks which have few, if any, counterparts in everyday experience. Under such conditions memory can appear severely limited and inaccurate. But the memory systems we now enjoy have evolved over millions of years for specific purposes, though like all specialised systems they can be made to look limited if tested on tasks for which they were not developed (a finely engineered racing car looks limited if you try to drive it across a field). Whenever a set of tasks appears to display our cognitive apparatus in a poor light it is more likely that the tasks are maladapted than that our cognitive systems are.

In recent years cognitive psychologists have shown an increasing willingness to step outside the laboratory in order to examine the cognitive system at work in everyday life (e.g. Harris & Morris, 1984; Neisser, 1982). One realisation which follows from such an exercise is that memory is as much about the future as it is about the past. Memory helps us to use our past experiences in order to better evaluate our present situation and better decide what to do next. We also store in our memories the plans for future actions. The amnesic patient NA found cooking difficult because he could no more retain a sequence of planned actions in memory than a sequence of past events (Kaushall et al., 1981), but so-called "prospective memory" (i.e. memory for future plans) has not been investigated systematically in amnesia. The sustained and reflective observation of the problems of amnesics in everyday life could pay substantial dividends in terms of increased understanding of both normal and impaired memory (cf. Schacter, 1983).

SUMMARY

If an event or piece of information is to be recalled at a later date, then three (possibly related) processes seem to be almost logically necessary. The event or item must be *registered* in memory, must be *retained* in memory, and must be capable of being *retrieved* from memory. Registration impairment causes an inability to form new memory traces, though old ones which comfortably preceded the onset of the amnesia should still be capable of recall (i.e. the patient shows anterograde but not retrograde amnesia). This pattern has been reported several times, including patients HM and NA. Retrieval deficits affect the recall of both old and new memories (anterograde and retrograde amnesia). Such deficits have never been demonstrated convincingly in the absence of registration impairment, but occur alongside a registration deficit in cases of transient global amnesia, traumatic amnesia, and Huntington's disease.

Both registration and retrieval impairments have been proposed as the sole cause of the memory impairments seen in alcoholic Korsakoff amnesics. Registration impairments are certainly present in these cases. The retrograde amnesia which would demonstrate a retrieval impairment is often hard to establish because of the gradual onset of the disease, though Butters (1984) and Butters and Cermak (1986) argue for a retrograde amnesia in their patient PZ.

The nature of the registration impairment may vary among amnesics. Patients with amnesia following electroconvulsive therapy forget abnormally rapidly, whereas patient NA and alcoholic Korsakoff amnesics forget at normal rates but only learn very slowly.

General cognitive and intellectual powers can survive the onset of amnesia, as can certain sorts of "memories". These include auditory–verbal short-term memory, some motor skills, and the sort of perceptual learning revealed in "repetition priming". It is important when claims of preserved types of memory are being made to show clearly that the learning of new material is intact as well as the recall of old material. This has *not* been established for semantic memories. Two broadly different views exist about why some sorts of "memory" may be preserved in some amnesic patients. One view asserts that only performance requiring explicit, conscious, intentional recall is impaired whereas performance which only requires implicit, incidental learning is preserved. The second view asserts that those sorts of memory which are preserved rely on distinct, unimpaired memory systems. Evidence for domain-specific losses of memory for spoken words, spellings, faces, objects, geographical knowledge, etc., certainly establish the existence of memory systems distinct from those damaged in amnesic patients.

FURTHER READING

Parkin, A. J. (1987). *Memory and amnesia*. Oxford: Basil Blackwell. An introduction to the subject, and a good place to begin learning about amnesia.

Squire, L. R. (1987). *Memory and brain*. New York: Oxford University Press. A thorough review of amnesia and the neural basis of memory.

Talland, G. A. (1965). *Deranged memory*. New York: Academic Press. Invaluable for its coverage of the early literature on amnesia.

Useful collections of advanced readings covering various aspects of work on amnesia are:

Whitty, C. W. M., & Zangwill, O. L. (Eds) (1977). *Amnesia* (2nd edn). London: Butterworths.

Cermak, L. S. (Ed.) (1982). *Human memory and amnesia*. Hillsdale, NJ: Lawrence Erlbaum Associates.

Lynch, G., McGaugh, J. L., & Weinberger, N. M. (Eds) (1984). *Neurobiology of learning and memory*. New York: The Guildford Press.

Weingartner, H., & Parker, E. S. (Eds) (1984). *Memory consolidation*. Hillsdale, NJ: Lawrence Erlbaum Associates.

References

Abadi, R. V., Kulikowski, J. J., & Meudell, P. (1981). Visual performance in a case of visual agnosia. In M. V. Van Hof & G. Mohn (Eds), *Functional recovery from brain damage*. Amsterdam: Elsevier.

Alajouanine, T., Ombredane, A., & Durand, M. (1939). *Le syndrome de désintégration phonétique dans l'aphasie*. Paris: Masson and Cie.

Alajouanine, T., Pichot, P., & Durand, M. (1949). Dissociations des altérations phonétiques avec conservation relative de la langue ancienne dans un cas d'anarthrie pure chez un sujet francais bilingue. *Éncephale, 28*, 245–246.

Alajouanine, T., Lhermitte, F., Ledoux, F., Renaud, D., & Vignolo, L. A. (1964). Les composants phonémiques et sémantiques de la jargon aphasie. *Revue Neurologique, 110*, 5–20.

Albert, M. L. (1973). A simple test of visual neglect. *Neurology, 23*, 658–664.

Albert, M. L., & Bear, D. (1974). Time to understand: A case study of word deafness with reference to the role of time in auditory comprehension. *Brain, 97*, 373–384.

Albert, M. L. Reches, A., & Silverberg, R. (1975). Associative visual agnosia without alexia. *Neurology, 25*, 322–326.

Albert, M. S. (1984). Implications of different patterns of remote memory loss for the concept of consolidation. In H. Weingartner & E. S. Parker (Eds), *Memory consolidation*. Hillsdale, N. J.: Lawrence Erlbaum Associates Inc.

Albert, M. S., Butters, N., & Levin, J. (1979). Temporal gradients in the retrograde amnesia of patients with alcoholic Korsakoff's Disease. *Archives of Neurology, 36*, 211–216.

Albert, M. S., Butters, N., & Brandt, J. (1981a). Development of remote memory loss in patients with Huntington's Disease. *Journal of Clinical Neuropsychology, 3*, 1–12.

Albert, M. S., Butters, N., & Brandt, J. (1981b). Patterns of remote memory in amnesic and demented patients. *Archives of Neurology, 38*, 495–500.

Alexander, M. P., Stuss, D. T., & Benson, D. F. (1979). Capgras syndrome: A reduplicative phenomenon. *Neurology, 29*, 334–339.

Allport, D. A. (1977). On knowing the meaning of words we are unable to report: The effects of visual masking. In S. Dornic (Ed.), *Attention and Performance VI*. Hillsdale, N. J.: Lawrence Erlbaum Associates Inc.

307

Allport, D. A. (1983). Language and cognition. In R. Harris (Ed.), *Approaches to language*. Oxford: Pergamon Press.

Allport, D. A. (1984). Speech production and comprehension: One lexicon or two? In W. Prinz & A. F. Sanders (Eds), *Cognition and motor processes*. Berlin: Springer-Verlag.

Allport, D. A. & Funnell, E. (1981). Components of the mental lexicon. *Philosophical Transactions of the Royal Society* (London), *B295*, 397–410.

Allport, D. A., Antonis, B., & Reynolds, P. (1972). On the division of attention: A disproof of the single channel hypothesis. *Quarterly Journal of Experimental Psychology, 24*, 225–235.

Anderson, J. R. (1976). *Language, memory and thought*. Hillsdale, N. J.: Lawrence Erlbaum Associates Inc.

Andrews, E., Poser, C. M., & Kessler, M. (1982). Retrograde amnesia for forty years. *Cortex, 18*, 441–458.

Assal, G., Favre, C., & Anderes, J. P. (1984). Non-reconnaissance d'animaux familiers chez un paysan: zooagnosie ou prosopagnosie pour les animaux. *Revue Neurologique, 140*, 580–584.

Atkinson, R. C. & Shiffrin, R. M. (1968). Human memory: A proposed system and its control processes. In K. W. Spence & J. T. Spence (Eds), *The psychology of learning and motivation*, Vol. 2. London: Academic Press.

Auerbach, S. H., Allard, T., Naeser, M., Alexander, M. P., & Albert, M. L. (1982). Pure word deafness: An analysis of a case with bilateral lesions and a defect at the prephonemic level. *Brain, 105*, 271–300.

Baddeley, A. D. (1983). Working memory. *Philosophical Transactions of the Royal Society* (London), *B302*, 311–324.

Baddeley, A. D. (1984a). Neuropsychological evidence and the semantic/episodic distinction. *Behavioral and Brain Sciences, 7*, 238–239.

Baddeley, A. D. (1984b). The fractionation of human memory. *Psychological Medicine, 14*, 259–264.

Baddeley, A. D. (1986). *Working memory*. Oxford: Oxford University Press.

Baddeley, A. D. & Lewis, V. (1981). Inner active processes in reading: The innner voice, the inner ear, and the inner eye. In A. M. Lesgold & C. A. Perfetti (Eds), *Interactive processes in reading*. Hillsdale, N. J.: Lawrence Erlbaum Associates Inc.

Baddeley, A. D. & Lieberman, K. (1980). Spatial working memory. In R. S. Nickerson (Ed.), *Attention and Performance VIII*. Hillsdale, N. J.: Lawrence Erlbaum Associates Inc.

Baddeley, A. D. & Warrington, E. K. (1973). Memory coding and amnesia. *Neuropsychologia, 11*, 159–165.

Baddeley, A. D. & Wilson, B. (1985). Phonological coding and short-term memory in patients without speech. *Journal of Memory and Language, 24*, 490–502.

Baddeley, A. D. & Wilson, B. (1986). Amnesia, autobiographical memory, and confabulation. In D. C. Rubin (Ed.), *Autobiographical memory*. Cambridge: Cambridge University Press.

Badecker, W. & Caramazza, A. (1985). On considerations of method and theory governing the use of clinical categories in neurolinguistics and cognitive neuropsychology: The case against agrammatism. *Cognition, 20*, 97–125.

Badecker, W. & Caramazza, A. (1986). A final brief in the case against agrammatism. *Cognition, 24*, 277–282.

Bálint, R. (1909). Die Seelenlähmung des Schauens, optische Ataxie, räumliche Störung der Aufmerksamkeit. *Monatsschrift für Psychiatrie und Neurologie, 25*, 51–81.

Barbur, J. L., Ruddock, K. H., & Waterfield, V. A. (1980). Human visual responses in the absence of the geniculo-calcarine projection. *Brain, 103*, 905–928.

Barton, D. & Hamilton, M. E. (in press). Social and cognitive factors in the historical development of writing. In A. Lock & C. Peters (Eds), *Handbook of human symbolic evolution*. Oxford: Oxford University Press.

Basso, A., De Renzi, E., Faglioni, P., Scotti, G., & Spinnler, H. (1973). Neuropsychological evidence for the existence of cerebral areas critical to the performance of intelligence tests. *Brain, 96*, 715–728.

Bauer, R. M. (1984). Autonomic recognition of names and faces in prosopagnosia: A neuropsychological application of the guilty knowledge test. *Neuropsychologia, 22*, 457–469.

Baxter, D. M. & Warrington, E. K. (1986). Ideational agraphia: A single case study. *Journal of Neurology, Neurosurgery and Psychiatry, 49*, 369–374.

Bay, E. (1962). Aphasia and non-verbal disorders of language. *Brain, 85*, 411–426.

Beattie, G. W. & Butterworth, B. (1979). Contextual probability and word frequency as determinants of pauses and errors in spontaneous speech. *Language and Speech, 22*, 201–211.

Beatty, W. W., Salmon, D. P., Bernstein, N., Martone, M., Lyon, L., & Butters, N. (1987). Procedural learning in a patient with amnesia due to hypoxia. *Brain and Cognition, 6*, 386–402.

Beaumont, J. G. (Ed.) (1982). *Divided visual field studies of cerebral organisation*. London: Academic Press.

Beauvois, M.-F. (1982). Optic aphasia: a process of interaction between vision and language. *Proceedings of the Royal Society* (London), *B298*, 35–47.

Beauvois, M.-F. & Dérousné, J. (1979). Phonological alexia: Three dissociations. *Journal of Neurology, Neurosurgery and Psychiatry, 42*, 1115–1124.

Beauvois, M.-F. & Dérousné, J. (1981). Lexical or orthographic dysgraphia. *Brain, 104*, 21–50.

Beauvois, M.-F. & Saillant, B. (1985). Optic aphasia for colours and colour agnosia: A distinction between visual and visuo-verbal impairments in the processing of colours. *Cognitive Neuropsychology, 2*, 1–48.

Beauvois, M.-F., Dérousné, J., & Bastard, V. (1980). Auditory parallel to phonological alexia. Paper presented at the Third European Conference of the International Neuropsychological Society, Chianciano, Italy, June 1980.

Bellugi, U., Poizner, H., & Klima, E. S. (1983). Brain organization for language: Clues from sign aphasia. *Human Neurobiology, 2*, 155–170.

Benson, D. F. (1979). Neurologic correlates of anomia. In H. Whitaker & H. A. Whitaker (Eds), *Studies in neurolinguistics*, Vol. 4. New York: Academic Press.

Benson, D. F. & Geschwind, N. (1967). Shrinking retrograde amnesia. *Journal of Neurology, Neurosurgery and Psychiatry, 30*, 539–544.

Benson, D. F. & Greenberg, J. P. (1969). Visual form agnosia: A specific defect in visual discrimination. *Archives of Neurology, 20*, 82–89.

Benson, D. F., Gardner, H., & Meadows, J. C. (1976). Reduplicative paramnesia. *Neurology, 26*, 147–151.

Benton, A. L. (1979). Visuoperceptive, visuospatial, and visuoconstructive disorders. In K. M. Heilman & E. Valenstein (Eds), *Clinical neuropsychology*. New York: Oxford University Press.

Benton, A. L. (1980). The neuropsychology of facial recognition. *American Psychologist, 35*, 176–186.

Benton, A. L. (1982). Spatial thinking in neurological patients: Historical aspects. In M. Potegal (Ed.), *Spatial abilities: Development and physiological foundations*. New York: Academic Press.

Benton, A. L. & Van Allen, M. W. (1972). Prosopagnosia and facial discrimination. *Journal of the Neurological Sciences, 15*, 167–172.

Bergson, H. (1896). *Matière et mémoire*. Paris: Alcan. (Translated as *Matter and memory*. London: Allen, 1911.)

Bernard, P. (1951). Essai psycho-pathologique sur le comportement dans le syndrome de Korsakoff. *La Raison, 2*, 93–101.

Berndt, R. S. (1987). Symptom co-occurrence and dissociation in the interpretation of agrammatism. In M. Coltheart, G. Sartori, & R. Job (Eds), *The cognitive neuropsychology of language*. London: Lawrence Erlbaum Associates Ltd.

Berndt, R. S. & Caramazza, A. (1980). A redefinition of the syndrome of Broca's aphasia: Implications for a neuropsychological model of language. *Applied Psycholinguistics, 1*, 225–278.

Bisiach, E. (1988). Language without thought. In L. Weiskrantz (Ed.), *Thought without language*. Oxford: Oxford University Press.

Bisiach, E. & Luzzatti, C. (1978). Unilateral neglect of representational space. *Cortex, 14*, 129–133.

Bisiach, E., Luzzatti, C., & Perani, D. (1979). Unilateral neglect, representational schema and consciousness. *Brain, 102*, 609–618.

Bisiach, E., Capitani, E., Luzzatti, C., & Perani, D. (1981). Brain and conscious representation of reality. *Neuropsychologia, 19*, 543–552.

Bisiach, E., Cornacchia, L., Sterzi, R., & Vallar, G. (1984). Disorders of perceived auditory lateralization after lesions of the right hemisphere. *Brain, 107*, 37–52.

Bisiach, E., Perani, D., Vallar, G., & Berti, A. (1986a). Unilateral neglect: Personal and extra-personal. *Neuropsychologia, 24*, 759–767.

Bisiach, E., Vallar, G., Perani, D., Papagno, C., & Berti, A. (1986b). Unawareness of disease following lesions of the right hemisphere: Anosognosia for hemiplegia and anosognosia for hemianopia. *Neuropsychologia, 24*, 471–482.

Blanc-Garin, J. (1986). Faces and non-faces in prosopagnosic patients. In H. D. Ellis, M. A. Jeeves, F. Newcombe, & A. Young (Eds), *Aspects of face processing*. Dordrecht: Martinus Nijhoff.

Blumstein, S. (1973). *A phonological investigation of aphasic speech*. The Hague: Mouton.

Blumstein, S. E. (1978). Segment structure and the syllable in aphasia. In A. Bell & J. B. Hooper (Eds), *Syllables and segments*. Amsterdam: North-Holland.

Blumstein, S. E., Cooper, W. E., Goodglass, H., Statlender, S., & Gottlieb, J. (1980). Production deficits in aphasia: A voice-onset time analysis. *Brain and Language, 9*, 153–170.

Blumstein, S. L., Tartter, V. C., Michel, D., Hirsch, B., & Leiter, E. (1977). The role of distinctive features in the dichotic listening perception of vowels. *Brain and Language, 4*, 508–520.

Bodamer, J. (1947). Die Prosop-Agnosie. *Archiv für Psychiatrie und Nervenkrankheiten, 179*, 6–53.

Bonhöffer, K. (1901). *Die akuten Geisteskrankheiten der Gewohnheitstrinker*. Jena: Fischer.

Bonhöffer, K. (1902). Zur Kenntis der Rückbildung motorische Aphasien. *Mitteilungen aus den Grenzbieten der Medizin und Chirurgie, 10*, 203–224.

Boomer, D. S. & Laver, J.D.M.H. (1968). Slips of the tongue. *British Journal of Disorders of Communication, 3*, 2–12. (Reprinted in V. A. Fromkin (Ed.) (1973). *Speech errors as linguistic evidence*. The Hague: Mouton.)

Bornstein, B (1963). Prosopagnosia. In L. Halpern (Ed.), *Problems of dynamic neurology*. Jerusalem: Hadassah Medical School.

Bornstein, B., Sroka, M., & Munitz, H. (1969). Prosopagnosia with animal face agnosia. *Cortex, 5*, 164–169.

Bowers, D. & Heilman, K. (1984). Dissociation between the processing of affective and nonaffective faces: A case study. *Journal of Clinical Neuropsychology, 6*, 367–379.

Bradshaw, J. L. & Gates, E. A. (1978). Visual field differences in verbal tasks: Effects of task familiarity and sex of subject. *Brain and Language, 5,* 166–187.

Bradshaw, J. L. & Nettleton, N. C. (1983). *Human cerebral asymmetry.* Englewood Cliffs, N. J.: Prentice-Hall.

Brain, Lord (1964). Statement of the problem. In A. V. S. De Reuck & M. O'Connor (Eds), *Ciba foundation symposium on disorders of language.* London: Churchill.

Brain, W. R. (1941). Visual disorientation with special reference to lesions of the right cerebral hemisphere. *Brain, 64,* 244–272.

Bramwell, B. (1897). Illustrative cases of aphasia. *The Lancet, i,* 1256–1259. (Reprinted in *Cognitive Neuropsychology,* 1984, *1,* 245–258.)

Brandt, J., Butters, N., Ryan, C., & Bayog, R. (1983). Cognitive loss and recovery in chronic alcohol abusers. *Archives of General Psychiatry, 40,* 435–442.

Brodmann, K. (1902). Experimenteller und Klinischer Beitrag zur Psychopathologie der polyneuritischen Psychose. I. *Journal der Psychologie und Neurologie, 1,* 225–247.

Brodmann, K. (1904). Experimenteller und klinischer Beitrag zur Psychopathologie der polyneuritischen Psychose. II. *Journal der Psychologie und Neurologie, 3,* 1–48.

Brooks, N. & Baddeley, A. D. (1976). What can amnesic patients learn? *Neuropsychologia, 14,* 111–122.

Brown, G. D. A. (1987). Resolving inconsistency: A computational model of word naming. *Journal of Memory and Language, 26,* 1–23.

Brown, J. W. (1981). Case reports of semantic jargon. In J. W. Brown (Ed.), *Jargonaphasia.* New York: Academic Press.

Brown, R. & McNeill, D. (1966). The "tip of the tongue" phenomenon. *Journal of Verbal Learning and Verbal Behavior, 5,* 325–337.

Brownell, H. H., Michel, D., Powerson, J., & Gardner, H. (1983). Surprise but not coherence: Sensitivity to verbal humor in right-hemisphere patients. *Brain and Language, 18,* 20–27.

Bruce, V. (1988). *Recognising faces.* London: Lawrence Erlbaum Associates Ltd.

Bruce, V. & Young, A. W. (1986). Understanding face recognition. *British Journal of Psychology, 77,* 305–327.

Bruner, J. S. (1969). Modalities of memory. In G. A. Talland & N. C. Waugh (Eds), *The pathology of memory.* New York: Academic Press.

Bruyer, R., Laterre, C., Seron, X., Feyereisen, P., Strypstein, E., Pierrard, E., & Rectem, D. (1983). A case of prosopagnosia with some preserved covert remembrance of familiar faces. *Brain and Cognition, 2,* 257–284.

Bryden, M. P. (1982). *Laterality: Functional asymmetry in the intact brain.* New York: Academic Press.

Bub, D. & Kertesz, A. (1982a). Evidence for lexicographic processing in a patient with preserved written over oral single word naming. *Brain, 105,* 697–717.

Bub, D. & Kertesz, A. (1982b). Deep agraphia. *Brain and Language, 17,* 146–165.

Bub, D., Cancelliere, A., & Kertesz, A. (1985). Whole-word and analytic translation of spelling to sound in a non-semantic reader. In K. E. Patterson, J. C. Marshall, & M. Coltheart (Eds), *Surface dyslexia: Neuropsychological and cognitive studies of phonological reading.* London: Lawrence Erlbaum Associates Ltd.

Bub, D., Black, S., Howell, J., & Kertesz, A. (1987). Speech output processes and reading. In M. Coltheart, G. Sartori, & R. Job (Eds), *The cognitive neuropsychology of language.* London: Lawrence Erlbaum Associates Ltd.

Buckingham, H. W. (1977). The conductive theory and neologistic jargon. *Language and Speech, 20,* 174–184.

Buckingham, H. W. (1980). On correlating aphasic errors with slips of the tongue. *Applied Psycholinguistics, 1,* 199–220.

Buckingham, H. W. & Kertesz, A. (1976). *Neologistic jargonaphasia*. Amsterdam: Swets and Zeitlinger B. V.

Buckingham, H. W., Whitaker, H., & Whitaker, H. A. (1978). Alliteration and assonance in neologistic jargonaphasia. *Cortex, 14,* 365–380.

Buerger-Prinz, H. & Kaila, M. (1930). Über die Struktur des amnestischen Symptomenkomplexes. *Zeitschrift für Neurologie und Psychiatrie, 124,* 553–595. (Translated in D. Rapaport (Ed.), *Organization and pathology of thought.* New York: Columbia University Press, 1951.)

Burnham, W. H. (1904). Retroactive amnesia: illustrative cases and a tentative explanation. *American Journal of Psychology, 14,* 118–132.

Burr, C. (1905). Loss of the sign language in a deaf mute from cerebral tumor and softening. *New York Medical Journal, 81,* 1106–1108.

Butters, N. (1984). Alcoholic Korsakoff's syndrome: an update. *Seminars in Neurology, 4,* 226–244.

Butters, N. & Albert, M. L. (1982). Processes underlying failures to recall remote events. In L. S. Cermak (Ed.), *Human memory and amnesia.* Hillsdale, N. J.: Lawrence Erlbaum Associates Inc.

Butters, N. & Cermak, L. S. (1980). *Alcoholic Korsakoff's syndrome: An information-processing approach.* New York: Academic Press.

Butters, N. & Cermak, L. S. (1986). A case study of the forgetting of autobiographical knowledge: implications for the study of retrograde amnesia. In D. C. Rubin (Ed.), *Autobiographical memory.* Cambridge: Cambridge University Press.

Butterworth, B. (1979). Hesitation and the production of verbal paraphasias and neologisms in jargon aphasia. *Brain and Language, 8,* 133–161.

Butterworth, B. (1980). Constraints on models of language production. In B. Butterworth (Ed.), *Language production,* Vol. 1. London: Academic Press.

Butterworth, B. (1985). Jargon aphasia: processes and strategies. In S. Newman and R. Epstein (Eds), *Current perspectives in dysphasia.* Edinburgh: Churchill Livingstone.

Butterworth, B. & Howard, D. (1987). Paragrammatisms. *Cognition, 26,* 1–37.

Butterworth, B., Swallow, J., & Grimston, M. (1981). Gestures and lexical processes in jargonaphasia. In J. W. Brown (Ed.), *Jargonaphasia.* New York: Academic Press.

Butterworth, B., Howard, D., & McLoughlin, P. (1984). The semantic deficit in aphasia: The relationship between semantic errors in auditory comprehension and picture naming. *Neuropsychologia, 22,* 409–426.

Campbell, R. (1987a). Cognitive neuropsychology. In G. Claxton (Ed.), *New directions in cognition.* London: Routledge and Kegan Paul.

Campbell, R. (1987b). One or two lexicons for reading and writing words; can misspellings shed any light. *Cognitive Neuropsychology, 4.* 487–499

Campbell, R., Landis, T., & Regard, M. (1986). Face recognition and lipreading: A neurological dissociation. *Brain, 109,* 509–521.

Campion, J. (1987). Apperceptive agnosia: The specification and description of constructs. In G. W. Humphreys & M. J. Riddoch (Eds), *Visual object processing.* London: Lawrence Erlbaum Associates Ltd.

Campion, J. & Latto, R. (1985). Apperceptive agnosia due to carbon poisoning. An interpretation based on critical band masking from disseminated lesions. *Behavioural Brain Research, 15,* 227–240.

Campion, J., Latto, R., & Smith, Y. M. (1983). Is blindsight an effect of scattered light, spared cortex, and near-threshold vision? *Behavioral and Brain Sciences, 6,* 423–486.

Capgras, J. & Reboul-Lachaux, J. (1923). L'illusion des "soisies" dans un délire systématisé chronique. *Bulletin de la Société Clinique de Médecine Mentale, 1,* 6–16.

Caplan, B. (1985). Stimulus effects in unilateral neglect. *Cortex, 21,* 69–80.

Caplan, D. (1981). On the cerebral localization of linguistic functions: Logical and empirical issues surrounding deficit analysis and function localization. *Brain and Language, 14,* 120–137.

Caplan, D., Kellar, L., & Locke, S. (1972). Inflection of neologisms in aphasia. *Brain, 95,* 169–172.

Caramazza, A. (1984). The logic of neuropsychological research and the problem of patient classification in aphasia. *Brain and Language, 21,* 9–20.

Caramazza, A. (1986). On drawing inferences about the structure of normal cognitive systems from the analysis of patterns of impaired performance: The case for single-patient studies. *Brain and Cognition, 5,* 41–66.

Caramazza, A. & Berndt, R. S. (1978). Semantic and syntactic processes in aphasia: A review of the literature. *Psychological Bulletin, 85,* 898–918.

Caramazza, A. & Berndt, R. S. (1985). A multi-component deficit view of agrammatic Broca's aphasia. In M. L. Kean (Ed.), *Agrammatism.* Orlando: Academic Press.

Caramazza, A. & Zurif, E. B. (1976). Dissociation of algorithmic and heuristic processes in language comprehension: Evidence from aphasia. *Brain and Language, 3,* 572–582.

Caramazza, A., Gordon, J., Zurif, E. B., & DeLuca, D. (1976). Right-hemispheric damage and verbal problem solving behavior. *Brain and Language, 3,* 41–46.

Caramazza, A., Basili, A. G., Koller, J. J., & Berndt, R. S. (1981). An investigation of repetition and language processing in a case of conduction aphasia. *Brain and Language, 14,* 235–275.

Caramazza, A., Berndt, R. S., & Basili, A. G. (1983). The selective impairment of phonological processing: A case study. *Brain and Language, 18,* 128–174.

Caramazza, A., Miceli, G., Silveri, M. C., & Laudanna, A. (1985). Reading mechanisms and the organisation of the lexicon: Evidence from acquired dyslexia. *Cognitive Neuropsychology, 2,* 81–114.

Casey, T. & Ettlinger, G. (1960). The occasional 'Independence' of dyslexia and dysgraphia from dysphasia. *Journal of Neurology, Neurosurgery and psychiatry, 23,* 228–236.

Cermak, L. S. (1976). The encoding capacity of a patient with amnesia due to encephalitis. *Neuropsychologia, 14,* 311–326.

Cermak, L. (1982). *Human memory and amnesia.* Hillsdale, N. J.: Lawrence Erlbaum Associates Inc.

Cermak, L. & Butters, N. (1973). Information processing deficits of alcoholic Korsakoff patients. *Quarterly Journal of Studies of Alcohol, 34,* 1110–1132.

Cermak, L. S. & O'Connor, M. (1983). The anterograde and retrograde retrieval ability of a patient with amnesia due to encephalitis. *Neuropsychologia, 21,* 213–234.

Cermak, L. S. & Reale, L. (1978). Depth of processing and retention of words by alcoholic Korsakoff patients. *Journal of Experimental Psychology: Human Learning and Memory, 4,* 165–174.

Cermak, L. S., Lewis, R., Butters, N., & Goodglass, H. (1973). Role of verbal mediation in performance of motor tasks by Korsakoff patients. *Perceptual and Motor Skills, 37,* 259–262.

Cermak, L. S., Talbot, N., Chandler, K., & Wolbarst, L. R. (1985). The perceptual priming phenomenon in amnesia. *Neuropsychologia, 23,* 615–622.

Charcot, J. M. (1883). Un cas de suppression brusque et isolée de la vision mentale des signes et des objetse (forms et couleurs). *Le Progres Medicale, 88,* 568–571.

Chedru, F. (1976). Space representation in unilateral spatial neglect. *Journal of Neurology, Neurosurgery and Psychiatry, 39,* 1057–1061.

Chiarello, C., Knight, R., & Mandel, M. (1982). Aphasia in a prelingually deaf woman. *Brain, 105,* 29–52.

Cicone, M., Wapner, E., Foldi, N., Zurif, E. B., & Gardner, H. (1979). The relation between gesture and language in aphasic communication. *Brain and Language, 8,* 324–349.

Code, C. (1987). *Language, aphasia and the right hemisphere.* Chichester: John Wiley.

Cohen, A. (1966). Errors of speech and their implications for understanding the strategy of language users. *Zeitschrift für Phonetik, 21,* 177–181. (Reprinted in V. A. Fromkin (Ed.) (1973). *Speech errors as linguistic evidence.* The Hague: Mouton.)

Cohen, G. & Faulkner, D. (1986). Memory for proper names: Age differences in retrieval. *British Journal of Developmental Psychology, 4,* 187–197.

Cohen, N. J. (1984). Preserved learning capacity in amnesia: Evidence for multiple memory systems. In L. R. Squire & N. Butters (Eds), *Neuropsychology of memory.* New York: Guilford Press.

Cohen, N. J. & Squire, L. R. (1980). Preserved learning and retention of pattern-analyzing skill in amnesia: Dissociation of knowing how and knowing that. *Science, 210,* 207–210.

Cohen, N. J. & Squire, L. R. (1981). Retrograde amnesia and remote memory impairment. *Neuropsychologia, 19,* 337–356.

Cole, M., Schutta, H. S., & Warrington, E. K. (1962). Visual disorientation in homonymous half-fields. *Neurology, 12,* 257–263.

Colella, R. (1894). La psicosi polyneuritica. *Annales de Neurologie, 12,* 1–66, 151–225, 449–521.

Coltheart, M. (1980a). Deep dyslexia: A review of the syndrome. In M. Coltheart, K. E. Patterson, & J. C. Marshall (Eds), *Deep dyslexia.* London: Routledge and Kegan Paul.

Coltheart, M. (1980b). Deep dyslexia: A right hemisphere hypothesis. In M. Coltheart, K. E. Patterson, & J. C. Marshall (Eds), *Deep dyslexia.* London: Routledge and Kegan Paul.

Coltheart, M. (1980c). Reading, phonological recoding, and deep dyslexia. In M. Coltheart, K. E. Patterson, & J. C. Marshall (Eds), *Deep dyslexia.* London: Routledge and Kegan Paul.

Coltheart, M. (1981). Disorders of reading and their implications for models of normal reading. *Visible Language, 15,* 245–286.

Coltheart, M. (1983). The right hemisphere and disorders of reading. In A. W. Young (Ed.), *Functions of the right cerebral hemisphere.* London: Academic Press.

Coltheart, M. (1986). Cognitive neuropsychology. In M. Posner & O. S. M. Marin (Eds), *Attention and Performance, XI.* Hillsdale, N. J.: Lawrence Erlbaum Associates Inc.

Coltheart, M. & Funnell, E. (1987). Reading and writing: One lexicon or two? In D. A. Allport, D. G. MacKay, W. Prinz, & E. Scheerer (Eds), *Language perception and production: Shared mechanisms in listening, reading and writing.* London: Academic Press.

Coltheart, M., Patterson, K. E., & Marshall, J. C. (Eds) (1980). *Deep dyslexia.* London: Routledge and Kegan Paul.

Coltheart, M., Sartori, G., & Job, R. (1987). *The cognitive neuropsychology of language.* London: Lawrence Erlbaum Associates Ltd.

Coriat, I. H. (1906). The experimental synthesis of the dissociated memories in alcoholic amnesia. *Journal of Abnormal Psychology, 1,* 109–122.

Coriat, I. H. (1907). The Lowell case of amnesia. *Journal of Abnormal Psychology, 2,* 93–111.

Corkin, S. (1965). Tactually-guided maze learning in man: Effects of unilateral cortical excisions and bilateral hippocampal lesions. *Neuropsychologia, 3,* 339–351.

Corkin, S. (1968). Acquisition of motor skill after bilateral medial temporal-lobe excision. *Neuropsychologia, 6,* 255–265.

Corkin, S. (1979). Hidden-figures test performance: Lasting effects of unilateral penetrating head injury and transient effects of bilateral cingulotomy. *Neuropsychologia, 17,* 585–605.

Corkin, S. (1984). Lasting consequences of bilateral medial temporal lobectomy: Clinical course and experimental findings in H. M. *Seminars in Neurology, 4,* 249–259.

Costello, A. de L. & Warrington, E. K. (1987). The dissociation of visuospatial neglect and neglect dyslexia. *Journal of Neurology, Neurosurgery and Psychiatry, 50,* 1110–1116.

Cotton, J. (1935). Normal "visual hearing". *Science, 82,* 592–593.

Coughlan, A. D. & Warrington, E. K. (1978). Word comprehension and word retrieval in patients with localised cerebral lesions. *Brain, 101,* 163–185.

Coughlan, A. D. & Warrington, E. K. (1981). The impairment of verbal semantic memory: A single case study. *Journal of Neurology, Neurosurgery and Psychiatry, 44,* 1079–1083.

Cowey, A. (1982). Sensory and non-sensory visual disorders in man and monkey. *Philosophical Transactions of the Royal Society* (London), *B298,* 3–13.

Cowey, A. (1985). Aspects of cortical organization related to selective attention and selective impairments of visual perception: A tutorial review. In M. I. Posner & O. S. M. Marin (Eds), *Attention and performance, XI.* New Jersey: Lawrence Erlbaum Associates Inc.

Cowie, R. (1985). Reading errors as clues to the nature of reading. In A. W. Ellis (Ed.), *Progress in the psychology of language,* Vol. 1. London: Lawrence Erlbaum Associates Ltd.

Craik, F. I. M. & Lockhart, R. S. (1972). Levels of processing: A framework for memory research. *Journal of Verbal Learning and Verbal Behavior, 11,* 671–684.

Craik, K. (1943). *The nature of explanation.* Cambridge: Cambridge University Press.

Critchley, M. (1942). Aphasic disorders of signalling (constitutional and acquired) occurring in naval signalmen. *Journal of the Mount Sinai Hospital* (New York), *9,* 363–375.

Critchley, M. (1962). Speech and speech-loss in relation to the duality of the brain. In V. Mountcastle (Ed.), *Interhemispheric relations and cerebral dominance.* Baltimore: Johns Hopkins University Press.

Cutler, A. (Ed.) (1982). *Slips of the tongue.* The Hague: Mouton.

Damasio, A. R. (1985). Disorders of complex visual processing: Agnosias, achromatopsia, Balint's syndrome, and related difficulties of orientation and construction. In M. M. Mesulam (Ed.), *Principles of behavioral neurology.* Philadelphia: F. A. Davis.

Damasio, A. R. & Benton, A. L. (1979). Impairment of hand movements under visual guidance. *Neurology, 29,* 170–178.

Damasio, A. R., Damasio, H., & Van Hoesen, G. W. (1982). Prosopagnosia: Anatomic basis and behavioral mechanisms. *Neurology, 32,* 331–341.

Damasio, A. R., Eslinger, P. J., Damasio, H., Van Hoesen, G. W., & Cornell, S. (1985). Multimodal amnesic syndrome following bilateral temporal and basal forebrain damage. *Archives of Neurology, 42,* 252–259.

Damasio, A., Bellugi, U., Damasio, H., Poizner, H., & Van Gilder, J. (1986). Sign language aphasia during left hemisphere amytal injection. *Nature, 332,* 363–365.

Dana, C. L. (1894). The study of a case of amnesia or "double consciousness". *Psychological Review, 1,* 570–580.

Darwin, C. J. (1971). Ear differences in the recall of fricatives and vowels. *Quarterly Journal of Experimental Psychology, 23,* 46–62.

Davidoff, J. B. & Ostergaard, A. L. (1984). Colour anomia resulting from weakened short-term colour memory. *Brain, 107,* 415–431.

Davies, L. (1984). *Word-finding difficulties: An information processing approach.* Unpublished undergraduate dissertation, Department of Psychology, University of Lancaster.

Day, J. (1977). Right-hemisphere language processing in normal right-handers. *Journal of Experimental Psychology: Human Perception and Performance, 3,* 518–528.

De Haan, E. H. F., Young, A., & Newcombe, F. (1987a). Face recognition without awareness. *Cognitive Neuropsychology, 4,* 385–415.

De Haan, E. H. F., Young, A., & Newcombe, F. (1987b). Faces interfere with name classification in a prosopagnosic patient. *Cortex*, *23*, 309–316.

Déjerine, J. (1892). Contribution à l'étude anatomo-pathologique et clinique des differentes variétés de cécité verbale. *Compte Rendu Hebdomadaire des Séances et Memoires de la Société de Biologie*, *4*, 61–90.

Déjerine, J. (1914). *Sémiologie des affections du systeme nerveux*. Paris: Masson.

Dell, G. S. (1986). A spreading-activation theory of retrieval in sentence production. *Psychological Review*, *93*, 283–321.

Denes, G. & Semenza, C. (1975). Auditory modality-specific anomia: Evidence from a case study of pure word deafness. *Cortex*, *11*, 401–411.

De Renzi, E. (1982a). *Disorders of space exploration and cognition*. Chichester: Wiley.

De Renzi, E. (1982b). Memory disorders following focal neocortical damage. *Philosophical Transactions of the Royal Society* (London), *B298*, 73–83.

De Renzi, E. (1986). Current issues in prosopagnosia. In H. D. Ellis, M. A. Jeeves, F. Newcombe, & A. Young (Eds), *Aspects of face processing*. Dordrecht: Martinus Nijhoff.

De Renzi, E., & Nichelli, P. (1975). Verbal and non-verbal short-term memory impairments following hemispheric damage. *Cortex*, *11*, 341–354.

De Renzi, E. & Spinnler, H. (1966). Visual recognition in patients with unilateral cerebral disease. *Journal of Nervous and Mental Disease*, *142*, 515–525.

De Renzi, E., Scotti, G., & Spinnler, H. (1969). Perceptual and associative disorders of visual recognition. *Neurology*, *19*, 634–642.

De Renzi, E., Faglioni, P., Scotti, G., & Spinnler, H. (1972). Impairment in associating colour to form, concomitant with aphasia. *Brain*, *95*, 293–304.

De Renzi, E., Faglioni, P., & Previdi, P. (1977a). Spatial memory and hemispheric locus of lesion. *Cortex*, *13*, 424–433.

De Renzi, E., Faglioni, P., & Villa, P. (1977b). Topographical amnesia. *Journal of Neurology, Neurosurgery, and Psychiatry*, *49*, 498–505.

De Renzi, E., Motti, F., & Nichelli, P. (1980). Imitating gestures: A quantitative approach to ideomotor apraxia. *Archives of Neurology*, *37*, 6–10.

De Villiers, J. (1974). Quantitative aspects of agrammatism in aphasia. *Cortex*, *10*, 36–54.

Drachman, D. A. & Arbit, J. (1966). Memory and the hippocampal complex. *Archives of Neurology*, *15*, 52–61.

Duncan, J. (1986). Disorganisation of behaviour after frontal lobe damage. *Cognitive Neuropsychology*, *3*, 271–290.

Dunn, R. (1845). Case of suspension of the mental faculties of the powers of speech and special senses. *Lancet*, *ii*, 536–538 and 588–590.

Efron, R. (1968). What is perception? In R. S. Cohen & M. W. Wartofsky (Eds), *Boston studies in the philosophy of science*, *4*. Dordrecht: Reidel.

Eisenson, J. (1962). Language and intellectual modifications associated with right cerebral damage. *Language and Speech*, *5*, 49–53.

Ellis, A. W. (1979a). Speech production and short-term memory. In J. Morton & J. C. Marshall (Eds), *Psycholinguistics series*, Vol. 2. London: Elek; and Cambridge, Mass.: MIT Press.

Ellis, A. W. (1979b). Slips of the pen. *Visible Language*, *13*, 265–282.

Ellis, A. W. (1980). Errors in speech and short-term memory: The effects of phonemic similarity and syllable position. *Journal of Verbal Learning and Verbal Behavior*, *19*, 624–634.

Ellis, A. W. (1982). Spelling and writing (and reading and speaking). In A. W. Ellis (Ed.), *Normality and pathology in cognitive functions*. London: Academic Press.

Ellis, A. W. (1983). Syndromes, slips and structures. *Bulletin of the British Psychological Society*, *36*, 372–374.

Ellis, A. W. (1984a). Introduction to Bramwell's (1897) case of word meaning deafness. *Cognitive Neuropsychology, 1,* 245–258.

Ellis, A. W. (1984b). *Reading, writing and dyslexia: A cognitive analysis.* London: Lawrence Erlbaum Associates Ltd.

Ellis, A. W. (1985a). The production of spoken words: A cognitive neuropsychological perspective. In A. W. Ellis (Ed.), *Progress in the psychology of language,* Vol. 2. London: Lawrence Erlbaum Associates Ltd.

Ellis, A. W. (1985b). The cognitive neuropsychology of developmental (and acquired) dyslexia: A critical survey. *Cognitive Neuropsychology, 2,* 169–205.

Ellis, A. W. (1987). Intimations of modularity, or, The modularity of mind. In M. Coltheart, G, Sartori, & R. Job (Eds), *The cognitive neuropsychology of language.* London: Lawrence Erlbaum Associates Ltd.

Ellis, A. W. (1988). Neurocognitive processing of faces and voices. In A. W. Young & H. D. Ellis (Eds), *Handbook of research on face processing.* Amsterdam: North-Holland.

Ellis, A. W. & Beattie, G. (1986). *The psychology of language and communication.* London: Lawrence Erlbaum Associates Ltd., and New York: The Guilford Press.

Ellis, A. W., Miller, D., & Sin, G. (1983). Wernicke's aphasia and normal language processing: A case study in cognitive neuropsychology. *Cognition, 15,* 111–144.

Ellis, A. W., Flude, B. M., & Young, A. W. (1987a). "Neglect dyslexia" and the early visual processing of letters in words. *Cognitive Neuropsychology, 4,* 439–464.

Ellis, A. W., Young, A. W., & Flude, B. M. (1987b). "Afferent dysgraphia" and the role of feedback in the motor control of handwriting. *Cognitive Neuropsychology, 4,* 465–486.

Ellis, A. W., Young, A. W., Flude, B. M., & Hay, D.C. (1987c). Repetition priming of face recognition. *Quarterly Journal of Experimental Psychology, 39A,* 193–210.

Ellis, H. D. (1986a). Processes underlying face recognition. In R. Bruyer (Ed.), *The neuropsychology of face perception and facial expression.* Hillsdale, N. J.: Lawrence Erlbaum Associates Inc.

Ellis, H. D. (1986b). Disorders of face recognition. In K. Poeck, H. J. Freund, & H. Gänshirt (Eds), *Neurology: Proceedings of the 13th World Congress of Neurology.* Berlin: Springer-Verlag.

Ellis, H. D. & Shepherd, J. W. (1974). Recognition of abstract and concrete words presented in left and right visual fields. *Journal of Experimental Psychology, 103,* 1035–1036.

Emmorey, K. D. (1987). The neurological substrates for prosodic aspects of speech. *Brain and Language, 30,* 305–320.

Etcoff, N. L. (1985). The neuropsychology of emotional expression. In G. Goldstein & R. E. Tarter (Eds), *Advances in clinical neuropsychology,* Vol. 3. New York: Plenum.

Ettlinger, G. (1956). Sensory deficits in visual agnosia. *Journal of Neurology, Neurosurgery and Psychiatry, 19,* 297–307.

Evans, J. J. (1966). Transient loss of memory: An organic mental syndrome. *Brain, 89,* 539–548.

Eysenck, M. (1984). *Handbook of cognitive psychology.* London: Lawrence Erlbaum Associates Ltd.

Fay, D. & Cutler, A. (1977). Malaproprisms and the structure of the mental lexicon. *Linguistic Inquiry, 8,* 505–520.

Ferro, J. M. & Santos, M. E. (1984). Associative visual agnosia: A case study. *Cortex, 20,* 121–134.

Feyereisen, P. & Seron, X. (1982a). Nonverbal communication and aphasia: A review. I. Comprehension. *Brain and Language, 16,* 191–212.

Feyereisen, P. & Seron, X. (1982b).   Nonverbal communication and aphasia: A review. II. Expression. *Brain and Language, 16,* 213–236.

Fisher, C. M. (1966).   Concussion amnesia. *Neurology, 16,* 826–830.

Fodor, J. (1983).   *The modularity of mind.* Cambridge, Mass.: MIT Press.

Fodor, J. A. (1985).   Précis of "the modularity of mind" (with commentaries). *The Behavioral and Brain Sciences, 8,* 1–42.

Francis, W. N. & Kucera, H. (1982).   *Frequency analysis of English usage: Lexicon and grammar.* Boston: Houghton Mifflin.

Franz, S. I. (1930).   The relations of aphasia. *Journal of Genetic Psychology, 3,* 401–411.

Freed, D. M., Corkin, S., & Cohen, N. J. (1984).   Rate of forgetting in H. M.: A reanalysis. *Society for Neuroscience Abstracts, 10,* 383.

Freud, A. (1891).   *On aphasia.* (Translated by E. Stengel. London: Imago, 1935.)

Freud, S. (1901).   *The psychopathology of everyday life.* Harmondsworth: Penguin, 1975.

Freund, C. S. (1889).   Ueber optische Aphasie und Seelenblindheit. *Archiv für Psychiatrie und Nervenkrankheiten, 20,* 276–297, 371–416.

Friederici, A. D. (1982).   Syntactic and semantic processes in aphasic deficits: The availability of prepositions. *Brain and Language, 15,* 249–258.

Friedrich, F. J., Walker, J. A., & Posner, M. I. (1985).   Effects of parietal lesions on visual matching: Implications for reading errors. *Cognitive Neuropsychology, 2,* 253–264.

Frith, U. (Ed.) (1980).   *Cognitive processes in spelling.* London: Academic Press.

Fromkin, V. A. (1971).   The non-anomalous nature of anomalous utterances. *Language, 47,* 27–52.

Fromkin, V. A. (Ed.) (1973).   *Speech errors as linguistic evidence.* The Hague: Mouton.

Fromkin, V. A. (Ed.) (1980).   *Errors in linguistic performance: Slips of the tongue, ear, pen and hand.* New York: Academic Press.

Fry, D. B. (1959).   Phonemic substitutions in an aphasic patient. *Language and Speech, 2,* 52–61.

Funnell, E. (1983).   Phonological processes in reading: New evidence from acquired dysgraphia. *British Journal of Psychology, 74,* 159–180.

Funnell, E. (1987).   Morphological errors in acquired dyslexia: A case of mistaken identity. *Quarterly Journal of Experimental Psychology, 39A,* 497–538.

Gabrieli, J. D. E., Cohen, N. J., & Corkin, S. (1983).   The acquisition of lexical and semantic knowledge in amnesia. *Society for Neuroscience Abstracts, 9,* 238.

Gainotti, G. (1976).   The relationship between semantic impairment in comprehension and naming in aphasic patients. *British Journal of Disorders of Communication, 11,* 57–61.

Gainotti, G., Miceli, G., Caltagirone, C., Silveri, M. C., & Masullo, C. (1981).   Selective semantic-lexical impairment of language comprehension in right-brain-damaged patients. *Brain and Language, 13,* 201–211.

Gardner, H., Ling, P. K., Flamm, L., & Silverman, J. (1975).   Comprehension and appreciation of humorous material following brain damage. *Brain, 98,* 399–412.

Gardner, H., Brownell, H. H., Wapner, W., & Michelow, D. (1983).   Missing the point: The role of the right hemisphere in the processing of complex linguistic materials. In E. Perecman (Ed.), *Cognitive processes in the right hemisphere.* New York: Academic Press.

Garner, W. R., Hake, H. W., & Eriksen, C. W. (1956).   Operationalism and the concept of perception. *Psychological Review, 63,* 149–159.

Garrett, M. F. (1975).   The analysis of sentence production. In G. H. Bower (Ed.), *The psychology of learning and motivation,* Vol. 9. New York: Academic Press.

Garrett, M. F. (1980).   Levels of processing in sentence production. In B. Butterworth (Ed.), *Language production, Vol. 1: Speech and talk.* London: Academic Press.

Garrett, M. F. (1982).   Production of speech: Observations from normal and pathological language use. In A. W. Ellis (Ed.), *Normality and pathology in cognitive functions.* London: Academic Press.

Garrett, M. F. (1984). The organization of processing structure for language production: Applications to aphasic speech. In D. Caplan, A. R. Lecours, & A. Smith (Eds), *Biological perspectives on language.* Cambridge, Mass.: MIT Press.

Gaur, A. (1984). *A history of writing.* London: The British Library.

Gazzaniga, M. S. (1983). Right hemisphere language following brain bisection; a 20 year perspective. *American Psychologist, 38,* 525–537.

Gelb, I. J. (1963). *A study of writing.* Chicago: Chicago University Press.

Geschwind, N. (1965a). Disconnexion syndromes in animals and man: I. *Brain, 88,* 237–294.

Geschwind, N. (1965b). Disconnexion syndromes in animals and man: II. *Brain, 88,* 585–644.

Geschwind, N. (1982). Disorders of attention: A frontier in neuropsychology. *Philosophical Transactions of the Royal Society* (London), *B298,* 173–185.

Geschwind, N. & Fusillo, M. (1966). Color-naming defects in association with alexia. *Archives of Neurology, 15,* 137–146.

Gillespie, R. D. (1937). Amnesia. *Archives of Neurology and Psychiatry, 37,* 748–764.

Glass, A. L. (1983). The comprehension of idioms. *Journal of Psycholinguistic Research, 12,* 429–442.

Glass, A., Gazzaniga, M., & Premack, D. (1973). Artificial language training in global aphasics. *Neuropsychologia, 11,* 95–103.

Gleason, J. B., Goodglass, H., Green, E., Ackerman, N., & Hyde, M. (1975). The retrieval of syntax in Broca's aphasia. *Brain and Language, 2,* 451–471.

Glisky, E. L., Schacter, D. L., & Tulving, E. (1986). Computer learning by memory-impaired patients: Acquisition and retention of complex knowledge. *Neuropsychologia, 24,* 313–328.

Glushko, R. J. (1979). The organization and activation of orthographic knowledge in reading aloud. *Journal of Experimental Psychology: Human Perception and Performance, 5,* 674–691.

Godfrey, J. J. (1974). Perceptual difficulty and the right ear advantage for vowels. *Brain and Language, 1,* 323–335.

Goldberg, E. & Bilder, R. M. (1985). Neuropsychological perspectives: Retrograde amnesia and executive deficits. In L. Poon (Ed.), *Handbook of clinical memory assessment in older adults.* Washington, D. C.: American Psychiatric Association.

Goldberg, E., Antin, S. P., Bilder, R. M., Gerstman, L. J., Hughes, J. E. O., & Mattis, S. (1981). Retrograde amnesia: Possible role of mesencephalic reticular activation in long-term memory. *Science, 213,* 1392–1394.

Goldberg, E., Hughes, J. E. O., Mattis, S., & Antin, S. P. (1982). Isolated retrograde amnesia: Different etiologies, same mechanisms? *Cortex, 18,* 459–462.

Goldblum, M. C. (1979). Auditory analogue of deep dyslexia. In O. Creutzfeldt, H. Scheich, & C. Schreiner (Eds), *Hearing mechanisms and speech.* (Experimental brain research, Supplementum 2.) Berlin: Springer-Verlag.

Goldblum, M. C. (1981). Un équivalent de la dyslexie profonde dans la modalité auditive. In *Études Neurolinguistiques* (Numéro special de la Revue Grammatica) 7 (1), 157–77. (Services des Publications de l'Université de Toulouse—Le Mirail.)

Goldblum, M. C. (1985). Word comprehension in surface dyslexia. In K. E. Patterson, J. C. Marshall, & M.Coltheart (Eds), *Surface dyslexia: Neuropsychological and cognitive studies of phonological reading.* London: Lawrence Erlbaum Associates Ltd.

Goldstein, K. (1915). *Die Transkortikale Aphasien.* Jena: Gustav Fischer.

Goldstein, M. N. (1974). Auditory agnosia for speech ("pure word deafness"): A historical review with current implications. *Brain and Language, 1,* 195–204.

Goodglass, H. (1976). Agrammatism. In H. Whitaker & H. A. Whitaker (Eds), *Studies in neurolinguistics,* Vol. 1. New York: Academic Press.

Goodglass, H. & Berko, J. (1960). Aphasia and inflectional morphology in English. *Journal of Speech and Hearing Research, 3,* 257–267.

Goodglass, H. & Geschwind, N. (1976). Language disorders (aphasia). In E. C. Carterette & M. Friedman (Eds), *Handbook of perception,* Vol. 7. New York: Academic Press.

Goodglass, H. & Hunt, J. (1958). Grammatical complexity and aphasic speech. *Word, 14,* 197–207.

Goodglass, H. & Kaplan, E. (1963). Disturbance of gesture and pantomime in aphasia. *Brain, 86,* 703–720.

Goodglass, H. & Kaplan, E. (1972). *Assessment of aphasia and related disorders.* Philadelphia: Lea and Febinger.

Goodglass, H. & Menn, L. (1985). Is agrammatism a unitary phenomenon? In M.-L. Kean (Ed.), *Agrammatism.* Orlando: Academic Press.

Goodglass, H., Klein, B., Carey, P., & James, K. J. (1966). Specific semantic word categories in aphasia. *Cortex, 2,* 74–89.

Goodglass, H., Fodor, I. G., & Schulhoff, C. (1967). Prosodic factors in grammar: Evidence from aphasia. *Journal of Speech and Hearing Research, 10,* 5–20.

Goodman, R. A. & Caramazza, A. (1986a). Dissociation of spelling errors in written and oral spelling: The role of allographic conversion in writing. *Cognitive Neuropsychology, 3,* 179–206.

Goodman, R. A. & Caramazza, A. (1986b). Phonologically plausible errors: Implications for a model of the phoneme–grapheme conversion mechanism in the spelling process. In G. Augst (Ed.), *New trends in graphemics and orthography.* Berlin: Walter de Gruyter.

Goodman, R. A. & Caramazza, A. (1986c). Aspects of the spelling process: Evidence from a case of acquired dysgraphia. *Language and Cognitive Processes, 1,* 1–34.

Goodman-Schulman, R. A. & Caramazza, A. (1987). Patterns of dysgraphia and the nonlexical spelling process. *Cortex, 23,* 143–148.

Goodwin, D. W., Crane, J. B., & Guze, S. B. (1969). Phenomenological aspects of the alcoholic "blackout". *British Journal of Psychiatry, 115,* 1033–1038.

Gordon, B. & Marin, O. S. M. (1979). Transient global amnesia: An extensive case report. *Journal of Neurology, Neurosurgery and Psychiatry, 42,* 572–575.

Gott, P. S. (1973). Language after dominant hemispherectomy. *Journal of Neurology, Neurosurgery and Psychiatry, 36,* 1082–1088.

Gough P. B. (1972). One second of reading. In J. F. Kavanagh & I. G. Mattingly (Eds), *Language by ear and by eye.* Cambridge, Mass.: MIT Press.

Gould, S. J. (1980). *The panda's thumb.* New York: W. W. Norton; and Harmondsworth: Pelican.

Gould, S. J. (1983). *Hen's teeth and horse's toes.* New York: W. W. Norton; and Harmondsworth: Pelican.

Graf, P., Squire, L. R., & Mandler, G. (1984). The information that amnesic patients do not forget. *Journal of Experimental Psychology: Learning, Memory and Cognition, 10,* 164–178.

Graf, P., Shimamura, A. P., & Squire, L. R. (1985). Priming across modalities and priming across category labels: Extending the domain of preserved function in amnesia. *Journal of Experimental Psychology: Learning, Memory and Cognition, 11,* 386–396.

Green, E. (1969). Phonological and grammatical aspects of jargon in an aphasic patient: A case study. *Language and Speech, 12,* 103–118.

Greenblatt, S. H. (1973). Alexia without agraphia or hemianopsia: Anatomical analysis of an autopsied case. *Brain, 96,* 307–316.

Gregor, A. (1909). Beiträge zur Psychopathologie des Gedächtnisses. *Monatschrift für Psychiatrie und Neurologie, 25*, 218–255, 330–386.

Grodzinsky, Y. (1984). The syntactic characterisation of agrammatism. *Cognition, 16*, 99–120.

Grünthal, E. (1923). Zur Kenntnis de Psychopathologie des Korsakowschen Symptomenkomplexes. *Monatschrift für Psychiatrie und Neurologie, 53*, 85–132.

Grünthal, E. (1924). Uber das Symptom der Einstellungstorung bei exogenen Psychosen. *Zeitschrift für Neurologie und Psychiatrie, 92*, 255–266.

Haggard, M. P. (1971). Encoding and the REA for speech signals. *Quarterly Journal of Experimental Psychology, 23*, 34–45.

Hamanaka, T. & Ohashi, H. (1974). "Aphasia" in pantomimic sign language. *Studia Phonologica, 8*, 23–35.

Hamsher, K. de S. & Roberts, R. J. (1985). Memory for recent U.S. Presidents in patients with cerebral disease. *Journal of Clinical and Experimental Neuropsychology, 7*, 1–13.

Harris, J. E. & Morris, P. E. (Eds) (1984). *Everyday memory, actions and absent-mindedness.* London: Academic Press.

Hart, J., Berndt, R. S., & Caramazza, A. (1985). Category-specific naming deficit following cerebral infarction. *Nature, 316*, 439–440.

Hatfield, F. M. & Patterson, K. E. (1983). Phonological spelling. *Quarterly Journal of Experimental Psychology, 35A*, 451–468.

Hay, D. C. & Young, A. W. (1982). The human face. In A. W. Ellis (Ed.), *Normality and pathology in cognitive functions.* London: Academic Press.

Hécaen, H. (1981). The neuropsychology of face recognition. In G. Davies, H. Ellis, & J. Shephered (Eds), *Perceiving and remembering faces.* New York: Academic Press.

Hécaen, H. & Angelergues, R. (1962). Agnosia for faces (prosopagnosia). *Archives of Neurology, 7*, 92–100.

Hécaen, H. & Marcie, P. (1974). Disorders of written language following right hemisphere lesions. In S. J. Dimond & J. G. Beaumont (Eds), *Hemisphere function in the human brain.* London: Elek.

Hécaen, H., Goldblum, M. C., Masure, M. C., & Ramier, A. M. (1974). Une nouvelle observation d'agnosie d'objet. Deficit de l'association ou de la categorisation, specifique de la modalité visuelle? *Neuropsychologia, 12*, 447–464.

Heeschen, C. (1985). Agrammatism versus Paragrammatism: A fictitious opposition. In M.-L. Kean (Ed.), *Agrammatism.* Orlando: Academic Press.

Heilbronner, K. (1906). Ueber Agrammatismus und die Storung der Innere Sprache. *Archiv für Psychiatrie und Nervenkrankheiten, 75*, 332–416.

Heilman, K. M. (1979). Neglect and related disorders. In K. M. Heilman & E. Valenstein (Eds), *Clinical neuropsychology.* New York: Oxford University Press.

Heilman, K. M. & Scholes, R. J. (1976). The nature of comprehension errors in Broca's, conduction, and Wernicke's aphasias. *Cortex, 12*, 258–265.

Heilman, K. M. & Watson, R. T. (1978). Changes in the symptoms of neglect induced by changing task strategy. *Archives of Neurology, 35*, 47–49.

Heilman, K. M., Scholes, R. J., & Watson, R. T. (1975). Auditory affective agnosia. *Journal of Neurology, Neurosurgery and Psychiatry, 38*, 69–72.

Heilman, K. M., Rothi, L., Campanella, D., & Wolfson, S. (1979). Wernicke's and global aphasia without alexia. *Archives of Neurology, 36*, 129–133.

Heilman, K. M., Bowers, D., Speedie, L., & Coslett, H. B. (1984). Comprehension of affective and nonaffective prosody. *Neurology, 34*, 917–921.

Hemphil, R. E. & Stengel, E. (1940). A study on pure word deafness. *Journal of Neurology, Neurosurgery and Psychiatry, 3*, 251–262.

Henderson, L. (1985).   The psychology of morphemes. In A. W. Ellis (Ed.), *Progress in the psychology of language,* Vol. 1. London: Lawrence Erlbaum Associates Ltd.

Heywood, C. A., Wilson, B., & Cowey, A. (1987).   A case study of cortical colour "blindness" with relatively intact achromatic discrimination. *Journal of Neurology, Neurosurgery and Psychiatry, 50,* 22–29.

Hier, D. B. & Kaplan, J. (1980).   Verbal comprehension deficits after right hemisphere damage. *Applied Psycholinguistics, 1,* 279–294.

Hier, D. B. & Mohr, J. P. (1977).   Incongruous oral and written naming: Evidence for a subdivision of the syndrome of Wernicke's aphasia. *Brain and Language, 4,* 115–126.

Hines, D. (1976).   Recognition of verbs, abstract nouns and concrete nouns from the left and right visual half-fields. *Neuropsychologia, 14,* 211–216.

Hines, D. (1977).   Differences in tachistoscopic recognition between abstract and concrete words as a function of visual half-field and frequency. *Cortex, 13,* 66–73.

Hirst, W. (1982).   The amnesic syndrome: Descriptions and explanations. *Psychological Bulletin, 91,* 435–460.

Hirst, W., Johnson, M. K., Kim, J. K., Phelps, E. A., Risse, G., & Volpe, B. (1986).   Recognition and recall in amnesics. *Journal of Experimental Psychology: Learning, Memory and Cognition, 12,* 445–516.

Holmes, G. (1918).   Disturbances of visual orientation. *British Journal of Ophthalmology, 2,* 449–468, 506–615.

Holmes, G. (1919).   Disturbances of visual space perception. *British Medical Journal, 2,* 230–233.

Holmes, G. & Horrax, G. (1919).   Disturbances of spatial orientation and visual attention, with loss of stereoscopic vision. *Archives of Neurology and Psychiatry, 1,* 385–407.

Holmes, J. M. (1973).   *Dyslexia: A neurolinguistic study of traumatic and developmental disorders of reading.* Unpublished Ph.D. thesis, University of Edinburgh.

Holmes, J. M. (1978).   "Regression" and reading breakdown. In A. Caramazza & E. B. Zurif (Eds), *Language acquisition and language breakdown: Parallels and divergences.* Baltimore: Johns Hopkins University Press.

Homan, R. W., Criswell, E., Wada, J. A., & Ross, E. D. (1982).   Hemispheric contributions to manual communication (signing and finger spelling). *Neurology, 32,* 1020–1023.

Hotopf, W. H. N. (1980).   Slips of the pen. In U. Frith (Ed.), *Cognitive processes in spelling.* London: Academic Press.

Hotopf, W. H. N. (1983).   Lexical slips of the pen and tongue: What they tell us about language production. In B. Butterworth (Ed.), *Language production,* Vol. 2. London: Academic Press.

Howard, D. (1985a).   Agrammatism. In S. Newman & R. Epstein (Eds), *Current perspectives in dysphasia.* Edinburgh: Churchill Livingstone.

Howard, D. (1985b).   Introduction to "On agrammatism" (*Über Agrammatismus*) by Max Isserlin, 1922. *Cognitive Neuropsychology, 4,* 303–307.

Howard, D. & Franklin, S. (1987).   Three ways for understanding written words, and their use in two contrasting cases of surface dyslexia. In D. A. Allport, D. MacKay, W. Prinz, & E. Scheerer (Eds), *Language perception and production: Common processes in listening, speaking, reading and writing.* London: Academic Press.

Howard, D. & Hatfield, F. M. (1987).   *Aphasia therapy.* London: Lawrence Erlbaum Associates Ltd.

Howard, D. & Orchard-Lisle, V. (1984).   On the origin of semantic errors in naming: Evidence from the case of a global aphasic. *Cognitive Neuropsychology, 1,* 163–190.

Humphreys, G. W. & Evett, L. J. (1985).   Are there independent lexical and nonlexical routes in reading? An evaluation of the dual route theory of reading. *The Behavioral and Brain Sciences, 8,* 689–740.

Humphreys, G. W. & Riddoch, M. J. (1984).   Routes to object constancy: Implications from neurological impairments of object constancy. *Quarterly Journal of Experimental Psychology, 36A*, 385–415.

Humphreys, G. W. & Riddoch, M. J. (1985).   Authors' correction to "Routes to object constancy". *Quarterly Journal of Experimental Psychology, 37A*, 493–495.

Humphreys, G. W. & Riddoch, M. J. (1987a).   *To see but not to see: A case study of visual agnosia.* London: Lawrence Erlbaum Associates Ltd.

Humphreys, G. W. & Riddoch, M. J. (1987b).   The fractionation of visual agnosia. In G. W. Humphreys & M. J. Riddoch (Eds), *Visual object processing.* London: Lawrence Erlbaum Associates Ltd.

Huppert, F. A. & Piercy, M. (1976).   Recognition memory in amnesic patients: Effect of temporal context and familiarity of material. *Cortex, 12*, 3–20.

Huppert, F. A. & Piercy M. (1977).   Recognition memory in amnesic patients: A defect of acquisition? *Neuropsychologia, 15*, 643–653.

Huppert, F. A. & Piercy, M. (1978).   Dissociation between learning and remembering in organic amnesia. *Nature, 275*, 317–318.

Huppert, F. A. & Piercy, M. (1979).   Normal and abnormal forgetting in organic amnesia: Effect of locus of lesion. *Cortex, 15*, 385–390.

Isserlin, M. (1922).   Über Agrammatismus. *Zeitschrift für die Gesamte Neurologie und Psychiatrie, 75*, 332–410. (Translated with Introduction by D. Howard in *Cognitive Neuropsychology*, 1985, *2*, 303–345.)

Jackson, J. H. (1874).   On the nature of the duality of the brain. *Medical Press and Circular, 1*, 19–43. (Reprinted in J. Taylor (Ed.), *Selected writings of J. H. Jackson*, Vol. 2. New York: Basic Books, 1958.)

Jacoby, L. L. (1984).   Incidental versus intentional retrieval: Remembering and awareness as separate issues. In L. R. Squire & N. Butters (Eds), *Neuropsychology of memory.* New York: Guilford Press.

Jacoby, L. L. & Witherspoon, D. (1982).   Remembering without awareness. *Canadian Journal of Psychology, 36*, 300–324.

Jakimik, J., Cole, R. A., & Rudnicky, A. I. (1985).   Sound and spelling in spoken word recognition. *Journal of Memory and Language, 24*, 165–178.

James, W. (1980).   *The principles of psychology.* New York: Holt.

Janis, I. (1950).   Psychological effects of electroconvulsive treatments I. Post-treatment amnesias. *Journal of Nervous and Mental Disease, 111*, 359–382.

Joanette, Y., Keller, E., & Lecours, A. R. (1980).   Sequences of phonemic approximations in aphasia. *Brain and Language, 11*, 30–44.

Job, R. & Sartori, G. (1984).   Morphological decomposition: Evidence from crossed phonological dyslexia. *Quarterly Journal of Experimental Psychology, 36A*, 435–458.

Johnson, M. K., Kim, J. K., & Risse, G. (1985).   Do alcoholic Korsakoff's syndrome patients acquire affective reactions? *Journal of Experimental Psychology: Learning, Memory and Cognition, 11*, 22–36.

Jones, G. V. (1983).   On double dissociation of function. *Neuropsychologia, 21*, 397–400.

Joseph, A. B. (1986).   Focal central nervous system abnormalities in patients with misidentification syndromes. *Bibliotheca Psychiatrica, 164*, 68–79.

Kadish, J. (1978).   A neuropsychological approach to the study of gesture and pantomime in aphasia. *South African Journal of Communication Disorders, 25*, 102–117.

Kaushall, P. I., Zetin, M., & Squire, L. R. (1981).   A psychosocial study of chronic, circumscribed amnesia. *Journal of Nervous and Mental Disease, 169*, 383–389.

Kay, J. (1985).   Mechanisms of oral reading: A critical appraisal of cognitive models. In A. W. Ellis (Ed.), *Progress in the psychology of language*, Vol. 2. London: Lawrence Erlbaum Associates Ltd.

Kay, J. & Ellis, A. W. (1987). A cognitive neuropsychological case study of anomia: Implications for psychological models of word retrieval. *Brain, 110,* 613–629.

Kay, J. & Marcel, T. (1981). One process not two in reading aloud: Lexical analogies do the work of nonlexical rules. *Quarterly Journal of Experimental Psychology, 33A,* 397–413.

Kay, J. & Patterson, K. E. (1985). Routes to meaning in surface dyslexia. In K. E. Patterson, J. C. Marshall, & M. Coltheart (Eds), *Surface dyslexia: Neuropsychological and cognitive analyses of phonological reading.* London: Lawrence Erlbaum Associates Ltd.

Kean, M.-L. (1977). The linguistic interpretation of aphasia syndromes: Agrammatism in Broca's aphasia, an example. *Cognition, 5,* 9–46.

Kean, M.-L. (1979). Agrammatism, a phonological deficit. *Cognition, 7,* 69–83.

Kean, M.-L. (Ed.) (1985). *Agrammatism.* New York: Academic Press.

Keller, E. & Gopnik, M. (Eds) (1987). *Motor and sensory processes of language.* Hillsdale, N. J.: Lawrence Erlbaum Associates.

Kertesz, A. (1979). *Aphasia and associated disorders: Taxonomy, localization and recovery.* New York: Grune and Stratton.

Kertesz, A. (Ed.) (1983). *Localization in neuropsychology.* New York: Academic Press.

Kertesz, A. & McCabe, P. (1975). Intelligence and aphasia. *Brain and Language, 2,* 387–395.

Kimura, D. (1981). Neural mechanisms in manual signing. *Sign Language Studies, 33,* 291–312.

Kimura, D. & Archibald, Y. (1974). Motor functions of the left hemisphere. *Brain, 97,* 333–350.

Kimura, D., Battison, R., & Lubert, B. (1976). Impairment of nonlinguistic hand movements in a deaf aphasic. *Brain and Language, 3,* 566–571.

Kinsbourne, M. & Warrington, E. K. (1962). A variety of reading disability associated with right hemisphere lesions. *Journal of Neurology, Neurosurgery and Psychiatry, 25,* 339–344.

Kinsbourne, M. & Warrington, E. K. (1963). Jargon aphasia. *Neuropsychologia, 1,* 27–37.

Kinsbourne, M. & Warrington, E. K. (1964). Observations on colour agnosia. *Journal of Neurology, Neurosurgery and Psychiatry, 27,* 296–299.

Kinsbourne, M. & Warrington, E. K. (1965). A case showing selectively impaired oral spelling. *Journal of Neurology, Neurosurgery and Psychiatry, 28,* 563–566.

Kinsbourne, M. & Wood, F. (1975). Short-term memory processes and the amnesic syndrome. In D. Deutsch & J. A. Deutsch (Eds), *Short-term memory.* New York: Academic Press.

Klatt, D. H. (1979). Speech perception: A model of acoustic-phonetic analysis and lexical access. *Journal of Phonetics, 7,* 279–312.

Kleiman, G. M. (1981). Speech recoding in reading. *Journal of Verbal Learning and Verbal Behavior, 14,* 323–339.

Klein, R. & Harper, J. (1956). The problem of agnosia in the light of a case of pure word deafness. *Journal of Mental Science, 102,* 112–120.

Kleist, K. (1916). Über Leitungsafasie und grammatische Störungen. *Monatschrift für Psychiatrie und Neurologie, 16,* 118–121.

Klima, E. S. & Bellugi, U. (1979). *The signs of language.* Cambridge, Mass.: Harvard University Press.

Knight, R. G. & Wooles, I. M. (1980). Experimental investigation of chronic organic amnesia: A review. *Psychological Bulletin, 88,* 753–771.

Kohn, S. E. (1987). Phonological production deficits in aphasia. In H. Whitaker (Ed.), *Phonological processes and brain mechanisms.* New York: Springer-Verlag.

Kohn, S. E. & Friedman, R. B. (1986).   Word-meaning deafness: A phonological-semantic dissociation. *Cognitive Neuropsychology, 3,* 291–308.

Kolb, B. & Whishaw, I. Q. (1985).   *Fundamentals of human neuropsychology.* New York: Freeman.

Kolk, H. H. J., Van Grunsven, M. J. F., & Keyser, A. (1985).   On parallelism between production and comprehension in agrammatism. In M.-L. Kean (Ed.), *Agrammatism.* Orlando: Academic Press.

Kopelman, M. D. (1985).   Rates of forgetting in Alzheimer-type dementia and Korsakoff's syndrome. *Neuropsychologia, 23,* 623–638.

Korsakoff, S. S. (1889).   Über eine besondere Form psychischer Störung, Kombiniert mit multiplen Neuritis. *Archiv für Psychiatrie und Nervenkrankheiten, 21,* 669–704. (Translated by M. Victor & P. I. Yakovlev in *Neurology,* 1955, *5,* 394–406.)

Kremin, H. (1985).   Routes and strategies in surface dyslexia and dysgraphia. In K. E. Patterson, J. C. Marshall, & M. Coltheart (Eds), *Surface dyslexia: Neuropsychological and cognitive studies of phonological reading.* London: Lawrence Erlbaum Associates Ltd.

Kuhl, P. K. & Meltzoff, A. N. (1982).   The bimodal perception of speech in infancy. *Science, 218,* 1138–1144.

Kurucz, J. & Feldmar, G. (1979).   Prosopo-affective agnosia as a symptom of cerebral organic disease. *Journal of the American Geriatrics Society, 27,* 225–230.

Kurucz, J., Feldmar, G., & Werner, W. (1979).   Prosopo-affective agnosia associated with chronic organic brain syndrome. *Journal of the American Geriatrics Society, 27,* 91–95.

Lakatos, I. (1974).   Falsification and the methodology of scientific research programmes. In I. Lakatos & A. Musgrave (Eds), *Criticism and the growth of knowledge.* Cambridge: Cambridge University Press.

Lambert, A. J. (1982).   Right hemisphere language ability: 2. Evidence from normal subjects. *Current Psychological Reviews, 2,* 139–152.

Landis, T., Regard, M., Graves, R., & Goodglass, H. (1983).   Semantic paralexia: A release of right hemispheric function from left hemispheric control? *Neuropsychologia, 21,* 359–364.

Landis, T., Cummings, J. L., Benson, D. F., & Palmer, E. P. (1986).   Loss of topographic familiarity: An environmental agnosia. *Archives of Neurology, 43,* 132–136.

Larsen, B., Skinhoj, E., & Lassen, N. A. (1978).   Variations in regional cortical blood flow in the right and left hemispheres during automatic speech. *Brain, 101,* 193–209.

Lashley, K. S. (1941).   Coalescence of neurology and psychology. *Proceedings of the American Philosophical Society, 84,* 461–470.

Lashley, K. S. (1951).   The problem of serial order in behavior. In L. A. Jeffress (Ed.), *Cerebral mechanisms in behavior.* New York: Wiley.

Lasky, E. Z., Weidner, W. E., & Johnson, J. P. (1976).   Influence of linguistic complexity, rate of presentation, and interphrase pause time on auditory-verbal comprehension of adult aphasic patients. *Brain and Language, 3,* 386–395.

Lebrun, Y. (1976).   Neurolinguistic models of language and speech. In H. Whitaker & H. A. Whitaker (Eds), *Studies in neurolinguistics,* Vol. 1. New York: Academic Press.

Lebrun, Y. (1985).   Disturbances of written language and associated abilities following damage to the right hemisphere. *Applied Psycholinguistics, 6,* 231–260.

Lebrun, Y. & Leleux, C. (1986).   Central communication disorders in deaf signers. In J.-L. Nespoulous, P. Perron, & A. R. Lecours (Eds), *The biological foundations of gestures: Motor and semiotic aspects.* Hillsdale, N. J.: Lawrence Erlbaum Associates Inc.

Lebrun, Y. & Rubio, S. (1972).   Reduplications et omissions graphiques chez des patients attients d'une lésion hémisphérique droite. *Neuropsychologia, 10,* 249–251.

Lebrun, Y., Buyssens, E., & Henneaux, J. (1973).   Phonetic aspects of anarthria. *Cortex, 9,* 126–135.

Lebrun, Y., Lessinnes, A., De Vresse, L., & Leleux, C. (1985).   Dysprosody and the non-dominant hemisphere. *Language Sciences, 7,* 41–52.

Lecours, A. R. (1975).   Methods for the description of aphasic transformations of language. In E. H. Lenneberg & E. Lenneberg (Eds), *Foundations of language development,* Vol. 2. New York: Academic Press.

Lecours, A. R. & Lhermitte, F. (1969).   Phonemic paraphasias: Linguistic structures and tentative hypotheses. *Cortex, 5,* 193–228.

Lecours, A. R. & Lhermitte, F. (1976).   The "pure form" of the phonetic disintegration syndrome (pure anarthria): Anatomico-clinical report of a historical case. *Brain and Language, 3,* 88–113.

Lecours, A. R., Nespoulous, J.-L., & Desaulniers, P. (1986).   Standard teaching on apraxia. In J.-L. Nespoulous, P. Perron, & A. R. Lecours (Eds), *The biological foundations of gestures: Motor and semiotic aspects.* Hillsdale, N. J.: Lawrence Erlbaum Associates Ltd.

Lecours, A. R., Osborn, E., Travis, L., Rouillon, F., & Lavallee-Huynh, G. (1980).   Jargons. In J. W. Brown (Ed.), *Jargonaphasia.* New York: Academic Press.

Lecours, A. R., Travis, L., & Osborn, E. (1980).   Glossolalia as a manifestation of Wernicke's aphasia: A comparison to glossolalia in schizophasia and in procession. In O. Höök & M. Taylor-Sarno (Eds), *Aphasia: Concepts of analysis and management.* Stockholm: Almquist & Wiksell.

Leech, G., Deuchar, M., & Hoogenraad, R. (1982).   *English grammar for today.* London: The Macmillan Press.

Lehiste, I. (1973).   Phonetic disambiguation of syntactic ambiguity. *Glossa, 7,* 107–122.

Lehiste, I. (1979).   Perception of sentence and paragraph boundaries. In B. Lindblom & S. Ohman (Eds), *Frontiers of speech communication research.* New York: Academic Press.

Lehiste, I., & Wang, W. (1977).   Perception of sentence and paragraph boundaries with and without information. In W. Dressler & R. Pfeiffer (Eds), *Phonologica, 1976.* Innsbruck: Institut für Sprachwissenschaft der Universitat Innsbruck.

Lehmann, W. P. (1973).   *Historical linguistics* (2nd ed.). New York: Holt, Rinehart and Winston.

Leischner, A. (1943).   Die Aphasie der Taubstummen. *Archiv für Psychiatrie und Nervenkrankheiten, 115,* 469–548.

Lenneberg, E. H. (1960).   A review of "Speech and brain mechanisms" by W. Penfield and L. Roberts. *Language, 36,* 97–112.

Lesser, R. (1978).   *Linguistic investigation of aphasia.* London: Edward Arnold.

Levin, H. S., Peters, B. H., & Hulkonen, D. A. (1983).   Early concepts of anterograde and retrograde amnesia. *Cortex, 19,* 427–440.

Levine, D. N. (1978).   Prosopagnosia and visual object agnosia: A behavioral study. *Brain and Language, 5,* 341–365.

Levine, D. N., Calvanio, R., & Popovics, A. (1982).   Language in the absence of inner speech. *Neuropsychologia, 20,* 391–409.

Levine, D. N., Warach, J., & Farah, M. (1985).   Two visual systems in mental imagery: Dissociation of "what" and "where" in imagery disorders due to bilateral posterior cerebral lesions. *Neurology, 35,* 1010–1018.

Levy, B. A. (1981).   Interactive processing during reading. In A. M. Lesgold & C. A. Perfetti (Eds), *Interactive processes in reading.* Hillsdale, N. J.: Lawrence Erlbaum Associates Inc.

Lewis, A. (1961).   Amnesic syndromes. *Proceedings of the Royal Society of Medicine, 54,* 955–961.

Lewis, S. W. (1987). Brain imaging in a case of Capgras' syndrome. *British Journal of Psychiatry, 150*, 117–121.

Lhermitte, F. & Beauvois, M.-F. (1973). A visual-speech disconnexion syndrome: Report of a case with optic aphasia, agnosic alexia and colour agnosia. *Brain, 97*, 695–714.

Lichtheim, L. (1885). On aphasia. *Brain, 7*, 433–484.

Lidz, T. (1942). The amnesic syndrome. *Archives of Neurology and Psychiatry, 47*, 588–605.

Lieberman, P. (1963). Some effects of semantic and grammatical context on the production and perception of speech. *Language and Speech, 6*, 172–187.

Liepmann, H. (1910). Beitrag zur Kenntnis des amnestischen Symptomenkomplexes. *Neurologie Zeitblatt, 29*, 1147–1161.

Lissauer, H. (1890). Ein Fall von Seelenblindheit nebst einem Beitrage zur Theorie derselben. *Archiv für Psychiatrie und Nervenkrankheiten, 21*, 222–270.

Lock, A. (1980). *The guided reinvention of language*. London: Academic Press.

Luria, A. R. (1970). *Traumatic aphasia*. The Hague: Mouton.

Luria, A. R. (1974). Language and brain: Towards the basic problems of neurolinguistics. *Brain and Language, 1*, 1–14.

Luria, A. R. (1976). *Basic problems in neurolinguistics*. The Hague: Mouton.

MacCallum, W. A. G. (1973). Capgras symptoms with an organic basis. *British Journal of Psychiatry, 123*, 639–642.

McCarthy, R. & Warrington, E. K. (1984). A two-route model of speech production. *Brain, 107*, 463–485.

McCarthy, R. & Warrington, E. K. (1986). Visual associative agnosia: A clinico-anatomical study of a single case. *Journal of Neurology, Neurosurgery and Psychiatry, 49*, 1233–1240.

McClelland, J. L. (1987). The case for interactionism in language processing. In M. Coltheart (Ed.), *Attention and Performance XII: The psychology of reading*. London: Lawrence Erlbaum Associates Ltd.

McClelland, J. L. & Elman, J. L. (1986). The TRACE model of speech perception. *Cognitive Psychology, 18*, 1–86.

McClelland, J. L. & Rumelhart, D. E. (1981). An interactive activation model of context effects in letter perception: Part 1. An account of basic findings. *Psychological Review, 88*, 375–407.

McClelland, J. L. & Rumelhart, D. E. (1985). Distributed memory and the representation of general and specific information. *Journal of Experimental Psychology: General, 114*, 159–188.

McClelland, J. L. & Rumelhart, D. E. (1986). Amnesia and distributed memory. In J. L. McClelland & D. E. Rumelhart (Eds), *Parallel distributed processing: Explorations in the microstructure of cognition, Vol. 2: Psychological and biological models*. Cambridge, Mass: MIT Press.

McGurk, H. & MacDonald, J. (1976). Hearing lips and seeing voices. *Nature, 264*, 746–748.

MacKain, K. S., Studdert-Kennedy, M., Spieker, S., & Stern D. (1983). Infant intermodal speech perception is a left hemisphere function. *Science, 219*, 1347–1349.

MacKay, D. G. (1970). Spoonerisms: The structure of errors in the serial order of speech. *Neuropsychologia, 8*, 323–350. (Reprinted in V. A. Fromkin (Ed.) (1973), *Speech errors as linguistic evidence*. The Hague: Mouton.)

McKenna, P. & Warrington, E. K. (1980). Testing for nominal dysphasia. *Journal of Neurology, Neurosurgery, and Psychiatry, 43*, 781–788.

McWeeny, K. H., Young, A. W., Hay, D. C., & Ellis, A. W. (1987). Putting names to faces. *British Journal of Psychology, 78*, 143–149.

Mack, J. L. & Boller, F. (1977). Associative visual agnosia and its related deficits: The role of the minor hemisphere in assigning meaning to visual perceptions. *Neuropsychologia, 15,* 345–349.

Malone, D. R., Morris, H. H., Kay, M. C., & Levin, H. S. (1982). Prosopagnosia: A double dissociation between the recognition of familiar and unfamiliar faces. *Journal of Neurology, Neurosurgery, and Psychiatry, 45,* 820–822.

Mann, V. A. & Liberman, A. M. (1983). Some differences between phonetic and auditory modes of perception. *Cognition, 14,* 211–235.

Marcel, A. J. (1983). Conscious and unconscious perception: An approach to the relations between phenomenal experience and perceptual processes. *Cognitive Psychology, 15,* 238–300.

Marcie, P. (1983). Writing disorders associated with focal cortical lesions. In M. Martlew (Ed.), *The psychology of written language: Developmental and educational perspectives.* Chichester: J. Wiley.

Marcus, S. M. (1981). ERIS—context-sensitive coding in speech perception. *Journal of Phonetics, 9,* 197–220.

Margolin, D. I. (1984). The neuropsychology of writing and spelling: Semantic, phonological, motor and perceptual processes. *Quarterly Journal of Experimental Psychology, 36A,* 459–489.

Margolin, D. I., Marcel, A. J., & Carlson, N. R. (1985). Common mechanisms in dysnomia and post-semantic surface dyslexia. In K. E. Patterson, J. C. Marshall, & M. Coltheart (Eds), *Surface dyslexia: Neuropsychological and cognitive processes in phonological reading.* London: Lawrence Erlbaum Associates Ltd.

Marin, O. S. M., Saffran, E. M., & Schwartz, M. F. (1976). Dissociations of language in aphasia: Implications for normal function. *Annals of the New York Academy of Sciences, 280,* 868–884.

Marr, D. (1976). Early processing of visual information. *Philosophical Transactions of the Royal Society* (London), *B275,* 483–524.

Marr, D. (1980). Visual information processing: The structure and creation of visual representations. *Philosophical Transactions of the Royal Society* (London), *B290,* 199–218.

Marr, D. (1982). *Vision.* San Francisco: W. H. Freeman.

Marr, D. & Nishihara, K. (1978). Representation and recognition of the spatial organization of three-dimensional shapes. *Philosophical Transactions of the Royal Society* (London), *B200,* 269–294.

Marshall, J. C. (1979). Disorders in the expression of language. In J. Morton & J. C. Marshall (Eds), *Psycholinguistics series,* Vol. 1. London: Elek; and Cambridge, Mass.: MIT Press.

Marshall, J. C. (1982). What is a symptom-complex? In M. Arbib, D. Caplan, & J. C. Marshall (Eds), *Neural models of language processes.* New York: Academic Press.

Marshall, J. C. (1986). Signs of language in the brain. *Nature, 322,* 307–308.

Marshall, J. C. (1987). The cultural and biological context of written languages: Their acquisition, deployment, and breakdown. In J. R. Beech & A. M. Colley (Eds), *Cognitive approaches to reading.* Chichester: John Wiley.

Marshall, J. C. & Fryer, D. M. (1978). Speak, Memory! An introduction to some historic studies of remembering and forgetting. In M. M. Gruneberg & P. E. Morris (Eds), *Aspects of memory.* London: Methuen.

Marshall, J. C. & Newcombe, F. (1966). Syntactic and semantic errors in paralexia. *Neuropsychologia, 4,* 169–176.

Marshall, J. C. & Newcombe, F. (1973). Patterns of paralexia: A psycholinguistic approach. *Journal of Psycholinguistic Research, 2,* 175–199.

Marshall, J. C. & Newcombe, F. (1980). The conceptual status of deep dyslexia: An historical perspective. In M. Coltheart, K. E. Patterson, & J. C. Marshall (Eds), *Deep dyslexia*. London: Routlege and Kegan Paul.

Marshall, J. C. & Patterson, K. E. (1983). Semantic paralexia and the wrong hemisphere: A note on Landis, Regard, Graves and Goodglass (1983). *Neuropsychologia, 21*, 425–427.

Marslen-Wilson, W. D. (1984). Function and process in spoken word recognition—A tutorial review. In H. Bouma & D. B. Bouwhuis (Eds), *Attention and Performance, X: Control of language processes*. London: Lawrence Erlbaum Associates Ltd.

Marslen-Wilson, W. D. & Teuber, H.-L. (1975). Memory for remote events in anterograde amnesia: Recognition of public figures from news photographs. *Neuropsychologia, 13*, 347–352.

Marslen-Wilson, W. D. & Tyler, L. K. (1975). Processing structure of sentence perception. *Nature, 257*, 784–786.

Marslen-Wilson, W. D. & Tyler, L. K. (1980). The temporal structure of spoken language understanding. *Cognition, 8*, 1–71.

Martin, A. D. & Rigrodsky, S. (1974). An investigation of phonological impairment in aphasia, Part 2: Distinctive feature analysis of phonemic commutation errors in aphasia. *Cortex, 10*, 329–346.

Martone, M., Butters, N., Payne, M., Becker, J. T., & Sax, D. S. (1984). Dissociations between skill learning and verbal recognition in amnesia and dementia. *Archives of Neurology, 41*, 965–970.

Mayer-Gross, W. (1943). Memory defects after ECT. *Lancet, ii*, 603.

Mayes, A. R. & Meudell, P. R. (1981). How similar is the effect of cueing in amnesics and in normal subjects following forgetting? *Cortex, 17*, 113–124.

Mayes, A. R. & Meudell, P. R. (1984). Problems and prospects for research on amnesia. In L. R. Squire & N. Butters (Eds), *Neuropsychology of memory*. New York: Guilford Press.

Mayes, A. R., Meudell, P. R., & Neary, D. (1978). Must amnesia be caused by either encoding or retrieval disorders? In M. M. Gruneberg, P. E. Morris, & R. N. Sykes (Eds), *Practical aspects of memory*. London: Academic Press.

Meadows, J. C. (1974a). The anatomical basis of prosopagnosia. *Journal of Neurology, Neurosurgery, and Psychiatry, 37*, 489–501.

Meadows, J. C. (1974b). Disturbed perception of colours associated with localized cerebral lesions. *Brain, 97*, 615–632.

Meckler, R. J., Mack, J. L., & Bennett, R. (1979). Sign language aphasia in a non-deaf-mute. *Neurology, 29*, 1037–1040.

Metz-Lutz, M.-N. & Dahl, E. (1984). Analysis of word comprehension in a case of pure word-deafness. *Brain and Language, 23*, 13–25.

Meudell, P. R. & Mayes, A. R. (1982). Normal and abnormal forgetting: Some comments on the human amnesic syndrome. In A. W. Ellis (Ed.), *Normality and pathology in cognitive functions*. London: Academic Press.

Meudell, P. R., Mayes, A. & Neary, D. (1980a). Orienting task effects on the recognition of humorous pictures in amnesic and normal subjects. *Journal of Clinical Neuropsychology, 2*, 75–88.

Meudell, P. R., Northen, B., Snowden, J. S., & Neary, D. (1980b). Long-term memory for famous voices in amnesic and normal subjects. *Neuropsychologia, 18*, 133–139.

Meyer, D. E. & Schvaneveldt, R. W. (1971). Facilitation in recognizing pairs of words: Evidence of a dependence between retrieval operations. *Journal of Experimental Psychology, 90*, 227–234.

Miceli, G., Mazzucchi, A., Menn, L., & Goodglass, H. (1983). Contrasting cases of Italian agrammatic aphasia without comprehension disorder. *Brain and Language, 19*, 65–97.

Miceli, G., Silveri, C., & Caramazza, A. (1985).   Cognitive analysis of a case of pure dysgraphia. *Brain and Language, 25*, 187–212.

Miceli, G., Silveri, C., & Caramazza, A. (1987).   The role of the phoneme-to-grapheme conversion system and of the graphemic output buffer in writing: Evidence from an Italian case of pure dysgraphia. In M. Coltheart, G. Sartori, & R. Job (Eds), *The cognitive neuropsychology of language*. London: Lawrence Erlbaum Associates Ltd.

Michel, F. (1979).   Preservation du language ecrit malgré un deficit majeur du language oral. *Le Lyon Medicale, 241*, 141–149.

Michel, F. & Andreewsky, E. (1983).   Deep dysphasia: An analogue of deep dyslexia in the auditory modality. *Brain and Language, 18*, 212–223.

Milberg, W. & Blumstein, S. E. (1981).   Lexical decision and aphasia: Evidence for semantic processing. *Brain and Language, 14*, 371–385.

Miller, D. & Ellis, A. W. (1987).   Speech and writing errors in "neologistic jargon-aphasia": A lexical activation hypothesis. In M. Coltheart, G. Sartori, & R. Job (Eds), *The cognitive neuropsychology of language*. London: Lawrence Erlbaum Associ ates Ltd.

Miller, G. A. (1956).   The magic number seven, plus or minus two: Some limits on our capacity for processing information. *Psychological Review, 63*, 81–93.

Miller, G. A. & Taylor, J. (1948).   Perception of repeated bursts of noise. *Journal of the Acoustical Society of America, 20*, 171–182.

Miller, J. L. (1987).   Rate-dependent processing in speech perception. In A. W. Ellis (Ed.), *Progress in the psychology of language*, Vol. 3. London: Lawrence Erlbaum Associates Ltd.

Miller, J. L., & Marlin, N. A. (1979).   Amnesia following electroconvulsive shock. In J. F. Kihlstrom & F. J. Evans (Eds), *Functional disorders of memory*. Hillsdale, N. J.: Lawrence Erlbaum Associates Inc.

Mills, C. K. (1912).   The cerebral mechanism of emotional expression. *Transactions of the College of Physicians of Philadelphia, 34*, 147–185.

Milner, B. (1966).   Amnesia following operation on the temporal lobes. In C. W. M. Whitty & O. L. Zangwill (Eds), *Amnesia*. London: Butterworths.

Milner, B., Corkin, S., & Teuber, H.-L. (1968).   Further analysis of the hippocampal amnesia syndrome: 14 year follow-up study of H.M. *Neuropsychologia, 6*, 215–234.

Mohr, J. P., Leicester, J., Stoddard, L. T., & Sidman, M. (1971).   Right hemianopia with memory and colour deficits in circumscribed left posterior cerebral artery territory infarction. *Neurology, 21*, 1104–1113.

Moll, J. M. (1915).   The "Amnestic" or "Korsakow's" syndrome with alcoholic aetiology: an analysis of thirty cases. *Journal of Mental Science, 61*, 424–443.

Mollon, J. D. (1982).   Colour vision and colour blindness. In H. D. Barlow & J. D. Mollon (Eds), *The senses*. Cambridge: Cambridge University Press.

Mollon, J. D., Newcombe, F., Polden, P. G., & Ratcliff, G. (1980).   On the presence of three cone mechanisms in a case of total achromatopsia. In G. Verriest (Ed.), *Colour vision deficiences, V*. Bristol: Hilger.

Monoi, H., Fukusako, Y., Itoh, M., & Sasanuma, S. (1983).   Speech sound errors in patients with conduction and Broca's aphasia. *Brain and Language, 20*, 175–194.

Monrad-Krohn, G. H. (1947).   Dysprosody or altered "melody of language". *Brain, 70*, 405–415.

Monsell, S. (1985).   Repetition and the lexicon. In A. W. Ellis (Ed.), *Progress in the psychology of language*, Vol. 2. London: Lawrence Erlbaum Associates Ltd.

Morrow, L., Ratcliff, G., & Johnston, C. S. (1985).   Externalising spatial knowledge in patients with right hemisphere lesions. *Cognitive Neuropsychology, 2*, 265–273.

Morton, J. (1964).   A model for continuous language behaviour. *Language and Speech, 7*, 40–70.

Morton, J. (1979). Facilitation in word recognition: Experiments causing change in the logogen model. In P. A. Kolers, M. Wrolstad, & H. Bouma (Eds), *Processing of visible language*, Vol. 1. New York: Plenum.

Morton, J. (1980a). The logogen model and orthographic structure. In U. Frith (Ed.), *Cognitive processes in spelling*. London: Academic Press.

Morton, J. (1980b). An analogue of deep dyslexia in the auditory modality. In M. Coltheart, K. E. Patterson, & J. C. Marshall (Eds), *Deep dyslexia*. London: Routledge and Kegan Paul.

Morton, J. (1981). The status of information processing models of language. *Philosophical Transactions of the Royal Society* (London), *B295*, 387–396. (Also published in H. C. Longuet-Higgins, J. Lyons, & D. E. Broadbent (Eds), *The psychological mechanisms of language*. London: The Royal Society and the British Academy, 1981.)

Morton, J. (1984). Brain-based and non-brain-based models of language. In D. Caplan, A. R. Lecours, & A. Smith (Eds), *Biological perspectives on language*. Cambridge, Mass.: MIT Press.

Morton, J. (1985a). Naming. In S. Newman & R. Epstein (Eds), *Current perspectives in dysphasia*. Edinburgh: Churchill Livingstone.

Morton, J. (1985b). The problem with amnesia: The problem with human memory. *Cognitive Neuropsychology, 2,* 281–290.

Morton, J. & Patterson, K. E. (1980). A new attempt at an interpretation, or, an attempt at a new interpretation. In M. Coltheart, K. E. Patterson, & J. C. Marshall (Eds), *Deep dyslexia*. London: Routledge and Kegan Paul.

Moscovitch, M. (1982). Multiple dissociations of function in amnesia. In L. S. Cermak (Ed.), *Human memory and amnesia*. Hillsdale, N. J.: Lawrence Erlbaum Associates Inc.

Mozer, M. C. (1983). Letter migration in word perception. *Journal of Experimental Psychology: Human Perception and Performance, 9,* 531–546.

Müller, G. E. & Pilzecker, A. (1900). Experimentelle Beiträge zur Lehre vom Gedächtnis. *Zeitschrift für Psychologie, Ergänzungsband, 1,* 1–300.

Myers, P. S. & Linebaugh, C. W. (1981). Comprehension of idiomatic expressions by right-hemisphere-damaged adults. In R. H. Brookshire (Ed.), *Clinical aphasiology: Conference proceedings*. Minneapolis: BRK Publishers.

Myerson, R. & Goodglass, H. (1972). Transformational grammars of three agrammatic patients. *Language and Speech, 15,* 40–50.

Nebes, R. D. (1975). The nature of internal speech in a patient with aphemia. *Brain and Language, 2,* 489–497.

Nebes, R. D., Martin, D. C., & Horn, L. C. (1984). Sparing of semantic memory in Alzheimer's disease. *Journal of Abnormal Psychology, 93,* 321–330.

Neisser, U. (1954). An experimental distinction between perceptual process and verbal response. *Journal of Experimental Psychology, 47,* 399–402.

Neisser, U. (1982). *Memory observed*. San Fransisco: W. H. Freeman.

Nespoulous, J.-L., Perron, P., & Lecours, A. R. (1986). *The biological foundations of gestures: Motor and semiotic aspects*. Hillsdale, N. J.: Lawrence Erlbaum Associates Inc.

Newcombe, F. (1969). *Missile wounds of the brain: A study of psychological deficits*. Oxford: Oxford University Press.

Newcombe, F. (1974). Selective deficits after focal cerebral injury. In S. J. Dimond & J. G. Beaumont (Eds), *Hemisphere function in the human brain*. London: Elek.

Newcombe, F. (1979). The processing of visual information in prosopagnosia and acquired dyslexia: Functional versus physiological interpretation. In D. J. Oborne, M. M. Gruneberg, & J. R. Eiser (Eds), *Research in psychology and medicine*, Vol. 1. London: Academic Press.

Newcombe, F. & Marshall, J. C. (1975).   Traumatic dyslexia: Localization and linguistics. In K. J. Zulch, O. Creutzfeldt, & G. C. Galbraith (Eds), *Cerebral localization.* Berlin: Springer-Verlag.

Newcombe, F. & Marshall, J. C. (1980a).   Response monitoring and response blocking in deep dyslexia. In M. Coltheart, K. E. Patterson, & J. C. Marshall (Eds), *Deep dyslexia.* London: Routledge and Kegan Paul.

Newcombe, F. & Marshall, J. C. (1980b).   Transcoding and lexical stabilization in deep dyslexia. In M. Coltheart, K. E. Patterson, & J. C. Marshall (Eds), *Deep dyslexia.* London: Routledge and Kegan Paul.

Newcombe, F. & Marshall, J. C. (1981).   On psycholinguistic classifications of the acquired dyslexias. *Bulletin of the Orton Society, 31,* 29–46.

Newcombe, F. & Marshall, J. C. (1984).   Varieties of acquired dyslexia: A linguistic approach. *Seminars in Neurology, 4,* 181–195.

Newcombe, F. & Ratcliff, G. (1974).   Agnosia: A disorder of object recognition. In F. Michel & B. Schott (Eds), *Les syndromes de disconnexion calleuse chez l'homme.* Lyon: Colloque International de Lyon.

Newcombe, F. & Russell, W. R. (1969).   Dissociated visual perceptual and spatial deficits in focal lesions of the right hemisphere. *Journal of Neurology, Neurosurgery and Psychiatry, 32,* 73–81.

Newcombe, F., Ratcliff, G., & Damasio, H. (1987).   Dissociable visual and spatial impairments following right posterior cerebral lesions: Clinical, neuropsychological and anatomical evidence. *Neuropsychologia, 25,* 149–161.

Newman, S. & Epstein, R. (Eds) (1985).   *Current perspectives in dysphasia.* Edinburgh: Churchill Livingstone.

Nolan, K. A. & Caramazza, A. (1982).   Modality-independent impairments in word processing in a deep dyslexic patient. *Brain and Language, 16,* 237–264.

Nooteboom, S. G. (1967).   Some regularities in phonemic speech errors. Institut voor Perceptie Onderzoek, Eindhoven, *Annual Progress Report,* No. 2, 65–70.

Ogden, J. A. (1985).   Autotopagnosia: Occurrence in a patient without nominal aphasia and with an intact ability to point to parts of animals and objects. *Brain, 108,* 1009–1022.

Ogle, W. (1867).   Aphasia and agraphia. *St. George's Hospital Reports, 2,* 83–122.

Okada, S., Hanada, M., Hattori, H., & Shoyama, T. (1963).   A case of pure word-deafness. *Studia Phonologica, 3,* 58–65.

Oldfield, R. C. & Wingfield, A. (1965).   Response latencies in naming objects. *Quarterly Journal of Experimental Psychology, 17,* 273–281.

Oppenheimer, D. R. & Newcombe, F. (1978).   Clinical and anatomical findings in a case of auditory agnosia. *Archives of Neurology, 35,* 712–719.

Oscar-Berman, N., Zurif, E. B., & Blumstein, S. (1975).   Effects of unilateral brain damage on the processing of speech sounds. *Brain and Language, 2,* 345–355.

Oxbury, J. M., Oxbury, S. M., & Humphrey, N. K. (1969).   Varieties of colour anomia. *Brain, 92,* 847–860.

Paillard, J., Michel, F., & Stelmach, G. (1983).   Localization without content: A tactile analogue of "blind sight". *Archives of Neurology, 40,* 548–551.

Pallis, C. A. (1955).   Impaired identification of faces and places with agnosia for colours. *Journal of Neurology, Neurosurgery and Psychiatry, 18,* 218–224.

Parisi, D. (1987).   Grammatical disturbances of speech production. In M. Coltheart, G. Sartori, & R. Job (Eds), *The cognitive neuropsychology of language.* London: Lawrence Erlbaum Associates Ltd.

Parker, E. & Noble, E. (1977).   Alcohol consumption and cognitive functioning in social drinkers. *Journal of Studies on Alcohol, 38,* 1224–1232.

Parkin, A. J. (1982).   Residual learning capability in organic amnesia. *Cortex, 18,* 417–440.

Parkin, A. J. (1987). *Memory and amnesia.* Oxford: Basil Blackwell.

Patterson, J. H. & Green, D. M. (1970). Discrimination of transient signals having identical energy spectra. *Journal of the Acoustical Society of America, 20,* 171–182.

Patterson, M. B. & Mack, J. L. (1985). Neuropsychological analysis of a case of reduplicative paramnesia. *Journal of Clinical and Experimental Neuropsychology, 7,* 111–121.

Patterson, K. E. (1978). Phonemic dyslexia: Errors of meaning and the meaning of errors. *Quarterly Journal of Experimental Psychology, 30,* 587–601.

Patterson, K. E. (1979). What's right with "deep" dyslexics. *Brain and Language, 8,* 111–129.

Patterson, K. E. (1980). Derivational errors. In M. Coltheart, K. E. Patterson, & J. C. Marshall (Eds), *Deep dyslexia.* London: Routledge and Kegan Paul.

Patterson, K. E. (1981). Neuropsychological approaches to the study of reading. *British Journal of Psychology, 72,* 151–174.

Patterson, K. E. (1982). The relation between reading and phonological coding: Further neuropsychological observations. In A. W. Ellis (Ed.), *Normality and pathology in cognitive functions.* London: Academic Press.

Patterson, K. E. (1986). Lexical but non-semantic spelling? *Cognitive Neuropsychology, 3,* 341–367.

Patterson, K. E. (1988). Acquired disorders of spelling. In G. Denes, C. Semenza, P. Bisiacchi, & E. Andreewsky (Eds), *Perspectives in cognitive neuropsychology.* London: Lawrence Erlbaum Associates Ltd.

Patterson, K. E. & Besner, D. (1984). Is the right hemisphere literate? *Cognitive Neuropsychology, 1,* 315–341.

Patterson, K. E. & Coltheart, V. (1987). Phonological processes in reading: A tutorial review. In M. Coltheart (Ed.), *Attention and Performance, XII: The psychology of reading.* London: Lawrence Erlbaum Associates Ltd.

Patterson, K. & Kay, J. (1982). Letter-by-letter reading: Psychological descriptions of a neurological syndrome. *Quarterly Journal of Experimental Psychology, 34A,* 411–441.

Patterson, K. E. & Morton, J. (1985). From orthography to phonology: An attempt at an old interpretation. In K. E. Patterson, J. C. Marshall, & M. Coltheart (Eds), *Surface dyslexia: Neuropsychological and cognitive studies of phonological reading.* London: Lawrence Erlbaum Associates Ltd.

Patterson, K. E., Marshall, J. C., & Coltheart, M. (1985). *Surface dyslexia: Neuropsychological and cognitive studies of phonological reading.* London: Lawrence Erlbaum Associates Ltd.

Perecman, E. & Brown, J. W. (1981). Semantic jargon: A case report. In J. W. Brown (Ed.) *Jargonaphasia.* New York: Academic Press.

Perenin, M. T. (1978). Visual function within the hemianopic field following early cerebral hemidecortication in man, II: Pattern discrimination. *Neuropsychologia, 16,* 696–708.

Perenin, M. T. & Jeannerod, M. (1978). Visual function within the hemianopic field following early hemidecortication in man, I: Spatial localization. *Neuropsychologia, 16,* 1–13.

Peterson, L. N. & Kirshner, H. S. (1981). Gestural impairment and gestural ability in aphasia: A review. *Brain and Language, 14,* 333–348.

Peuser, G. (1978). *Aphasie.* Munchen: Wilhelm Fink Verlag.

Pickett, L. (1974). An assessment of gestural and pantomime deficit in aphasic patients. *Acta Symbolica, 5,* 69–86.

Poeck, K. (1983). What do we mean by "aphasic syndromes"? A neurologist's view. *Brain and Language, 20,* 79–89.

Poizner, H., Bellugi, U., & Iragui, V. (1984). Apraxia and aphasia for a visual-gestural language. *American Journal of Physiology: Regulative, Integrative and Comparative Physiology, 246,* R868–R883.

Pollack, I. & Pickett, J. M. (1964). The intelligibility of excerpts from fluent speech: Auditory versus structural context. *Language and Speech, 6,* 151–165.

Pöppel, E., Held, R., & Frost, D. (1973). Residual visual function after brain wounds involving the central visual pathways in man. *Nature, 243,* 295–296.

Posner, M. I. (1980). Orienting of attention. *Quarterly Journal of Experimental Psychology, 32,* 3–25.

Posner, M. I., Cohen, Y., & Rafal, R. D. (1982). Neural systems control of spatial orienting. *Philosophical Transactions of the Royal Society* (London), *B298,* 187–198.

Posner, M. I., Walker, J. A., Friedrich, F. J., & Rafal, R. D. (1984). Effects of parietal injury on covert orienting of visual attention. *Journal of Neuroscience, 4,* 1863–1874.

Posner, M. I., Rafal, R. D., Choate, L. S., & Vaughan, J. (1985). Inhibition of return: Neural basis and function. *Cognitive Neuropsychology, 2,* 211–228.

Potter, J. M. (1980). What was the matter with Dr. Spooner? In V. A. Fromkin (Ed.), *Errors in linguistic performance: Slips of the tongue, ear, pen and hand.* New York: Academic Press.

Potter, M. C. & Faulconer, B. A. (1975). Time to understand pictures and words. *Nature* (London), *253,* 437–438.

Potts, C. S. (1901). A case of transient motor aphasia, complete anomia, nearly complete agraphia and word blindness occurring in a left-handed man; with special reference to the existence of a naming center. *Journal of the American Medical Association, 36,* 1239–1241.

Ratcliff, G. (1979). Spatial thought, mental rotation and the right cerebral hemisphere. *Neuropsychologia, 17,* 49–54.

Ratcliff, G. (1982). Disturbances of spatial orientation associated with cerebral lesions. In M. Potegal (Ed.), *Spatial abilities: Development and physiological foundations.* New York: Academic Press.

Ratcliff, G. & Cowey, A. (1979). Disturbances of visual perception following cerebral lesions. In D. J. Oborne, M. M. Gruneberg, & J. R. Eiser (Eds), *Research in psychology and medicine.* New York: Academic Press.

Ratcliff, G. & Davies-Jones, G. A. B. (1972). Defective visual localization in focal brain wounds. *Brain, 95,* 49–60.

Ratcliff, G. & Newcombe, F. (1973). Spatial orientation in man: Effects of left, right, and bilateral posterior cerebral lesions. *Journal of Neurology, Neurosurgery, and Psychiatry, 36,* 448–454.

Ratcliff, G. & Newcombe, F. (1982). Object recognition: Some deductions from the clinical evidence. In A. W. Ellis (Ed.), *Normality and pathology in cognitive functions.* London: Academic Press.

Reason, J. T. & Lucas, D. (1984). Using cognitive diaries to investigate naturally occurring memory blocks. In J. Harris & P. E. Morris (Eds), *Everyday memory, actions and absentmindedness.* London: Academic Press.

Reider, N. (1941). A note on the influence of early training on the development of aphasic manifestations. *Bulletin of the Menninger Clinic, 5,* 1–4.

Repp, B. H. (1982). Phonetic trading relations and context affects: New experimental evidence for a speech mode of perception. *Psychological Bulletin, 92,* 81–110.

Riddoch, G. (1917). Dissociation of visual perceptions due to occipital injuries, with especial reference to appreciation of movement. *Brain, 40,* 15–57.

Riddoch, G. (1935). Visual disorientation in homonymous half-fields. *Brain, 58,* 376–382.

Riddoch, M. J. & Humphreys, G. W. (1983). The effect of cueing on unilateral neglect. *Neuropsychologia, 21,* 589–599.

Riddoch, M. J. & Humphreys, G. W. (1987a).   A case of integrative visual agnosia. *Brain*, *110*, 1431–1462

Riddoch, M. J. & Humphreys, G. W. (1987b).   Visual object processing in optic aphasia: A case of semantic access agnosia. *Cognitive Neuropsychology, 4*, 131–185.

Rinnert, C. & Whitaker, H. A. (1973).   Semantic confusions by aphasic patients. *Cortex, 9*, 56–81.

Rochford, G. & Williams, M. (1965).   Studies in the development and breakdown of the use of names. I. The relationship between nominal dysphasia and the acquisition of vocabulary in childhood. *Journal of Neurology, Neurosurgery and Psychiatry, 25*, 222–227.

Roeltgen, D. P., Sevush, S., & Heilman, K. M. (1983).   Phonological agraphia: Writing by the lexical-semantic route. *Neurology, 33*, 755–765.

Rollins, H. A. & Hendricks, R. (1980).   Processing of words presented simultaneously to eye and ear. *Journal of Experimental Psychology: Human Perception and Performance, 6*, 99–109.

Roman-Campos, G., Poser, C. M., & Wood, F. B. (1980).   Persistent retrograde memory deficit after transient global amnesia. *Cortex, 16*, 509–518.

Rosati, G. & Bastiani, P. de (1979).   Pure agraphia: A discrete form of aphasia. *Journal of Neurology, Neurosurgery and Psychiatry, 42*, 266–269.

Rosch, E. (1978).   Principles of categorization. In E. Rosch & B. B. Lloyd (Eds), *Cognition and categorization.* Hillsdale, N. J.: Lawrence Erlbaum Associates Inc.

Rosch, E., Mervis, C. B., Gray, W. D., Johnson, D. M., & Boyes-Braem, P. (1976).   Basic objects in natural categories. *Cognitive Psychology, 8*, 382–439.

Rose, F. C. & Symonds, C. P. (1960).   Persistent memory defect following encephalitis. *Brain, 83*, 195–212.

Ross, E. D. (1981).   The aprosodias. *Archives of Neurology, 38*, 561–569.

Ross, E. D., Harney, J. H., de Lacoste-Utamsing, C., & Purdy, P. D. (1981).   How the brain integrates affective and propositional language into a unified behavioral function. *Archives of Neurology, 38*, 745–748.

Ross, E. G. & Mesulam, M.-M. (1979).   Dominant language functions of the right hemisphere? *Archives of Neurology, 36*, 144–148.

Roy, E. A. (1982).   Action and performance. In A. W. Ellis (Ed.), *Normality and pathology in cognitive functions.* London: Academic Press.

Rozin, P. (1976).   The psychobiological approach to human memory. In M. R. Rosensweig & E. L. Bennett (Eds), *Neural mechanisms of learning and memory.* Cambridge, Mass.: MIT Press.

Rubens, A. B. (1979).   Agnosia. In K. M. Heilman & E. Valenstein (Eds), *Clinical neuropsychology.* New York: Oxford University Press.

Rubens, A. B. & Benson, D. F. (1971).   Associative visual agnosia. *Archives of Neurology, 24*, 305–316.

Rumelhart, D. E. & McClelland, J. L. (1981).   Interactive processing through spreading activation. In A. M. Lesgold & C. A. Perfetti (Eds), *Interactive processes in reading.* Hillsdale, N. J.: Lawrence Erlbaum Associates Inc.

Russell, W. R. (1935).   The after-effects of head injury. *Edinburgh Medical Journal, 41*, 129–144.

Russell, W. R. & Nathan, P. W. (1946).   Traumatic amnesia. *Brain, 69*, 280–300.

Ryan, C., Butters, N., & Montgomery, L. (1980).   Memory deficits in chronic alcoholics: Continuities between the intact alcoholic and the alcoholic Korsakoff patient. In H. Begleiter (Ed.), *Advances in experimental medicine and biology: Biological effects of alcohol,* Vol. 126. New York: Plenum Press.

Ryle, G. (1949).   *The concept of mind.* London: Hutchinson.

Saffran, E. M. (1982). Neuropsychological approaches to the study of language. *British Journal of Psychology, 73,* 317–337.

Saffran, E. M., Marin, O. S. M., & Yeni-Komshian, G. H. (1976a). An analysis of speech perception in word deafness. *Brain and Language, 3,* 209–228.

Saffran, E. M., Schwartz, M. F., & Marin, O. S. M. (1976b). Semantic mechanisms in paralexia. *Brain and Language, 3,* 255–265.

Saffran, E. M., Bogyo, L. C., Schwartz, M. F., & Marin, O. S. M. (1980a). Does deep dyslexia reflect right-hemisphere reading? In M. Coltheart, K. E. Patterson, & J. C. Marshall (Eds), *Deep dyslexia.* London: Routledge and Kegan Paul.

Saffran, E. M., Schwartz, M. F., & Marin, O. S. M. (1980b). Evidence from aphasia: Isolating the components of a production model. In B. Butterworth (Ed.), *Language production,* Vol. 1. London: Academic Press.

Saffran, E. M., Schwartz, M. F., & Marin, O. S. M. (1980c). The word order problem in agrammatism, II. Production. *Brain and Language, 10,* 249–262.

Sanders, H. I. & Warrington, E. K. (1971). Memory for remote events in amnesic patients. *Brain, 94,* 661–668.

Schacter, D. L. (1983). Amnesia observed: Remembering and forgetting in a natural environment. *Journal of Abnormal Psychology, 92,* 236–242.

Schacter, D. L. (1985). Multiple forms of memory in humans and animals. In N. M. Weinberger, J. L. McCaugh, & G. Lynch (Eds), *Memory systems of the brain.* New York: The Guilford Press.

Schacter, D. L. (1987). Implicit memory: History and current status. *Journal of Experimental Psychology: Learning, Memory and Cognition, 13,* 501–518.

Schacter, D. L. & Tulving, E. (1982). Amnesia and memory research. In L. S. Cermak (Ed.), *Human memory and amnesia.* Hillsdale, N. J: Lawrence Erlbaum Associates Inc.

Schacter, D. L., McAndrews, M. P., & Moscovitch, M. (1988). Access to consciousness: Dissociations between implicit and explicit knowledge in neuropsychological syndromes. In L. Weiskrantz (Ed.), *Thought without language.* Oxford: Oxford University Press.

Schneider, K. (1912). Über einige klinisch-pathologische Untersuchungsmethoden und ihre Ergebnisse. Zugleich ein Beitrag zur Psychopathologie der Korsakowschen Psychose. *Zeitschrift für Neurologie und Psychiatrie, 8,* 553–616.

Schneider, K. (1928). Die Störungen des Gedächtnisses. In O. Bumke (Ed.), *Handbuch der Geisteskrankheiten,* Vol. 1. Berlin: Springer.

Schouten, M. E. H. (1980). The case against a speech mode of perception. *Acta Psychologica, 44,* 71–98.

Schuell, H. (1950). Paraphasia and paralexia. *Journal of Speech and Hearing Disorders, 15,* 291–306.

Schwartz, M. F. & Schwartz, B. (1984). In defence of organology. *Cognitive Neuropsychology, 1,* 25–42.

Schwartz, M. F., Marin, O. S. M., & Saffran, E. M. (1979). Dissociations of language function in dementia: A case study. *Brain and Language, 7,* 277–306.

Schwartz, M. F., Saffran, E. M., & Marin, O. S. M. (1980a). Fractionating the reading process in dementia: Evidence for word-specific print-to-sound associations. In M. Coltheart, K. E. Patterson, & J. C. Marshall (Eds), *Deep dyslexia.* London: Routledge and Kegan Paul.

Schwartz, M. F., Saffran, E. M., & Marin, O. S. M. (1980b). The word order problem in agrammatism, I. Comprehension. *Brain and Language, 10,* 249–262.

Schwartz, M. F., Linebarger, M. C., & Saffran, E. M. (1985). The status of the syntactic deficit theory of agrammatism. In M.-L. Kean (Ed.), *Agrammatism.* Orlando: Academic Press.

Scoville, W. B. & Milner, B. (1957). Loss of recent memory after bilateral hippocampal lesions. *Journal of Neurology, Neurosurgery and Psychiatry, 20,* 11–21.

Searleman, A. (1983).   Language capabilities of the right hemisphere. In A. W. Young (Ed.), *Functions of the right cerebral hemisphere*. London: Academic Press.

Sejnowski, T. J. & Rosenberg, C. R. (1986).   Parallel networks that learn to pronounce English text. *Complex Systems, 1,* 145–168.

Seltzer, B. & Benson, D. F. (1974).   The temporal pattern of retrograde amnesia in Korsakoff's disease. *Neurology, 24,* 527–530.

Semmes, J., Weinstein, S., Ghent, L., & Teuber, H.-L. (1963).   Correlates of impaired orientation in personal and extrapersonal space. *Brain, 86,* 747–772.

Sergent, J. (1984).   Processing of visually presented vowels in cerebral hemispheres. *Brain and Language, 21,* 136–146.

Seymour, P. H. K. (1979).   *Human visual cognition*. West Drayton: Collier MacMillan.

Shallice, T. (1979a).   Case-study approach in neuropsychological research. *Journal of Clinical Neuropsychology, 1,* 183–211.

Shallice, T. (1979b).   Neuropsychological research and the fractionation of memory systems. In L. G. Nilsson (Ed.), *Perspectives in memory research*. Hillsdale, N. J.: Lawrence Erlbaum Associates Inc.

Shallice, T. (1981a).   Neurological impairment of cognitive processes. *British Medical Bulletin, 37,* 187–192.

Shallice, T. (1981b).   Phonological agraphia and the lexical route in writing. *Brain, 104,* 413–429.

Shallice, T. (1982).   Specific impairments of planning. *Philosophical Transactions of the Royal Society* (London), *B298,* 199–209. (Reprinted in D. E. Broadbent & L. Weiskrantz (Eds), *The neuropsychology of cognitive function*. London: The Royal Society.)

Shallice, T. (1984).   More functionally isolable subsystems but fewer "modules"? *Cognition, 17,* 243–252.

Shallice, T. & Jackson, M. (1988).   Lissauer on agnosia. *Cognitive Neuropsychology, 5,* 153–192.

Shallice, T. & McCarthy, R. (1985).   Phonological reading: From patterns of impairment to possible procedures. In K. E. Patterson, J. C. Marshall, & M. Coltheart (Eds), *Surface dyslexia: Neuropsychological and cognitive studies of phonological reading*. London: Lawrence Erlbaum Associates Ltd.

Shallice, T. & McGill, J. (1978).   The origins of mixed errors. In J. Requin (Ed.), *Attention and Performance, XII*. Hillsdale, N. J.: Lawrence Erlbaum Associates Inc.

Shallice, T. & Saffran, E. (1986).   Lexical processing in the absence of explicit word identification: Evidence from a letter-by-letter reader. *Cognitive Neuropsychology, 3,* 429–458.

Shallice, T. & Warrington, E. K. (1970).   Independent functioning of verbal memory stores: A neuropsychological study. *Quarterly Journal of Experimental Psychology, 22,* 261–273.

Shallice, T. & Warrington, E. K. (1974).   The dissociation between short-term retention of meaningful sounds and verbal material. *Neuropsychologia, 12,* 553–555.

Shallice, T. & Warrington, E. K. (1977).   The possible role of selective attention in acquired dyslexia. *Neuropsychologia, 15,* 31–41.

Shallice, T. & Warrington, E. K. (1980).   Single and multiple component central dyslexic syndromes. In M. Coltheart, K. E., Patterson, & J. C. Marshall (Eds), *Deep dyslexia*. London: Routledge and Kegan Paul.

Shallice, T., Warrington, E. K., & McCarthy, R. (1983).   Reading without semantics. *Quarterly Journal of Experimental Psychology, 35A,* 111–138.

Shallice, T., McLeod, P., & Lewis, K. (1985).   Isolating cognitive modules with the dual-task paradigm: Are speech perception and production separate processes? *Quarterly Journal of Experimental Psychology, 37A,* 507–532.

Shankweiler, D. & Harris, K. S. (1966). An experimental approach to the problem of articulation in aphasia. *Cortex, 2,* 277–292.

Shankweiler, D. & Studdert-Kennedy, M. (1967). Identification of consonants and vowels presented to left and right ears. *Quarterly Journal of Experimental Psychology, 19,* 59–63.

Shimamura, A. P. (1986). Priming effects in amnesia: Evidence for a dissociable memory function. *Quarterly Journal of Experimental Psychology, 38A,* 619–644.

Shoumaker, R. D., Ajax, E. J., & Schenkenberg, T. (1977). Pure word deafness (auditory verbal agnosia). *Diseases of the Nervous System, 38,* 293–299.

Shraberg, D. & Weitzel, W. D. (1979). Prosopagnosia and the Capgras syndrome. *Journal of Clinical Psychiatry, 40,* 313–316.

Shuttleworth, E. C. & Wise, G. R. (1973). Transient global amnesia due to arterial embolism. *Archives of Neurology, 29,* 340–342.

Smith, A. (1966). Speech and other functions after left (dominant) hemispherectomy. *Journal of Neurology, Neurosurgery and Psychiatry, 29,* 467–471.

Smith, S. & Holmes, G. (1916). A case of bilateral motor apraxia with disturbance of visual orientation. *British Medical Journal, 1,* 437–441.

Smyth, M. M. & Silvers, G. (1987). Function of vision in the control of handwriting. *Acta Psychologica, 65,* 47–64.

Smyth, M. M., Morris, P. E., Levy, P., & Ellis, A. W. (1987). *Cognition in action.* London: Lawrence Erlbaum Associates Ltd.

Snodgrass, J. G. & Vanderwart, M. (1980). A standardised set of 260 pictures: Norms for name agreement, image agreement, familiarity and visual complexity. *Journal of Experimental Psychology: Human Perception and Performance, 6,* 174–215.

Soderpalm, E. (1979). *Speech errors in normal and pathological speech.* (Travaux de l'Institut de Linguistique de Lund, XIV.) Malmo: CWK Gleerup.

Squire, L. R. (1981). Two forms of human amnesia: An analysis of forgetting. *Journal of Neuroscience, 1,* 635–640.

Squire, L. R. (1982). The neuropsychology of human memory. *Annual Review of Neuroscience, 5,* 241–273.

Squire, L. R. (1987). *Memory and brain.* New York: Oxford University Press.

Squire, L. R. & Cohen, N. J. (1984). Human memory and amnesia. In G. Lynch, J. L. McGaugh, & N. M. Weinberger (Eds), *Neurobiology of learning and memory.* New York: The Guilford Press.

Squire, L. R. & Slater, P. C. (1978). Anterograde and retrograde memory impairment in chronic amnesia. *Neuropsychologia, 16,* 313–322.

Squire, L. R., Wetzel, C. D., & Slater, P. C. (1978). Anterograde amnesia following ECT: An analysis of the beneficial effects of partial information. *Neuropsychologia, 16,* 339–348.

Squire, L. R., Cohen, N. J., & Nadel, L. (1984). The medial temporal region and memory consolidation: A new hypothesis. In H. Weingartner & E. S. Parker (Eds), *Memory consolidation.* Hillsdale, N. J.: Lawrence Erlbaum Associates Inc.

Starr, A. & Phillips, L. (1970). Verbal and motor memory in the amnesic syndrome. *Neuropsychologia, 8,* 75–88.

Stemberger, J. P. (1984). Structural errors in normal and agrammatic speech. *Cognitive Neuropsychology, 1,* 281–314.

Stemberger, J. P. (1985). An interactive activation model of language production. In A. W. Ellis (Ed.), *Progress in the psychology of language,* Vol. 1. London: Lawrence Erlbaum Associates Ltd.

Stern, L. D. (1981). A review of theories of human amnesia. *Memory and Cognition, 9,* 247–262.

Studdert-Kennedy, M. (1983). On learning to speak. *Human Neurobiology, 2,* 191–195.

Sumby, W. H. & Pollack, I. (1954). Visual contribution to speech intelligibility in noise. *Journal of the Acoustical Society of America, 26*, 212–215.

Summerfield, Q. (1979). Use of visual information for phonetic perception. *Phonetica, 36*, 314–331.

Swinney, D. A. & Cutler, A. (1979). The access and processing of idiomatic expressions. *Journal of Verbal Learning and Verbal Behavior, 18*, 523–534.

Symonds, C. (1953). Aphasia. *Journal of Neurology, Neurosurgery and Psychiatry, 16*, 1–6.

Syz, H. (1937). Recovery from loss of mnemonic retention after head trauma. *Journal of General Psychology, 17*, 355–387.

Taft, M. (1985). The decoding of words in lexical access: A review of the morphographic approach. In D. Besner, T. G. Waller, & G. E. MacKinnon (Eds), *Reading research: Advances in theory and practice*, Vol. 5. New York: Academic Press.

Tallal, P. & Newcombe, F. (1978). Impairment of auditory perception and language comprehension in dysphasia. *Brain and Language, 5*, 13–24.

Talland, G. (1965). *Deranged memory*. New York: Academic Press.

Taylor, A. & Warrington, E. K. (1971). Visual agnosia: A single case report. *Cortex, 7*, 152–161.

Teuber, H.-L. (1955). Physiological psychology. *Annual Review of Psychology, 6*, 267–296.

Teuber, H.-L., Milner, B., & Vaughan, H. G. (1968). Persistent anterograde amnesia after stab wound of the basal brain. *Neuropsychologia, 6*, 267–282.

Tiberghien, G. & Clerc, I. (1986). The cognitive locus of prosopagnosia. In R. Bruyer (Ed.), *The neuropsychology of face perception and facial expression*. Hillsdale, N. J.: Lawrence Erlbaum Associates Inc.

Tissot, R., Mounin, G., & Lhermitte, F. (1973). *L'agrammatisme*. Paris: Dessart.

Tranel, D. & Damasio, A. R. (1985). Knowledge without awareness: An autonomic index of facial recognition by prosopagnosics. *Science, 228*, 1453–1454.

Tucker, D. M., Watson, R. T., & Heilman, K. M. (1977). Discrimination and evocation of affectively intoned speech in patients with right parietal disease. *Neurology, 27*, 947–950.

Tulving, E. (1972). Episodic and semantic memory. In E. Tulving & W. Donaldson (Eds), *Organization of memory*. New York: Academic Press.

Tulving, E. (1983). *Elements of episodic memory*. Oxford: Oxford University Press.

Tulving, E. (1984). Multiple learning and memory systems. In K. M. J. Lagerspetz & P. Niemi (Eds), *Psychology in the 1990's*. Amsterdam: Elsevier Science.

Tulving, E., Schacter, D. L., & Stark, H. A. (1982). Priming effects in word-fragment completion are independent of recognition memory. *Journal of Experimental Psychology: Learning, Memory and Cognition, 8*, 352–373.

Tzavaras, A., Luaute, J. P., & Bidault, E. (1986). Face recognition dysfunction and delusional misidentification syndromes (D.M.S.). In H. D. Ellis, M. A. Jeeves, F. Newcombe, & A. Young (Eds), *Aspects of face processing*. Dordrecht: Martinus Nijhoff.

Underwood, J. & Paulson, C. (1981). Aphasia and congenital deafness: A case study. *Brain and Language, 12*, 285–291.

Ungerleider, L. G. & Mishkin, M. (1982). Two cortical visual systems. In D. J. Ingle, M. A. Goodale, & R. J. W. Mansfield (Eds), *Analysis of visual behavior*. Cambridge, Mass.: MIT Press.

Vallar, G. & Baddeley, A. (1984a). Fractionation of working memory: Neuropsychological evidence for a phonological short-term store. *Journal of Verbal Learning and Verbal Behavior, 23*, 151–162.

Vallar, G. & Baddeley, A. (1984b). Phonological short-term store, phonological processing and sentence comprehension: A neuropsychological case study. *Cognitive Neuropsychology, 1*, 121–141.

Van Galen, G. P. (1980). Handwriting and drawing: A two-stage model of complex motor behaviour. In G. Stelmach & J. Requin (Eds), *Tutorials in motor behaviour*. Amsterdam: North-Holland.

Van Harskamp, F. (1974). Some considerations concerning the utility of intelligence tests in aphasic patients. In Y. Lebrun & R. Hoops (Eds), *Intelligence and aphasia*. Amsterdam: Swets and Zeitlinger.

Van Lancker, D. (1987). Nonpropositional speech: Neurolinguistic studies. In A. W. Ellis (Ed.), *Progress in the psychology of language*, Vol. 3. London: Lawrence Erlbaum Associates Ltd.

Van Lancker, D. & Canter, G. J. (1982). Impairment of voice and face recognition in patients with hemispheric damage. *Brain and Cognition, 1*, 185–195.

Van Lancker, D., Cummings, J. L., Kreiman, J., & Dobkin, B. H. (1988). Phonagnosia: A dissociation between familiar and unfamiliar voices. *Cortex, 24.*

Van Zomeren, A. H. & Deelman, B. G. (1978). Long term recovery of visual reaction time after closed head injury. *Journal of Neurology, Neurosurgery and Psychiatry, 41*, 452–457.

Vernon, M. D. (1929). *The errors made in reading.* Medical Research Council Special Report Series, No 130. London: HMSO.

Victor, M. & Yakovlev, P. I. (1955). S. S. Korsakoff's psychic disorder in conjunction with peripheral neuritis. *Neurology, 5*, 394–406.

Vignolo, L. A. (1982). Auditory agnosia. *Philosophical Transactions of the Royal Society* (London), *B298*, 49–57.

Volpe, B. T., LeDoux, J. E., & Gazzaniga, M. S. (1979). Information processing of visual stimuli in an "extinguished" field. *Nature, 282*, 722–724.

Wales, R. & Kinsella, G. (1981). Syntactic effects in sentence completion by Broca's aphasics. *Brain and Language, 13*, 301–307.

Warren, C. & Morton, J. (1982). The effects of priming on picture recognition. *British Journal of Psychology, 73*, 117–129.

Warrington, E. K. (1975). The selective impairment of semantic memory. *Quarterly Journal of Experimental Psychology, 27*, 635–657.

Warrington, E. K. (1979). Neuropsychological evidence for multiple memory systems. In *Brain and mind.* Ciba Foundation Symposium 69 (New series). Amsterdam: Excerpta Medica.

Warrington, E. K. (1982). Neuropsychological studies of object recognition. *Philosophical Transactions of the Royal Society* (London), *B298*, 15–33.

Warrington, E. K. (1987). Visual deficits associated with occipital lobe lesions in man. In C. Chagass, R. Gattass, & C. Gross (Eds), *Pontificae Academia Scientarium Scripta Varia, 54*, 247–261.

Warrington, E. K. & James, M. (1967a). Disorders of visual perception in patients with localized cerebral lesions. *Neuropsychologia, 5*, 253–266.

Warrington, E. K. & James, M. (1967b). An experimental investigation of facial recognition in patients with unilateral cerebral lesions. *Cortex, 3*, 317–326.

Warrington, E. K. & McCarthy, R. (1983). Category specific access dysphasia. *Brain, 106*, 859–878.

Warrington, E. K. & Shallice, T. (1969). The selective impairment of auditory verbal short-term memory. *Brain, 92*, 885–896.

Warrington, E. K. & Shallice, T. (1972). Neuropsychological evidence of visual storage in short-term memory tasks. *Quarterly Journal of Experimental Psychology, 24*, 30–40.

Warrington, E. K. & Shallice, T. (1979). Semantic access dyslexia. *Brain, 102*, 43–63.

Warrington, E. K. & Shallice, T. (1980). Word-form dyslexia. *Brain, 30*, 99–112.

Warrington, E. K. & Shallice, T. (1984).   Category-specific semantic impairments. *Brain*, *107*, 829–854.

Warrington, E. K. & Taylor, A. M. (1973).   The contribution of the right parietal lobe to object recognition. *Cortex*, *9*, 152–164.

Warrington, E. K. & Taylor, A. M. (1978).   Two categorical stages of object recognition. *Perception*, *7*, 695–705.

Warrington, E. K. & Weiskrantz, L. (1968).   New method of testing long-term retention with special reference to amnesic patients. *Nature*, *277*, 972–974.

Warrington, E. K. & Weiskrantz, L. (1970).   Organizational aspects of memory in amnesic patients. *Neuropsychologia*, *9*, 67–71.

Warrington, E. K. & Weiskrantz, L. (1973).   An analysis of short-term and long-term memory defects in man. In J. A. Deutsch (Ed.), *The physiological basis of memory*. New York: Academic Press.

Warrington, E. K. & Zangwill, O. L. (1957).   A study of dyslexia. *Journal of Neurology, Neurosurgery and Psychiatry*, *20*, 208–215.

Waugh, N. C. & Norman, D. A. (1965).   Primary memory. *Psychological Review*, *72*, 89–104.

Wechsler, D. (1917).   A study of retention in Korsakoff psychosis. *Psychiatric Bulletin of the New York State Hospital*, *2*, 403–451.

Weintraub, S., Mesulam, M.-M., & Kramer, L. (1981).   Disturbances in prosody: A right-hemisphere contribution. *Archives of Neurology*, *38*, 742–744.

Weiskrantz, L. (1968).   Treatments, inferences, and brain functions. In L. Weiskrantz (Ed.), *Analysis of behavioural change*. New York: Harper and Row.

Weiskrantz, L. (1980).   Varieties of residual experience. *Quarterly Journal of Experimental Psychology*, *32*, 365–386.

Weiskrantz, L. (1986).   *Blindsight: A case study and implications*. Oxford Psychology Series, 12. Oxford: Oxford University Press.

Weiskrantz, L., Warrington, E. K., Sanders, M. D., & Marshall, J. (1974).   Visual capacity of the hemianopic field following a restricted occipital ablation. *Brain*, *97*, 709–728.

Weiss, M. & House, A. (1973).   Perception of dichotically presented vowels. *Journal of the Acoustical Society of America*, *53*, 51–58.

Wells, R. (1951).   Predicting slips of the tongue. *Yale Scientific Magazine*, December 1951. (Reprinted in V. A. Fromkin (Ed.), 1973. *Speech errors as linguistic evidence*. The Hague: Mouton.)

Welman, A. & Lanser, J. (1974).   Intelligence or intellectual tests in aphasic patients. In Y. Lebrun & R. Hoops (Eds), *Intelligence and aphasia*. Amsterdam: Swets and Zeitlinger.

Wernicke, C. (1874).   *Der Aphasische Symptomencomplex*. Breslau: Cohn and Weigart. (Translated in G. H. Eggert. *Wernicke's works on aphasia*. The Hague: Mouton, 1977.)

Weston, M. J. & Whitlock, F. A. (1971).   The Capgras syndrome following head injury. *British Journal of Psychiatry*, *119*, 25–31.

Wetzel, C. D. & Squire, L. R. (1980).   Encoding in anterograde amnesia. *Neuropsychologia*, *18*, 177–184.

Whiteley, A. M. & Warrington, E. K. (1977).   Selective impairment of topographical memory: A single case study. *Journal of Neurology, Neurosurgery and Psychiatry*, *41*, 575–578.

Whitty, C. W. M. (1977).   Transient global amnesia. In C. W. M. Whitty & O. L. Zangwill (Eds), *Amnesia* (2nd edn). London: Butterworths.

Whitty, C. W. M. & Zangwill, O. L. (1977).   Traumatic amnesia. In C. W. M. Whitty & O. L. Zangwill (Eds), *Amnesia* (2nd edn). London: Butterworths.

Wickelgren, W. A. (1968).   Sparing of short-term memory in an amnesic patient: Implications for strength theory of memory. *Neuropsychologia*, *6*, 235–244.

Wilbrand, H. (1892). Ein Fall von Seelenblindheit und Hemianopie mit Sectionsbefund. *Deutscher Zeitschrift für Nervenkrankheiten, 2,* 361–387.

Wilcox, J. & Waziri, R. (1983). The Capgras symptom and nondominant cerebral dysfunction. *Journal of Clinical Psychiatry, 44,* 70–72.

Williams, M. (1953). Investigations of amnesic defects by progressive prompting. *Journal of Neurology, Neurosurgery and Psychiatry, 16,* 14–18.

Williams, M. & Smith, H. V. (1954). Mental disturbances in tuberculous meningitis. *Journal of Neurology, Neurosurgery and Psychiatry, 17,* 173–182.

Williams, M. & Zangwill, O. L. (1952). Memory defects after head injury. *Journal of Neurology, Neurosurgery and Psychiatry, 15,* 54–58.

Williams, M. D. & Hollan, J. S. (1981). The process of retrieval from very long-term memory. *Cognitive Science, 5,* 87–119.

Wingfield, A. (1968). Effects of frequency on identification and naming of objects. *American Journal of Psychology, 81,* 226–234.

Winner, E. & Gardner, H. (1977). The comprehension of metaphor in brain-damaged patients. *Brain, 100,* 717–729.

Winnick, W. A. & Daniel, S. A. (1970). Two kinds of response priming in tachistoscopic recognition. *Journal of Experimental Psychology, 84,* 74–81.

Winocur, G., Oxbury, S., Roberts, R., Agnetti, V., & Davis, C. (1984). Amnesia in a patient with bilateral lesions to the thalamus. *Neuropsychologia, 22,* 123–143.

Winograd, T. (1975). Understanding natural language. In D. Bobrow & A. Collins (Eds), *Representation and understanding.* New York: Academic Press.

Woods, R. T. & Piercy, M. (1974). A similarity between amnesic memory and normal forgetting. *Neuropsychologia, 12,* 437–445.

Woodworth, R. S. (1938). *Experimental psychology.* New York: Holt, Rinehart and Winston.

Yamadori, A, & Albert, M. L. (1973). Word category aphasia. *Cortex, 9,* 83–89.

Yamadori, A., Osumi, Y., Masuhara, S., & Okubo, M. (1977). Preservation of singing in Broca's aphasia. *Journal of Neurology, Neurosurgery and Psychiatry, 40,* 221–224.

Yarnell, P. R. & Lynch, S. (1973). The "ding": Amnesic states in football trauma. *Neurology, 23,* 196–197.

Yealland, L. R. (1916). Case of gunshot wound involving visual centre, with visual disorientation. *Proceedings of the Royal Society of Medicine, 9,* 97–99.

Young, A. W. (1982). Methodological and theoretical bases of visual hemifield studies. In J. G. Beaumont (Ed.), *Divided visual field studies of cerebral organisation.* London: Academic Press.

Young, A. W. (1987). Cerebral hemisphere differences in reading. In J. R. Beech & A. M. Colley (Eds), *Cognitive approaches to reading.* Chichester: Wiley.

Young, A. W. (1988). Functional organisation of visual recognition. In L. Weiskrantz (Ed.), *Thought without language.* Oxford: Oxford University Press.

Young, A. W. & De Haan, E. H. F. (1988). Boundaries of covert recognition in prosopagnosia. *Cognitive Neuropsychology, 5.*

Young, A. W. & Deregowski, J. B. (1981). Learning to see the impossible. *Perception, 10,* 91–105.

Young, A. W. & Ellis, A. W. (1985). Different methods of lexical access for words presented in the left and right visual hemifields. *Brain and Language, 24,* 326–358.

Young, A. W. & Ellis, H. D. (1988). Childhood prosopagnosia. *Brain and Cognition.*

Young, A. W. & Ratcliff, G. (1983). Visuospatial abilities of the right hemisphere. In A. W. Young (Ed.), *Functions of the right cerebral hemisphere.* London: Academic Press.

Young, A. W., Ellis, A. W., & Bion, P. J. (1984). Left hemisphere superiority for pronounceable nonwords, but not for unpronounceable letter strings. *Brain and Language, 22,* 14–25.

Young, A. W., Hay, D. C., & Ellis, A. W. (1985a). The faces that launched a thousand slips: Everyday difficulties and errors in recognizing people. *British Journal of Psychology, 76,* 495–523.

Young, A. W., Hay, D. C., McWeeny, K. H., Flude, B. M., & Ellis, A. W. (1985b). Matching familiar and unfamiliar faces on internal and external features. *Perception, 14,* 737–746.

Young, A. W., Ellis, A. W., Flude, B. M., McWeeny, K. H., & Hay, D. C. (1986). Facename interference. *Journal of Experimental Psychology: Human Perception and Performance, 12,* 466–475.

Zaidel, E. (1982). Reading by the disconnected right hemisphere: An aphasiological perspective. In Y. Zotterman (Ed.), *Dyslexia: Neuronal, cognitive and linguistic aspects.* Oxford: Pergamon Press.

Zaidel, E. & Peters. A. M. (1981). Phonological encoding and idiographic reading by the disconnected right hemisphere: Two case studies. *Brain and Language, 14,* 205–234.

Zangwill, O. L. (1964). Intelligence in aphasia. In A. De Reuck & M. O'Connor (Eds), *Disorders of language.* London: Churchill.

Zeki, S. (1978). Functional specialization in the visual cortex of the rhesus monkey. *Nature, 274,* 423–428.

Zihl, J., Von Cramon, D., & Mai, N. (1983). Selective disturbance of movement vision after bilateral brain damage. *Brain, 106,* 313–340.

Zola-Morgan, S., Cohen, N. J., & Squire, L. R. (1983). Recall of remote episodic memory in amnesia. *Neuropsychologia, 21,* 487–500.

Zollinger, R. (1935). Removal of left hemisphere: Report of a case. *Archives of Neurology and Psychiatry, 34,* 1055–1064.

Zubin, J. (1948). Memory functioning in patients treated with electric shock therapy. *Journal of Personality, 17,* 33–41.

Zurif, E. B., Caramazza, A., Myerson, R., & Galvin, J. (1974). Semantic feature representations for normal and aphasic language. *Brain and Language, 1,* 167–187.

Subject Index

Author Index

349